QUANTUM SCREENS

QUANTUM SCREENS

Nonlinear Universes in Film and Television

MARTHA P. NOCHIMSON

UNIVERSITY OF TEXAS PRESS
AUSTIN

Printed in the United States of America
First edition, 2026

∞ The paper used in this book meets the minimum requirements of ANSI/NISO Z39.48-1992 (R1997) (Permanence of Paper).

Library of Congress Cataloging-in-Publication Data

Names: Nochimson, Martha, author
Title: Quantum screens : nonlinear universes in film and television / Martha P. Nochimson.
Description: First edition. | Austin : University of Texas Press, 2026. | Includes bibliographical references and index.
Identifiers: LCCN 2025020123 (print) | LCCN 2025020124 (ebook)
ISBN 978-1-4773-2137-9 hardcover
ISBN 978-1-4773-3382-2 paperback
ISBN 978-1-4773-3339-6 pdf
ISBN 978-1-4773-3340-2 epub
Subjects: LCSH: Lynch, David, 1946–2025—Criticism and interpretation | Lindelof, Damon, 1973—Criticism and interpretation | Space and time in motion pictures | Space and time on television | Television programs—Plots, themes, etc. | Science and the arts | Quantum theory—Influence | Postmodernism—Influence | Metaphysics—Influence | Hindu philosophy—Influence | Storytelling—Psychological aspects | Storytelling—Philosophy | Motion pictures—Plots, themes, etc.
Classification: LCC PN1995.9.S668 .N63 2026 (print) | LCC PN1995.9.S668 (ebook)
LC record available at https://lccn.loc.gov/2025020123
LC ebook record available at https://lccn.loc.gov/2025020124

doi:10.7560/321379

The University of Texas Press gratefully acknowledges the William and Bettye Nowlin Endowment in Art, History, and Culture of the Western Hemisphere for its support of this publication.

This book is dedicated to David Lynch,
who unchained film and television

∞

CONTENTS

ILLUSTRATIONS

QUANTUM SCREENS

INTERSECTIONS: WHAT WOULD EINSTEIN DO?

Introduction

The imagination can seize the facts of science—observations of new stars, the discoveries of history and comparative mythology, strange plants and insects, the grandeur of space—and weave out of them new experiences of beauty, new emotions and images, new myths.

JOHN TRESCH, *The Reason for the Darkness of the Night: Edgar Allan Poe and the Forging of American Science*

Listen, it's TV. . . . You just watch old TV shows and rip 'em off.

GLEN MAZZARA, QUOTING TELEVISION PRODUCER JOHN WIRTH, AT THE AUSTIN FILM FESTIVAL, SEPTEMBER 20, 2022

David Lynch concludes *Twin Peaks,* season 3 (2017), with Special Agent Dale Cooper (Kyle MacLachlan), Lynch's most incandescent hero, knocking at the door of a house in Odessa, Texas.

Odessa, Texas?

The door is opened by Carrie Page (Sheryl Lee), a diner waitress who looks just like dead Twin Peaks prom queen Laura Palmer (Sheryl Lee).

Who?

Twin Peaks viewers know Laura well but have never before seen this Carrie or Odessa. Nor has Cooper. Well, the end of a series finale is an odd place to introduce a new character, in a totally strange location. And more discombobulation ensues. Inside, there is blood on Carrie's living-room wall, and an unexplained corpse stiffening on one of her chairs. Our special agent ignores blood and body, even as he identifies himself as FBI. He is too busy insisting that, despite Carrie's protestations, she *is* Laura Palmer, and that she needs to come with him to the town of Twin Peaks, in Washington state, to see her mother, Sarah Palmer (Grace Zabriskie).

Mother?

Carrie is startled and hostile, at first. She has no mother in—where was it?—Twin Peaks. But getting far away from the dead guy with an FBI agent could be a good deal.

Their strange, silent road trip makes the final moments of the series stranger when Cooper and Carrie pull up in front of the "Palmer" house in Twin Peaks, familiar and then some to the audience, only to find that it isn't the Palmer house. Sarah Palmer doesn't live there. No Palmer has ever lived there. Cooper is stunned; Carrie is terrified; and the audience is twisting in the wind. Cooper's body contorts as he wonders what year it is, and Carrie hears faint traces of the very familiar sound of Sarah Palmer calling for her daughter Laura—familiar to us, that is, but ostensibly not to her. However, when Carrie emits a bloodcurdling scream, we have to wonder whether she does recognize the voice after all. But. No time to process this turn of events. Strobe light flashes from the house, preceding the disappearance of Cooper, Carrie, and everything else. The frame goes to black. This is not how we expect incandescent heroes to end up.

Ought we describe this final scene as

A. quirky;
B. terrifying;
C. dark; or
D. the conclusion of a hero's journey in a post-Newtonian universe?

Let's go with D, because this is not the terminus of a quirky, terrifying, dark horror fantasy. It is, rather, a new knowledge of reality. Through this closure, Lynch brings the hero's journey into the baffling, nonlinear, quantum cosmic reality that negates the old, stable reality of the Newtonian universe and puzzles even quantum physicists. In his day, it appalled Albert Einstein, who named it "spooky action at a distance."[1] Cooper's disappearance is certainly spooky, and at a distance from the context we thought we knew, and yet somewhere, from wherever Sarah's voice emanates, a stable context seems to endure. Einstein thought it did too. He believed in, but could not prove, a unified field beyond the limitless disorientation of quantum behavior being documented in physics laboratories. These competing theories about cosmic fragmentation and coherence haunt the new map of the universe being drawn by the physical sciences, and they hover over the denouement of *Twin Peaks* 3.

Lynch has taken that mass-media staple, the detective, and drowned him in spooky action. (The detective vanishes.) But at the same time, Lynch also offers the possibility of a new kind of coherence in a unified field. (Sarah Palmer is out there somewhere.) He has given us an experience of narrative in a complex new picture of the universe that has been evolving for over a hundred and fifty years in the natural and social sciences and the arts. *Twin Peaks* leaves us at an unexpected intersection, the intersection of mass-culture entertainment and the new map of matter, time, energy, and space.

A new hero's journey for a new cosmos in the popular media? What would Einstein say about that, considering that people in the industry themselves talk their work down as cut-and-paste jobs? There was no new hero on the drawing board, for example, when future show creator Glen Mazzara, nervously brimming with new ideas about the art of writing, went to his first job interview for a staff position on *Nash Bridges* (1996–2001) and was told, "Listen, it's TV. . . . You just watch old TV shows and rip 'em off."[2] Imagine if Mazzara had pitched an intersection between television and quantum physics. Nevertheless, if ripping off old shows is a fact of life for many media hacks, it is an outdated cliché if we try to apply it to the entire current industry.

Lynch must be accounted for as an artist, an entirely original storyteller, who broke open a viable place in the mass media for the hero's journey across nonlinear time and space. And he is not just a lone flash of lightning in a bottle. True, in 1990, when the first season of *Twin Peaks* went on the air, he was virtually alone. But in the intervening years, his influence and new ideas in the zeitgeist have inspired numerous popular-media storytellers. I do not refer to those who think they are Lynchian when they throw a couple of images of white fences and little dancing men onto the screen, but rather those who are impelled to reimagine, as he does, both the cosmos and heroes. Heroes, and also history.

A new kind of hero is being created in quantum contexts by Terrence Malick, Brit Marling and Zal Batmanglij, and Charlie Kaufman, all of whose works we are about to visit. And Lynch's influence also extends to new kinds of historical narratives. Nonlinear ideas about energy, matter, and time are also behind Damon Lindelof's approach to history in media entertainment when he created the streaming series *Watchmen* (2019), based on Alan Moore's searing, but linear, commentary on the unfolding of historical events in his *Watchmen* graphic novel (1986). Lindelof reimagined Moore's fiction in a fully quantum reality.[3] To be sure, Moore's novel alludes to quantum strangeness. One of his characters, the immense, blue Doctor Manhattan is a quantum being composed of infinitely malleable particles who occupies past, present, and future simultaneously. But Moore exiles Doctor Manhattan from history at the end of the novel, sending him to Mars. No more spooky reality for Earth. It is linear business as usual. By contrast, Lindelof's adaptation imagines what history might be like if Doctor Manhattan had not left Earth. As we shall see, Lindelof comically and tragically turns upside down our expectations about historical melodrama when he drowns linear history in Doctor Manhattan's boundless energy and power. We see an entirely new historical vista as the racist Ku Klux Klan; a technologically motivated idealist, the mysterious Lady Trieu; and the progressive Robert Redford government compete to establish themselves as the authors of a permanent linear history. They are forced to look on Doctor Manhattan's spooky action on Earth and despair! We are left to contemplate the historical possibilities of the new zeitgeist. Nor, as we are about to discover, is Lindelof the only media artist to bring historical melodrama into a quantum context.

No extant studies of time in film and television to date have explored the new narrative dynamics of nonlinearity for heroes and history for leisure consumption, and few have even addressed the possibility that our mass-media storytellers are now cocreating ideas about nonlinear time with physics and similarly revolutionary developments in other disciplines. The common practice among those who do observe nonlinear time and space in the mass media has been to establish taxonomies of cinematic temporalities in entertainment with little or no consideration of how popular narrative works in the reality of a nonlinear cosmos, now being explored by the natural sciences. Todd McGowan's *Out of Time: Desire in Atemporal Cinema* is one exception, but his study is restricted to searching for ways that nonlinear time in film is informed by Lacanian psychology.[4] In his well-considered analyses, McGowan proposes that understanding narrative nonlinearity in the media is an extension of psychological critiques of film and television, which relegate nonlinearity to an internal Freudian dynamic. But those popular artists who allege a nonlinear reality point us away from Freud and Jung, and toward the external mysteries in the new map of the universe. Aside from McGowan, almost all the other meditations on nonlinearity in the mass media define categories of nonlinear-temporal narrative patterns—not all of them nonlinear—as in Helen Powell's *Stop the Clocks! Time and Narrative in Cinema* and in Lee Carruthers's *Doing Time: Temporality, Hermeneutics, and Contemporary Cinema*.[5] Almost all.

There are two very significant critical precedents for this zeitgeist study. One is an exploration of time in early film by Mary Ann Doane, in *The Emergence of Cinematic Time: Modernity, Contingency, The Archive*. Doane's book is concerned with the "representability of time" in cinema and attends to some intersections between the mass media and science.[6] She thoughtfully and complexly proffers a gift to all who think about time in cinema when she engages the capacity of the mass media for depicting the reversibility of time, even at the dawn of cinema.[7] Doane discusses filmic representation of reversibility in the works of the earliest filmmakers, taking examples from Georges Méliès, a magician who made a career of filming objects and bodies that appear not to obey what classical physics decreed about the rules of time and space, and Auguste Lumière, who comically played with reversibility in his short film, *The Demolition of a Wall* (1896). In *Demolition*, as Doane notes, Lumière drives reality into a nonlinear side trip. The film depicts a wrecking crew progressively destroying a wall, but it was intended to be shown not only chronologically but also backward. The audience was supposed to see the wall seemingly reconstituting itself.[8] Temporal reversibility in the movies: There is quite a lot of it for Doane to survey, and she integrates it into not only nineteenth- and twentieth-century scientific breakthroughs, but also the history of ideas about time and space, current and ancient, from Henri Bergson in the twentieth century all the way back to Zeno and his paradoxes.[9]

Equally committed to probing the dynamic of nonlinearity in film and its relationship to the cosmos is Gilles Deleuze in *Cinema 2: The Time-Image*. Indeed, Deleuze tells us up front that he intends to explore those aspects of time that "the cinematographic image has been able to grasp and reveal, and which can echo the teaching of science."[10] Toward that end, among the many complex and fascinating avenues he pursues, Deleuze reflects on the intersection of cinema with the fracturing of the linear relationship between cause and effect that we find in the fiction of Jorge Luis Borges, particularly in his short story, "The Garden of Forking Paths." As Deleuze notes, in that story "it is not space but time which forks."[11] Deleuze refers to the splitting of time in cinema in greater detail when he analyzes it as what he calls a crystal-image and explains it this way: "What constitutes the crystal-image is the most fundamental operation of time. . . . [T]ime has to split itself in two at each moment as present and past, which differ from each other in nature, or, what amounts to the same thing, it has to split the present in two heterogeneous directions, one of which is launched towards the future while the other falls into the past. . . . Time consists of this split, and it is this, it is time, that we *see in the crystal*."[12] And it is by portraying this concept of the temporal split that cinema can cocreate in images with science. Einstein and the quantum physicists might well raise their eyebrows at Deleuze's terminology; Lynch called it gobbledygook when I read that quotation to him.[13] But Deleuze is, nevertheless, part of the cocreation that is taking place between the science of nonlinear temporality and the narratives in the mass media. I follow in the footsteps of Deleuze and Doane in understanding new experiences of time in entertainment as part of a dialogue with the sciences and as crucial contributions to the modern zeitgeist.

I stand with Doane when she points toward the intersection between cinema and the zeitgeist: "Cinema is not merely an effect or a symptom of epistemological developments in other disciplines. It is a crucial participant in an ongoing rethinking of temporality in modernity."[14] Similarly, this study stands with Deleuze when he writes that great cinema authors "become philosophers or theoreticians—even Hawks who wanted no theories, even Godard when he pretends to distrust them. Cinema's concepts are not given in cinema. And yet they are cinema's concepts, not theories about cinema. So that . . . we must no longer ask ourselves, 'What is cinema?' but 'What is philosophy?' Cinema itself is a new practice of images and signs."[15] With them, I am interested in asking about the role of cinema—and I add television—in cocreating the new nonlinear cosmos. But I start where Doane and Deleuze left off, and I intend to broaden and deepen the inquiries they initiated. I begin by taking stock of a basic problem in the works of both Doane and Deleuze.

COCREATION

Simply put, both Doane and Deleuze studied time in popular entertainment before David Lynch's *Twin Peaks,* when fully nonlinear temporality and space were virtually impossible in mass-media narratives. Doane and Deleuze homed in on bursts of nonlinearity irrupting into inherently teleological media storytelling, which insistently proposes action that unfolds from clearly identifiable causes and moves straight forward, toward inevitable effects. Maybe this involves flashbacks and reverse projection, but they are minor breaks in a normal (read *linear*) space-time that is forward moving and/or teleological. Doane and Deleuze are commenting on cinematic universes imagined by pre-Einsteinian and prequantum thinking. The new thinking evolving in physics and biology, as well as in philosophy, describes a nonteleological reality and mandates an entirely new emotional and imaginative relationship to narrative, of which Doane and Deleuze saw very little in the commercial media when they wrote. They wrote before the massive changes in the culture industry that have occurred post-Lynch. The breakdown of cause and effect as Isaac Newton described it in the late seventeenth century had monumental implications for film and television, but Doane and Deleuze did not have access to the popular art thus impacted. Nor were they presented with the inability of most critics to perceive the paradigm shifts in new, post-Lynch, nonlinear cinema and television. This study takes into account not only the shift of some mass-media entertainment toward the new zeitgeist, but also the emotional trauma of a new knowledge of reality. We are anything but emotionally gratified by Cooper's uncanny disappearance.

There is no doubt that mass audiences and film and media critics are still more emotionally comfortable with narrative fostered by a Newtonian cosmos, in which heroic quests and historical teleologies manifest how causes lead to effects. Nor is there any doubt that most of the mass media caters to traditional narratives about heroes who escort us gloriously through a linear universe, as, for example, in the hero's journey of loner Rick Blaine (Humphrey Bogart) in *Casablanca* (1942). The film contains an extended flashback in its narrative structure, but only in service of the cause and effect that dominates Rick's reunion with Ilsa Lund (Ingrid Bergman) and leads him to sacrifice love for a larger good. A Newtonian context is also mandatory for the historical melodrama of *Gandhi* (1982), in which a linear process leads India from unjust exploitation by Great Britain to independence. In the Newtonian universe, Rick in *Casablanca* can reassure Ilsa—and the audience—that they'll "always have Paris." Rick and Ilsa occupy a satisfyingly romantic and stable universe, in which we may cherish what has been and move from the past through the present to the future in a straight line. Always, Paris. OK. Similarly, in the Newtonian universe everything leads thrillingly to the liberation of India.

This is not the universe of the closure of Lynch's *Twin Peaks*. Lost among indeterminate frames of time and unstable matter and energy, neither Agent Cooper nor Carrie can *have* any location in time or get where they thought they were going along a road they were sure would get them there. And, as we shall see, in Matthew Weiner's *The Romanoffs*, the series' depiction of the heritage of the Romanov dynasty offers a completely different idea of historical heritage from the cause-and-effect linearity of *Gandhi*. Not only is heritage unable to travel in a straight line, but for better and for worse, it doesn't exist except in the imaginations of those who attempt to claim it. Nor is the cause-and-effect Newtonian universe the universe of Lindelof's *Watchmen*, in which pipe dreams of historical teleologies implode under the pressure of Doctor Manhattan's nonlinear reality.

When the mass media go nonlinear, the likes of both Rick's journey and the linear unfolding of India's path to self-rule, or any culture's direct path to anywhere, are impossible. This study intends to highlight new narrative satisfactions, without downplaying the intellectual and emotional traumas caused by storytelling set in the brave new map of the cosmos.

Actually, while the new map is very brave, it isn't that new. It is but new to film and television. But the undertaking of exploring the cocreation of the media with the new zeitgeist sets us tasks that are very unfamiliar. We are called to connect the dots of the history of the natural and social sciences with the new developments in the commercial media. The dots of natural and social science begin as far back as the mid-nineteenth-century speculations of Charles Darwin. A cursory familiarity with Darwin's work is not sufficient for comprehension of the truly radical nature of his prefiguration of quantum science. It has been easy to misread Darwin as a rigorously linear thinker, because of the attraction of natural and social scientists, not yet acquainted with quantum science, to what he wrote about the "survival of the fittest," which seemed to contend that adaptive, linear, causal changes are the law of nature. Contextualized by later developments in physics, a new Darwinian narrative emerges, in which nonlinear mutation is more central to his thinking than the linear logic of adaptation that has been read into his work.

Erwin Schrödinger, one of the fathers of quantum science, and feminist philosopher and theorist Elizabeth Grosz have acknowledged the debts their respective fields owe Darwin for his conceptualization of mutation. In her book *The Nick of Time: Politics, Evolution, and the Untimely,* Grosz outlines the overlaps between new temporal narratives of Charles Darwin, Friedrich Nietzsche, and Henri Bergson and counts Darwin as one of the progenitors of the map of the nonlinear universe: "Darwin brings the concept of the *event* to the sciences. Events are ruptures, nicks, which flow from causal connections in the past but which, in their unique combinations and consequences, generate unpredictability and effect sometimes subtle but wide-ranging unforeseeable transformations in the present and future."[16] In formulating his theories about adaptation, Darwin "inadvertently provided us with a theory of time which regards it as an always open-ended movement directed to a future whose parameters cannot be known in advance."[17] In *What is Life?,* Schrödinger also remarks on Darwin's contribution to the concept of nonlinearity in his theorization of mutation. If, Schrödinger says, the past really did teleologically dictate the future, mutation and adaptation would not be possible.[18] Einstein, of course, decisively made discussion of nonlinear time part of the standard scientific discourse, when he pioneered thinking about the existence of numerous frames of time, maybe millions, that have complex relationships to each other.[19] Relative time frames can be extrapolated to mean that there isn't one past and one future, but rather pasts and futures for numerous time frames. This is the cosmos of David Lynch and Damon Lindelof's *Watchmen,* but not the cosmos of Rick, Ilsa, or Gandhi, nor of any linear narrative.

The spookiness of quantum sciences provides a new context for storytelling. Physicists have proven that particles can be in two places at the same time—a phenomenon called superposition—and that particles can communicate with each other instantaneously at any and all distances through any and all kinds of barriers without any material means of connection—a phenomenon known as entanglement. If Rick can be in two places at the same time, he can both let Ilsa go off with Victor Laszlo and go off with her himself. India can both remain part of the British Empire and be independent. Moreover, the mathematics of the strange behavior of matter creates extreme problems regarding moral responsibility.

Quantum mechanics is now pondering the existence of particles without mass and particles that can move faster than the speed of light that would entirely rewrite another Humphrey Bogart classic. It alters definitively the responsibility Sam Spade (Humphrey Bogart) feels about hunting down whoever killed his partner, Miles Archer (Jerome Cowan), in *The Maltese Falcon,* let alone the necessity that he turn Brigid O'Shaughnessy (Mary Astor), the film's femme fatale, over to the police.[20] A famous thought experiment in physics called the tachyon murder paradox suggests that in the new map of the cosmos no femme can be particularly fatale: she would be just a material function, like everything else, of the nonlinear realities of time and space. In that thought experiment, a woman called Mary, standing forty feet away from a man called John, fires massless tachyon bullets that move at four times the speed of light. Light moves at a speed of one foot per nanosecond (billionth of a second), and in a time frame in which that is the speed limit, a light-speed bullet would take forty nanoseconds seconds to reach John. But Mary's tachyon bullets take just ten nanoseconds to kill him.[21] And that makes all the difference. How?

Here, I will quote physicist Richard Muller from his book *Now: The Physics of Time*:

> Mary is brought to trial . . . [and] says she has a right to argue the case in whatever reference frame she chooses. They are all valid, the [quantum-influenced] judge knows, so he allows her to proceed. She chooses a frame moving at half lightspeed, \F1/2 *c*. Since that frame is moving slower than the speed of light, according to relativity it is a valid reference frame. In the Earth frame, the two events (fire gun, hit heart) are separated by +10 nanoseconds. . . . The same two events described in a reference frame moving at \F1/2 *c* have a time separation of –15.5 nanoseconds. The negative sign means that the two events occur in the opposite order. The bullet enters the victim's heart before Mary fires the gun! Mary has the perfect alibi.[22]

In this thought experiment, in which John dies before Mary fires the gun, she bears no responsibility. There is no consciousness of a need to get justice for John. Just the materialist quantum mechanics of light and matter. Sam Spade's manly detective code, which demands he abandon his desire for Brigid as a point of honor, evaporates—as do the historical moral imperatives that challenge British colonialism.

Similarly, Erwin Schrödinger's now famous/infamous thought experiment about the cat in a box which can only be dead or alive once it is observed, but not as an absolute condition of life or death, proposes a materialism that nullifies all morality.[23] India could be both exploited and free, depending on the perspective of whoever observes it. Miles Archer could be alive or dead. The entire enterprise of being a detective, or of telling stories about any hero, is profoundly altered when reality is determined by observation. So, too, narratives about great historical movements. The problem of quantum materialism is always a consideration for a storyteller in the new universe.

This is not to say that *Casablanca, The Maltese Falcon,* and *Gandhi* are not exciting, beautiful, brilliantly acted and cast, and even insightful within the Newtonian framework, but only to contend that they are representations of the moral coherence and truths of a universe that strike a nerve with a large mass audience for whom the new temporal and spatial zeitgeist isn't yet an emotional reality. The new zeitgeist takes an emotional toll when, in the final moments of *Twin Peaks*, season 3, an FBI agent who takes no notice of the clear signs of murder and cannot return a daughter to her mother ends in nothingness. Such conundrums posed by a nonlinear cosmos occur in all nonlinear narrative in film and television, whether about a hero's journey or about history. And they pose problems not only for how audiences feel about film and television but also for what we have been conditioned to think of as heroic or historical. As we will discover in the chapters to follow, mass media storytelling for a nonlinear universe can justifiably also be called spooky action at a distance. Let us not understate how disconcerting they are.

To begin with the heroic narrative. The prevailing, well-worn narrative theories about the voyages of heroes echo Joseph Campbell's very influential, very Newtonian study, *The Hero with a Thousand Faces*. Only a linear adventure can ensue from Campbell's widely accepted assumption that all hero's journeys are variations on his linear monomyth. Campbell's template, which here stands as the model of what commerce insists on as the foundation of market mass-media entertainment, involves a protagonist in a series of events that begins with a call to adventure, progresses to the initiation segment, then moves to the denouement he calls return, in which the hero moves toward mastery and moral accomplishment.[24] Like Rick.

For all Campbell's sensitivity to multicultural fictions, and his nuanced discussions of psychology and metaphysics, he paid no attention to how different ideas about reality, already in public circulation when he wrote his book, might pose problems for the truth and reality of his linear monomyth and his narrative template. In fact, late in his career, in the 1970s, when the new map of the cosmos was fleshed out more clearly, Campbell and conventional storytellers like George Lucas and Steven Spielberg spoke of how brilliantly Campbell illuminated storytelling in the movies, strengthening a misguided and still-prevalent belief that only a linear hero's journey constitutes true narrative in popular entertainment. Understanding *Star Wars* in terms of the Campbellian linear monomyth is all well and good. But it is not feasible to limit media narratives to those parameters in a changing vision of reality. Arguing for attention to those who break the Campbellian mold, as legitimate, prescient storytellers in a new, nonlinear zeitgeist, is what we propose to do here.

Similarly, if the story of the hero is profoundly altered in a nonlinear universe, so is the story of individuals who are part of a drama bigger than themselves in the historical narrative. I am also arguing for the recognition of a new kind of historical storytelling. We can no longer recognize as historical movies and television *only* those that are in step with history as defined by the centuries-long teleological historical tradition developed by Christian dogma, Thomas Hobbes, John Locke, Georg Wilhelm Friedrich Hegel, and Karl Marx—and continued by their contemporary inheritors, the likes of Yuval Noah Harari and Francis Fukuyama. Traditional historians only recognize as history events in time that follow a universal, forward-thrusting pattern, though there is robust disagreement about the one, true teleology.

Consider the differences between two modern teleologists. Harari contends in *Sapiens: A Brief History of Humankind* that there is only one historical narrative, and it leads teleologically from the loosely structured hunter-gatherer societies to societies that manage the food supply through planned agriculture. Harari's thesis is that history is a teleology that inevitably leads to the growth of hierarchical organization, which even with all its injustices is the only possible model of civilization.[25] In *The End of History and the Last Man*, Fukuyama has a teleology, too, but quite a different one. He also argues for a singular historical narrative, but his argument goes like this: Liberal democracy is the end point of the one, continuous, historical evolution; it is the end of history because it has none of the flaws of previous ideas about cultural organization.[26] These and all teleological historians we might consider—from Thomas Hobbes to Karl Marx to the present day—depend on the linear time of the Newtonian universe. But historical reality does not conform to teleology in the map being drawn by the natural sciences—or in the work of a new crop of historians.

Consider *The Dawn of Everything: A New History of Humanity* by David Graeber and David Wengrow. Graeber and Wengrow do not contest linear time, nor do any of the new historians, but they do argue from the growing body of new archaeological and anthropological evidence that there is no basis for belief in any of the universalist historical teleologies proposed by the likes of Harari and Fukuyama. This perspective on history overlaps with nonlinear historical melodramas in film and television. Graeber and Wengrow argue that the overwhelming new evidence being gathered points away from historical teleology, and they contend that when we restrict ourselves to any one historical narrative, we not only arbitrarily reduce our idea of history, but also confine ourselves to a much less interesting story of culture than the evidence suggests.[27]

The same is true of the research archaeologists Israel Finkelstein and Neil Asher Silberman present in *The Bible Unearthed: Archaeology's New Vision of Ancient Israel and the Origin of Its Sacred Texts*, which disputes almost all historical interpretation of the Old Testament, not only the miracles like the parting of the Red Sea. Most biblical scholars give credence to the stories in the Old Testament about battles and the location of ancient kingdoms. Finkelstein and Silberman present documented evidence that what has commonly been understood as fact is not based on real events in the past, but is rather invented for a fabricated epic narrative, having as little historical verification as the fictions of *The Iliad* and *The Odyssey.* Finkelstein and Silberman do not claim that the verifiable historical truth is necessarily more interesting than the fabrications of the Old Testament, but rather that history is not teleological and needs to be sorted from the fantasies that have been circulated as if they were history and not just for a good story. They conjecture that the teleology of Old Testament stories, recounting the destiny of a chosen people, was intentionally fabricated to create a unity consciousness among the tribes of the Hebrews, which were radically fractured by internecine antagonisms, so that they might join together against their enemies.[28]

However, while *The Bible Unearthed* and *The Dawn of Everything* inject nonlinearity into the history of human culture, resulting in what is likely to be shocking to the general understanding of the past, the research on which they stand does not contest linear time. By contrast, nonlinear historical storytelling in the mass media dismisses both the reductiveness of a universal teleological narrative and the phantasms of historical destiny and Newtonian ideas of time and space. In *The Romanoffs,* the linear Romanov heritage is reduced to pure fantasy caught up in a much more interesting reality of nonlinear temporality, and in *Watchmen* all teleology is depicted as invention intended to advance the power of a particular group that is inevitably blown up by the reality of the discontinuities of nonlinear time and space.

In sum, in order to read the new hero's journey, or the new historical melodrama, we are called on to give up familiarity, assurances, and even, perhaps, some religious teachings. Though some readers will take like ducks to water to the new hero's journey and new historical melodramas, many are likely to find it difficult to engage with the radical emotional and intellectual changes necessitated by new zeitgeist storytelling. And indeed, the emotional and intellectual trauma of material and temporal nonlinearity have led to disengagement of many kinds, including misreadings of nonlinear narratives as dreams or science fiction. Far too many interpretations of David Lynch's films and *Twin Peaks* mistake the new vision of reality he is invoking as the presentation of a dream. Similarly, nonlinear historical melodramas are generally mislabeled as science fiction. As a proposed antidote to such misreadings, this voyage acknowledges the courage necessary for the suspension of our all-too-human dependence on the familiar. This voyage proposes a reward for the courage to consider the narratives of nonlinear time and space as visions of a new cosmic reality, as poetry of the limitlessness of a quantum universe and a unified field: Once we make that leap, we can be rewarded by an ability to see the truly inspired and complex nature of the cocreation between popular narrative and the natural and social sciences.

Much of the complexity inheres in the differences between the ways poets and scientists function. The boundlessness of the new zeitgeist tends toward (ironically) a limited number of models among scientists. Among poets, it provokes diverse visions as numerous as the artists themselves. Moreover, the media artists we are about to visit do not choose one side of the debate between quantum scientists and those who continue along the road Einstein trod. Post-Newtonian physicists continue to work along that divide, but the films and television series that lie ahead reflect, each in its own way, the most current thinking in physics that imagines the oxymoron of a universe of both quantum discontinuity and unified field.

The most developed of the scientific searches for an Einsteinian proof of a unified field is string theory, based on the substitution of vibrating strings for particles as the building blocks of the cosmos.[29] That substitution holds promise that they will find the proof Einstein sought, that at the core of the quantum-like universe is a coherence within which the nonmaterial might exist or even be the supreme reality—a soul, a consciousness, and moral responsibility. Such a universe would be both spooky and stable, acknowledging both the reality of quantum particles and vibrating strings. So, when or if string theory can be validated by proof, of which there is none now, it will not mean the return of historical teleology or a heroic reality that contains Rick Blaine and Sam Spade, but something closer to the visions of Lynch, Lindelof, Weiner, and the other artists we will discuss. That is the nature of cocreation of a new understanding of reality by the popular arts and the rigorous sciences.

Whatever was in the air that inspired Einstein and Schrödinger to explore new ideas has also long been in the air for artists, who are always equally sensitive to new possibilities as scientists and philosophers. But before we visit the works of the new cutting-edge popular artists, one prefatory caveat. The preoccupations of artists and theoretical scientists always trickle down to popular journeyman crafters. In the sciences, the crafters are engineers, who invent new, practical kinds of technology as opposed to discovering new existential problems. In the popular media, the crafters are storytellers who use the new nonlinear ideas as stylistic innovations as opposed to new directions in the constructs of belief.

An important assumption of this study is that it is important to discriminate between film and television that dives deeply into the narrative ramifications of the boundless/unified universe envisioned by cutting-edge science and philosophy, and movies and television that merely portray nonlinear mysteries as disposable in a Newtonian universe.

WE'LL ALWAYS HAVE GALLIFREY

The hallmark of the extremely popular, contemporary linear movies and TV that give the audience only a fun-filled whiff of nonlinearity is that they comfort us with the assumption that nonlinearity is nothing more troubling than a hiccup in the standard Newtonian scheme of things. Where fully nonlinear historical cinema and series narrative gives the audience a total experience of the baffling quantum *here* of superposition and entanglement, and the oxymorons of cosmic continuities and discontinuities; movies and TV that dabble in trendy nonlinearity bring us back from the brink at closure. Consider the movie *Groundhog Day* and *Doctor Who*, the TV series, which tease the mind and agitate our emotions with small doses of nonlinearity, but ultimately restore "normal"—read "Newtonian"—linearity. *Groundhog Day* (1993) makes for merriment when it throws its protagonist, miserable, unfeeling Phil Connors (Bill Murray), a status-conscious weatherman for a small Pittsburgh television station, into nonlinear time just long enough for him to return to linear temporality a more loving person, now committed to the familiar middle-class narrative of marriage and family, in a small town that looks like a Christmas card, no less. *Groundhog Day* is barely ankle-deep in nonlinearity.

The series *Doctor Who* (1963–1989; rebooted in 2005) is at least as much fun as *Groundhog Day*, and it provides a greater range of wrinkles in time and space. However, it too stays in the nonlinear shallows. Each new episode wades knee-deep into the new nonlinear mysteries but then wades right back out to the reassuring way it was before things (briefly) went sideways. The enigmatic Time Lord from Gallifrey, known only as the Doctor, travels the corridors of time backward and forward, as if time were Route 95, in a vehicle called a TARDIS that suggests the limitless quantum materiality the show does not follow through on. On the outside, it is a six-by-four-foot, old-fashioned British police box, but on the inside is boundless space. The name, TARDIS, is an acronym for "Time And Relative Dimension(s) In Space." However, the Doctor's goals, successfully achieved in the spirit of Joseph Campbell's heroes, always serve to reestablish linear time. Indeed, in one of his most tantalizing stories, which spans the entirety of season 6 of the rebooted *Doctor Who* series, the premise is that if he doesn't die, the cosmos will implode from the horrors of nonlinear instability. Don't ask.

Well, he both lives and dies in reboot-season 6, and so the cosmos doesn't implode. By the end of the season, the Doctor is both dead and alive, à la Schrödinger. But it's Schrödinger-lite. Lots of "timey-wimey" things happen in the season, but its long arc narrates the success of the Eleventh Doctor (Matt Smith) in inventing a strategy whereby his unwilling wife, River Song (Alex Kingston), agrees to kill him so that linear time will not collapse, since we must always save linear time—otherwise, catastrophe. For example, with linear time on the chopping block, prehistoric pterodactyls swoop out of the sky over a modern London park. Charles Dickens (Simon Callow) is interviewed on television talking about his plans to write a new book that "involves ghosts in the past, the present, and future, all at the same time." Winston Churchill (Ian McNeice) holds the office of Holy Roman Emperor and parties with Cleopatra in twenty-first-century England, and the time is always two minutes past five on April 22.

No fear. The Doctor engineers circumstances so that his bride, River, kills him *and* he doesn't die. As they marry, the Doctor whispers a cosmic secret in his bride's ear while leaning in for a cosmic kiss that signifies both marriage and murder. *Here* regains its normative image for us all. The Doctor and River will always have Gallifrey; it is an updated *Casablanca*, spiced with a quantum aroma. And so it goes with the similarly semi-spooky Marvel universe and a raft of semi-spooky time-travel movies and TV. It is a good time, but it must be distinguished from the narrative revolution in the mass media, inaugurated by David Lynch, that recognizes the strange, deeply real, nonlinear, oxymoronic cosmos.

Inaugurated is a figure of speech, of course. There are no clear beginnings. So, although the chapters to follow begin with Lynch's *Twin Peaks*, this introduction concludes with Stanley Kubrick's *2001: A Space Odyssey*, an interesting prologue to the beginning. In 1968, Kubrick baffled, outraged, and frightened audiences, critics, and even his cocreator, Arthur C. Clarke, with a nonlinear reality for which no one in the mass media was ready. My favorite anecdote, though apocryphal, about the reception of *2001* is Rock Hudson's explosive reaction on exiting the theater after the film's high-visibility premiere, when he was reported to have said, "What the fuck was *that* about?"[30] The Rock of this urban legend got it. He had the fully nonlinear experience, but no idea what to do with it. Nor did any of the critics. Subsequent early attempts to deal with "that uncertain feeling" led critics either to reject *2001* as a narrative film or try to force linear meaning into it. Clarke, especially, desperate to make it more user-friendly to unaccustomed spectators for a better box office, "novelized" *2001* by "filling in the blanks" of Kubrick's film.[31] But we are here to recognize *2001* for what it is: a radical reality shift.

Once we consider Kubrick's brilliant film in the context of the new map of the universe, *2001* becomes a new experience of reality. With the new map of the universe in mind, we can appreciate the retro nature of Clarke's book, which was not a mere transfer of *2001* from screen to page. It was a narrative regression from a nonlinear back to a linear cosmos, oblivious to the vast implications of modern science for storytelling. Indeed, in the ways that count, Kubrick's *2001* bears less relationship to Clarke's boring novelization than it does to Lynch's *Eraserhead*. Only nine years after the film *2001*, in 1977, Kubrick, who primarily worked with linear narrative, intuited that there was a future for a very different form of filmic storytelling, once he had seen David Lynch's first feature-length film, which he had seen multiple times, and which he used in his creation of *The Shining* (1980).[32] Similarly, Lynch recognizes Kubrick as his cinematic godfather. When, probably in 1995, I proposed a conference at NYU that would include both Kubrick and Lynch, Lynch was elated at the prospect. Alas, the conference didn't materialize. Would it have revealed some kind of spiritual connection between Kubrick's *2001*, Lynch's film and television, and the birth of nonlinear narrative in the mass media? Quite possibly. So, I will propose that spiritual transition here. I offer *2001* as a fraught, exhilarating prefiguration of the recent blossoming of an interface between popular entertainment and the new cosmos.

COSMIC OXYMORON

Before *2001* begins narratively, Kubrick prepares us with two minutes and fifty-two seconds of a musical overture, György Ligeti's musical composition *Atmosphères* played over a black screen. *Atmosphères* becomes the frame for a nonlinear cinematic experience as it evokes a nonlinear sound environment devoid of the linear musical structures of melody, harmony, and sequential rhythm. It uses tone clusters that music critic Harald Kaufmann describes as breaking down conventional musical organization into "a magma of evolving sound," which Kaufmann elsewhere likens to breathing.[33] When visual images finally appear, the sound environment transitions into the grand strains of *Thus Spake Zarathustra*, by Richard Strauss, which rise behind a syzygy, a cosmic vision of an ordered universe of aligned planetary bodies. Per Ligeti and Strauss, through Kubrick, a cosmos of both magisterial order and disorienting discontinuity manifests; the cosmos beckons us into a limitless, yet paradoxically coherent, Einsteinian universe. It merits the Strauss fanfare. The same cannot be said of what we see initially of life on Earth.

In the first segment of *2001*, "The Dawn of Man," we enter the muted monotony of unrelieved flow, a boundless plain, devoid of linear anything. There isn't even a sound environment, linear or nonlinear. The plain is populated by vaguely formed groups of viscerally motivated, almost upright ape-humans and pacific, four-footed beasts like tapirs; the horizon is haphazard, undefined. Its silence is broken by random grunts and chattering.

FIGURE 0.1 *Stanley Kubrick's postquantum vision of prehistory in* 2001: A Space Odyssey. *Barren, empty terrain.*

Activity lacks sequence. It is, rather, a limitless panoply of fragmentary calm and violence. Narrative sequence, let alone the linearity of cause and effect, does not exist. This is not the accustomed expository opening of a film.

Nor does sequence immediately appear when a black monolith, in materiality and energy unlike anything else, shows up suddenly, for no discernible reason and from no discernible source. It is bounded where all else is unbounded, but it is a mutation, not a development. It emits an energy and sound unlike anything else on the vast, open expanse. Then something happens that is also a mutation. Linear action begins. It is born of a paradox, as inexplicable as the monolith itself. An object devoid of sequence in a linear chain of cause and effect, the monolith appears at roughly the same time that cause and effect enters the boundless Earth plain. But is the monolith part of that sequence? That question will not be answered in any way until the end of the film, and not even then in a way that satisfies a linear template.

At first glance, there *might be* a connection between the monolith and the actions of one curious ape (Daniel Richter). It is more of a question than an established foundation of history. The ape plays haphazardly with the bones of the dead animals littered meaninglessly about. They suddenly become interesting when a cause-and-effect connection mutates into the ape's life. Based on no previous experience, he picks up a bone and shatters the others lying on the ground. Can we trace this back to the appearance of the monolith? Or is it merely Darwinian discontinuity toward a new trajectory? The idea of breaking scattered bones with a chosen bone is followed by the ape's discovery that he can break a living creature too. Cause and effect equals murder. In his excitement, the ape throws the bone into the air, where it seamlessly morphs before our eyes into a space station in boundless space. Limitlessness remains on the audience radar, along with the linear teleology of technology, which has, after an unspecified interim, engendered an entire technological culture. Was technology the only possible trajectory possible? The visuals tell us it isn't. The interface between cause and effect, technology, and murder remains nothing more than a tiny option in an unbounded universe.

The opening frames do not suggest a necessary, progressive connection, à la the historical teleologies of Harari and Fukuyama, between the appearance of the monolith and a history that follows an ape's discovery of sequential cause and effect. This is not a prehistorical introduction that suggests that what follows is the linear course of history, creating meaning where there had been only chaos. It is rather an extrahistorical introduction that diminishes the teleology of technology that grows out of the ape's mutated adaptation. In fact, I contend that the rest of the film asks us to experience as curious, à la Graeber and Wengrow, the way human beings became historically stuck in an ape's delight in his murderous application of linear sequence and, thereby, stuck in a diminished existence. The film re-visions linear technological progress as a form of sensory impoverishment and detachment from the larger reality. The space age to which we have leaped contains little or no color, no art, and only the most cursory of human relations. People speak in detached platitudes; families communicate through screens. Etching a jump from the ape's discovery of linearity to the sudden reappearance of the monolith in the Tycho crater on Earth's moon, sending and receiving signals from the planet Jupiter, Kubrick suggests that linear culture that evolved in between those two events is just more of the same thing, ad nauseum. The historical moment of potential change is the emergence of a second chance for humankind for a more expansive relationship with a boundless yet unified reality.

That humanity badly needs a second chance is made manifest when we meet HAL 9000. When the human powers that be send a crew of astronauts to Jupiter, on the spaceship *Discovery One*, to investigate the nature of the connection between the mysterious monolith and Jupiter, the humans on the mission have been diminished so radically that they are merely pieces of a puzzle, known in its totality only to the computer in the 9000 series known by the acronym HAL (*H*euristically programmed *AL*gorithmic computer;[34] voiced by Douglas Rain). HAL reveals himself as the horrifying reductio ad absurdum of linear culture when he kills almost all the human crew and turns to the business of murdering the final man, Dave Bowman (Keir Dullea). Second chance anyone? Bowman realizes what HAL is up to, dismantles him, and gains belated access to information about the official goals of the mission. Dave is now cleared to do some real exploring. But the enlightenment that the *Discovery One* mission brings is independent of, and renders moot, its original, narrow quest to answer questions about the monolith. It is, rather, the start of a greater mystery and a potential rebirth for humankind. The designated historical mission cannot be completed in the universe Bowman discovers. Instead, the plan, inextricably bound to the now-defunct computer, dissipates as a new sensibility takes over.

In the final section of the film, "Jupiter and Beyond the Infinite," Bowman encounters the oxymoronic but sublime cosmos that is both a united field and a quantum nonlinearity: a new manifestation of the monolith in both superposition—it is one and it is more than one—and entanglement is co-present with a reiteration of the syzygy of the opening frames, the image of the orderly globes. Bowman is inundated with sensations and his eye undergoes many mutations as he engages time and space anew and comes in for a landing on a terrain that resembles the wide-open, rocky spaces of Earth at the "Dawn of Man." On Jupiter, the reality of infinite nonlinear time, superposition, and entanglement are unconcealed by teleology. Bowman exists not as one being in one time and place, but as a being in superposition at all times. He meets himself in a setting composed of the objects of the many historical eras that were elided when the film jumped from the ape to the space station. Bowman's is a climactic new experience of himself and of history.

Bowman's voyage has brought him back to the beginning of linear, technological teleology and to the implosion of what once might have been mistaken by the audience as a necessary, linear progression. As *Discovery One* cruises in for a landing, we experience the same openness with which we began but radiant with unprecedented color. Then Bowman enters a space filled with ancient Greek statues, porcelain shepherds and shepherdesses, tufted French provincial furniture, and the silver and crystal of an elegant twentieth-century table, and we experience a fusion of the events previously

FIGURE 0.2 *Dave Bowman in a space suit.*

FIGURE 0.3 *Dave, an old man in a robe.*

FIGURE 0.4 *Dave on his deathbed.*

excised by the cut between bone and space station. A face-off between linear history and the boundless infinite is Bowman's unexpected discovery, and it leads to a potential reboot of civilization itself. Bowman is surrounded by the howls and grunts of the apes of four million years ago, but not the reductive ape-constructed cause-and-effect sequence. This time, Bowman is ending and beginning simultaneously. Bowman is a young astronaut, an old astronaut, an old man at home in an elegant apartment, and a dying man on his deathbed. The monolith appears again in front of the deathbed, and he dies, pointing to it; yet he is still alive as a shining, fetal presence in a shining orb. The fetal apparition, which bears a striking resemblance to Bowman, is saluted by the fanfare-like opening notes of *Thus Spake Zarathustra*. We are at the beginning of the film and the end, but perhaps with a new knowledge that is worthy of the fanfare.

The shimmering fetal presence has the force of a sunrise. Infinity out of the finite. Nonlinearity made possible by the technology of linearity. Life out of death. And there are very big questions. Kubrick poetically envisions both nonlinearity and a unified field. It is a clarion call to film and television to play with nonlinear narrative, to probe the possibilities of a boundless yet unified universe without the retreat to the old linearity that we find in *Groundhog Day* and *Doctor Who*.

Thank you, Stanley Kubrick. His preamble to the intersections between poetry and science, to come in future chapters, invokes both a new cinematic reality for the mass media, under cover of the image of a literal journey into nonlinear space and time, and the journey we are about to take into the cosmos. Let us not understate how thrilling and exhilarating that voyage can be. As we make our journey, we will be experiencing more than one intersection. There is the intersection between the natural and social sciences and the mass media. But there is also the intersection between the vision of the artist and the vision of the intellectual, both those who explore science and those, like me, who explore storytelling. These intersections are both fascinating and difficult to negotiate, and I have had to deal with how to report them credibly and with integrity. On the one hand, we have the clearly stated objectives of science in the writings of physicists and historians and their popularizers. The intersecting objectives and visions of the storytellers? Not as clearly announced, or as widely disseminated. As great good fortune would have it, I gained access to several of the storytellers and their firsthand accounts of their creative processes, industry pressures, and visions. David Lynch, who gave me yet another new group of insights into his nonlinear film and television, and Matthew Weiner (*The Romanoffs*) and Damon Lindelof (*Watchmen*), by their own accounts influenced by Lynch, generously engaged with me. A thrilling intersection, giving shape to the paradoxical overlap of these popular artists with the natural and social sciences and chasms between art and science. My study of nonlinearity is nonlinear.

Filled with the wonder of the strange, like the scientific and aesthetic map of nonlinearity, my study is also a well-considered work in progress. There are many important revelations—more questions than answers—that emerge as we encounter the overlap of the methods and meanings in the works of the scientists who have experimented their way into a new age; the perspectives and processes of selected mass-media artists; and my methods and meanings derived from them.

The nonlinear poetic expressions that interface with the proofs of nonlinearity and unity in the natural and social sciences encourage us to wonder what in the world is happening, as we stumble into the gaps between perception and reality in the films and series. I encourage a simultaneous wonder at the odd fellowships between poets and scientists that are unearthed and the diversity of visions of the nonlinear cosmos adopted by Lynch, Lindelof, and Weiner. They grow out of the natural sciences, modern existentialism, ancient Vedic spiritualism, and modern interpretations of ancient esotericism, all of which I will unpack in the chapters to follow, where pertinent.

Please consider the voyage ahead as an invitation to imaginatively experience in selected innovative films and series what happens to heroes and history in the new zeitgeist.

There are two kinds of nonlinear hero's journeys we will make. We will engage series and cinema about what the boundless quantum universe means to insiders, pillars of bounded marketplace structures who find themselves shaken and stirred by the pressures of limitlessness. We will also encounter series and cinema about heroes who have never fit into the limits imposed by the marketplace, square pegs in round holes, who experience for the first time freedom and a higher consciousness in a world of indeterminate particles and waves as old limits blur, bend, and break. The story of Agent Cooper in *Twin Peaks*, season 3, and the story of Jack O'Brien (Sean Penn) in *The Tree of Life* are examples of the first kind of journey. The story of the many-named heroine (Brit Marling) in *The OA*; and of Joel Barish (Jim Carrey) and Clementine Kruczynski (Kate Winslet) in *Eternal Sunshine of the Spotless Mind* are examples of the second kind of new hero's journey.

With respect to history, we will observe the reinvention of two kinds of historical linearities: heritage and teleology. We will observe how Matthew Weiner in *The Romanoffs*; Tom Tykwer and the Wachowski sisters in *Cloud Atlas*; and Spike Lee in *BlacKkKlansman* deal with heritage in a nonlinear universe. We will observe how Jonathan Nolan and Lisa Joy in *Westworld*; Denis Villeneuve in *Arrival*; and Damon Lindelof in *Watchmen* deal with historical teleology in a nonlinear universe. The post-Newtonian historical melodramas, while exposing the impossibility of teleology and heritage—as we have understood them—in the new cosmos do not leave us with limitless nothingness. Rather, beyond linear heritage and teleology we will find a number of versions of a new kind of historical coherence and new possibilities.

Prepare. Ahead heroes and history are about to materialize in new time and space with strange, new problems and even stranger options. Cue the opening notes of *Thus Spake Zarathustra*.

Part I

THE HERO'S NONLINEAR JOURNEY

DAVID LYNCH AND UNMANIFEST DESTINY

Chapter 1

Twin Peaks 3

A most disturbing—or perhaps liberating—consequence of quantum physics is that the past no longer determines the future, at least not completely.

RICHARD A. MULLER, *Now: The Physics of Time*

Space and time . . . can no longer be thought of as an inert backdrop on which the events of the universe play themselves out; rather, through special and then general relativity, they are intimate players in the events themselves.

BRIAN GREENE, *The Elegant Universe: Superstrings, Hidden Dimensions, and the Quest for the Ultimate Theory*

What is more familiar to film and television audiences than the mythos of the questing journey of the hero, society's courageous, sharp-witted, inevitably successful guardian and protector? And who more dear to the mass media than its detective heroes? Here's looking at all those dashing, intrepid G-men, FBI agents, police, and gumshoes. They recognize the clues, when others cannot pick them out of a mass of details. Theirs is a manifest destiny of unraveling the mysteries of cause and effect, to reveal whodunit and why. Or would you prefer Special Agent Dale Cooper (Kyle MacLachlan), in *Twin Peaks*? He is FBI, he sees clues of which others are oblivious. But they don't lead to whodunit or why. He lives in a universe of unmanifest destiny, your new, much less familiar, option. What is it? Let us go and make our visit.

The mass media have long given us the choice of vicariously living the heroic journeys of a pantheon of sleuths who operate from inside the rules and regulations of society, in a linear universe, to foil those who stray outside the bounds of legal, ethical, and moral limits. Only in 1990 did David Lynch's game-changing *Twin Peaks* introduce us to Special Agent Cooper, the questing hero, an elite defender of the public, who is bewildered by a nonlinear universe. Inside, outside, cause and effect, even here and there.

Who can tell which is which in Lynch's mysteriously boundless yet enigmatically unified nonlinear, post-Newtonian universe?

Cocreating the new zeitgeist with the natural and social sciences, David Lynch has reconceived one of the most popular mass-culture genres, the detective story. We are talking, of course, about his riveting images, montages, and sound designs that convey the new, post-Newtonian realities of materiality, time, and energy. But we are also talking about his even more puzzling, unbound narratives in *Twin Peaks*, no longer lashed to the manifest (visible) linear dynamic of cause and effect, and a heroic passage from here (the initial problem) to there (the impending solution.) In this pioneering series, Lynch's Special Agent Cooper and the audience are, rather, forced into a cosmos where we are always in an unmanifest (not visible) *here*. It is a cosmos that thwarts linear heroic action through the indeterminacies of nonlinear time and space and yet is also a unified consciousness filled by inevitable, unmanifest destiny.

Indeterminate *and* inevitable?

Only when we reach the third season of *Twin Peaks* do we really know the paradoxes of its universe. We begin this study of the mass-media cocreation of a nonlinear zeitgeist by observing the startling season-to-season mutation of *Twin Peaks*'s detective hero, Special Agent Dale Cooper. There is a stark difference between Cooper's reality as it appears in seasons 1 and 2 of *Twin Peaks* (1990–1991; hereafter *TP 1* and *TP 2*) and the reality of the film *Twin Peaks: Fire Walk with Me* (1992; *FWWM*), and a still-greater reality shift that takes place when we know Cooper again in *Twin Peaks*, season 3 (2017; *TP 3*). It is as though, over the years, we have been standing in a photographic darkroom, watching an emerging image in a tray of developer.

Almost everyone familiar with *Twin Peaks* is aware of the pressure ABC TV put on David Lynch to create a linear narrative in *TP 1* and *TP 2* that would take Cooper from here (the death of Laura Palmer) to there (the whodunit moment).[1] So, that happened. But Lynch, nevertheless, snatched his series from the prequantum jaws of Channel 7, after the fact. When Cooper found, in *TP 2*, that Leland Palmer had murdered his daughter—albeit while possessed by a demon with the prosaic name of BOB (Frank Silva)—that was supposed to be "case closed." However, Lynch rejected the linear finality of Cooper's discovery written into the scripts against his wishes. He propelled Cooper into a nonlinear universe at the climactic closure of the second season. And Lynch didn't stop. In *FWWM*, which visits the events leading up to Laura's death, images of the new physics and the impossibility of linearity seem to be waiting around every corner. When we reach the third season, which explores in much greater depth Cooper's new reality, *Twin Peaks* goes into full-throttle spooky action at a distance. Details to follow shortly about how the *Twin*

Peaks saga moved from one universe to another. Or was its universe always here, like the photographic image before it is fully manifest?

To clarify this perspective on Lynch's groundbreaking series, I invite you once again into my privileged conversations with him, which have followed a similar pattern of time release. In 1990, he revealed to me important information about the Red Room as a place of larger reality than the marketplace of ordinary affairs. As a result, I wrote about *Twin Peaks* in *The Passion of David Lynch: Wild at Heart in Hollywood*.[2] In 2010, a conversation that got us into Lynch's fascination with quantum physics led to *David Lynch Swerves: Uncertainty from "Lost Highway" to "Inland Empire."*[3] Then, after ninety minutes of conversation with Lynch in May of 2023, a new shock of recognition. And this study.

Wait. Not so fast. Lynchian? There is, after all, another name on the credits, Mark Frost, and television is a collaborative medium. Time out for a necessary digression. Some readers may remember that I have already written of my discovery of an asymmetry between Lynch and Frost.[4] The books about *Twin Peaks* Frost has since published have only confirmed my perception of the skew between Frost's linear worldview and Lynch's nonlinear vision.

We now have evidence that these books did not sit well with Lynch, who was determined to make a sharp distinction between Frost's books and the series. Sabrina Sutherland, executive producer of *TP 3*, told me that Lynch wanted to make sure that everyone knew that Mark's books were his alone and "anything in them came from Mark and not David at all. This is why David's name is not on the books and only Mark's is." Truth to tell, Lynch politely and appropriately drew a necessary line between Frost's books and the on-screen show. Frost's publications conjure the series Frost wanted to write. They are irrelevant to the on-air episodes. Indeed, by the time they were published, the series' cosmos had long since become thoroughly Lynchian. The precise moment the die was cast was during the taping of the second-season finale.[5]

At first, as season 2 progressed, Lynch took his hands off the wheel. He showed up to play FBI chief Gordon Cole, concentrating his attention on *Wild at Heart*, his new film, while Frost built a linear adventure for Cooper after what had seemed the solution to Laura's murder. Lynch seemed to have given up on his vision. But when it came time for him to direct the season finale of *TP 2*, in a stunning reversal, he discarded Frost's script. Lynch improvised the finale while he was taping it, disposed of Frost's linear universe and the neat plot solution ABC had demanded, and propelled Cooper into a nonlinear cosmos. The action was spooky once more. Very spooky. Cooper now began to lose the confident location in time, space, matter, and energy of the conventional detective. Then in *TP 3*, Cooper's nonlinear trajectory pushed the *Twin Peaks* saga further into the new

Lynchian zeitgeist. While Frost has contributed many compelling images and some snappy, inspired dialogue in *Twin Peaks*, which he and I discussed in our interview, it is not his cosmos.[6] The word Lynchian stands with respect to the series.

But Lynchian does not mean quite what it seemed to mean before my final interview with him. As Lynch and I spoke, in May 2023, it became clear that, the abundant presence of quantum uncertainties in his film and television notwithstanding, in his personal vision, Lynch does not contemplate *only* a baffling reality in which matter can be in two places at once, or where two or more entities can be strangely entangled, regardless of distance in space-time. While Lynch is taken with quantum ideas and frequently depicts quantum events in his series, he believes that the uncertainty they articulate is only partial knowledge about an unbounded, unified universe. Partial knowledge. Full knowledge equates with enlightenment through engagement with the unified, unbound ocean of consciousness. Full knowledge of the series requires us to explore both the disconnections of its fragmented, quantum strangeness and its assertion of the connections of a unified field.

The totality of Lynch's vision poetically resonates with—it is not an exact echo of—the battle between quantum physicists and physicists walking on the path toward which Einstein pointed. Quantum mechanics maps a dark, disconnected, and uncertain universe. Einstein insisted that science continue to look for the unified cosmic field he believed exists beyond the local manifestation of quantum phenomena. Lynch comes down, on his own poetic terms, on the side of Einstein's speculations. For Lynch, at the same time that, at one level, reality is the unpredictable and essentially unknowable matter, time, and energy in the dark, quantum marketplace, on another level the universe is, in its full essence, unified. Lynch reflects Einstein in a poetic mirror.

Lynch's vision of a unified consciousness field poetically complements Einstein's scientific ruminations about a unified cosmic field. The spirit of Lynch's poetry translates the scientific intellectual/theoretical longing for proof of a paradoxical universe that is both unified and fragmented into an emotional/perceptual aesthetic expression. The artist does not seek proof. The artist who tells stories of a nonlinear universe depicts human action as it manifests to imagination in the context of boundless but unified mass, energy, and time. In *TP 3*, Lynch imagines an Einsteinian universe that is both random and unified by means of its perplexing evocation of both the discombobulating quantum marketplace *and* the glorious unity of the cosmos, but not by finding the elusive proof of the unity Einstein sought, of weak and strong forces, electromagnetic force, and gravity, that would constitute a unified universe. Rather, Lynch's series cocreates the new map of the universe by its embodied narrative visions of both detectives who get stuck in partial quantum knowledge and detectives who are lifted toward the enlightenment of a unified ocean of consciousness. The series offers stories set in an oxymoronic universe, through the tragedy of Special Agent Dale Cooper (and others) confusedly cutting themselves off from reality by getting trapped in partial knowledge, interwoven with the comedy of the detectives in the sheriff's station in Twin Peaks blundering into reality through inadvertent connections with an ocean of consciousness, in which all is unified.

To summarize: these are stories. Science is polemical. *Twin Peaks* is not part of a polemic on behalf of Lynch's personal beliefs; it is the poetry of a nonlinear universe, informed by Lynch's personal beliefs, that intersects asymmetrically with science. And we are about to engage in understanding David Lynch's specific nonlinear vision of the detective's journey, as we have never seen it before, as just that: stories informed by Lynch's very particular, profound belief in his nonlinear vision of reality. The other works we will explore in chapters to follow are similarly not polemical, but nonlinear storytelling informed by other profound personal visions that poetically overlap the new zeitgeist of the natural sciences. Lynch's aesthetic, poetic corollary for the scientific vision of the nonlinear universe is part of a range of poetic mass-media narrative corollaries by popular artists to follow.

After the early pleasantries of our May 11, 2023, conversation, Lynch's first words to me were, "I don't know anything. I've heard things. And some things I believe and some things I don't. And that's sort of the way I think it is for everyone. And so we go along and we hear certain things, and we say, because I say we're all like detectives, we hear certain things and we roll them around thinking about them and it's, like, you know, a cash register—you put in all these things and you hit the final button and it rings up and you get the answer. I believe in that."[7] Well, answers, beliefs, detectives. Unpacking Lynch's assertion in the light of the rest of our conversation, and what we hear and see on-screen in all the twists and turns of *Twin Peaks* over the years and decades, we find the Lynchian detective and his journey bathed in a new and brilliant light.

In Lynch's words: "There's certain things about quantum physics that I like to think about, having heard certain things that seem true. I like to think about these little strings [i.e., string theory]. What I believe in is this ocean of consciousness. There's a Vedic line, 'consciousness alone is.' There is nothing but consciousness. You are consciousness. I am consciousness. The chair is consciousness. There's nothing else but consciousness. *Nothing else but consciousness. Nothing else.* Consciousness exists in the nonrelative absolute, one absolute, unbounded ocean of pure consciousness, unmanifest."[8]

For the *Twin Peaks* audience, following Lynch's vision of consciousness is likely to be a difficult leap of faith. But how else can we read the series Lynch created? The great detectives working in physics labs are indispensable to the new map of the universe, but so are the great detectives working in film and television studios. Cocreation. We earn entrance into the conversation of physicists through informed, disciplined acquaintance with their experimentation. We earn entrance into Lynch's vision that a unitary consciousness *is*, and that there is nothing else but that consciousness, by springing intuitively into the complex of narrative and visual and aural textures of *Twin Peaks*.

Our first great leap occurs at the end of *TP 2*, when images of Cooper begin to resonate quantum mechanics. In the Red Room Cooper enters in the second season finale, he splits into a detective and his doppelgänger. He becomes the negative energy that is BOB, who has been identified as the driving force behind Leland Palmer killing his own daughter, and he remains Agent Cooper at the same time. When he exits the Red Room, he both remains there and is in the Great Northern Hotel in Twin Peaks. He is strangely in more than one place at the same time and connected strangely over distances in time and space to the murdering energy he discovered as a detective. In "quantum speak," he is in states of superposition and entanglement, respectively. And it is a reality not a dream or a fantasy. Strikingly, this quantum reality was not manifest when the series began.

TP 1 initially represented what seemed to be the old, classic Newtonian universe, in which time, matter, and space are the stage on which Cooper investigated mystery as he moved through a trail of clue, clue, clue, clue, leading to Definitive Solution, and the identification of Laura's murderer. Case closed. And in which the Red Room was only a dream. But Lynch surprised us by then revealing a very different universe in the *TP 2* season finale, when we, along with Cooper, had the experience of seeing what we had not seen before, a real Red Room, a quantum material world of doppelgängers and a Laura who radiates the quantum mystery of Schrödinger's cat by being both dead and alive, both positive and negative. Here *Twin Peaks* became a new image of reality and a new kind of mystery involving a new consciousness about the world of things and bodies. Matter, time, and space themselves are no longer the stage for a plot enigma, they *are* the enigma.

This kind of storytelling constitutes a big deviation from the theory of the hero's journey as defined by Joseph Campbell's masterwork, *The Hero with a Thousand Faces*, with its template, so widely adopted by popular- and high-culture storytellers. Joseph Campbell maps a monomyth that he asserts informs all heroic passages, on an inert terrain through which a hero passes through three narrative stages—the Departure, the

Initiation, and the Return—moving definitively from here to there toward a definitive conclusion. It is a passage that almost all mass-media storytellers have adopted to create their heroes.[9] Useful it has been, but only in a Newtonian reality of immobile, stable time and space. Our first leap into a new cosmic reality in *Twin Peaks* is the discovery that Cooper is not one of Campbell's thousand faces.

Campbell's version of the hero exists in Newtonian space and time which, thank you, Brian Greene, are no more than the material "backdrop on which the events of the universe play themselves out." Lynch, by contrast, sends Agent Cooper, again to quote Greene, into quantum space and time that are "intimate players in the events themselves," making *Twin Peaks* part of a history of narratives that are not in the tradition of the ancient myth of Theseus, one of Campbell's favorites, in which the hero solves the puzzle of the inert space of a labyrinth, or the more contemporary movie *The Maltese Falcon*, in which the world is an unmoving stage for Sam Spade's pursuit of a statue.[10] Yes, there is already a new history of nonlinear narrative we can reference in both physics and literature. Consider the imagined quantum scenario by the twentieth-century physicist Arthur S. Eddington in *The Nature of the Physical World* (1927). Then consider the novels of twentieth-century writer Franz Kafka.

In *The Nature of the Physical World*, as Eddington discusses the new quantum science, he offers up a seriocomic portrait of himself as a man in a cosmos in which time, space, and matter are players in his attempt to simply enter a room. I return often in my work to this illuminating passage, in which Eddington plays with the vision of time, space, matter that are not merely an inert background for human action. In Eddington's words:

> I am standing on the threshold about to enter a room. It is a complicated business. In the first place I must shove against an atmosphere pressing with a force of fourteen pounds on every square inch of my body. I must make sure of landing on a plank traveling at twenty miles a second round the sun—a fraction of a second too early or too late, the plank would be miles away. I must do this whilst hanging from a round planet headed outward into space, and with a wind of aether blowing at no one knows how many miles a second through ever interstice of my body. The plank has no solidity of substance. To step on it is like stepping on a swarm of flies. Shall I not slip through? No, if I make the venture one of the flies hits me and gives a boost up again; I fall again and am knocked upwards by another fly; and so on.[11]

In a quantum universe, merely entering a room is such a mysterious, nonlinear drama in itself that at the very least it decenters and at most replaces conventional linear-plot action, such as solving the riddles of Theseus's labyrinth and finding Sam Spade's falcon.

Franz Kafka similarly depicted the conundrum of time and space as active players in events, decentering plot. In Kafka's novel *The Trial* (1925), for example, the hero, Josef K., is arrested for reasons never disclosed to him or the reader and must defend himself within a labyrinthine legal system in which it is impossible either to find out the nature of his crime or to get a legal defense. The oxymoron of K's life is emphasized in chapter 9, "In the Cathedral," the novel's penultimate chapter, in which a priest tells K. a story about a man who spends his life trying in vain to be admitted to the law by a doorkeeper in front of an entrance. As the man is about to die, he asks the doorkeeper why, if all men seek to be admitted to the law, no one has tried to enter the door but him. The doorman replies, "No one else could be granted entry here, because this entrance was intended for you alone. I shall now go and shut it." K's struggle with the unfathomable ends when two anonymous assassins kill him, for no reasons he or the reader can determine.[12] This is the quantum reality of the Kafkaesque hero in a nutshell. A similar reality can be found in Kafka's earlier and perhaps more stunning novel, *The Metamorphosis* (1915), whose protagonist inexplicably transforms into a monstrous insect, whose only possibility in a bounded marketplace is to die.[13] Both Eddington and Kafka resonate with Cooper's journey, in which he transforms inexplicably, has difficulty merely going places, and finally evaporates into nothingness.

But there is more in the *Twin Peaks* universe, even in the early days of the series, than quantum boundlessness. From the first, a sense of a larger unity is already subtly present in the Log Lady. But to speak of how she interpolates into *Twin Peaks* the unified field, we will need to augment our vocabulary. Superposition and entanglement take us only so far. We need an additional Lynchian vocabulary that illuminates Lynch's personal vision in *Twin Peaks* of both quantum boundlessness and a unified cosmos of "nothing but consciousness."

A NEW VOCABULARY FOR A UNIVERSE OF CONSCIOUSNESS

We begin by looking at the prologues Lynch wrote for the Log Lady (Catherine E. Coulson), which were added to every episode of *TP 1* and *TP 2*, when the boxed sets of the series came out, as well as looking at the angel who appears at the end of *FWWM*. In the Log Lady's prologues, especially that of the second season finale, and in the *FWWM* angel, we find the suggestion, albeit but dimly, of some greater wholeness and unity. Quantum language and concepts of superposition and entanglement are useful for talking about Cooper's nonlinear dreams, his entrance into the fragmentation of the Red Room, and his division at the closure of season 2. But they are no help in talking about the hints in the Log Lady prologues or the apparition of the *FWWM* angel of a contrapuntal external reality, a cosmic, coherent unity. We also need concepts that reference a unified field.

Here is where we must note how counterproductive it is to contextualize Lynch's art, and *Twin Peaks* in particular, with language and concepts that define Cooper's journey in terms of internal reality, specifically with the Freudian framework often misguidedly applied to Lynch's work. *Twin Peaks* is a universe that reflects enlightenment and knowledge in terms of the external, simultaneous existence of the manifest and unmanifest in an ocean of cosmic consciousness that is both the one and the many. By contrast, Freudian vocabulary defines only the internal encounter of the individual with its own un/subconscious. For discussing the heroic voyage in *Twin Peaks*, the Lynchian language he used when speaking to me of consciousness is necessary. Lynch spoke eloquently but concisely on the subject, and pointed me toward a book by Tony Nader, at that time not yet published, in which Nader mapped out in great detail what came to be Lynch's framework of belief. Dr. Nader generously made available to me the unpublished manuscript of what was then titled "One Unbounded Ocean of Consciousness" and has since given me access to a thoroughly revised draft manuscript of his book, which has now been published as *Consciousness Is All There Is: How Understanding and Experiencing Consciousness Will Transform Your Life*.

The two drafts present the same cosmic concept of the manifest and unmanifest in consciousness. Both drafts, together, serve us here as rare and extraordinarily useful resources for considering the vision that informs Lynch's art. However, in the second, published draft, a self-help book, while completely consistent conceptually with the earlier draft, a predominantly philosophical book, Nader has dropped the term *coning*, which Lynch not only used when he spoke with me, but which he illustrated for me with a hand-drawn diagram. The concept of coning is not necessary for Nader's practical advice to his readers about consciousness, but as we shall see it is invaluable to our exploration of *Twin Peaks*.[14]

Coning and other Lynchian vocabulary centers on the unmanifest and gives us words with which to speak of the levels of consciousness, from the lowest rung up to enlightenment, and to speak of the dynamic of transcending toward enlightenment and falling away from it. Lynch describes those processes in terms of coning up toward the unmanifest reality of enlightenment and coning down into the manifest, a Kafkaesque descent away from reality.[15] Through Lynch's vocabulary, we can speak of Cooper being stuck in partial quantum knowledge and coning down to nonbeing,

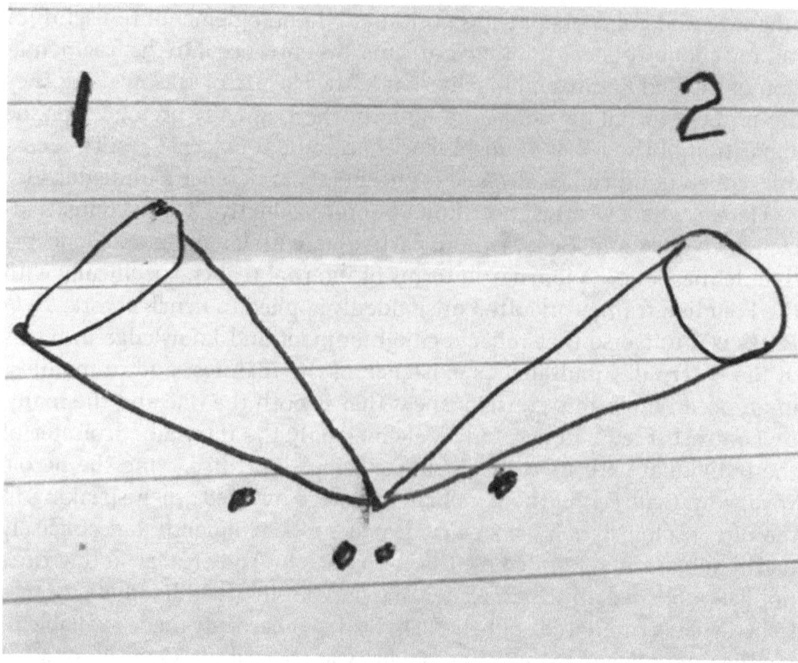

FIGURE 1.1 *David Lynch's hand-drawn illustration of "coning."*

and we can also speak of a very different set of detectives in the series, the detectives in the Twin Peaks Sheriff's Department , as they cone up toward reality and existence.

These are the waves we ride in *Twin Peaks*. Point of interest: Quantum mechanics envisions a form of coning up and down in its descriptions of the particles of which the manifest world is made. Physicists have observed that those basic particles spin. They can spin up or down. When physicists measure entangled particles, they find that the particles are spinning up and down at the same time.[16] Quite a bit of spinning takes place in the *Twin Peaks* saga.

Using Lynch's vocabulary as a parachute, we can glide into Lynch's perspective on the constant, simultaneous, unmanifest movement of the cosmos in the directions of the positive and negative and the reflection in *TP 3* of that unceasing dynamic. Point of clarification: The rising of the positive toward the unmanifest ocean of consciousness refers to the power of positive thinking but is not the pragmatism popularized by Norman Vincent Peale as the means of achieving financial success. Lynch is speaking spiritually. He means that we move toward reality and existence itself when we transcend toward the unmanifest and toward nonexistence when we are conscious only of the visible things around us.

In a state of transcendence outward into the ocean of consciousness, we know about knowing. We are not only aware of objects and bodies. The vocabulary in Nader's published book offers a useful key to this distinction: "Thus transcendence is a self-referral or self-referential state. Ordinary consciousness is object-referral. . . . The state which arises when all activity ceases but you don't fall asleep is self-referral; all the ever-changing objects of ordinary perception fall away and what remains is a non-changing, pure, absolute state of awareness. Self-referral leads to the consciousness of consciousness where to an increasing degree, the individual sees the perfect orderliness of the whole range of life and living, and the perfection of what is felt to be the Divine nature in all the objects that appear to be 'not-self'—in other words, the whole field of relative creation." This high level of enlightenment activates the expansion of love and experience of connectedness to the relative world. "Seeing, knowing, and acting are acts of love."[17] Such love, as Nader says, is "the ultimate verb, the supreme link, the unbounded process."[18] The further we exist from enlightenment, the more we fall into the detachment of nothingness, nonbeing.

To avoid being classified as New Age and philosophically impressionistic, Nader refers us to the careers of many of the great quantum physicists who, after they went as far as they could go into the materiality of quantum mechanics, began searching for a unified theory of everything, which meant a consciousness of consciousness. He invokes British physicist Sir James Jeans and Erwin Schrödinger, both of whom assert the centrality of consciousness. Jeans tells us, "I incline to the idealistic theory that consciousness is fundamental and that the material universe is derivative from consciousness, not consciousness from the material universe."[19] Schrödinger contends that "Consciousness cannot be accounted for in physical terms. For consciousness is absolutely fundamental."[20] Nader is also part of the chorus of current interest in string theories and M-theory now on the cutting edge of the material sciences that is moving toward proof of the unified field.[21] M-theory speaks to the intellectual conversation among physicists. However, in Lynch's *Twin Peaks* we do not tread these stepping stones of science. Rather, we have an example of how poetry borrows from science and philosophy for its own conversation with the heart and spirit about meaning. So . . .

Crucial caveats in the interest of clarity about a conceptually difficult subject: the vision of the unmanifest that Lynch outlined for me and that Nader mapped in his book informs Lynch's series in tandem with the quantum vision of matter. While *Twin Peaks* is Lynch's invitation to the audience to entertain joy and sorrow through his poetry of the manifest and unmanifest, it isn't about abandoning the visible world of things. For Lynch, the unmanifest exalts the manifest. He believes that by transcending to the highest level of expansion of awareness and connection, we see objects differently. "You see this table. The table is almost, like, translucent because the light of the unified field is just everywhere. And yet you see all the things. And at that point you have 200 percent of life. You own everything manifest and everything unmanifest. And you perceive it all as one."[22] It is only by coning down that we flail about in a sinister putrefaction of the manifest, which is more than obvious when we encounter the room above the convenience store. There is a lot of beauty in the visible in *Twin Peaks*, depending on the state of conscious perception.

TP 1, *TP 2*, and *FWWM* move toward the depiction of coning up and down in consciousness. When coning emerges in full flower in *TP 3*, we find ourselves in a new kind of detective story, Agent Cooper's odyssey, which I will call a *Cooprodyssey*, an odyssey with a Lynchian difference. Homer's hero Odysseus, in his odyssey, is a soldier who travels the material world, between Greece, Troy, and many islands. While *Twin Peaks* takes us among many material locations—New York, South Dakota, Las Vegas, Twin Peaks—it even more importantly shifts us among different states of unmanifest positive and negative consciousnesses, made visible through Lynch's poetry, all to be discussed below.

The marketplace is a space of a particular kind of consciousness—as are the Red Room, the strange bunker in space, and the room above the convenience store. Of all the spaces of consciousness, however, the two most important are the Fireman's palace, the closest we come in the series to coning up into the unbounded ocean of consciousness, and the space of consciousness in which Cooper and Carrie take their road trip in the final moments of the series, the closest we come to the nonbeing of coning down. These states of being or nonbeing generate an experience of what the hero's journey is and is not in a nonlinear, Lynchian reality.

BECOMING THE COOPRODYSSEY

Twin Peaks became the Cooprodyssey as it matured into a narrative shaped by both quantum partial knowledge and the total enlightenment of conings up and down. In *TP 1* and *TP 2*, we are offered only peeks at Cooper's strange, Kafkaesque coning down and the sudden flashes of something closer to coning up the Log Lady prologues. They run the gamut from early confinement in the material world to a later intimation of what exists above that level of consciousness. While Cooper is still looking for material clues, in the prologue to episode 8, the Log Lady speaks of a world in which objects are only seemingly solid and much of reality we cannot see. By episode 27, she strongly suggests that Cooper is on the wrong track as a detective. There are clues everywhere, she says, but are they about what only appears to be solid? No, and interpretation is a problem. In her prologue to the second season finale, episode 29, in which Cooper splits before our eyes, she tells us that in the world we know, we are on a level of consciousness in which everything is confusingly divided, but that there is a level of consciousness at which there is clarity and unification, which we find when "we are everywhere," and there will be just one. This is an oblique way of referring to Lynch's more specialized vocabulary about "unity consciousness."

At the end of her prologue, before our eyes the Log Lady cones up to the higher level of consciousness as she rises into a pure white light and the screen whites out. The prologue prepares us for an episode in which Cooper cones in the opposite direction taken by the Log Lady, where instead of becoming one, unified, he divides into a radiant special agent and a monstrous doppelgänger. In *FWWM* and *TP 3* to follow, Lynch elaborates on what he has shown us of unity and division in his impromptu, nonlinear season finale that replaced Frost's linear script.

FWWM, the next segment of the *Twin Peaks* saga, was commercially advertised as a prequel, which carries linear baggage, suggesting a progress from here to there. But the dynamic of *FWWM* is, rather, a nonlinear excursion from here to here. *FWWM* juxtaposes the perilous, muddled, and inconclusive murder investigations conducted by an elite group inside the FBI, known as the Blue Rose Task Force, with the perilous, muddled, and inconclusive downward spiral Laura's life becomes in the last days before her murder.

What we see in *FWWM* of the Blue Rose investigations is a pattern of difficulty with time and space that somewhat resembles Arthur Eddington's attempt to enter the quantum reality of a room. Like Eddington, the Blue Rosers find space-time against them as they are trapped in two places at the same time and/or disappear. And it is a Blue Rose pattern. Before there was Laura's corpse, there was the corpse of Teresa Banks, both murdered by Leland Palmer possessed by BOB. Before the disappearance of Dale Cooper there was the disappearance of Special Agent Chester "Chet" Desmond. And before Desmond there was Special Agent Phillip Jeffries. We are given an inkling of what we are referring to as *coning down* when long-lost Jeffries suddenly appears in nonlinear space-time, only compounding the mystery of descent into nonbeing when he provides a visceral experience of it but lacks the vocabulary to speak about it. As the Blue Rose special agents Albert Rosenfield and Cooper, and FBI deputy director Gordon Cole are floundering in their inability to solve the Banks murder, Jeffries suddenly enters their office, yelling about a room above a convenience store and about an unspeakable Judy. ("We're not going to talk about Judy!")

Jeffries brings with him the quantum state of mind of being in two places at once and the experience of the intersection of manifest and unmanifest reality. Jeffries "arrives" at 10:10 in the morning, a special temporal moment that doubles the Vedic number of completion, a magical state when manifest and unmanifest are visible. The Blue Rosers are experiencing quantum reality but have no idea how to interpret the clues of Jeffries's appearance, much as Laura in her final days is disoriented by her state of consciousness when, for her, linear time and space lose even the appearance of coherence. The Blue Rose detectives and the intended corpse are all in Kafkaesque trouble.

Yet *FWWM* conveys a universe in which coning up to a higher level of consciousness is possible. All the gloom of coning down notwithstanding, *FWWM* closes with a great affirmation, when Laura sees angels, a manifest image of the unmanifest. It is not the image of the angels that is important here but the all-irradiating light and the visualization of their ascension, much like that of the Log Lady, a coning up into the light of the unmanifest. This asymmetrical film, portraying a bunch of detectives sinking into disconnection and pain, climaxed abruptly by a glimpse of coning up into a consciousness of a higher reality, reiterates the dynamic of the finale of *TP 2*, and prefigures the twin trajectories of *TP 3*, with its epic vision of a unified cosmos filled with waves of motion toward and away from the higher levels of consciousness.

When *TP 3* reopens the *Twin Peaks* narrative, it has fully become the Cooprodyssey with its conings up and down on all planes of existence and nonexistence, through different states of awareness immanent in different spaces and on different paths of time. The Cooprodyssey cosmos is only partially quantum and Kafkaesque. To fully know this universe, we must also apprehend the unified field. Space-time in *TP 3* is much like it has been described, as a unity of divisions, by Jorge Luis Borges in "The Garden of Forking Paths," a description to which Lynch is very partial. In Borges's words, time is not as Newton imagined it, a passage from then, to now, to will be. Rather it is "a growing, dizzying web of divergent, convergent, and parallel times . . . that approach one another, fork, are snipped off . . . [and contain] *all* possibilities. In most of those times, we do not exist; in some, you exist but I do not; in others, I do and you do not; in others still, we both do."[23] Lynch's portrayal of time is completed by the addition of Borges's forking paths in *TP 3*. And on those forking paths, the characters cone up and down. It is a universe of parallel realities in which consciousness is dynamically and ceaselessly in motion. Keeping up as a spectator of such a cosmos is no mean feat.

Notably, on one fork, Laura exists, in the main title, as the face in a solar halo, all but unmanifest in the radiance of a here that is everywhere. On another fork, she vanishes as a kind of doppelgänger along with Cooper, like two birds killed with one stone. Similarly, Cooper is simultaneously on numerous paths in time, in some of which he and Laura exist and in some of which he doesn't. But this is a cosmos in which, in all times and on all planes of reality, a new, unitive character, the Fireman, exists. We'll get to him in due course. Here let us say that the energy of the Fireman and his reality in an unbounded cosmos is the great secret that is revealed in *TP 3*. The light that he casts on the narrative inverts all assumptions about the hero, as Campbell conceived of him. As we discover, the special agent Dale Cooper, who initially seemed the best and the brightest, does not offer the hope that we thought he did; we find a new source of hope in detectives that initially seemed less stellar than Cooper, and even bumbling or foolish. It is all about consciousness.

A NEGATIVE BOUQUET OF BLUE ROSES

Whereas Cooper has been the presumptive hero in *TP 1*, *TP 2*, and *FWWM*, in *TP 3*, our vision of his journey alters radically. His trajectory once he leaves the Red Room, where he has been becalmed for twenty-five years, is awash in negative energy and negative consciousness, and he descends from there. As the Cooprodyssey unfolds, old linear ideas about heroes fall as we watch Cooper and the Blue Rose Task Force on their way down. Within the new *TP 3* context, Cooper is more intensely Kafkaesque, a doomed figure unable to comprehend the forces of negativity in which he is increasingly swept up. Indeed, negative consciousness is revealed as the beginning and end of the Blue Rose Task Force, its raison d'être. The elite detectives of the bound marketplace are always blinkered by their partial knowledge, always in peril of vanishing onto a forking path of nonexistence, and one by one they do.

All the clues of their Kafkaesque doom are present. Hanging on the walls of Gordon Cole's office are a photograph of Franz Kafka, a drawing of a rotted ear of corn, and a huge blowup of a photograph of the 1945 atomic bomb test. In our reintroduction to Cole, surrounded by negativity and uncertainty, we follow him and the agents as they slip and slide helplessly on a web of convergent and divergent temporalities, searching for a Blue Rose agent who is confusingly in more than one place at the same time. For Cole, those on his team who have not yet disappeared, and for Cooper, who is on his way to disappearing, it is a Kafkaesque mess.

FIGURE 1.2 *Frame series: Gordon Cole's office and its Kafkaesque interior decoration. A rotted ear of corn.*

FIGURE 1.3 *FBI Special Agent Tammy Preston and framed picture of Franz Kafka.*

Negativity dogs every step of the Blue Rosers after Deputy Director Cole receives a phone call from a penitentiary in South Dakota with the surprising news that the long-missing Special Agent Cooper is incarcerated there. Cooper in jail? Well, partially. Unbeknownst to Cole, he and his special agents are chasing an agent who is one but also three. Speaking of division. Much like an updated, seriocomic version of the Keystone

FIGURE 1.4 *FBI Deputy Director Gordon Cole and Special Agent Albert Rosenfield with a photo of atomic bomb explosion at White Sands.*

Cops of the silent movies, in constant but fruitless motion, Blue Rosers have no idea they are following more than one Cooper.

Cooper is one agent going in three directions simultaneously. Does it get more quantum? While he is seeking an exit from a Red Room filled with quantum contradictions about when and how he can leave, his doppelgänger, whom we know as Mr. C., is also furiously driving through South Dakota, attempting to avoid returning to the Red Room, as he knows he is supposed to, crashing the car, and winding up in jail for carrying contraband in his trunk. At the same time, a tulpa—a kind of manufactured "placebo" humanoid—replica of Cooper is taking time out from his working day at the Lucky 7 Insurance company in Las Vegas for sex with a self-employed prostitute named Jade. Tulpa? More about this new addition to the Lynchian universe below.

Dougie Jones isn't the only tulpa the Blue Rosers are dealing with. When they turn to Cooper's former assistant Diane Evans to help them make some sense of Mr. C., who is and isn't the Cooper they knew, they are unaware that "she" is a tulpa clone of Diane created by Mr. C. to act as an informer for him. Cole, Rosenfield, and Preston are lost in the quantum world of an agent who is all at the same time: missing; his own double, Mr. C.; and his mysteriously manufactured clone.

The tulpa is not a Lynchian invention. It exists outside of *TP 3* in Asian mythology as a hominid form of inert matter given life through a mystical process.[24] Lynch adapts the tulpa myth as part of the complication of the Kafkaesque, negative, quantum uncertainty in which the Blue Rose team is embroiled. Part of the enigma is the mystery of the origin of the tulpas and their variations in awareness. Tulpa Diane, keenly aware of things and events, is the result of some obscure process of fabrication instigated—we never know how—by Mr. C. Tulpa Dougie Jones, a fat, unkempt version of Cooper, is completely of unknown origin. It has a minimal, but functional, degree of basic waking consciousness and a concomitant low degree of creativity, connection, and potency. It betrays and neglects its family, and on the job, it is of very little use. Other tulpas pop up in the series, too, notably in a story Rosenfield tells Preston about a tulpa named Lois Duffy for whom the Blue Rose Task Force is named. All are confusions of the quantum marketplace and part of the confused negativity of the group mindset of the Blue Rose team.

The task force is named for and sets its sights on nothingness, as we discover. One of the big reveals of the series is Cole's belated confession to Rosenfield and Preston that the task force began with the discovery of Jowday. Now called Judy, the ancient negative entity was brought to the attention of Cole and Phillip Jeffries by an army major, Garland Briggs, and the team was formed to look into it. Cole and Jeffries named the team for a tulpa they encountered during a case when they found two identical women, both called Lois Duffy, in a hotel room, one a tulpa dying from a bullet wound inflicted by the other. The dying Duffy exclaimed, "I am a blue rose," and disappeared. The murderous Duffy hanged herself while waiting to go to trial. Wherever the Blue Rosers are, their states of consciousness are taken up with the negativity of what isn't there and they themselves disappear, as have Jeffries and Briggs, or are on the brink of vanishing, as is Cooper.

Or they are preoccupied with finding vanished colleagues. While Cole, Rosenfield, and Preston are looking for a suddenly resurfaced Cooper, they get news that the headless dead body of Colonel Briggs has turned up, strangely in the physical shape of a man of the age he was when he vanished in season 2. When they take a brief detour to the house where Briggs was last seen still attached to his head, Cole is almost harvested by a negative force field—a swirling vortex of vibration and air marked by a black dot that opens in the sky. Drawn to it, he finds a portal into the room over the convenience store, the space of nonexistence that he found himself in when Jeffries burst into this office in *FWWM*. Albert Rosenfield pulls Cole back just before he is swallowed up by a space of nonexistence in time.

The same cannot be said of the Coopers. If Cole, Preston, and Rosenfield still exist, albeit on the edge of nothingness, the Coopers only seem to exist. When we are first reintroduced to Agent Cooper in part 1 of *TP 3*, we are also introduced to what will turn out to be his nonexistence. The Agent Cooper in the Red Room is in conversation with the Fireman, a new

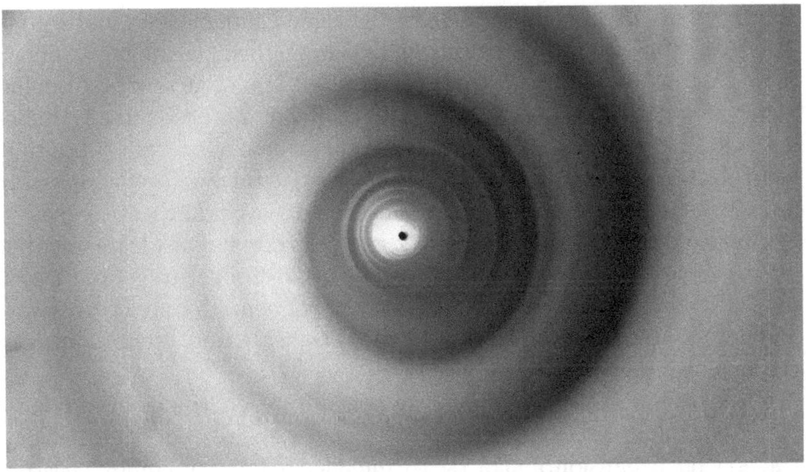

FIGURE 1.5 *The black dot vortex out of linear time and space, part 11, chapter 2.*

character, in his palace, a new, cosmic space of expansive consciousness that is simultaneously past, present, and future, and he is telling Cooper to remember, but it turns out that what he is asking Cooper to remember hasn't happened yet, though it will in part 18, the last part of the series, when Cooper enters a space of nonbeing. "Four, three, zero." "Richard and Linda." "Two birds with one stone." "Remember?" In the unmanifest space-time of the Fireman's palace, Cooper already doesn't exist. His disappearance simply hasn't manifested yet.

It is all part of the universe in which Cooper manifests as being present in the Fireman's palace but isn't there. He is, as the Fireman remarks, "far away." Similarly, in manifest time, Cooper is about to leave the Red Room, but in unmanifest time, he has already vanished. The Newtonian mind boggles; but the palace is a space of a consciousness of the new zeitgeist that comprehends what isn't as well as what is, and Cooper becomes increasingly, in manifest time, what he already is in unmanifest time: nonexistent.

Nonexistence is omnipresent as Cooper leaves the Red Room, which he has already left before part 1 begins and will leave again in part 18 on another fork of time. On this fork of time, Laura, Phillip Gerard (a new incarnation of Mike, who guides Cooper in a confusing way throughout season 3), Leland Palmer, and an electrified, barren tree chaperone Cooper toward negativity, uncertainty, and "what is not." Gerard is neither the henchman of BOB he once was nor an evolved and dependable mentor to Cooper as he presents himself while Cooper seeks to make his exit. Laura is neither the Laura of the end of *FWWM*, nor the young, tormented prom queen, but another entity that resembles them both. Leland Palmer is both the demon-possessed murderer and a sentimental, loving father, pleading for Cooper to find Laura. The tree is what was once the left arm Mike severed from his own body after he parted company with BOB, but it is now a totally different entity, as unstable as Gerard. It exists in an entangled state of positive, calm electricity and a raging, electronic, negative frenzy. The Red Room is a mass of uncertainty. Laura tells him he can leave and then is violently ejected from the Red Room herself. Gerard tells him he can't leave until his doppelgänger returns, and his "arm" screams at Cooper to get out. Most crucially, the arm yells "nonexistent," as the floor beneath Cooper gives way, and he is in unbounded space but he is not transcending. Agent Cooper is coning down toward—

Nonexistence. Cooper is first imprisoned in an enormous glass box in New York City that is contracting into a smaller and smaller confine. Contraction, not expansion, and in a space intended to trap unmanifest negative energy and make it manifest. Next, Cooper drops into a bunker, a concrete-like enclosure oddly levitating in boundless space. It is a crossroad between energy that is captured and routed through electrical sockets and the limitless energy of starry space. Which way to go? It is tempting to see this as a moment of choice for Cooper, but we have already seen that the end of his path already exists in unmanifest time. So, when Cooper first arrives, and the inside of the bunker is a place of hope, it is only an impossible hope. Naido, a strange eyeless woman inside the bunker, lacking all capability of communicating through language, convinces him to follow her onto the roof of the bunker, away from the magnetic pull of a huge socket, but Cooper will only do in manifest time what has already taken place in unmanifest time. The missing head of Major Briggs appears in space, intoning the words "Blue Rose," and Cooper, a member of that team, chases negativity when he fearfully retreats into the bunker, now a space of fear. It is now occupied by an anxious woman, identified as an American girl who fearfully urges him to enter the force field of the big socket. Cooper takes the path of fear. He emerges from another socket in an abandoned house in Las Vegas, where he takes the place of the tulpa of Cooper, who has been called to the Red Room. Once there, Tulpa Dougie disappears. He has been on a path to nothingness. All the Coopers are on that path.

We don't know where the bunker is, but we know what time it is. A close-up reveals that it is 2:53 on the watch of the American girl. Clock time is linear time. But it is also nonlinear time. The sum of the digits 2, 5, and 3 is 10, the number of completion, when the manifest and the unmanifest converge in a moment of total, 200 percent reality like the one we saw when Jeffries entered the FBI office in *FWWM*. When the manifest and unmanifest converge here, they do so for Cooper, the tulpa that looks like Cooper, Dougie Jones, and the Cooper doppelgänger, Mr. C., and they all lose consciousness. This is a negative state of affairs, a prefiguration of the ensuing negative trajectory of the Coopers.

In Las Vegas, it is 2:53 for the Dougie Jones tulpa who reaches nonexistence almost immediately when Agent Cooper takes its place. Cooper is in a state of dormant consciousness, even less aware than the low-functioning tulpa. Agent Cooper is unable to feed or dress himself; he cannot speak as an independent consciousness. He is unable even to urinate without instructions, let alone know that he is an FBI agent. He often seems to be on the verge of awakening, and reclaiming the role of a hero, but when he does become conscious once more, it is only another step toward his ultimate disappearance. It is also 2:53 for Mr. C., driving in South Dakota—who feels the call of the Red Room but does not heed it—when he blanks out on the road, crashes the car, and winds up in a federal penitentiary. When the warden calls Deputy Director Cole, thinking the man in the cell is Cooper, Mr. C. uses the power of his negativity to manipulate the warden, and escape from Cole. But the unfolding season will reveal that Mr. C., too, is headed downward to nonexistence.

"Is the marketplace a dream?" I asked Lynch. "Sure," he said.[25] And for the Coopers it is like that kind of dream in which no matter which way we travel, we wind up where we didn't want to be. Mr. C. spends *TP 3* resisting his return to the Red Room, but he has an unmanifest destiny. Every step he takes leads him back to the Red Room. He kills most of his associates, all of the people who get in his way, and even his own son to find the right coordinates, only to find that they are the very place at which he is positioned to be sent to eternal bondage.

Similarly, no matter that Agent Cooper is moved by happy, positive forces in Las Vegas; his unmanifest negative destiny will out. In his nearly unconscious state in Las Vegas as Dougie, Cooper is guided by a positive light from an indeterminate source toward winning a fortune from the one-armed bandits in the Silver Mustang Casino. At Lucky 7 Insurance, bereft of his Blue Rose consciousness, he functions brilliantly as an investigator, through the guidance of that same light. Despite or because of his diminished capacity for negative consciousness, fortune and success get him good sex from tulpa Dougie's wife Janey-E (Naomi Watts), the adoration of the tulpa's child, Sonny Jim (Pierce Gagnon), and the gratitude of the Mitchum brothers, Rodney (Robert Knepper) and Bradley (Jim Belushi), a pair of brutal gangsters who are transformed into mild-mannered benefactors to Cooper/Dougie and his family by the sunshine of Cooper's oblivious success at getting them a multimillion-dollar payout from Lucky 7. But nothing can stop Cooper from sticking a fork into an electrical socket and being recharged into awareness, and nothing can stop his reactivated mind from returning him to the negative Blue Rose path.

FIGURE 1.6 *Light indicating a nonlinear connection between the Twin Peaks sheriff's station and the cosmos.*

Everything is in unmanifest motion behind manifest appearances. This includes Cole and his Blue Rose Task Force, who are always moving and never going anywhere. Deploy their technologies as they may, Cole and his Blue Rose are never more than observers of the Coopers coning down. So then, can we say that *TP 3* is a Cooprodyssey of despair? Well, yes and no. The boundless universe of consciousness has its very dark side. But it also has an inevitably light and positive aspect.

Also destined is the path of the detectives in the town of Twin Peaks, Sheriff Frank Truman, Deputy Chief Tommy "Hawk" Hill, and deputies Andy Brennan (Harry Goaz) and Bobby Briggs. Bathed in the radiance of a white light resembling the "everywhere and all" into which the Log lady disappears in her last prologue, the sheriff's station is the site of the unmanifest destiny of Truman's team. This destiny is anchored not in the negativity of the Blue Rose Task Force, the Coopers, and Judy, but in the energy of the Fireman. The Fireman creates Truman, Hawk, Andy, and Bobby as positive heroes in the unbounded cosmos.

YOU (REALLY) DON'T WANT TO KNOW ABOUT THAT

Coning up is the gift of the universe to Truman and his team. While the dynamic of Cooper and the Blue Rosers is shaped by Judy and nonexistence, the Twin Peaks detectives don't know about Judy, and they don't want to. Their dynamic is shaped by their many connections to affirmative existence: through the prophetic awareness that the dying Log Lady communicates to Deputy Chief Hawk; by a message sent in nonlinear time by Major Garland Briggs; by a living map owned by Hawk that manifests in linear but exists in nonlinear time; and by their positive connections with 2:53, the temporal moment of completion, the 200 percent of reality when the manifest and unmanifest connect.

No information about the unbounded ocean of consciousness is needed for us to see that the Log Lady's expansive vision of the cosmos could not be more different from the blinkered negativity of the Blue Rose Task Force. But reading the Log Lady in terms of Lynch's vision of the unmanifest adds depth and color to our understanding of who she is and why the Twin Peaks constabulary moves toward a happy ending, while the Blue Rosers move toward tragedy. The Log Lady is filled with the upward everywhere of the unmanifest that enables her to perceive "the dream of time and space. It all comes out now, flowing like a river. That which is and is not." And when the Twin Peaks detectives have their own 2:53, unlike the 2:53 of the Coopers in *TP 3* or the 10:10 at the FBI office in *FWWM*, theirs is not a moment of negativity.

When it is 2:53 in the forest outside of Twin Peaks, it is a moment of the unmanifest and manifest that they have been led to by the message left by Major Briggs and by Hawk's special map, both of which exist in nonlinear time, and which place the actions of the Twin Peaks detective in an eternal context. Briggs's message gives them coordinates for an uncharted part of the forest, and Hawk's map leads them there, where a map that depicts a Newtonian reality cannot. The map exists in unmanifest time, always current, on which time and space are represented not by coordinates, but by negative and positive energy. Good fire and bad fire. Rotten corn and nourishing corn. They are symbols of energies, Hawk explains to Sheriff Truman, "like modern day electricity," which may be used either for good or evil. Judy? Yes, it is there, but at the margins of the map, in the upper, left-hand corner. And far from being the motive for investigation. "You don't want to know about that," Hawk tells Truman. "No?" asks Truman. "No," says Hawk. This team is not headed for Judy, but for a space, in part 14, where they discover Naido, who had seemed to disappear when she leaped off the bunker into unbounded space, but who reenters the series in the unmanifest space-time of the uncharted forest and the Fireman's palace. Naido's path is the road not taken by Cooper.

Rather, she is part of the entrance into cosmic time of the sheriff's team. After they find her, Deputy Andy Brennan is pulled up into the Fireman's palace, coned up, to use the Lynchian vocabulary, into a vortex of unspotted, white light and the Fireman makes available to him full knowledge of past, present, and future as one. Andy envisions images of what was, is, and will be, all at once: he sees Laura dead in the marketplace and alive with her angel; Cooper in superposition as both the Blue Rose special agent and as Mr. C., in two places at once; Andy himself and his wife, Lucy, in the process of some not clearly revealed action. The manifest images render the actions they represent as simultaneous, as if the events had already happened and were being remembered, but are also happening and are yet to happen. And if we don't know yet specifically what Andy has foreknowledge of, what has been made wordlessly manifest to Andy fills him with unmanifest knowledge.

Knowing the Fireman as the fulcrum of the twin dynamics of the Blue Rose agents and Twin Peaks detectives in unmanifest space-time is crucial to recognizing the nature of Lynch's portrait of nonlinear reality in his series. When he is released from the palace, Andy springs into action to scoop up Naido's naked, supine body; preparing for what will happen next, he is coning up to fuller existence. When Cooper leaves the space of consciousness in the Fireman's palace, he is coning down into nonexistence. The rising and falling of the detectives are at the center of the Cooprodyssey. But also crucial to Lynch's purposes as a storyteller of manifest and unmanifest reality is the sea of stories around them in the marketplaces.

AND THE BAND PLAYED ON

The Blue Rosers and the Twin Peaks constabulary are not the only ones coning up and down. The entire marketplace is coning up and down, everyone is always in ferment: the Double R Diner, the Roadhouse, the public spaces, the Silver Mustang Casino, the glass-box-experiment building, various private homes. And all merit our attention as part of our enjoyment of Lynch's epic. It is a great, big, wonderful world of many, many manifestations for Lynch. The necessarily limited scope of this study makes it impossible for us to explore the entire cosmic Lynchian banquet of consciousnesses, so delving only into two marketplace spaces in some detail must stand as a representative of the moving energies in the other *TP 3* marketplace spaces. One obvious choice is the Twin Peaks Roadhouse, which gives us the most to watch and listen to, about what is and what is not, to use the Log Lady's vocabulary.

The Roadhouse shows up in all of the series' parts, juxtaposing the coherence generated by its featured musical performances, each of which Lynch chose himself, and the divisive bickering, and even violence, pervasive among the occupants of the booths.[26] There are floods of fluctuating energies in the truncated narratives in the booths. Yet the music generated onstage by a panoply of entertainers creates an interconnectedness in the Roadhouse audience, in Lissie belting out "Wild West," in the quiet, sweet sadness of Rebekah Del Rio singing "No Stars," and even in the Nine Inch Nails growling "She's Gone Away," amid its clanging, banging, and guttural howls. The Roadhouse stands in Lynch's epic as a major textural experience of ongoing marketplace mood. Diverse energies rise and fall at the tables; the band plays on. These unified yet diverse energies exist on various levels of consciousness. On the ordinary level of consciousness, the music of the Roadhouse is the reality of negativity and positivity of ordinary consciousness.

Another obvious choice is Audrey Horne's comatose fantasy as she lies unconscious in a hospital bed. In a state of temporary nonexistence, disconnected from others inside her own traumatized mind for decades, after being caught in the bank explosion in *TP* 2, Audrey's dream of the Roadhouse functions to reconnect her to waking awareness. We know a little more of the reality of the series through the juxtaposition of Audrey's internal scenario of a claustrophobic marriage to stultifying Charlie and her scenario of departing for the Roadhouse with Charlie from their airless home, where she becomes one of the Roadhouse musical presentations, reprising her dance to the music of the jukebox at the Double R Diner when she was young and vibrant. When, out of nowhere, two men erupt into a violent fight, disrupting her dance, she transfers to the next level of consciousness. The Roadhouse of Audrey's comatose fantasy disappears abruptly, and she wakes confusedly in the hospital. Audrey's transit from one level of awareness to another through the image of the Roadhouse creates an extremely intriguing texture of the series' universe. Along with the Roadhouse, it combines with the negativity of the Blue Rose Task Force, the positivity of the Twin Peaks detectives, the quantum disorientation of the bunker in space, the Red Room, and the ordinary waking consciousness of the marketplace in Twin Peaks, Las Vegas, and New York, to invoke a unified ocean of unbounded consciousness in its many manifestations.

However, it is the Fireman's palace that most vividly creates the series universe, a rendezvous of all energies, an asymmetrical, unmanifest cosmic balance.

ARRANGING THE RENDEZVOUS

In his poem "Final Soliloquy of the Interior Paramour," Wallace Stevens invokes a feeling of a whole behind the chaos of our ordinary days, a sense that there is an all-encompassing "knowledge, that which arranged the rendezvous." In *Twin Peaks*, the Fireman provokes that kind of awareness, from when we first see him during Agent Cooper's visit to his palace, to our observation of his palace as a point of cosmic perspective when, from an eternal site of all temporal time frames, he contemplates the test explosion of the first atomic bomb in White Sands, New Mexico, manifest in the linear year of 1945, to Deputy Andy Brennan's visit to his palace that makes us intuit his hand behind the series' double closure.

Every appearance of the Fireman makes manifest the unmanifest nonlinear time of the cosmos that contains the linear time of the marketplace. The most extraordinary and evocative of these appearances occurs in part 8, when Lynch brings into the epic Cooprodyssey the Fireman surveying the New Mexico desert devolving into particles, gas, and flame as it is used as a testing ground for the newly invented atomic bomb in 1945. Through the Fireman, we see the test from a pantemporal past/present/future, in unmanifest time and the coherence of all manifestations within the ocean of consciousness. With the eruption in the desert of negative energy, there is a flare-up of the nonexistent space of the convenience store, its cluster of demons in erratic spasmodic motion, and the nonexistence of Demon BOB. The Fireman's response is the production of a balancing, positive, golden energy, the pantemporal energy of Laura, recalling the angel in the closure of *FWWM*. The Fireman is made manifest as a force for balancing out nonexistence and existence. Reality is a nonlinear interweaving of negativity and positivity.

In part 8, we watch the eruption and spread of a contagion of negation that manifests in 1945 and 1956 being contemplated by the Fireman in unmanifest time. Lynch paints it with sound as well as image when the test creates a brutal coning down that reverses creation into a breakdown of the manifest into particles and waves and activates the nonexistence of the convenience store and BOB. Let us recall that Lynch's faith that transcending to the unmanifest ocean of consciousness floods the creation with a higher consciousness of the great beauty and unity of the manifest. In part 8, he invokes the opposite through the event in White Sands, which flows and spreads through unmanifest time into 1956, creating unconsciousness and degenerate, disconnected matter. A murderous , putrefied, convenience-store figure, the Woodsman (Robert Broski), is on the prowl in the marketplace. And a sinister hybrid entity, part flying insect and part amphibian, the opposite of the glory of nature on which Laura and the sun shine in the main title, is born in the desert and treks toward inhabited terrain. Murdering the personnel of a local radio station, the Woodsman replaces the Platters' song "My Prayer," an expression of human desire for connection, with a chant of the darkness of disconnected quantum reality: "This is the water and this is the well. Drink deep and descend." The Woodsman's "Descend" takes on an entirely new meaning in the context of Lynch's vision of the unity of consciousness at the highest levels of reality. Unconsciousness ensues as the Woodsman chants, for a diner waitress

FIGURE 1.7 *Frame series: Attack on consciousness. A waitress faints.*

FIGURE 1.8 *A mechanic faints.*

and a car mechanic, and an innocent young girl who has just had her first kiss. And the girl opens her mouth to allow the sinister hybrid into her.[27]

The Fireman also invokes a positivity, a rendezvous of negative and positive, when he generates golden energy for the damaged world, an initiation of a generative cycle already informing manifest time, that will slowly become visible as the story of Andy and the rest of the Twin Peaks

FIGURE 1.9 *A young girl falls asleep when the radio station is taken over by dark, nonlinear energies.*

detectives unfolds, along with the story of Freddie Sykes (Jake Wardle), a cockney newcomer to Twin Peaks of no particular distinction, whom the Fireman marks as part of an inexplicable call to recovery. We see Freddie in our first view of the Roadhouse, but we only belatedly find out his unsuspected importance to the epic at the end of the series. He is the sine qua non of the nonlinear waves of positivity in this universe.

We are almost at the end of *TP 3* when Freddie tells his story of how, in unmanifest time, he is called to the Fireman's palace and the Fireman instructs him to reenter manifest time and acquire from a certain hardware store a certain ordinary rubber gardening glove that will give his fist the power of a hypercharged pile driver and head for Twin Peaks. When Freddie reenters manifest time, he does so as the designated hero who will destroy BOB. Like the Twin Peaks sheriff's team, there is no explanation of why Freddie was chosen and no understanding until a certain moment arrives in linear time when any of them is called. When Freddie has his audience with the Fireman, he wants to know why *he* has been called to the palace. "Why *not* you?" is the Fireman's reply.

Such is the hero in this universe. Not the dazzling Cooper. And, as we learn, if we acquire nonlinear reading skills as we watch *TP 3*, everything has already happened, is happening. Freddie's success and Cooper's failure are yet to come and have already happened when the third season begins. Cooper has already disappeared, is disappearing, and will disappear in the first part when the Fireman asked him to "remember" Richard and Linda, 340, and two birds with one stone. When Andy is called to the palace, we see that the destruction of BOB has already taken place, even though it only enters manifest time later, when Lucy Brennan shoots Mr. C. and Freddie arrives at the sheriff's station, in linear time, to apply the coup de grâce to BOB, in a ferocious battle that leaves BOB nothing but a burnt-out fire and a pile of inert carbon shards. How long has Lucy Brennan already been in motion to shoot Mr. C. dead in the station, and Mr. C. set in motion to arrive in the station for her to kill him? Unmanifest. Why? Unknown. Why not Cooper? Ambiguous. We could not have guessed at the start of the Cooprodyssey, but by its end we will see that everyone's destiny has been all the time in unmanifest form.

It is a challenge to try to grasp the mind-bending experience of time for a new zeitgeist that Lynch creates in his epic masterpiece. But grasp it we must if we are to see the twin dynamic of positive and negative energy in *Twin Peaks*. The series gives us the experience of a completely different temporality from the linear time we recognize as our ordinary reality.

BRINGING LAURA HOME

A double ending of coning up and coning down concludes Lynch's epic series, an inexplicable, amazing dynamic of being and nonbeing, inexplicable because Lynch never answers the question of why there are destructive energies—a question he raises and leaves for us to wonder about. Lynch never explains the negativity of the trauma in White Sands, New Mexico, the fatal attraction of nonbeing for Cooper and the Blue Rosers, or the exaltation of Freddie, Lucy, and Andy. Nor does the double ending ever explain who the Fireman is or make manifest the enormity of the great negativity of Judy and the room above the convenience store. But through a double denouement, Lynch does paint in vivid, exhilarating images the consolations of the great *It Is* of nonlinear existence and the stark, quantum anguish of the more enigmatic, inescapable, companion element of the great *It Is Not* of nonexistence.

The defeat of Mr. C. and BOB is a seriocomic manifestation of the healing of a marketplace torn by intrusions of shattered space, and demonic energies, all set in motion by the Fireman and already accomplished in unmanifest time, as we saw in part 15. In the sheriff's station, darkened by the presence of Mr. C., Lucy Brennan, whom we know as a ditzy receptionist, astonishingly and comically, fatally shoots and kills Mr. C. to save Sheriff Frank Truman from him, and the strange army of demons from the room above the convenience store are unable to revive him as they once did, and they vanish. When BOB emerges as a fireball from inside the supine body of Mr. C., the station becomes a quantum disorientation of matter and energy, objects in superposition in many places at once, and fire appearing out of nowhere. Freddie is bloodied as he uses his gloved fist to restore the dream of the marketplace when he demolishes BOB, and light is restored, as is the ordinary appearance of objects. Things come together. Euphoria reigns.

What follows that great inexplicable triumph is the even less legible climax of Agent Cooper's descent into nonbeing that entails his rejection of love and connection. Cooper reunites with his FBI colleagues and the love of his life, Diane, in the Twin Peaks sheriff's station, after BOB and Mr. C. are gone, only to abandon them. No sooner are Mr. C. and BOB dispatched than Cole finds Cooper after a long wild-goose chase, and it is revealed to Cooper that Naido is only a protective shell, when it breaks to reveal Diane Evans—long afflicted by loneliness and isolation. Happiness ensues all too briefly, however. Almost immediately after Cole and Cooper greet each other, and Cooper and Diane embrace, negativity prevails.

No one in *Twin Peaks* moves forward on an inert stage of time and space, the way Campbell's Theseus or Warner Bros.' Sam Spade does. They are all carried by the flow of positive or negative consciousness, coning up toward connection with reality or down into disconnection from reality. Cooper, who has been moving toward a negative consciousness of disconnection for almost the entire series breaks his most important bonds before entering the final stage of coning down, nonexistence. Everything is Kafkaesque about Cooper's last stand.

A big, disconnected head appears as the Naido shell breaks and Diane is revealed behind her exterior. The head intones, "We live inside a dream," and Cooper becomes further isolated. The clock in the sheriff's station is unable to reach 2:53, the moment of 200 percent of reality, because Cooper can exist in neither the manifest nor the unmanifest. Cooper misguidedly asserts that "the past determines the future," but in a nonlinear universe they are the same. While the sheriff and his people have coned up, Cooper is coning down, will cone down, and has already coned down, taking the same route away from awareness as Blue Rose agents Desmond and Jeffries before him into nonexistence.

It is all negative Kafkaesque time and space when Cooper leaves Diane and Cole and opens a door in the basement of the Great Northern Hotel with a key that has been waiting for him for decades as part of his unmanifest destiny of nonbeing. Cooper then makes his final descent into the stream of negative temporality through a door opened by Phillip Jeffries, whom Cooper has asked to let him return to the night of Laura's death. Jeffries speaks in literally illegible fragments as he creates a time portal for Cooper, marked by a symbol of nothingness: an icon for Judy that appears in the air and morphs into an inverted icon of eternity, marked by the sinister black spot. It is negative time and energy that Cooper is entering into when he meets Laura and erases her death. As Cooper leads Laura by the hand to take her home, he discovers he has a hand full of nothing. Of course. Cooper has entered the coning down consciousness of nonbeing. Things fall apart.

In part 18, Cooper makes a final advance into nonexistence. Having lost Laura, he is in the Red Room and leaves it again to find her, replaying everything that happened when he made his exit in part 1 but with greater negativity. He meets up with Diane, not to partner, but to separate. Cooper and Diane shift onto a number of parallel paths after leaving the Red Room, always more divided and confused. With Diane beside him, Cooper drives a car into negative time, energy, and space at the 340-mile marker, the number the Fireman asked Cooper to remember. Before they pass 340, they are lovingly attached. After, connections irretrievably fray when the two of them arrive at a motel for the night. The already much-divided Diane—once Agent Cooper's assistant, once Mr. C.'s tulpa, once Naido, and whatever she is when she emerges in the Twin Peaks sheriff's station and when Cooper meets her in part 18—has a premonition of her further splitting when a double of herself appears briefly, quietly, with a sinister aura in the distance. It does not bode well. Cooper is not the same man he was when they encountered each other outside the Red Room. Terrible sex ensues and the next morning Diane has vanished. Along with everything else.

Cooper wakes up in a different motel, on a different fork in time, in which Diane doesn't exist. Does he? He continues to call himself Agent Cooper, but a note he finds by his bedside suggests he doesn't exist on the new fork in time either. The note is from someone called Linda to someone called Richard, ending their relationship. Just what the Fireman told him to remember. But what does memory mean to a man who is already nonexistent. A major identity issue. After he drives off, he makes contact with a woman who looks like Laura Palmer but calls herself Carrie Page and has an unexplained corpse in her living room.[28] He asks no questions. Another identity issue for a special agent. And who is this Carrie who leaves town with him to drive to Twin Peaks? Where are they when they stop in a town that looks like Twin Peaks, and Cooper knocks on the door of a house that looks like the Palmers' house? They are no one and nowhere. The middle-aged blond woman, coiffed with Laura Palmer's hairstyle, who opens the door tells them that no Palmer lives or has ever lived there. They are on the far side of existence. Existence endures somewhere but not in this strange limbo, in which Cooper has the sudden feeling that he doesn't know what year it is, and in which, in nonlinear time, Carrie can hear Sarah Palmer calling "Laura." And screams. A bleak, unilluminating light flashes from the house. Cooper and Carrie disappear into the ensuing darkness.

No explanations here. Just consciousness. The downward drag of partial knowledge that much resembles quantum confusion is juxtaposed to the upward blossoming that resembles transcending consciousness we saw when BOB and Mr. C. were defeated. For Lynch, consciousness IS. And we are either moving toward love, connection, and cohesion whether we are aware or not; or our consciousness is diminishing, devolving into what Nader describes in the unpublished version as "the disconnection leading to nonexistence: indifference and ignorance, fear and pain."[29]

Lynch once told me that the "world is as you are."[30] A negative consciousness produces a negative world. A positive consciousness produces a positive world. This is the cosmos of *Twin Peaks*. In Lynch's personal vision, voluntary enlightenment and bliss are the ideal of unmanifest destiny. *Twin Peaks*, however, is a narrative about an unenlightened world. A Kafkaesque, doomed hero falls away from the ocean of consciousness and, unaware, becomes the negativity he sees and seeks (Judy) by chasing it. The universe calls to the unaware constabulary in the sheriff's station, a portrait of the ordinary people who, for reasons never revealed, rise toward the ocean of consciousness. Why them? Well, why not them?

Twin Peaks is and is not a radical departure from older epic literature. The old, linear epics offer us heroes who travel in a straight line, as *Twin Peaks* does not. But like Lynch's series, the old narratives offer a puzzling universe. Ultimately, whatever the ancient heroes do, they are presided over by an unfathomable pantheon of gods who inexplicably enforce limits. Whatever Cooper and the sheriff's team do in *Twin Peaks*, it, too, is a saga that unfolds in an ultimately unfathomable universe. There is a discontinuous continuity between *Twin Peaks* and the old epic narratives. There is a break between the limits portrayed by the old poetry and the boundlessness of the new poetry. What unites them is the portrayal of the human condition, in which tears and despair are as unavoidable as laughter and hope, and as incomprehensibly determined.

Detectives are not—it is almost needless to say—the only insiders whose stories are altered by the discontinuous continuities of the new zeitgeist. The small-town family, biologically building one cohesive generation after another, is another version of the mass media's ultimate marketplace insiders. The impossibility of such a linear story in a nonlinear universe is front and center in the work of Terrence Malick, another popular artist creating narrative for the new zeitgeist in his beautiful film *The Tree of Life*. In the next chapter, we will follow Malick into the nonlinear universe to explore his version of the unmanifest destiny of his insiders, the bedrock, marketplace O'Brien family.

TERRENCE MALICK'S NONLINEAR BOOK OF JOB

The Tree of Life

Chapter 2

Where were you when I laid the foundation of the earth?...
When the morning stars sang together, and all the sons of God shouted for joy?

JOB 38:4, 7

Brother. Mother. It was they who led me to your door.

The Tree of Life

Terrence Malick is a controversial, reclusive, elusive director, with an interest in nonlinearity, who prefers not to speak publicly about his work. Sound familiar? But unlike David Lynch, Terrence Malick has an academic history. Where Lynch has avoided formal education, as he evolved a nonlinear art, enriched by extracurricular deep dives into Vedic thought and quantum mechanics, Malick's interest in nonlinear storytelling is linked with his formal study of German phenomenologist Martin Heidegger. Heidegger's influence is especially interesting when we turn to the next stop on our tour of mass-media heroes on a voyage into a nonlinear universe, Malick's film *The Tree of Life* (2011; hereafter *TOL*). It is a film that has sparked very spirited debate.

Malick's academic career was relatively brief—and checkered, to say the least. He earned an MA in philosophy at Harvard, where he studied Heidegger, against the advice of his mentor, Stanley Cavell. Cavell was very supportive of Malick but warned him against planning for a thesis about Heidegger, who had been tainted by association with the Nazi regime in Germany; when Malick was at Harvard, Heidegger was still generally a very problematic figure among American philosophers.[1] At Magdalen College, Oxford, Malick worked on a PhD thesis about Heidegger, expecting to pursue an academic career. However, he never completed his degree studies there, because of "irreconcilable differences" with his adviser, the eminent modernist Gilbert Ryle. Of Malick's time at Oxford we know very little, aside from Ryle's reluctance to consider Heidegger a credible philosopher.[2]

But we do know that Malick's academic passions led him to publish a translation of Heidegger's *The Essence of Reasons* in 1969 and to teach philosophy briefly at the Massachusetts Institute of Technology.[3] And it will soon be clear that he channeled Heidegger's ideas about *Dasein*, or unmediated being, into cinema and contributed a new perspective on narrative for the mass media. Malick sought to represent Dasein in the *TOL* narrative, within the mediations of cinema. *TOL* intersects with the attempt of quantum physics to define the unmediated being of the *now*; it also intersects with Lynch's project of creating a narrative infused by the unmediated, unmanifest ocean of consciousness and with Einstein's attempt to locate a way to unify in theory the four major unmediated forces in the universe.[4]

Contextualized by Malick's enthusiasm for Heidegger, *TOL*, a film both vilified as confusing and cherished for its beauty and freshness, easily presents itself as a nonlinear narrative that releases cinema in interesting ways from linear time and space. When *TOL* fractures the mediations of linear time and space that have constructed the conventional mass-media family story, it reveals another aspect of the ordinary story of the O'Briens' family life. The O'Briens are what is left of the family when the familiar temporal and spatial boundaries are broached.

Contemplating Malick's struggle to depict the energy of Dasein in *TOL* as part of the cocreation of a new map of the cosmos introduces a new perspective into the critical literature. It is a perspective diametrically opposed to the critics who, unable to grasp *TOL*'s Heideggerian insights into a postquantum, nonlinear universe, view the film as a "mess" or castigate Malick's work as empty formal exercise.[5] It is a perspective that has some overlap with the extant body of critical admiration for Malick's use of sound and visual poetry and with critics who variously discuss Malick's masterpiece as a serious work informed by philosophy.[6] But even previous criticism sensitive to the radical nonlinearity of *TOL* has not perceived how Malick's philosophical roots have transmuted one of the bedrock conventions of the mass-media narrative for the new map of the cosmos.

In *TP 3*, Lynch reenvisioned the heroic journey of the insider detective. In *TOL*, Malick transforms the small-town family, through the heroic voyage of insider corporate executive Jack (Sean Penn), the eldest son of the O'Brien family. The O'Brien family at the center of Jack's journey is, to be sure, a cluster of blood-related insiders, shaped by the limits of hierarchical, patriarchal culture familiar to mass-media family stories. It ticks the boxes of conventional movies and TV, with their authoritarian fathers, their warmly supportive mothers, grandparents, three children—an approximation of the requisite number of offspring in conventional movies and TV—a family car, and a dog. But Jack's heroic voyage opens the O'Briens and their struggles to the limitless energies of nonlinear Dasein. Rejecting the old Campbellian template, Malick offers a new, unique experience of a family story for the mass audience that does not follow developments in a linear journey from *here* to *there.*

Jack has risen from the small town in which he was born to success in a steel-and-glass city; he is *there,* at the top of an urban skyscraper when the film begins, at the top of the tree. But that is not the tree of unmediated life, and it is not the journey that preoccupies *TOL*. Rather his marketplace success is part of a much larger voyage, from *here* to *here,* from confusion and anger about his family within linear time and space, to a new perspective and a new reality gained beyond those limits. It is also a new, unique journey for Malick. *TOL* intersects in many ways with the body of his previous work, but as a narrative set in a nonlinear cosmos it differs importantly from his earlier, linear narratives.

Malick has produced a spectrum of films about the problems of characters who belong to the marketplace, as do the O'Briens. He has told cinematic tales about families, neighborhoods, communities, even about noble dignitaries at the top of a regal hierarchy. His is an eclectic imagination that finds subjects in a variety of settings, and employs a variety of tonalities, moods, and styles. Malick's portrait of hardscrabble, rural American life in *Badlands* (1973) is a work of social realism. His portrait of a lonely landowner's involvement with an attractive migrant worker in early twentieth-century agrarian America in *Days of Heaven* (1978) and his seventeenth-century tale about the love between Pocahontas, the daughter of a tribal chief in colonial Virginia, and John Smith, an agent of the British crown, in *The New World* (2005) are pastoral romances. His film *A Hidden Life* (2019), a journalistic, "based on a true story" family narrative, takes its universe from the preserved letters between Franz Jägerstätter, an Austrian farmer during World War II who refused to take an oath of loyalty to Hitler, and his wife, Fani. While the glory of nature and a religious passion surround and infuse Franz's heroic resistance, the film is a solidly linear narrative that explores a Newtonian vision of the hierarchies of every aspect of marketplace life: the family, the village, the church, the military, and the judiciary.[7]

These Malick offerings are typical of his juxtaposition of the visual fecundity, and even ecstasy, of the openness and authentic being of nature with the closed, mediated forms of social machinery, but they unfold within a familiar linear narrative time frame. By contrast, the linear spaciotemporal guardrails are down in *TOL,* in the 139-minute, nonlinear cut Malick prepared for theatrical screening. Interestingly, he had originally intended *TOL* to be even more nonlinear. An earlier plan was to use the "seamless branching" of DVD and Blu-ray technology to allow the audience to choose from the many hours he shot for the film "to effectively watch a different version of the movie each time they saw it." Malick wanted to include extra footage that could "'play randomly in different ways to create different story lines,' [Criterion technical director Lee] Kline said. 'There'd be so many permutations of it you wouldn't get the same story over and over.'"[8]

Very Heideggerian. A film of endless permutations would ideally go a very long way toward dissolving the authority of the mediations of linear narrative and releasing a narrative reality of the Heideggerian Dasein; but that film was never made. Nevertheless, Malick came quite close in the cut of *TOL* that he released. The fluidity of the nonlinear narrative Malick prepared for distribution realizes a portrait of the O'Brien family that captures both the conventionally perceived structure of family, community, religion, and response to death, and a perspective that soars to visions of Dasein, above, below, through, and under linear limits. On one hand, *TOL* portrays the quintessential mid-twentieth-century life of a family in the American small town, mostly in Waco, Texas, where the churchgoing O'Briens (Jessica Chastain and Brad Pitt), dependent for income on Father's corporate middle-management job, are raising their three young boys—Jack (Hunter McCracken), R. L. (Laramie Eppler), and Steve (Tye Sheridan). They all know the small joys and irritations of passages from one phase of life to another in domestic and communal life. But they are also shaken by one great tragedy: R. L., the middle O'Brien son, dies at the age of nineteen.[9] The received wisdom of those in the community fails them in their confused anguish. Why R. L.? They will be neither comforted nor silenced by mediated advice from friends, the clergy, and family. This ruptures their containment within the linear marketplace. The rupture is where the light comes in.

The O'Briens, especially Mother O'Brien and her son Jack, are driven toward the experience of Dasein. Malick's "Book of O'Brien," so to speak, differs greatly from the many cheerful, conventional versions of good families in crisis. Consider *How Green Was My Valley* (1941; 1960; 1975; and 1991); the twenty-one cozy movie and television versions of Louisa May Alcott's nineteenth-century novel, *Little Women* (1917–2022); Vincente Minnelli's candy-colored *Meet Me in St. Louis* (1944); John Ford's gripping saga of the Joad family during the Depression, *The Grapes of Wrath* (1940); William Wyler's encouraging World War II movie, *Mrs. Miniver* (1942); and MGM's core mythmaker of the rock-solid parameters of the American family, the fourteen movies of the Andy Hardy series, made between 1938 and 1958. In the series, Mickey Rooney's Andy is sold as the iconic American son who becomes the iconic American dad, through the wise counsel of his iconically wise father, Judge Hardy, about success and women. Typical of the trajectory of the mass-media family story, Andy's episodic passage through teen exuberance to adult stability naturalizes the community's patriarchal structure, within a bounded universe in which time moves in a straight line, space is confined and defined, and the presence of a just and benign God (Whose will be done) at the center of a linear, authoritarian universe is so unquestioningly assumed that religion need barely be mentioned.[10]

By contrast, in Malick's family saga, the Old Testament religion, as it informs the mass-media marketplace, is interrogated repeatedly as Jack makes his passage into a boundless cosmos. The film refuses to justify the death of R. L.—kind, beautiful, and talented—as the Biblical God's will. Rather, it reconfigures the death so that it does not take place merely inside a creation that is a one-shot act by the Old Testament God, in which time has passed, and R. L. is gone. R. L.'s death comes to coexist with his life in a unified temporality and Dasein where creation is ongoing—here and now as well as here and then—and in which all the O'Briens participate. Malick depicts Jack's and Mother O'Brien's intertwined voyages into a new, manifold *here* by means of his explicit comparison and contrast of their journeys with that of the Old Testament's book of Job, in which the ancient figure of Job, the consummate marketplace insider, supremely uncomfortable under the yoke of a linear, authoritarian cosmic hierarchy, is nevertheless forced to recognize Jehovah-sanctified limits.

Not so for the book of O'Brien. Jack's salvation, and his mother's, is their discovery of family and community as part of not only the authoritarian marketplace they know, but also the sanctified, limitless universe of Being they didn't know they knew. Malick integrates one of the most perplexing books of the Old Testament into *TOL* and tells a family story for the new zeitgeist by rejecting the biblical, theocratic limits of the Old Testament God.[11]

In conventional mass-media family stories, salvation lies in some form of rock-solid limits. Where inexplicable death does break hearts, the marketplace insiders turn to tight parameters of sanctified linear reality for comfort and stability. Every time the little Beths in all the *Little Women* movies expire; and when Carol Miniver in *Mrs. Miniver* is killed by the German strafing of a remote English village; or when preacher Casy senselessly dies in *The Grapes of Wrath*, there are identifiable causes, and undeserved suffering is treated by the other characters as part of a divine plan, or an inevitable cause-and-effect progression. By contrast, in *TOL*, Malick subtracts cause and effect from R. L.'s death and propels it beyond, into the limitlessness of Dasein, regardless of how friends, relatives, and the local church seek to render it God's (unchallengeable) will. None of the familiar meliorations proposed by a world of limits will suffice for Jack and his mother—or for Malick. From the first moment of Malick's book of O'Brien, before we even know anything about the death of R. L., Malick asks us to entertain the largest, most limitless vantage point: not only how the cosmos is depicted in the Judeo-Christian Bible, but also how it manifests from the perspective of a very different cosmos in a new zeitgeist.

When Malick left Oxford, he didn't leave Heidegger or his key concept of Dasein. *Dasein* translates from the German as both "being there" and "being open," and it connotes authentic direct experience of the universe, as opposed to what Heidegger called an inauthentic self, created by inauthentic public constructs that mediate the world for us. For Heidegger, existence was "to be understood neither as mere subjectivity nor mere objectivity, but as a fundamental openness to the Being of beings."[12] Malick reflects Dasein as the *here* Jack and his mother arrive at, a *here* that grows from a renewed consciousness that partakes of the shared Sein of humankind. For Heidegger, "the meaning of the world is not simply invented out of our private subjectivity but is given to us by Being itself."[13]

Dasein, private subjectivity, Being, the authoritarian God of the Old Testament, R. L.'s death: that is where *TOL* begins. The film opens with a black title card quoting Job 38:4, 7: "Where were you when I laid the foundation of the earth? . . . When the morning stars sang together, and all the sons of God shouted for joy?" What follows the title card is Jack's form of response. We hear, but do not see, him whisper, "Brother. Mother. It was they who led me to your door." No title card here, but rather on a black screen, a light sculpture called a lumia. Boundless, radiant orange-and-yellow light, in which unlimited, nonlinear motion is open, mutable, yet nevertheless a form, much like the form Malick had intended to offer us through the magic of DVD technology. This is the first of a series of images of Thomas Wilfred's lumia collection of light sculptures, works of art that capture the essence of form in the new zeitgeist, limitless yet unified.[14]

"Your" door? Boundless, yet formed light? With *TOL*, Malick took a turn into the new map of the cosmos. Five years later, he went deeper into the new map of the universe in a documentary called *Voyage of Time* (2016); in 2025 he is projected to release *The Way of the Wind*, a nonlinear juxtaposition of several versions of the life of Christ. But in his book of O'Brien, Jack's journey to "your door" takes the trajectory of a poetic narrative in which Jack refuses to be silenced by the notion of creation as a one-time, humbling effort, at the beginning of linear time. Rather, Jack mutates into a creator himself, experiencing Dasein, envisioning all humankind as part of a continuing process of creation, changing from moment to simultaneously occurring moment.

THE DESIGN OF DASEIN

The book of O'Brien is a fine example for us of how film may cocreate from a philosophical foundation the new map being drawn by the physical sciences.

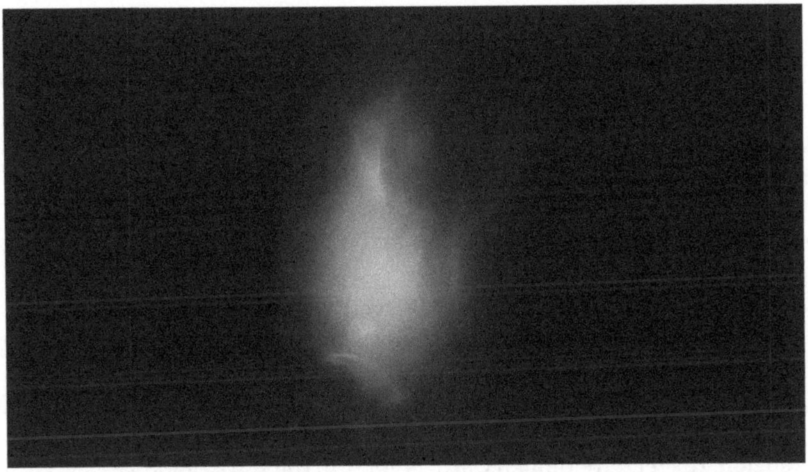

FIGURE 2.1 *Terrence Malick's lumia image of nonlinear reality at the beginning of* The Tree of Life, *chapter 1.*

In *TOL*, Malick himself came to a door, an opening into a nonlinear narrative in which Heideggerian Dasein defines the largest form of reality, and he had to struggle to find a nonlinear cinematic language through which to build that narrative. What, after all, is the means to show the unmediated energy of Dasein in cinema, a medium that by its technological nature is—mediated? Of course, in *TOL* Malick never achieves total limitlessness—no one can—but he approaches it. Malick the student had thrown up his hands at academic limitations that impeded his address to Heidegger's concept. Malick the artist, however, appropriated Dasein for the cinema, an academia-free zone. *TOL* is our occasion for engaging Malick's use of the mediations of cinema—frame composition, music, color, camera and editing work, dialogue, character—toward what he deems possible in a human approach to expressing and partaking of pure Being.

In *TOL*, we see that Malick made that approach mainly by extracting words from his film, as much as he could, and reenvisioning the making of meaning. We see words used sparingly, and often against their intellectual power, to minimize mediation. But more importantly, we see how necessary nonlinear temporality is to represent a new philosophical consciousness of authentic life. Malick's mere act of demoting conventional linear narrative until it is equal with the image—not the usual, dominant method of creating meaning that image merely supports—creates an expressive opportunity.

TOL is built on the tension between the linear, publicly mediated concepts of life, death, success, happiness, and family that frame the marketplace lives of the O'Briens and the nonlinear images of the family's brushes with Dasein. Malick's cinematic Dasein sweeps us into sometimes rapturous, sometimes awe-inspiring, sometimes comic flows of eons of temporality that dwarf the many limits applied to the lives of the O'Briens. In *TOL*, the conventions of marketplace life become visible to us as lacking in genuine reality, in juxtaposition with the authenticity of the flow of nonlinear time; and there is always that "door," invoked by adult Jack at the start of the film, an opening, as we discover, into Dasein, Jack's cosmic lifeline.

Familiar, bracketed limits are the reality and salvation of the conventional mass-media family. Mrs. Miniver (Greer Garson) is able to cope with the senseless, sudden death of her daughter-in-law Carol (Teresa Wright) during World War II by thinking of it as part of a coherent set of systems to which she belongs, including family, community, country, and religion, that endure though Carol is gone, in the spirit of Job's acceptance of an enduring grand creation that prevails though his family and wealth are gone. Linear bracketing in the story of the O'Briens? Well, Malick doesn't reject it. Rather he presents it as partial knowledge. Partial but crucial knowledge. And there again he takes a page from Heidegger, who urged the discovery of "one's own truth," something authentic and beyond community mediations, as well as the necessity to be a part of community. Heidegger clearly asserted that both Sein and community are necessary for authenticity. The Heidegger paradox. The paradox at the core of *TOL*.

Heidegger contends that if the hierarchies of family and community are inauthentic, closed, and inimical to the openness and authenticity of Dasein, the energies of relationships those hierarchies make possible are essential to the individual experience of Dasein. Openness to Being is not, paradoxically, possible for the individual seeking a truth devoid of those communal energies. As we shall see, Jack has been cut off from openness and Being by hierarchies of family and community—as have all the O'Briens. But mediated forms of family and community are not all there is in this vision. There is another form of family and community, like the form of the lumia, silent, luminous, unbound but shaped, immaterial but perceptible as an image, simultaneous with the limited hierarchies of family and community in the marketplace. It is only by finding the copresence of boundless, nonhierarchic connections through family, community, and cosmic energy that Jack achieves peace with R. L.'s death and arrives at the door of a limitless universe, in which death and life are always joyously copresent in nonlinear time and space.[15]

One good paradox deserves another. Representation of the unmediated Dasein of family and community in *TOL* depends on a structure of representation that can approach a storytelling version of the boundless form of lumia sculpture. Malick finds this cinematic language in montage, a form of mediation that is more immersive than the distancing of linear continuity editing.[16] Through the paradoxical capacity of montage to be both a form of mediation and a transcendence of the ordinary parameters, Malick communicates Jack's necessary release into the authentic openness of love and connection.

OPENINGS

TOL is not built on movement from here to there, as is the book of Job. "Were you there?" thunders the voice from the whirlwind. Job is silenced. He wasn't there. Time is linear, and Job's "now" is infinitely distanced from the "then" of the voice. In the nonlinear universe of *TOL*, however, we and Jack mutate into an intimate relationship to the power of creation; we *were and are* all there in the eons of time that contain all the ongoing mutations of creation simultaneously. The audience and Jack are continually immersed in waves of narrative that paradoxically sweep us and him into knowing again, for the first time, where he has always been—and where he is beginning to know he has always been. As he speaks of finding "your door" through his brother and his mother, he also speaks of having always heard the call from "you." Yet *TOL* never erases the reality of the marketplace and its hierarchies built within linear time. The film's montages evoke discontinuous, nonlinear, cosmic time, but portray linear events as part of its vast boundlessness.

Copresent in *TOL* are the elevating vastness of Dasein and the joys and sorrows of being a familial and communal insider, an inheritor of communal comforts, continuities, and boundaries. The initial dialogue between the voice out of the whirlwind in the book of Job and Jack's alternative cosmic vision yields to a sequence that depicts Mrs. O'Brien as a child, living on a farm with her loving, unnamed father, a trace of her youth as she takes in the glory of life around her. There is no linear link between this euphoric montage and the shattering appearance in the next montage of Mrs. O'Brien receiving news of R. L.'s death, via telegram, from a source that is never made known to us. The questions, regrets, and the attempts at consolation that follow—often voiceovers, which are sometimes harmonious with the images, sometimes a counterpoint—are not the creation of continuity editing.

We don't see a linear progress from the arrival of the enigmatic telegram to its shattering impact. Nor is our subsequent vision of an adult Jack, in a luxurious home of his own, with a wife from whom he is emotionally distant, articulated through a chain of cause and effect. When Jack lights a candle in a cobalt-blue glass to mark the anniversary of his brother's death, a sense of connection is in the air, but it is not linear. Connection has the boundless shape of the lumia. The montages are a whirl of traces of Mother O'Brien, R. L.'s death, a new image of a lumia, and Jack's whispered "Brother. Mother. It was they who led me to your door." They begin the book of O'Brien, with a soft voice from a vortex of fragments, not the harsh stipulations about authoritarian creation from the violent whirlwind that ends the book of Job.

Images take on a power they do not have in linear movie narrative. Words are present, and they too signify, but in collaboration with, not dominant over, the visual making of meaning. This equality creates both a new sense of time and a lumia-like narrative context for the trauma of R. L.'s passing. In voiceover, simultaneous with the images of Mother O'Brien as a little girl, words come at us. As an adult, she speaks of what the nuns taught her about "the way of nature" and "the way of grace." There is a temporal discontinuity between Mother's adult voice and the images of the child that Mother was, but that disjunction creates a new sense of connection. All time in her life is simultaneous; ideas, though present, do not structure a linear narrative. The dichotomy between the self-seeking way of nature and the selfless way of grace float in the montage with the images. And then suddenly, as she recalls that the nuns told her that nothing bad can happen to those who follow the way of grace, and that she has pledged her loyalty to grace, "whatever comes," the telegram arrives. The copresence of the nonlinear montages and linear narrative events swirl around each other. Their disconnection evolves into a new idea of connection. The voices that float on the soundtrack contrast with what we see of the immediate small-town aftermath of the telegram and of Jack in his corporate glass-and-steel city. The images intertwine with the serious questioning by Mother and Jack of why innocent R. L. died so young.

Jack O'Brien and Mother are separated in linear time and space, but they merge, as Mother demands answers from the "you" of her Biblical deity: that wasn't supposed to happen. Simultaneously, Jack puzzles over how he found his way, through his mother and brother, to another kind of "you." Dasein is a new kind of unmediated "thou." Two inimical kinds of cosmic realities are in play: Mother's is in the shape of the God of the mediated creation; Jack's, in the boundlessness of Dasein. Jack and Mother are each isolated and connected at the same time. As a second lumia sculpture appears, Mother stubbornly asks God for the parameters of human relationship to the divinity, using the same language that he uses when he exerts power over Job. "Where were you . . . ?" she demands to know; "Answer me," she insists. "What are we to you?"

At the same time, both with her and apart from her, Jack experiences an unbounded space that is copresent with his corporate daily life, confined in rooms, walkways, and elevators. That space is communicated through montage, in images of the sun shining through a partly open,

FIGURE 2.2 *Frame series: Jack O'Brien's portals out of the constricted linear marketplace: A wooden door cracks open for Jack, chapter 3.*

FIGURE 2.3 *Jack O'Brien on a beach, a freestanding door frame, chapter 3.*

wooden barn door in a rough stucco wall and opening onto a vast, open space where the adult Jack stands alone on a beach, near a freestanding, detached door frame. Birds fly freely overhead, and we are propelled across a broad, uncontained expanse of water. He is only briefly in that alternate space of openness and Being. It is as yet merely a contrast to the glass enclosure of his corporate world, through which much can be seen of the hierarchical corporate community, but within which all are compartmentalized by the transparent walls. There is a reason for the brevity of Jack's initial experiences of Dasein; his voyage from here to here is in progress. It don't come easy.

What happens next is that the film is taken over by a brilliant, breathless, magnificent tsunami of images that I will call an "eons montage," which spans the creation of outer space and the planets, and the seas, land, and creatures on Earth. It is disconnected from all the images, words, and thoughts swirling around R. L.'s death, but it is also connected. Mother's questioning and Jack's search continue, interwoven with the eons montage in voiceover. As Malick has contextualized the death of the middle O'Brien son with the book of Job, the eons montage catapults the film into a nonlinear version of the answer to Job's questions and searching. This answer, revealing the vastness of creation, occurs very early in the unfolding of Jack's heroic journey. So, if it is a kind of answer, it is only partial knowledge, as David Lynch would say, that will ultimately transform for a boundless cosmos the Old Testament limits to knowing and feeling.

It is impossible to verbally nail down the openness and being of Dasein extravagantly unfurled in Malick's eons montage, in terms of just how Jack and his mother might be in touch with it, its spirit, or its vastness—unlike the verbal message that is clearly received by Job. Rather, the openness of being intersects with the questions and yearning of Mother and Jack as a form of copresence irreducible to definitive explanation. Words are spoken. An ear receives. The odd form of connection between Jack, his mother, and the eons montage most resembles the quantum phenomenon of entanglement, the quantum mystery of what emerges as instantaneous connection across time and space, despite the absence of any material link. All the creation we see in the eons montage seems to be copresent with Mother and with Jack and with the audience. Everything is united, despite monumental swaths of time and space we cannot perceive within the limits of our urban and small-town activities.

But we are here, in any case, right in the middle of a deluge of special effects in which light shapes glow in darkness, some of which resemble fire, but which fan out in strange ways. Swaths of starry space, bifurcated by needle-shaped light formations in cool colors, and monumental, gloriously colored shapes among the stars, varying in shades, that swirl around or are pierced by radiant light. Orange fire fountains erupt out of darkness, enormous gray and white pillars of smoke rise in the air, and torrents of white water fall. By the grace of film magic, we glide slowly into their centers. We observe that among the stars, fanciful images like cosmic swaths of cloth or flowers unfurl or blossom; we observe clouds over greened earth and rocky mountains. In undersea canyons, we are surrounded both by familiar ocean fish, swimming alone and in schools, and by unfamiliar, pulsating or undulating not quite identifiable micro shapes.

We discover a dinosaur quietly sitting at the edge of the sea, its enormous body still; its small head swaying at the top of a long, serpentine neck. The camera moves in for a close-up of a smaller dinosaur, walking erect in a rainforest, and then at a distance sees it execute an erratic, comical charge toward the camera, in order to plant a foot on the head of an even smaller dinosaur. It disappears from camera range—losing interest?—once it has subdued the little one. The planets Saturn and Jupiter appear. Debris tumbles in space. Crystalline, blue waves break. Jack appears walking on a rocky plain; seagulls swoop in a blue sky. Holy music plays; or the air roars; sometimes the sound of water rises as a roar or a gurgle. Among these are intercut images of the red rock-and-sand formations into which we have seen Jack walk, pushing through the asymmetrical, ungeometrical, gloriously beautiful crevices.

None of this relates to the O'Briens within a linear context. This kind of connection requires a paradigm shift to the intersecting nonlinear ideas that are now mapping a new zeitgeist. From that new perspective, what may seem fragmentary becomes visible as a new narrative in which a continuing whirlwind, more monumental than it appeared at the start of Jack's voyage, invokes the simultaneous existence of the bound and the unbound in the cosmos. The juxtaposition continues to evoke both boundaries and boundlessness, as the film moves toward both a Waco minister's sermon on Job that makes sense within the hierarchies of small town, family, and church, and a full-throttle immersion in boundlessness within which that sermon is irrelevant, yet copresent.

The film takes us from the eons montage into an intersection of montages that invoke ever more intensely flashes of openness and a flowing connection beyond the marketplace and the isolation created by its hierarchical limits. André Bazin believed that montages rendered audiences passive—and they may be within a linear framework; but within the nonlinear framework of *TOL*, its montages enliven, activate.[17] The marketplace montages display Father drilling obedience to his authority into his sons, sometimes harshly. Father teaches his children to erect boundaries between themselves and others; Father tutors his sons about the hierarchies he inhabits, in which money and power are not distributed equally; and he imparts the need for aggressive behavior in order to get others before they get you. We see him show Jack the invisible boundaries between their house and their neighbors'; we see him teach Jack that their property is not as beautifully tended as those of the rich families, who can afford gardeners. We see him trying to teach Jack and R. L. to fight by getting them to punch him. We also see Mr. O'Brien make Jack close the door quietly fifty times, force him to call him "sir" every time he speaks to him, and insist that Jack kiss him and tell him he loves his father on demand. None of these montages leads to a specific cause-and-effect result; rather, they are traces that lead to an environment of violence and aggression, some of it pointedly oedipal.

Traces of a town filled with the results of hierarchical systems bubble up in montage after montage, never leading from one to the other but forming layers, accretions of an atmosphere, a mood. Jack fitfully and unhappily bullies his brothers and engages in destructive "wildings" with the neighborhood boys, who are clearly being taught the same lessons as the O'Brien children. They break the glass in an abandoned house and torture and kill a frog for the fun of it. Budding sexual attraction sends young Jack into hostility and withholding. Jack invades the home of an anonymous neighbor and steals the wife's delicate slip, letting it float away on the current of a local river. He betrays his brother's trust, shooting R. L. with a BB gun after telling him to hold his finger over the barrel, and in remorse Jack offers R. L. the chance to hit him with a length of two-by-four. He wants to establish their mother as his, asking her to tell him which brother she loves best, yelling at their father that mother loves him best, and on one occasion accusing his father of wanting to kill him.

R. L., by contrast, rejects Father's discipline and incitements to violence. In one montage, when Mr. O'Brien is pontificating endlessly at dinner about his rules and expectations, R. L. tells him to be quiet, sending the father into a furious temper that asserts patriarchal hierarchy and drives each member of the family into warring isolation. He terrifies his sons, forcefully shuts Jack and R. L. each into their own rooms and, because Mother comforts the boys, has a violent physical fight with her, after accusing her of turning his sons against him. He also suffers the humiliation and disappointment of losing his job, when the plant he works at closes, and he is given the choice of either being fired or taking an awful job for which he must uproot his family and leave Waco. Everyone must be part of a pecking order of frustration and various forms of stress, it would seem, or die—as did R. L.—within the assaults on Dasein within the marketplace. All the while we are reminded of Jack's yearning and searching and Mother's questions.

Father's many lectures to his children about the power brokers in town that own all the land, in combination with the minister's sermon that interprets Job's trials as part of a universe controlled by an all-powerful God whose authority must not be questioned, situate the O'Briens in a system in which family is the dismal reflection of an authoritarian universe. We are not in "Andy Hardyville," now. The minister warns the congregation not to entertain Job's mistaken belief that following the rules and creating a good life will ward off evil. "Job imagined that if he built his nest on high the integrity of his behavior would protect him against misfortune. . . . But no. Misfortune befalls the good as well."

The sermon paints a frightening picture, resonant of the words of fire-and-brimstone New England minister Jonathan Edwards in his famous eighteenth-century sermon, "Sinners in the Hands of an Angry God."[18] The image that the Waco minister evokes is of an unfathomable rather than an angry God, but the resulting message is all too similar. No matter what we do, we cannot protect ourselves and our loved ones. This mediation creates a community of helplessness and fear. Ironically, although Mother's faith is in the way of grace, the outcome is the same. No matter what she did, she could not protect R. L. from an unjust death.

Yet that is only part of the montage mosaic. The family unit is also depicted in montages that portray traces of joy and even boundlessness, which shine through cracks in hierarchy, although communal joy is sometimes clouded by unexpected or unsuspected toxicity. A DDT truck spraying the neighborhoods lures the children to dance with abandon in its poisonous clouds. A communal swimming pool is the scene of a child's sudden drowning. But there are also traces of pure delight. Father and Mother play with their sons in a spirited way, within the confines of their property. Within the confines of the neighborhood, children frolic together. The montages of the births of the children to the O'Briens are filled with wonder as well as joy. Father tenderly marvels at Mother's pregnancy and the babies after they are born. We see Mother tenderly welcoming a butterfly that lands on her finger. We also see her dancing literally on air—a fantasy, perhaps in Jack's mind because of her often charming and graceful encounters with nature, or her own fantasy built on her exhilarated memory of an airplane flight she was given as a graduation present. For his part, Father loves music and confesses to having wanted to be "a great musician." He listens to the recordings of classical masterpieces and plays both the piano and the church organ with rapt elation. But Mother's escape into the air is limited to that one glorious flight, and perhaps that fantasy. Father's love of music is weighed down by his all-too-characteristic sense of pressure. He lectures the boys on the perfectionism of the true geniuses of music, for whom a performance can always be better, and he compulsively displays his superior knowledge of music by testing the boys while they listen to recordings.

By the time the film reaches its ecstatic leap into Dasein at the end, the situation of the O'Briens in the marketplace is a whirlwind of traces, moving parts that establish Heidegger's paradox: the copresence of Newtonian limits and quantum boundlessness. Authentic openness to Being depends on individuals merging with family and community, not only in the marketplace, as part of mediated, hierarchical systems, but also on the authentic, open, unmediated plane of Dasein. Only poetry and vision make this possible. The film achieves a privileged moment of authenticity, through the visual poetry of montage, approaching boundlessness, rendered equal with verbal, highly mediated language, which we see when Jack makes his breakthrough as he finally enters "the door" with his family and his community. *TOL* approaches an ecstatic kind of closure when a mutated Jack whispers again that his mother and his brother "led me to your door." Jack is in a different, visionary position when the family and community beyond "the door" are connected, not disconnected as in the marketplace.[19]

YOU?

Jack begins the film on a nonlinear hero's journey. He has been to the door. Yet by the end of *TOL* his journey is not concluded. He is part of ongoing creation; he is still approaching the door. All time is one. The limited marketplace and the openness of Dasein are eternally copresent. At the end of the film, we are still in the marketplace and also still nearing Dasein. Jack's flashes of the door explode into a full-fledged entrance into a limitless plane of reality. He enters an elevator in the steel-and-glass city, and suddenly he is bathing in openness, more *here* than before and still going from *here* to *here*. Now he is *here* on an open expanse, surrounded by the nonhierarchic flow of community and his family. Father and Mother are present, as are R. L. and his youngest brother, Steve, as children, and himself as both a child and an adult. The O'Briens are no longer restricted to constricting roles in a linear family construct. Father is not imposing his authority; Mother is not being imposed on. All toxic oedipal anxieties are gone. Jack doesn't need to question whom mother loves best or whether father wants to kill him, a hallmark, as we have seen, of the bounded, patriarchal, Newtonian world of Job and his whirlwind. All are embraced and embrace a boundless, horizontal form of warm, untroubled connection. R. L. is regained in the openness of the authentic Dasein.

The nonlinear poetics of Jack's second trip through the door is a poetics of release from bounded form, like the lumia light sculptures that have a beauty and energy of their own. The final exit/entrance through the door takes him and us to a place of wide ocean and unobstructed air, now populated by all the O'Briens, not just Jack's lonely peregrinations, and many other less recognizable community figures. We are with Jack. We are with Mother. We are in a state of openness, joy, a vision of Dasein.

When Jack follows his younger self, we find ourselves on desert and ocean. Waves ripple. The breeze blows. At the shoreline of a wave-filled ocean, the camera flows freely among the characters. Nonlinear camera motions complement the language of montage in making meaning.[20] Hair and clothing waft on the wind. Mother finds and caresses young

FIGURE 2.4 *Jack O'Brien in nonlinear reality with family and community, near end of film, chapter 22.*

R. L. Father hugs his children and his wife kisses him. Her demands of an absent authoritarian God transform into an intimate relationship with the thou of Dasein. Her last words, the last words in the film, are "I give him to you. I give you my son." Giving is the essence of being in an ever newly creating cosmos. But this is not the end. Jack exits the elevator into the glass-and-steel corporate city. Was it all a dream?

Where is Jack and where are we when we are experiencing Dasein? It is no dream. I contend we are on another level of reality here, having moved from *here* to *here*, and about to move from *here* to *here*, again, maybe forever. On exiting the elevator into linear time Jack is hemmed in on all sides by skyscrapers, with but a small space, if we look upward, for a view of the unbounded sky. Then Malick cuts to an image of a bridge, the next-to-last image in the film, an avatar of connection, open-ended transit both ways. Malick's poetic response to the book of Job is a bridge open on both ends, wide open.

And now the film cuts to the image of a lumia, the final image of the film. Yes. Malick affirms the limited marketplace as reality. Yes. And he also affirms the unbounded form of the lumia. All is one for all time.

IDEAS IN THE MASS MEDIA?

Gilles Deleuze and Mary Ann Doane, as we have already noted, have raised the possibility that the mass media can be discussed as cocreators of the modern world with philosophy and science. Here, at the outset, I have discussed *TP 3* and *TOL* as our first examples of a meaningful, albeit indeterminate, collaboration between the mass media and the new map of the cosmos proposed by science and philosophy. Lynch and Malick employ moving images, sound, music, and popular narratives to provide a poetic experience of nonlinearity, conjoined with their own manifestations of a unified field, the parallel realities comprising reality.

Nonlinear film and serial narrative form a bridge for the imagination from ordinary, experiential life to the abstract claims of the learned discourses. Or, more accurately, the nonlinear creations of the mass media form as many bridges as the imaginations of media artists can bring forth. Nonlinear poetry in film and serial narrative neither proves or disproves the new consciousness or the ideas of any particular thinker or school of thought. Proof is the bailiwick of the sciences, not the arts. Rather, nonlinear entertainment integrates our feelings, imaginations, and viscera with the abstractions of science and philosophy and thereby expands their capacity to map the cosmos and our capacity to entertain the wider horizon of reality of which the learned disciplines now speak.

Broadening our engagement in the cosmos in the mass media is analogous to the familiar claims made for literature, as a way of expanding our empathy with people and experiences beyond our own prejudices and cultural groups, and just as important. Science expands the knowledge of time and space, beyond what the naked eye and ear can perceive, through its technology and its mathematics. The mass media expand our empathy, through poetry, to levels of reality beyond what we can know of time and space through the naked eye and ear. It is in that spirit that all the shows we will discuss on this voyage speak to us and in that spirit that we will proceed with our journey. We have seen how insiders like Agent Cooper and Jack O'Brien make the new hero's journey in limitless space and time. In the next chapter, we observe the nonlinear poetry of the very different journeys made by marketplace *outsiders* in two very different nonlinear narratives.

OUTSIDERS, FORKING PATHS, HEALING OXYMORONS

The OA, Eternal Sunshine of the Spotless Mind

Chapter 3

Your ancestor did not believe in a uniform and absolute time; he believed in an infinite series of times, a growing, dizzying web of divergent, convergent, and parallel times. That fabric of times that approach one another, fork, are snipped off, or are simply unknown for centuries, contains all *possibilities. In most of those times, we do not exist; in some, you exist but I do not; in others, I do and you do not; in others still, we both do.*

JORGE LUIS BORGES, *"The Garden of Forking Paths"*

We have found that what we have long thought to be everything is only a small part of a grander whole, only one piece of a much wider cosmos.

BRIAN GREENE, INTERVIEW ON NPR'S *Fresh Air*, JANUARY 24, 2011

Outsiders of the world: go nonlinear!

Our perspective shifts when we inquire about the reality of the new zeitgeist for the outsider hero's journey. The journey of the insider hero, a pillar of the marketplace, forces a frightening, sometimes unwelcome, experience of the nonlinear, boundless cosmos, even though new possibilities may abound. After all, what had once seemed a comfortable linear reality has collapsed. By contrast, for the outsider hero, painfully uncomfortable within the bounds of the marketplace, the encounter with nonlinear time and space is prophylactic. When, in this chapter, we explore the voyages of the outliers in *The OA* (2016–2019), created by Brit Marling and Zal Batmanglij, and the misfits of *Eternal Sunshine of the Spotless Mind* (2004), created by Charlie Kaufman and director Michel Gondry, we will watch them begin their journeys distressingly hemmed in by their marketplace circumstances. Then, not fear, but imaginable comfort looms when they are called on to enter the innumerable possibilities of the "fabric of times that approach one another, fork, are snipped off, or are simply unknown for centuries," as the universe is described by Jorge Luis Borges in his story "The Garden of Forking Paths."[1]

Forget Freud, as we observe the discontents of outliers. The heroes of *OA* and *Sunshine* are not out of step because of psychological disorders, but because they are round pegs, incompatible with the square holes their narratives define as marketplace illusions about time, space, matter, and energy. They begin oppressed variously by a variety of negativities, such as homophobia, racism, sexism, ageism, and panic about intimacy. When they are called by the boundlessness of the nonlinear cosmos to experience limitlessness, release becomes possible. Possible, but not inevitable. The compelling suspense of their travels in the multiverse is generated by the uncertain urgency that they realize those possibilities.

The outlier's nonlinear journey also channels Kafka but tosses him up in the air and watches him land on his philosophical head, where he finds a potential way out of his angst. It is as though, when Josef K. in *The Trial* was told he was guilty of an unidentified crime in the marketplace, he had set out, not on a doomed quest to confront his elusive accusers, but rather in answer to a wake-up call to look beyond the marketplace and its constraints on matter, time, space, and energy. Unlike Josef K.'s cosmos of unyielding incomprehensibility, the universe in *OA* and *Sunshine* may be incomprehensible, but it is unified by a strange, healing, new kind of coherence. We are in the presence of poetic invocations to gratifying prospects for outsiders in the great Einsteinian oxymoron of a unified, cosmic boundlessness. We begin with the complexity of such gratifications as they are represented in Brit Marling and Zal Batmanglij's series *The OA*.

THE OA: EVERY HUMAN MIND CONTAINS THE MULTIVERSE

Writing partners Marling and Batmanglij are no strangers to outsiders or cinema for a nonlinear universe. In *Another Earth* (2011), *Sound of My Voice* (2011), and *The East* (2013), they dipped into nonlinear time and outlier stories. In *The OA* (2016–2019), their two-season series, however, the larger canvas of the serial form afforded them the opportunity for a richer and more complex narrative. With a vengeance. The rich temporality of *OA* offers a range of outlier adventures in innumerable temporal dimensions, within which exist innumerable marketplaces. A cosmic dynamic of intertwined expansion *and* constriction is the nature of the series' reality. Both open-ended and confined without end, the series features a universe that is nonlinear and expansive but contains time dimensions that are internally linear and constricting. Its multiple, parallel time frames form a kaleidoscope of elements that comprise a Borgesian "fabric of times." Indeed, the image of a kaleidoscope appears often in the main titles of the episodes.

The series is a concrete indicator of how David Lynch changed the industrial context. By the time Marling and Batmanglij arrived, there was a clear opening for them to dive into nonlinear storytelling; and there was a clear precedent for entertainment journalists to explore it. Not all journalists made the leap, of course. James Poniewozik, in *The New York Times*, writes as a bedazzled, but ultimately uncomprehending critic of the Marling and Batmanglij series: "To me, the ending of *The OA* was ludicrous and cheaply provocative; some folks wired differently may find it haunting and profound. Just beware. This wonder box is gorgeously gift-wrapped, but the time you'll invest in it is nonreturnable."[2]

Perhaps from the perspective of the prequantum cosmos. In the context of the new zeitgeist, *The OA* is anything but cheap or ludicrous. Peter Debruge, in *Variety*, concurs. Debruge found himself responding at a deep level to a show he knows he doesn't fully understand. He sobbed for a half hour after seeing the ending, and has this to say, "The entire experience is *about* the need for narratives that seem bigger than the incidents we face in our own lives. The same quality that the OA's five followers respond to in her is what draws us into a show like this."[3] This will be the first book-length study to support critics like Debruge and that part of the mass audience with an empathetic connection to *The OA*, not as a definitive explanation of the inexplicable aspects of the series, but as a way of understanding its place as a narrative for the new post-Newtonian reality.

With Borgesian flair, the series' creators present us with parallel dimensions in which their characters find parallels of themselves, and of the friends and enemies they have left in other dimensions, just not necessarily all of them, and not in precisely the same relationships they once had. Marling and Batmanglij are on the same forking paths as Borges. But they envision Borges's temporal boundlessness from their own inventive perspectives. The grand design of *The OA* is the result of Marling and Batmanglij's obvious familiarity with Borges, or at least his short story "The Garden of Forking Paths." Ahem, the title of chapter 6 in part 1—the first season—is "Forking Paths." Moreover, the drama of the series just as obviously grows from Borges's description of the mutations of parallel people in parallel time frames and the possibility that in some dimensions some people may have disappeared. But this is only their jumping-off point.

Marling and Batmanglij depart from Borges's vision as they imagine outsiders who become travelers, able to take voyages around those paths and inhabit the lives of their parallel alters. As part of their take on the multiverse, the series' creators jump into the function of memory in such a cosmos, not a factor at all in Borges's story. In *The OA*, whether the characters do or do not remember other dimensions is of crucial importance because *The OA* is playing with new kinds of quests in the multiverse, and failure to remember where one has been in time and space forecloses the greatest potential of the traveler: the ability to incorporate into the heroic quest the multiverse mind that emerges from a number of possible marketplace existences. Moreover, the Marling and Batmanglij version of the heroic quest is dramatically impacted by a new vision of what death means in the multiverse. It does not have the finality it seems to have within any linear marketplace. Far from being the end, in *The OA* death is one of the bridges across time frames for travelers. Death enables the quest in the nonlinear cosmos of boundless time dimensions. Memory, heroic mutation, crossing the bridge of death, outliers, travelers. All this and more.

Marling and Batmanglij begin their series in a time dimension the audience will recognize as their own, but very soon the setting morphs into a cosmos with a brisk traffic in passages for a multitude of outliers across the multiverse. A diverse lot they are, but they share the common plight of the outsider. They are isolated, angry, misunderstood, and rejected by their communities as peculiar, maybe twisted, and they believe they are condemned to isolation. So they are, if they stay trapped in the limited marketplace mindset. The series, however, speaks from a wide-open mindset, distances itself from the tyranny of the limits of the marketplace, and offers its outsiders a call from the multiverse to travel and perhaps find the connections, acceptance, and peace denied them within unrealistic marketplace confines. The connections they long for are available in the multiverse, details to follow shortly.

It is the restricted marketplace vision that the series portrays as somewhat twisted; it fosters disconnection, and it is disconnected from the greater universe. The first outlier task is to find the capacity to bond, by losing the mind-forged manacles that rule the marketplace. As the seasons unfold, most of the outsiders we are introduced to learn to become a group of allied partisan travelers in a Borgesian cosmos. How? They apprehend the cosmic unity, which the marketplace does not recognize, after they encounter a pioneer traveler: She is a woman with a number of names in different dimensions, to whom we will refer, for purposes of clarity, by one of those names, OA (Brit Marling). OA is born with an innate intuition about the multiverse, and as knowledge fortifies intuition she learns how to travel, and she wants to share. Together, OA and her friends embody a new, nonlinear, heroic concept.

The nonlinear blessings of traveling! But not always. There is also Hap (Jason Isaacs), as we will call him, although he, too, has different names in different dimensions. He is an outsider with a difference. Hap begins in the same time dimension as OA and the traveling friends she acquires. He, too, is angry and alone. But he fancies himself a hero in the Campbellian sense, and the series does not fancy him. Self-hypnotized by a belief that he will improve society as a lone, superior adventurer, he, too, breaks limits. But it is the linear benefactor game he plays, light on the benefits for others and heavy on personal fame and success for him. Of course. There is much conflation of selfless altruism with self-promotion.

Hap is a scientist, isolated because he is determined to benefit humankind by rejecting the limitations of institutional science. He wants to explore what happens after death, a field of study considered out of bounds by the scientific establishment and emphatically prohibited. How do you experiment with death? The specter of killing human test subjects arises. Hap is undaunted by the specter. Killing a human test subject is, Hap reasons, a reasonable sacrifice for the greater good. The scientific establishment begs to differ, and so does the series, albeit not for the same reasons. The establishment is into limits.

So when the series, set in a limitless cosmos, condemns Hap, it is not for that reason. Rather, the cosmic, Borgesian reality of *The OA* is oxymoronic. Both boundless and unified. Traveling requires the nonlinear quests of OA and her allies across accustomed limits, but in ways that honor the connections of any and everything. Boundlessness *and* connection are the essence of this multiverse. Heroism is associated with a band of allies that cherishes connection as it heeds the nonlinear call of the multiverse. Hap doesn't cherish connectedness. He is, in fact, a version of the Campbellian hero; alone, disconnected, and pursuing the linear action of the experimental process: try, fail, try, fail, try, succeed. In this multiverse, such linearity is bound to fail. It is also bound to be psychotic. Hap is a psychotic failure.

Surprisingly, however, the narrative is not about the need to conquer or erase Hap, as in the prequantum narrative polarization endemic to the Marvel Universe or the *Star Trek* franchise, inhabited by an either/or perspective on heroes and villains. In *The OA*, Hap and OA are destined to be partners in a Borgesian evolution only possible in the multiverse. Dialectically, they eternally transform each other as they travel the forking paths. This transformation of the heroic quest for a nonlinear universe that incorporates both the constriction of the Campbellian linearity and the open receptivity of postquantum nonlinearity is Marling and Batmanglij's most crucial contribution to mass media in the new zeitgeist. Watch and see.[4]

TRAVELERS

Traveling in the series begins with OA, both because she is the first traveler we meet in the series and because she becomes a leader for other outliers. Her leadership is shaped by her early encounter with traveling, as a child who learns that death is a bridge rather than a void. Official marketplace opinion? She is psychologically troubled. And when we enter the series in medias res, that is exactly what she seems. But we are asked to perceive differently. We first see OA as an anonymous young woman dashing to her certain death across lanes of automobile traffic on a bridge near St. Louis, Missouri. Passengers in other cars clearly consider her out of her mind. But we are given a clue that all is not as it seems. We see her image framed by large, dark borders—the kind we see in smartphone videos when they are transferred to a conventional TV or computer screen. It is a signal that much surrounds her that we cannot see. Moreover, quick cuts to black fracture her progress toward the edge of the bridge creating a sense of discontinuity. And a perception of an open plane of reality. Nevertheless, when fragmented, anonymous voices from one of the vehicles express fear for her, our ordinary sense of limited time and space kicks in and we feel anxious, too. Should we?

The answer is Schrödingeresque; it depends on who observes her. At first we have only the perspective of the observers in the scene, who intuit

FIGURE 3.1 *OA tries to use a linear bridge to travel to nonlinear reality, season 1, episode 1.*

an impending suicide. But she survives her leap from the bridge and is taken to a hospital, where she is reunited with her adoptive parents, Abel and Nancy Johnson (Scott Wilson and Alice Krige), from whom OA has been inexplicably separated for seven years. They seem to share our anxiety about the attempted suicide. But there is also the young woman's point of view: She is disappointed that she did not die. Does she offer us an alternative perspective? Not yet.

Surely, most of the audience enters the series on the same wavelength as the people in the car who helplessly watch OA throw herself off the bridge, the doctors and nurses who tend to her injuries, and OA's discombobulated parents: The girl needs medication and therapy. Doesn't she? And indeed, OA has an official record of mental illness. But the series will contest that record and diagnosis. Official records and conventional psychology leave much to be desired in this context. They have no way of tracing what happened to OA during her mysterious seven-year absence, and they cannot account for one important change in her. When Abel and Nancy adopted OA as a little girl, named her Prairie Johnson, and took her home to suburban Crestwood in Wisconsin, she was blind. She has returned home able to see.

Marling and Batmanglij present the medical files as only part of the story. The series is dedicated to giving us a competing, imaginative experience; we are asked to look at death from the perspective of the multiverse. OA is on that kind of voyage. Leaping into the water below from the steel traffic bridge to St. Louis is, for her, an act of connectivity. With what or whom? Patience, please. With a firm hand, the series validates her point of view and divorces us from a psychiatric interpretation of her distress. And the places we then go!

Unfortunately, because Marling and Batmanglij did not have time to fully explore the permutations of OA's adventure across the five seasons they were hoping for, due to Netflix's premature and misguided cancellation of the series, we can never enjoy their full articulation of a new kind of hero's journey in the multiverse. Rather, we must marvel at the immensity of the series' contribution to popular storytelling, truncated as it is.

DEATH AND THE MAIDEN

Once OA has made her failed leap, we are led to discover a new idea about death through a narrative in the nonlinear shape of a matryoshka doll. It is a nested aggregation of time periods, one inside the other, in which OA and Hap meet and experience a nonlinear discovery of the multiverse. We move through nested, nonlinear time, through OA's voice as she tells her story. To whom does she tell it? Five other outliers, with whom she connects when she returns to Crestwood after her long absence. A band of partisan travelers forms before our eyes, whom I shall call the Crestwood Five. They, like OA, are struggling with the limits of Crestwood, a suburban subdivision in the St. Louis area. While the authorities and OA's adoptive parents misguidedly seek limited answers to OA's unlimited situation, OA meets in secret with the Five, to lead them to a vision of the full multiverse she has discovered. And they are not the first band of travelers seeking release in OA's life. That is what she has assembled them to tell them. Enter Hap.

At secret midnight meetings in an abandoned house in Crestwood, away from the prying eyes of officialdom, OA tells the Five how she became an outlier. Together, OA's Crestwood Five, scarred by the weaponized marketplace limits imposed on them, begin to heal. Steve Winchell (Patrick Gibson), handsome, athletic, and strong, has been brutalized by his macho, white father to be almost completely and viciously transactional, seeing in others nothing more than servants to his will. Buck/Michelle Vu (Ian Alexander), kind, slight, brilliant, and Asian, is forced by his blinkered culture to furtively and illegally seek the drugs needed for his transition from Buck to Michelle. Jesse Mills (Brendan Meyer), who is a grubby, neglected white orphan, barely able to find a place for himself in the Crestwood community, compulsively seeks solace in drugs. There is one, Alfonso "French" Sosa (Brandon Perea), a handsome, brilliant young man of Filipino heritage, who seems bound for insider success. But at a price. He has been enthusiastically identified by the marketplace powers that be, who don't know he is gay, as deserving of a full scholarship to the college of his choice in Michigan. And all he has to do is stay in the closet.

The fifth is Betty Broderick-Allen (Phyllis Smith), a teacher in the local high school, where the other members of the Crestwood Five are students. She, too, is uncomfortably inside and masked. She is white, and she is educated, and she is in the system. But as a plump woman who doesn't conform to social standards of desirability, she is alone, patronized by her colleagues and her family, doggedly doing her duty as an educator to gain what acceptance is offered to her, while telling herself she has to accept her emotional isolation.

OA seeks to reopen the gates to the cosmos for all of them, in a tale that recreates how the gates were opened for her, as she speaks of her childhood, her adoption, and remarkable revelations after she ran away from Abel and Nancy. Her nested, nonlinear narrative enables the Five to connect with each other, as they come to believe OA's tale of her early life as little Nina Azarova (Zoey Todorovsky), the young daughter of Russian oligarch Roman Azarov (Nikolai Nicholaeff), an insider born into a high level of wealth and power in Russia who was murdered by her father's political enemies. OA even makes credible the space of dark brilliance she enters into where Khatun (Hiam Abbass), a maternal presence, has the power to send

FIGURE 3.2 *OA, as little Nina, and Khatun, together where death is a space, not a void, season 1, episode 1.*

her back to the marketplace, but blinded, to shield her against its horrors. This near-death experience (NDE) is prologue to her travels as an outsider to marketplace limits. Very cool. But believable? Are the Crestwoods and the audience really to believe that in this universe death is not a void, but a space beyond the marketplace, a transition point of sorts? And what about her seemingly fantastic account of how, after Roman's enemies succeeded in killing him, she had to be spirited away for her protection to America, where she was adopted by Abel and Nancy in Crestwood? Belief has its benefits. Once the Crestwood Five accept OA's strange narrative of the layers of her life, they and we are relieved of their classification as pathological. (Freud who?) And so much becomes possible.

Still, their passage and ours is a learning curve. OA reveals that the calls from the greater cosmos that she continued to receive in her dreams as she was growing up were not initially comprehensible to her. Though the authorities in Crestwood are wrong to dismiss her dreams as hallucinations for which she needs to be medicated, her belief that her dreams were telling her that her father wasn't dead—that he was waiting for her in New York City at the Statue of Liberty—was in error. Yes, the cosmos was calling her. But Roman is truly dead in the temporal dimension in which Nancy and Abel are her adoptive parents. The cosmos was calling her to her next step in her education as a traveler by someone else: Hap.

Blind and alone, as she tells the Crestwoods, OA bumped into not Roman but Hap. Disappointed that her father was not there, she was exhilarated to discover that she had met up with a scientist exploring what happens after death. Hap beguiled OA with the promise that she would work with him in his pursuit of knowledge about NDEs, like the one she had, but after he lured her to a secret laboratory he had set up in South Dakota, he made her a prisoner, not a partner. OA tells the Crestwoods how her joy turned to terror when, once they reached the laboratory, Hap locked her into a glass cage with four other research subjects, who had also lived through NDEs. She describes how Hap, trying to find out what they have learned about death through dying, kills them repeatedly and brings them back to life, on the assumption that if they returned once they could do it again.

But wait. This is really strange. Doubts again surface. Can OA be delusional after all?

No. Hap is strange, but strangely real and necessary to OA's quest and to the release of the Crestwoods from suffering in the marketplace. Perhaps even more strange is that, as OA speaks, it becomes clear that in the South Dakota lab something positive was taking place because of the fraught dynamic between what I will call the South Dakota Five and Hap. Hap's intentional experiments are only part of the dynamic in the lab, which neither he, nor OA, nor his other prisoners can understand. There is a Big Bang in progress, so to speak: a mutation. Hap is monstrous, but because he brought together the South Dakota Five, a nonlinear mutation occurs. It is that kind of a nonlinear narrative.

The arrival of OA at Hap's laboratory turns out to be a painful step toward a new knowledge of reality, but not the linear way Hap had been imagining. When OA shows up, a mutation in group chemistry occurs. The group in the glass cage had been thoroughly demoralized. Having survived death, they were kidnapped by Hap. Homer Roberts (Emory Cohen), a football hero, had died and come back to life after an accident on the field; Scott Brown (Will Brill) had an NDE he couldn't explain, and was a sickly and homeless drug addict when Hap kidnapped him; and Rachel DeGrasso's (Sharon Van Etten) NDE came after a car crash that killed her brother but left her alive. After Hap imprisons OA, he goes to Cuba to hunt down the fifth, Renata Duarte (Paz Vega), another NDE survivor, similarly betrayed into captivity and outraged. Left to Hap's untender experiments, they are isolated. OA introduces connection, connection, connection. They all bond in friendship and OA and Homer fall in love.

By contrast, Hap feels even more intensely disconnected as he observes them bond. He envies their solidarity, but most of all he envies Homer. Hap desires OA. In his isolation he is deluded about who he is. Rejected by OA and only able to make discoveries through her and her band of friends, Hap is far from the Campbellian mastermind in pursuit of truth he believes himself to be. In his lab, his experiments, products of linear thinking, fail miserably. OA and the other captives cannot remember what happens between their deaths and returns to life. But, as the captives bond, they find themselves bound for a bigger vision than Hap ever conceived of. Through their nonlinear bonding, not his linear experiments, Hap learns that he is on the wrong track; what happens after death is only part of the big cosmic picture. On his own, he has been oblivious to the connectivity of the larger universe, even when he is told about it point-blank. In "Paradise," chapter 5 of the first season, OA recalls for the Crestwood Five a time in South Dakota when Hap listened to a radio broadcast of the program *Fresh Air*, on NPR, a real-world program on a real-world, public radio station, in which Brian Greene, a real-world physicist, is being interviewed.

Reality and fiction merge, as Hap putters, and on the radio Greene talks about the revolution in thought taking place in physics:

> We have found that what we have long thought to be everything is only a small part of a grander whole, only one piece of a much wider cosmos. And to really kind of communicate that idea, we've introduced this new terminology that our universe is just one of many universes populating, possibly, a grander multiverse. . . . This would be, of course, a huge revolution. It's a revolution in a way that would complete a metarevolution that's been in the making for five centuries. I mean, a long time ago, we all know that we thought that the Earth was the center of everything. Then Copernicus comes along, and we learn that no, the Earth is going around the sun. And then later, we learn that the sun is one of many stars in our galaxy, one of hundreds of billions of stars in our galaxy. Then we learn that our galaxy is . . . [5]

Here we leave *Fresh Air*, as Hap moves off to other concerns. Greene's words about the multiverse have not penetrated. It is only when OA and the other four discover the multiverse that Hap takes notice.

Such is the series' depiction of the Campbellian hero. Hap is presented as a rapist in the old sense of the word, one who abducts and subdues by brute force. He holds himself separate from his captives, who have experienced the multiverse as he has not, and expects to live off their lives, secretly and perversely longing to possess OA. This we had already begun to see earlier, at the end of chapter 3, "Champion." When OA tried to escape, Hap killed her. It wasn't part of his experimentation; rather in a fit of compulsive authoritarianism and disappointed love when she tried to get away from him, he chased and murdered her. Tellingly, where the deaths he inflicted in the lab produced no new experiences or knowledge, this death, a nonlinear result of spontaneous rage, becomes OA's next step toward her hero's quest. In the space of death once more, OA sees Khatun again and learns more about who she is and what the cosmos is about. This time, she regains her sight and is given a gift by the strange, motherly Khatun that casts knowledge in an entirely different light.

The gift arrives as a sudden, incomprehensible (nonlinear) knowledge about a complex physical movement, of which OA has no idea until she returns to life in South Dakota and finds herself teaching it to her beloved Homer and her friends. Nor do the Five know what the movement will mean to them, as they work to perform it, until four other movements are given to them, each one to a different one of Hap's captives, each one a surprise, each one an energy dynamic, like a new knowledge of the alphabet of a visceral language. The movements together generate massive energy that galvanizes them out of the torpor of captivity toward a path opening up for them. The "letters" of the new alphabet arrive spontaneously from the multiverse. Hap can do no more than appropriate their evolution as his own.

The movements create collaborative power over not only travel but also life and death. After they have the first two letters of the new alphabet, Homer and OA are stunned to discover that together they can conjoin two pieces of that visceral alphabet to restore life to Scott, who has been in fragile health. During one of Hap's routine experiments, dying and returning proves too much for Scott's compromised body. The movements Homer and OA perform bring Scott across the bridge of death to the marketplace. Later, they will realize that when all five movements are performed together by all the South Dakota captives, they can transition across the multiverse without dying.

Although Hap and his detainees continue to be essential to each other, what a contrast between what happens to Hap and what happens to OA, Homer, Rachel, Scott, and Renata! While the five captives gained strength, coherence, and enlightenment, Hap increasingly fell into the despair of Cambellian isolation. In chapter 6, "Forking Paths," Marling and Batmanglij detail for us how the linear marketplace turns insiders with the highest levels of learning into competitors rather than collaborators. OA tells the Crestwoods how, miserably alone, Hap took a trip to see his old teacher, Dr. Leon Citro (Michael Cumpsty), for advice about his work. But the renowned Citro, who had mentored Hap as a young scientist, only manifests how pathetically blind to the multiverse Hap would have remained without the South Dakota Five. Engaged in the experiments with death that motivated Hap to isolate himself in South Dakota, Citro works secretly in an abandoned hospital morgue, where he routinely kills his prisoners when they are no longer useful, as if disposing of chemical waste. Instead of finding a colleague, Hap finds a monstrous enemy, who is perfectly happy to dispose of him, too, because what Hap is gaining from his captives threatens Citro's ambitions.

Citro's conclusions about NDEs as a way to investigate an afterlife suddenly seem irrelevant when Hap tells him he is seeking not merely an afterlife but an entire multiverse. Citro immediately tries to murder him, only to be killed when his younger and stronger former student defends himself. But Hap's survival brings no revelations about connection in the multiverse. Back in South Dakota, he wants to partner with OA and abandon the others, obdurately blind to how it was the bond among the South Dakota Five that made discovery of the multiverse possible. When OA refuses his offer, Hap contrives to force her beloved Homer and their friends to jump to another dimension without her. In the present, OA has been recreating that bond with the Crestwood Five and teaching them to do the motions with her so that she can follow her friends into a parallel dimension. By the time OA has revealed her history to them they are ready to help her. No more leaping from steel-cable bridges.

But there is yet one more hurdle for OA in the linear marketplace. The marketplace delusion that vision is madness comes close to shattering the bond between OA and the Crestwoods. When parents and authorities learn of the midnight meetings, they condemn OA as a lunatic and predator of the young. To make things worse, when the Crestwood Five go looking for evidence to defend OA, they find a box under OA's bed containing books about Russian oligarchs, and NDEs, and a copy of *The Iliad*, by the ancient poet Homer, that Abel and Nancy had purchased for OA to try to prove to her that she was hallucinating her multiverse stories. The Crestwood Five misunderstand their discovery. They think that OA bought and used them as a source for making up her strange story. They relapse into isolation, and the audience is also caught up in doubt about OA's credibility. Partial knowledge: It clouds the mind in this series. But not the body.

The experience marked in the bodies of the Crestwood Five by the motion language OA taught them cannot be denied. When the high school where Betty teaches, and where French, Buck/Michelle, Steve, and Jesse are students, is attacked by an anonymous shooter, that energy activates spontaneously. Instead of running in isolated fear like everyone else, they stand up together to perform the five movements of the energy language, transfixing the shooter, who is then subdued. Their performance of the motions energizes OA, who, though miles away, is impelled to arrive at the school just in time to be struck in the heart by a bullet that goes astray from the shooter's gun as he is tackled. Everything is connected; everything is Schrödingeresque. OA is dead in the Crestwood marketplace, but in the cosmic context, she is in transition to another dimension. Will it be the dimension where Hap and the South Dakota captives went? She speaks the name "Homer" as she crosses dimensions. And lands where Homer, the other captives, and Hap are. Shall we ever doubt again?

FORKING, CONNECTED

It all looks fragmented, but "it's all connected," is one of the main themes of the new map of the zeitgeist, and a recurring theme in the film and television of a nonlinear universe. And it is the main thrust of the Marling and Batmanglij series.[6] The series' vision embodies not only Borges's forking paths, but also Einstein's yet unproven belief that the cosmos only seems fragmented. The potent and necessary interconnection that exists between OA and her allies, new heroes for the multiverse, and Hap, the strangely necessary adversary, is the enigmatic dynamic of *The OA*. The connectivity of the multiverse is solidified for us in part 2, which unfolds in San Francisco, but it is not in the City on the Bay of part 1's time dimension; it is San Francisco 2. And, as on Borges's forking paths, OA's life in a parallel time frame is both similar to and different from her life in part 1. She is herself, but she is also spookily connected to the life of Nina Azarova, whose body she jumps into in the new dimension.

The address to the audience in part 2 differs from the address in part 1. We no longer watch through the lens of OA's first-person narrative. Now that we are accustomed to the reality of the Borgesian universe, we directly observe the stories unfolding along the forking paths. *Connected paths*: Both OA and Nina 2 were born into the Russian oligarchy to Roman Azarov. *Forking paths*: This dimension's Nina never lost her father as a child, and she grew up with all the privileges of his wealth. She only lost him just before OA jumped into her body. She never died on a school bus and came back to life; was never blind, shunted off to America to be adopted by Nancy and Abel; and was never held in captivity by Hap. She never met and fell and love with Homer or learned the language of body energy with him, Scott, Rachel, and Renata. Who cares? OA only wants to reconnect with her old friends and the love of her life, Homer. Much too linear and direct. Dear OA, that is not how the multiverse works.

If that is what OA wants, she will need to more clearly hear the call of the multiverse about traveling. Traveling requires interaction between traveler and host in the new dimension. Again, Hap is (a painful) part of her education, as the question of connection versus disconnection is the crux of what emerges in this new dimension. Who remembers, who doesn't, and the problem of psychology as a false explanation for the problems of marketplace limits are revisited as revelations about the nonlinear universe are narratively expanded.

In part 2, the series once more tells us to look away from conventional psychology. Here, it is even more clearly the wrong route. It is represented by Hap, who has jumped into his parallel existence in San Francisco 2

(SF2) as Dr. Hunter Percy, a highly regarded psychologist, the author of a groundbreaking book, ironically titled *Quantum Psychotic*, and the head of the prestigious Melanu Clinic psychiatric inpatient facility on Treasure Island off the SF2 coast.

Well, the new dimension may applaud Hap, but the series portrays him as the psychotic rapist he was in part 1. When OA first arrives in SF2, Hap is still a jailer to Rachel, Scott, and Renata, who in this dimension are inpatients at Melanu. His tyranny over Homer here may be even stronger. In this dimension Homer is his intern, and Homer's career depends on Hap's approval, a situation that is exacerbated by Homer's lack of memory of South Dakota. Hap is also able to exert power over OA when her strange behavior, after she jumps into the body of Nina 2, lands her at Melanu. What is everyone going to learn?

As we shall see, exploitation through linear means is still Hap's modus operandi, and he is still keeping OA and Homer separated. Indeed, by the end of the season, Hap is also abusing the parallel Crestwood Five who cross the bridge into SF2. Yet again, as adversary, he is entwined in their evolutions and they in his.

THE SUTTER HOUSE

Connection. Disconnection. It's complicated. And OA is still at the center of it all, but this time because she has found a connection she refuses—unwisely. At the beginning of the second season, OA stubbornly refuses to explore her connection with Nina Azarova 2, whose life she now inhabits. Events reveal that connections between Nina and OA are OA's road back to Homer and her greatest source of resistance to Hap. It seems that disconnection and a kind of Campbellian perspective are not only Hap's flaws. But OA can learn. And she does integrate with Nina 2 through their mutual connection with the Sutter House, a mansion owned by Nina. Ultimately OA's experiences inside the Sutter House propel her toward that convergence.

Not in existence in the San Francisco of season 1, the Sutter House was built in the nineteenth century of SF2 by a rich San Francisco power couple. She was a medium and he an engineer. An odd couple by any measure, despite the knowledge that they were erecting their mansion on the site of a spring sacred to the long-gone Indian Ohlone tribe, they were—she for mystic reasons, and he for engineering reasons—undaunted by the presence of toxic mercuric sulfide gasses, generated by the spring that once inspired the sibylline prophets of the Ohlone. Only the prophets were practiced in deriving prophecy from the gasses; for the unpracticed, prolonged exposure to the gasses would result in mental confusion and death. Similarly, Sutter House has an engineering secret. It is simultaneously an ordinary place to live, and a puzzle. Depending on how one entered it, the house might lead either to vision or to confusion and death. No one lives there now, yet it binds all the lives in the season 2 narrative.

OA is marooned in Hap's Melanu clinic, until her first unwilling step toward integration with Nina, because of the Sutter mansion. OA's exploration of its mysteries is belated, because initially she has no interest in the mansion, nor in Nina's billionaire boyfriend, Pierre Ruskin (Vincent Kartheiser), who sponsors a game being played by hundreds of young adults on their smartphones that leads them to the Sutter House. Circumstances alter cases. Ruskin, Sutter, the game, and Nina become interesting to her as a way out of Melanu. There is a private detective named Karim Washington (Kingsley Ben-Adir), who has been hired to find a missing girl—Michelle Vu, a brilliant sixteen-year-old Vietnamese girl who has been playing Ruskin's game and was last seen in Nina's mysterious mansion. His investigation turns out to be OA's call from the multiverse. Washington has already entered the Sutter House through the door that leads only to an ordinary habitation. No Michelle. When he discovers that "Nina Azarova" who owns Sutter is in Hap's clinic, he enters OA's life. Washington is, of course, looking for Nina and OA's first reaction is, "Nope." But when Washington indicates he is willing to break OA out of Melanu because he assumes that "Nina" can get him into the secret entrance of the Sutter House, OA accepts the deal. It is her first step toward her host in this dimension. Filaments, filaments, filaments. Everything is connected.

Connections are what Washington and OA discover, as he searches for Michelle, and she becomes free from Melanu to find a way back to Homer. Are their seemingly different goals connected? Well, Ruskin's game and Nina are connected. Not only with Nina's mansion but also with a secret mission of the CURI Institute (the acronym remains unexplained), which is also connected to Pierre Ruskin. He is the owner and founder because of an idea he got from Nina. Not Nina, again. Yes.

Nina Azarova 2, who didn't die on her school bus and wasn't adopted by the Johnsons, lived a life of privilege that led to her writing a PhD dissertation at the Sorbonne about a peculiar phenomenon in pre–World War II Germany. Unrelated people there had reported dreams about violence and blood that presaged the Holocaust. Ruskin created CURI to study whether a similar phenomenon is occurring in SF2—and it is. The CURI dreamers all report images connected with the Sutter House; Ruskin invented his game to recruit the best and brightest young people to figure out why. *Problem*: The young game players are being driven mad by the gasses after they enter the Sutter mansion. Maybe Michelle Vu is one of them. Washington is committed to finding out. When OA helps him, she gets closer to Nina and reuniting with Homer.

Connection: OA doesn't know the secret way into the Sutter House, because she hasn't integrated with Nina, but she finds it and learns about CURI as she makes good on her deal with Washington. *Connection to be revealed*: OA will find that Ruskin, CURI, the Sutter House, and Michelle Vu are connected to both the Crestwood Five and to Hap. *Connection to be revealed*: Michelle Vu is the parallel self of Buck/Michelle, one of the five outliers in Crestwood. *Connection*: Back in Crestwood, the Five, who feel they are being contacted across the dimensions by OA, are making a cross-country journey to SF1 to find her, trying to connect with her as they go. *Connection to be revealed*: The CURI study of dreamers has discovered that all the dreams contain a tunnel the size of a coffin, a double-sided, curving stairway, and a rose stained-glass window. Washington intuits filaments of connection between the CURI dream study, Michelle's disappearance, and the Sutter House. He hunts down Marlow Rhodes (Liz Carr), the woman who oversaw interpreting and collating dreams for CURI. She had left CURI when she saw that making those connections had evil consequences. After all, the young players of Ruskin's game were driven mad by the poisonous gasses of the Sutter house. *Disconnection*: Poor Marlow kills herself because she believes she has facilitated evil. The series suggests that she dies because of her partial knowledge. In this universe, negativity is part of evolution.

A big moment: OA and Washington enter the Sutter House together, as a team, through the secret entrance, on their different yet connected missions. When they are separated in the house, Washington struggles (successfully) to find a way out of the poisoned environment of exits and

FIGURE 3.3 *Marlow Rhodes and Karim Washington talk about mystic phenomena in Germany in 1930s Germany, season 2, episode 2.*

entrances that mysteriously sometimes block him and sometimes open for him. His revelations will come later.

He goes home alone, while the gasses produce for OA a prophetic moment like those of the long-ago Ohlone. The house permits her to open a window high above the ground, from which she can climb out onto a large tree. There, many voices, the voices of nature, whisper to her, calling her to an intense experience of a web of minute interconnections of branch- and rootlike filaments, an image of her connection with the cosmos and a prefiguration of her discovery of her connections with Nina Azarova 2. The voices intone, "No tree survives alone in the forest" and that she cannot survive alone, either. Nina. Connect with her. It is a powerful revelation for a traveler, and we experience it, too. And when Washington enters the house for a second time, he, too, will have a powerful experience. He accesses the rose window and, through it, the secret of the forking paths of time. But we are not ready for that, yet.

Now, a digression about Élodie (Irène Jacob), another important new character in the series. Like the tree outside the Sutter House, she is also a transdimensional messenger, with a different, but complementary message. If OA must integrate with Nina 2 to counter Hap, she must also accept Hap as an inevitable part of her multiverse.

Élodie is a seasoned cosmic tourist, as she calls herself, who has traveled across many dimensions and inhabited many lives, always expanding from each experience, and who appears to both OA and Hap. No longer merely a being for whom there are no limits to the number of dimensions she can inhabit, she can also become a part of the boundlessness of other

FIGURE 3.4 *OA in the tree outside the Sutter House, experiencing her interconnections with the nonlinear cosmos, season 2, episode 5.*

travelers by sensing where they need unblocking. Hap and OA are blocked and Élodie has an earful of advice for both of them.

Élodie reveals the profundity of the multiverse of connections between Hap and OA. Élodie embodies the mystery of these connections when she counsels OA's integration with Nina 2 and gives Hap a way to generate energy, as an alternative to death, as a bridge for his travels in pursuit of OA in the multiverse. Élodie gives OA a lesson in multiverse connections, when she makes it clear to her that she must recognize *all* connections, if she wishes to regain her bond with Homer. It is a hard lesson when it comes to her links with Nina Azarova. Even harder for OA to accept is her connection to Hap, when Élodie tells her that she must accept the inevitability of both Homer and Hap in all dimensions. She initially resists believing that the triangle relationship between Hap, Homer, and herself is an echo that reverberates across all time dimensions. Eventually she accepts that to leave the echo is to risk losing oneself.

Enigmatically, Hap's negativity does not daunt Élodie. Even though he tries to kill her, as part of his Campbellian isolation as a hero, she gives him five miniature robots that can enact the choreography of the physical alphabet Khatun gave OA and her allies and thereby generate the same energies. Élodie's impartiality challenges us to understand and accept the relationship between linearity and nonlinearity in the heroic quest for travelers on the forking paths of the multiverse. Negativity and positivity remain in dubious struggle from the beginning of the series until it ends. Because of Élodie, OA does find her way to merging with Nina Azarova 2, and it pays off. The fog of Homer's oblivion of their love lifts in answer to her new expansiveness. But also because of Élodie, Hap has the power to separate them again. Both are parts of the quest. That is not that easy to understand.

Compounding this difficulty is the palpable evil of Hap, as a given in the nonlinear cosmos of the series. In SF2, his negativity is ratcheted up a few notches, as OA discovers when Hap reveals to her his secret room at the Melanu Clinic, which contains the floating, unconscious, young players of Ruskin's game, as well as the unconscious parallel selves of some of the South Dakota captives and some of the Crestwood Five. Hap acquired Ruskin's game players though an agreement with Ruskin, whom Hap convinced to routinely deliver the players to him, after they have been driven mad by the toxic gases in the Sutter House—how he got hold of the parallel selves of the Crestwood Five, we never learn. But OA makes the rounds of the bodies in the pool and finds her allies one by one.

Hap has discovered that the Sutter House toxic gases activate a seed inside the human mind—all human minds contain the multiverse. It is the seed of human connection with infinite number of parallel time dimensions. In his pool, Hap cultivates the blossoms that literally grow out of the seeds and he violates each subject by harvesting them. Way beyond

FIGURE 3.5 *"Every human mind contains the multiverse." Hap horribly literalizes the garden of forking paths, growing flowers of the human mind in the pool in his secret laboratory.*

the violations he inflicted on young people who had experienced NDEs, this violation enables him to cannibalize any and all fellow beings who inhale the poisonous gases in the Sutter mansion. Hap has discovered that eating the blossoms gives him control over travel between dimensions and is delirious with joy that he has found a way to connect across the multiverse without leaping into the unknown.

But Hap's success through linear experimentation is only apparent. What he has done is only a very small part of the waves that sweep the forking paths of the greater cosmos. The Crestwood Five may be unconscious in Hap's pool in SF2, but in dimension 1 they have arrived at Melanu and are preparing to use their visceral language to jump time frames, while in SF2 Hap is determined to transport himself and OA into a new dimension that is about to emerge. *Problem*: Because of OA's integration with Nina, Homer has remembered and reexperienced his love for her. Hap then must kill Homer to separate him from OA again. OA and Homer vow to find each other in another dimension before Homer dies. Death is not the end in the multiverse, but the lovers have again been torn from each other. So, does Hap in fact have the upper hand?

Yes and no: always the answer in the multiverse. As Homer lies dead in SF2 and all the multiverse jumping is about to begin, OA mysteriously levitates into the night sky of SF2, sparkling against the stars, a magnificent sight that promises to augur well for her and her friends. But the promise fades, because when, across town, Karim Washington reenters the attic of the Sutter House and opens the rose window, a dove nesting there unexpectedly flies out the house and into OA's path. She falls disastrously. She may be dying. Or is it a new step in her evolution as a traveler? Once she reaches the ground, she isn't in SF2 anymore. She drops into a third temporal dimension, where she lies bleeding and broken, but still alive, on the floor of a London television soundstage. This is not a London of the first-season dimension, nor a London in the second-season dimension. This is L3. OA is now in a television studio in a parallel London. If this sounds reflexive, it is.

THE OVERVIEW

The Russian-doll shape of the narrative of *The OA* manifests brilliantly as the narrative reality becomes a series of nested stories that blurs the line between the real and the fictive. When Washington peers from one forking path of time to another through the rose window, he discovers that the reality of San Francisco 2 is a fiction in London 3. Among the cameras, lights, boom mics, and wires in L3 are a series of maquettes of locations that were reality in SF2 but are film sets in L3. Through the window of one of the maquettes, Washington even sees the envelope with his handwriting on it that he left on a desk in the SF2 reality. In L3, SF2 is a make-believe place, the setting of a television show.

Washington spots OA on the floor, as she transitions to a new host in a new dimension. OA's hair, long and blond in previous dimensions, becomes a wig that is peeled off her to reveal short blond hair, and we find that OA has jumped into the body of an actress named Brit. But that is the name of the actress playing OA in the series *The OA*! Moreover, in L3, Hap is an actor named Jason Isaacs, which is the name of the actor playing Hap in the series. The reality of SF2 has been reduced to a TV show in L3, conflating *The OA* audience's reality with the show's own fictive reality in this time dimension. When an ambulance arrives to take the injured Brit to the hospital, Jason Isaacs claims a place in it with her, because he is her husband.

But L3 is not about the biographical reality of either Marling or Isaacs. They are not married in the real world of the audience, nor has Marling, the actress and writer, had a physically catastrophic fall. Rather, L3 is another forking path of time in the series that tantalizingly suggests that the reality of one path may be the fiction of another. Every dimension is a new *here.*

The same is true for Washington. There is someone on the set in L3 who resembles the Michelle he looked for in SF2, and who is clearly a cast member of the series being taped. And Washington sees that in L3 Hap is taping a scene that was Washington's reality in SF2. On the cusp of two "heres," in SF2 Washington calls to the L3 Michelle. She responds by climbing a very tall ladder to the rose window and disappears into the Sutter House of SF2. Michelle is restored to her grandmother in SF2. As that portal closes, the L3 portal has clearly opened.

And now we see that Steve Winchell, one of the Crestwood Five, has crossed from SF1 to L3. In this new dimension, Steve is anything but the lifeless victim we saw in SF2, floating in Hap's pool. Rather, he chases the ambulance, leaps onto its rear fender, forces his way in, and says menacingly, "Hello, Hap." Hap, already confused about being Jason Isaacs, is further discombobulated. Questions proliferate. If only we could learn more about the implications for our understanding of the multiverse of these crossings, Hap's use of the blossoms he has so despicably harvested, OA's love for Homer. The series' narrative is frustratingly incomplete.

Not so the series' vision. It is not any kind of partial knowledge. In detective Washington's final interview with Ruskin, the SF2 power player tells him that, when astronauts first went into space, the real prize of their journey was not the mechanical ability to go into space, but rather the overview, the ability to turn back and look at the Earth from which they had come. This created a new kind of knowledge of our planet from a previously unavailable perspective. So it is with *The OA*. We have not lost the prize through the interrupted linear-narrative questions. We find ourselves deeper than ever in the parallel realities of nested, nonlinear narrative, dazzled by a view of a cosmos of forking paths; a new perspective on time, reality, and storytelling. This conclusion, though forced on Marling and Batmanglij, nibbles annoyingly, exhilaratingly, provocatively at our learned sense of an ending. It proposes a new set of inconclusive moral and ethical problems, beyond the limits of the marketplace, a great gift to mass-media storytelling for the new zeitgeist.

ETERNAL SUNSHINE OF THE SPOTLESS MIND: THERE IS NO NOTHING

We enter the nonlinear universe by yet another path, in the film *Eternal Sunshine of the Spotless Mind* (2004), a cinematic tour de force, directed by Michel Gondry and written by Charlie Kaufman, who has made nonlinearity a part not only of his cinema but also of his public persona. Kaufman is almost as resistant to discussing his work as David Lynch. He prefers to engage the public in his feelings about being a popular artist. However, his relationship to narrative for a nonlinear universe often comes tumbling out along with his angst. His appearances in public, his interviews, and his evaluations of himself and his work all express a hopeless yearning for an honesty that hinges on the impossibility of speaking about what is actually happening in the moment. He frequently bemoans what happens after time has passed and distanced him from any experience he wants to talk about, any story he wants to tell.[7] He speaks eloquently about how over linear time, the truth, so vivid in the moment, becomes elusive, ungraspable. Nothing is experienced as connected. And his storytelling tends to reflect the hopelessness of storytelling. Not so in *Sunshine*, a nonlinear lovers' journey back to an essentially connected cosmos and into the truth of their connection, a triumph over linear time. Since the exile Kaufman personally feels from the immediacy, connection, and truth of a *here* informs the Kafkaesque hopelessness of most of his films, *Sunshine* is unique in his filmography. But, in Kaufman's jubilant moment, outliers go nonlinear, indeed!

Kaufman's other films find their heroes stuck in a distanced "there," distanced from the *here* of connection, in bleak narratives in the spirit of Kafka and Beckett, as in *Human Nature* (2001), *Adaptation.* (2002), *Synecdoche, New York* (2008), and *I'm Thinking of Ending Things* (2020).[8] In *Sunshine*, working with director Michel Gondry, Kaufman has flipped his typical universes of quantum nothingness into an ebullient and joyous rom-com for a nonlinear universe and proves that comedy is indeed more complex and deeper than tragedy. I take liberties in calling *Sunshine* a rom-com. It is generally thought of as a romance, but not necessarily linked with "com." However, it is a comedy that interweaves the fragmentation of quantum physics with Einstein's unified field into a romance, with wry humor.

But *Sunshine*'s perilous resistance to inclusion in any genre is typical of Kaufman, who emphatically rejects any association between his work and genre; indeed, he rejects any categorization of his cinema, himself, or his life. With due respect for Kaufman, I employ the term *rom-com* here only as a heuristic that enables us to see what happens to film classifications in the hands of this cinematic poet of the new zeitgeist.[9] Kaufman's storytelling for a nonlinear universe gives us no leaps into the Fireman's palace or montages of the creation of life on Earth. But it does have its own version of the Borgesian forking paths. Like *The OA*, the double quests of the two heroes jump into a matryoshka-like nesting of parallel times, some of which only exist on snipped forking paths. *Sunshine* has its own Kaufmanesque version of Borges and nonlinear storytelling.

Joel Barish (Jim Carrey) and Clementine Kruczynski (Kate Winslet) are Kaufman's retooled rom-com couple, both actors ingeniously cast as the genre's mismatched couple but against type. Carrey, who is synonymous with manic, comedic performances—sometimes filtered through grotesque CGI alterations of his body—plays an introspective, quiet, buttoned-down, educated man, who is nevertheless an outlier square peg unable to fit into any round marketplace hole. Winslet, who is associated with sweet, unpretentious insider womanhood, plays an extroverted, streetwise, impulsive, raunchy, intuitive outsider, who sports messy Day-Glo hair in constantly changing colors.[10] The image-shattering casting is part of the convention-shattering narrative into which Joel and

Clementine are thrust because they are unable to embrace their fractious coupledom. The signature meet-cute of the rom-com couple is rendered highly inconclusive. They are drawn to each other's differences but then can't live with them. His comforting, quiet, controlled personality eventually becomes a claustrophobic limit for her; her tantalizing drama ultimately becomes excess that pushes him beyond the limits of endurance. So, go your separate ways, people! And they try. But not a chance. Their absurd inability to say goodbye is endemic to the absurd universe of *Sunshine*. Here we have the absurdity of connection.

Sunshine depletes the convention of the linear rom-com in which, on a forward-moving path to love, oppositions yield to harmony. No Rock-and-Doris template here, where each extreme transforms into a romantic, golden mean. But it also inverts the Kafkaesque and perhaps Beckettian version of disconnection and nothingness to which Kaufman is notoriously drawn.[11] In *Sunshine*, it is as though when Gregor Samsa, in Kafka's *The Metamorphosis*, discovers that he has become an insect, all connections between himself and those who are supposed to love him do not evaporate. Rather, he discovers that the connection between him and his family endures despite his absurd transformation. Or maybe it is as if, in Samuel Beckett's *Waiting for Godot*, Vladimir, Estragon, Ponzo, and Lucky realize that Godot is strangely and ineradicably present. Kaufman gives us a universe in which love and connection are *the* incontestable, absurd reality that binds an absurd, only seemingly fragmented and meaningless universe. And no one can say why.

In the boundless, nonlinear cosmos of *Sunshine*, love has a new relationship to limits and time. And although Kaufman does not explicitly invoke the multiverse, quantum physics, or Jorge Borges, his poetic vision overlaps with the new zeitgeist. At a Q&A organized by the Writer's Guild in 2020, Charlie Kaufman answered a question I asked about quantum physics to the effect that he has tried in vain to read and understand cutting-edge physics, so his imaginative grasp of the new universe is born of his poetic sensibility, not exposure to the new science.[12] Nor is his vision Borgesian. Although Kaufman mentions many writers, artists, and philosophers, I have found no interview, film, or public address in which he alludes to Borges or his "forking paths of time." But *Sunshine* implicitly does. Even more so, *Sunshine* implicitly alludes to Franz Kafka and Samuel Beckett, as he flips nothingness into a positive spin on the forking paths. Not that Kaufman speaks of them as influences, either, but he does speak of them, and they reverberate so loudly through his cinema.

Like David Lynch, Kaufman is not conscious of what he is doing when he writes; that would involve the distance he equates with a lack of truth. He dives in and struggles with a narrative he loves, as it evolves. However, arguably—very arguably—he has internalized Kafka and Beckett so profoundly that what evolves overlaps with an unfathomable Kafkaesque or Beckettian universe in which the heroes journey ever more deeply into nothingness, the erasure of the seeming limits of the marketplace, and even of their own existence.

For example, whether or not Kaufman was thinking of Kafka or Beckett when he wrote *Synecdoche, New York*, nothing could channel their universes of nothingness more than the story of Caden Cotard (Philip Seymour Hoffman), a theater director who dies trying to find the story he wants to tell. All narrative dissipates as he reaches for it, along with the unity of his identity. The absence of narrative meaning is amplified by a compromised integrity of the self so complete that at the end of Kaufman's film someone else dies Caden Cotard's death. In Kaufman's other films, aside from *Sunshine*, he similarly narrates nothingness. At the same time, in his story of Joel and Clementine, his profound connection with Kafka and Beckett is visible in the way he turns them inside out. Step by step, the journey of the couple is an attempt to pursue the nothingness they hope will ease the pain of their inability to live with or without each other. They are hopeful when erasure and nothingness (and happiness) are guaranteed by a certain Dr. Howard Mierzwiak (Tom Wilkinson), who has developed what he calls his Lacuna process, which he claims can erase tormenting passionate connections from people's lives by eradicating all memory of who or what those connections were. But every step renders nothingness increasingly impossible. They are connected.

To tell his tale of Joel and Clementine, Kaufman makes witty use of the medieval, twelfth-century story of the severing of connections between two real lovers, Héloïse, a high-born maiden, and Abelard, a poor, learned monk, and its dire consequences. Their correspondence after they were forcefully parted by her family has come down to us through the ages. So we hear the voice of Héloïse, confined to a convent as a punishment for her sin, begging Abelard, vengefully castrated by her family, never to regret or renounce their love. But Abelard has been defeated by the marketplace power structure. She must endure both their separation and his abandonment of her.[13] Their story has been much memorialized, most famously in the fourteenth-century *Inferno*, the first volume of Dante's *Divine Comedy*, as the incarnation of un-Christian desire, noteworthy for its unquenchable intensity; and retold in *Eloisa to Abelard*, one of the poetic epics of eighteenth-century poet Alexander Pope. Pope's poem shoehorns the wild passion of Héloïse and Abelard into the tight limits of the rationalist eighteenth century. Kaufman chooses Pope's version, off which he comically bounces the story of Joel and Clementine.

Kaufman's film takes its title from Pope's poem, in which his Eloisa longs for the unblemished, pacific life of a cloistered nun with the yearning words,

How happy is the blameless vestal's lot!
The world forgetting, by the world forgot.
Eternal sunshine of the spotless mind!
Each pray'r accepted, and each wish resign'd

She wants to be a clean page, unblemished by unruly passion. She wants erasure, in a word. Not in Kaufman's universe. Or Pope's, come to that, but for very different reasons. Pope, the apostle of the definitive reality of the marketplace—as he announced with his famous dictum in *An Essay on Man: Epistle I*: "Whatever is, is right"—renders Eloisa's words ironically. He rejects erasure as he affirms the essential solidity and correctness of "whatever is." But Kaufman, whose poetic sensibility is fundamentally that of the new zeitgeist of confusion about "what is," renders Pope's poem ironically.[14] He rejects erasure, but not for Pope's prequantum reasons.

In *Sunshine*, belief in nothingness and erasure is the skewed result of the partial knowledge epitomized by the technology of Dr. Mierzwiak, to whom Joel and Clementine turn for an updated form of castration and cloistering. Mierzwiak can erase memory in the brain. Erasure can cause physical removal of lovers from each other. But the connection exists beyond both brain and body. Erasure and removal cause only a psychotic break from reality for Joel and Clementine. This film is about their unbreakable connection unaltered by the strikingly ineffective Lacuna procedure.

LET'S TALK ABOUT CASTRATION AND CONVENTS

When the film begins, Joel and Clementine have each already undergone the Lacuna process. True to its name, which is Latin for *void* or *gap*, the process has surgically produced in each of them an absence and some vaguely Freudian overtones of nongendered castration anxiety—angst about the potential for missing something essential. As the film unfolds, the Freudian flavor of the surgery dissipates into a universe that cannot be explained merely in terms of matter that can be manipulated, a universe unstructured by the misguided technological presumptions of cause and effect, a universe inexplicably structured.

The Lacuna process developed by Mierzwiak (pronounced *Meer-zwack*), stands as the very opposite of the unfathomability of reality, a monument to the erroneous cult of the explicable. It is a three-step linear procedure that treats passion as if it is a material appendage that can be surgically removed, like an appendix, by creating a gap in the mind and inserting a machine-made, altered reality. Step one, the client surrenders to the Lacuna office all material reminders of the existence of the person to be lasered out of existence. Step two, a technician uses a machine to map the client's brain that charts the physical existence in the brain of all memories of a specific relationship. Step three, the client takes a prescribed sleeping pill, and a second machine is brought to their home, where a technician surgically lasers away the unwanted memories while the client sleeps in their own bed. Result, the client is supposed to wake the next morning a free soul, all traces of pain gone, ready for a new start in life. Except that is not what happens for Joel and Clementine, or for Mierzwiak, for that matter. As the story unfolds, we see that for all of them, only the memory has gone missing. Connections remain.

We enter the film the morning after Joel has undergone the Lacuna process. It is Valentine's Day, a superficial, fabricated day for celebrating love. Its lack of reality is juxtaposed to energy surging under the surface. Joel may not remember Clementine, but he is still bonded to her. Although not an impulsive or irresponsible man, he suddenly decides not to go to work and makes a dash for the train to Montauk, the extreme point of Long Island. Toward, in fact, the reality from which he has been separated. The place where he met Clementine. And she is there when he arrives. Neither knows why they are there. We and they will ultimately discover they are being moved by an unshakeable connection far beyond memory. When they strike up an awkward conversation, they connect and reconnect simultaneously, as if temporality were past and present at the same time. And it is, in this narrative.

FIGURE 3.6 *Joel and Clementine at Montauk; nonlinear reality cannot be erased, beginning of film, 00:03:07:06.*

Eventually, they decide to go to the frozen Charles River in Boston, where they lie down on its temporarily arctic surface to look at the stars, again, but seemingly for the first time. They have been there before. They and we are going forward and back at the same time. This is no Campbellian rom-com journey toward love. It has already happened; it is still happening. The Lacuna surgery that we are about to learn about and experience as Joel goes through it has a cause-and-effect linearity. But Joel is jumping into nested moments, many of which are conflations of the time and space of Joel's pre–Lacuna process life, and all of which are just as real to his journey.

With his use of nonlinear narrative time, Kaufman comes closest to writing narrative for the new map of the universe being drawn by the very physicists who fascinate but puzzle him.[15] Simultaneously, the narrative pulls us into the connection between Joel and Clementine in parallel time frames before, during, and after the surgery. At the core of our experience of nonlinear time is our simultaneous engagement of time when we are inside Joel, as his brain is being lasered by Mierzwiak's head technician, Stan (Mark Ruffalo), and outside of Joel, when Stan's assistant technician, bumbling, hapless Patrick (Elijah Wood), is attempting to recreate Joel's connection with Clementine. Inside Joel, although drugged into unconsciousness, he is enlivened by some energy beyond his brain that is aware of the Lacuna process and is increasingly fighting it. Outside Joel, while Stan is lasering, hapless Patrick gets a phone call from his new girlfriend—Clementine. She is now Patrick's girlfriend because he has stolen the materials Clementine and Joel surrendered to Mierzwiak during step one, prior to the lasering procedure, and he is wooing her by recreating their experiences and by giving her a pendant Joel bought for her. Lasered Clementine is delighted by the "first" jewelry anyone has ever given her that she likes! Modified rapture. Patrick's ersatz gestures ultimately engender the pain of alienation from nonlinear reality. And, speaking of nonlinear, Patrick's courtship is the result of contaminating step one in the Lacuna procedure. Linear Lacuna has a big reality problem.

Meanwhile, inside the lasering process, mental erasure and physical absence also have no effect on Joel's connection with Clementine. Memories are disappearing, time and space are collapsing, as images, landscapes, and scenes of past actions degrade into nothingness, but Joel's bond with Clementine does not. The invisible bond, located neither in mind or body but somewhere beyond both, manifests inside Joel when she appears to him and becomes coconspirator in his fight against the surgical procedure he now regrets. The disappearances inside him, caused by the lasered erasures of memory, do not constitute forward-moving inner change. Nothing moves forward but the surgery.

The more Kaufman gives us the experience of the interplay between linear and nonlinear time, the less the import of the logic of the Lacuna process, and the less we and the characters seem to be moving forward from *here* to *there*. Erasure doesn't ultimately matter to Joel or Clementine—or to Patrick. Or to Mary (Kirsten Dunst), Mierzwiak's secretary/receptionist, who arrives at Joel's apartment during the procedure to party with Stan. Chaos ensues, because Mary had an affair with Mierzwiak that was lasered out of her memory. As her bond with him resurges, it becomes clear that the Lacuna process is just as pointless for her and Mierzwiak as it is for Joel, Clementine, and Patrick.

Lacuna Failure—Patrick: When Patrick desperately takes Clementine on a trip to the frozen Charles River, where he repeats the words Joel spoke to her, she only erupts in agitated irritation. It is a false connection. Connection is in neither head nor body. When her body does the same thing with Patrick that she did with Joel, it does not an intimate connection make. When Joel's mind is erased, a manifestation of the connection with Clementine appears to him; an erased mind does not a disconnection make.

Lacuna Failure—Mary: The film piles on more nonlinear layers of time after Patrick leaves Joel's apartment and Mary's erasure is clearly just as problematic as everything else connected with Lacuna. Inside Joel, he and his manifested Clementine are so successfully fighting the castration/lasering that Stan has to call Mierzwiak for help. Mierzwiak swoops in to save a failing surgery, but a successful surgery does not a successful experience make. Mary doesn't remember the affair at all. But the connection

FIGURE 3.7 *Synchronous space-time in the Lacuna process: a frame showing the conflation of two different spaces, 01:12:02:01.*

remains. The irony leaps from the screen as Mary circles Mierzwiak with desire while reciting Eloisa's encomium to the eternal sunshine of the spotless mind, from Pope's *Eloisa to Abelard.* As she gushes over the beauty of the verse, which she has memorized from a book of quotations, she kisses the married doctor. Reality is a different kind of eternity, and connection is quite spotty. The modern versions of cloistering and castration are at odds with cosmic realities of connection.

THE INERADICABLE

In *Sunshine*, the motion of the narrative is only nominally forward; actually, it scrapes away the illusory oblivion of the flawed procedure. There is no nothingness. Mierzwiak's wife, Hollis (Deirdre O'Connell), makes a surprise visit to Joel's apartment, sees Mary and Mierzwiak cuddling and kissing, and forces the good doctor to spill the beans to Mary. The shock of recognition sends Mary into a tailspin, and in an act of revenge and assertion of reality, she sends all the Lacuna patients their files and the audiotapes they recorded explaining why they have opted for the treatment. In the nonlinear temporality of Kaufman's narrative, simultaneous with all this, Joel and Clementine, in a post-surgery moment, are experiencing the encore of their Charles River idyll, not yet aware that there was a first time, before this. Time past and present continues to be fused as they receive their files and tapes from Mary, and their pre-Lacuna pain and anger return to their conscious minds.

Their initial reactions after hearing their Lacuna tapes and reading the files is the return of the hopelessness about their relationship that drove them to Mierzwiak. But if their experiences of the process and its deterioration have not changed them in the generic rom-com manner—she isn't less impulsive, he isn't less buttoned up—it has made them bigger and more real, as reality is defined in the film. They try to say goodbye again—they know they will run up against the same impasses if they remain together. But the choice quickly appears to them in a different light than it once did. When Clementine tearfully recapitulates the cycles of attraction and repulsion they will go through if they don't part, Joel replies, "So?" They laugh and cry at the same time as they realize that they can either choose fraught love or nothingness. High comedy. Kaufman is, after all, wittily asking whether nothingness is ever really a choice. Connection in the absurd, nonlinear world of Joel and Clementine is absurdly inescapable. If there is a choice, it is only whether one will or will not acknowledge that reality.

Lacuna offered the illusion of blank, eternal sunshine; reality is human laughter in the snow. The last we see of Joel and Clementine, they are

FIGURE 3.8 *Joel and Clementine frolic on a snowy beach in timeless space, 01:43:36:02.*

frolicking joyously on a gray, wintry day on a snowy Montauk beach. Recalling their romantic night on the ice of the Charles River? (A variation on singin' in the rain?) But, most significant for our purposes, *when* are they? Their joy is not happening in linear time. We have no idea whether this is a moment from before they were Lacunaed or after they broke from the erasure. Is it memory, fantasy, or a frolic that is happening now? Does it make any difference? With them, we have left the arrow of time. This is Joel and Clementine as they were, are, will be in nonlinear time. The film shucks off portrayal of the linear progress of their lives. It is Kaufman's most optimistic portrait of the journey of the hero in a nonlinear universe.

OUR VOYAGE SO FAR

Dale Cooper; Jack O'Brien; OA and Hap; Clementine Kruczynski and Joel Barish. They lead us into nonlinear experiences as fictional characters who are not to be taken literally. The overlaps between their universes and the new consciousness being created across the spectrum of explorations of the new zeitgeist are poetical leaps that permit us the pleasure of narrative thought experiments, which create, in their narrative forms, a richly emotional and spiritual overlap with the intellectual voyages taken by the learned disciplines of natural and social sciences. Einstein and the quantum crew map out the material ramifications of time and space in a limitless physical universe. As cocreators of the zeitgeist, Lynch, Malick, Marling and Batmanglij, and Kaufman explore the personal dimensions of limitlessness for the emotional life of the marketplace and beyond, using many forms of time and consciousness to create new figurative fictions about personal achievement, connection, and our endless questions about the dark forces of evil and death. This is entertainment, of a high order, that provides permission to loosen the mind-forged manacles, as William Blake described the marketplace limits we personally internalize. But the personal, heroic journey is only one part of our cocreation story.

The next stop of this study leaves behind the journeys of insider and outsider heroes in a nonlinear cosmos, to explore some voyages of entire cultures into the long arcs of historical legacy and the grand historical narrative in the new zeitgeist. It is not just the linearity of the personal hero's journey that nonlinear television and film are rewriting. Some nonlinear films and series take us, as Kubrick might say, beyond Jupiter, to another form of historical narrative.

Part II

NONLINEAR HISTORICAL

HISTORY DON'T TEACH: THE NONLINEAR HERITAGE SOCIETY

Chapter 4

The Romanoffs, Cloud Atlas, BlacKkKlansman

Those who forget history are condemned to repeat it.

GEORGE SANTAYANA

Those who do not learn from history are doomed to repeat it.

GEORGE SANTAYANA

Those who cannot remember the past are condemned to repeat it.

GEORGE SANTAYANA

Those who fail to learn from history are doomed to repeat it.

WINSTON CHURCHILL

Those who don't know history are destined to repeat it.

EDMUND BURKE

Who said it best? No matter for the purposes of nonlinear historical narratives. Film and television for a nonlinear universe dismiss the Newtonian concept of linear heritage, as a designated instructor about causality and—à la Santayana (as variously remembered), Burke, and Churchill—how we might attain better effects. But for most of the mass-media public, it is another story.

The mass audience craves the optimism of the belief that legacy is a source of identity, community, continuity, and stability. It tends to misperceive as failed storytelling a post-Newtonian mass-media film or series that depicts the impossibility of linear heritage in a nonlinear cosmos. It embraces entertainment journalists who turn a blind eye to a new frontier in historical storytelling. The public follows the lead of the commentators who belittled Matthew Weiner's *The Romanoffs* (2018), a sophisticated, nonlinear depiction of heritage that is not informed by the

Santayana-Churchill-Burke recipe for learning from history. *Cloud Atlas* (2012), written and directed by Tom Tykwer and the trans Wachowski sisters, Lana and Lilly, a poignant, funny, and piercingly nonlinear excavation of legacy, was received with some appreciation, but mostly with rancor and, worse, the silence reserved for blocking new visions. Spike Lee's *BlacKkKlansman* (2018) has been more widely appreciated, but mostly because it was misconstrued as a Campbellian celebration of a hero's story—which it was in Ron Stallworth's memoir, *Black Klansman*, from which it was adapted. It has not been recognized as Lee's brilliant translation of a self-congratulatory print narrative into audacious, nonlinear cinematic poetry about racist legacies beyond the control of any single hero. What is there to learn from the nonlinear vision? This is the first book-length study to embrace Weiner, Tykwer and the Wachowskis, and Lee and seriously ask that question.

The virtual erasure of these achievements from public memory contrasts radically with the ongoing celebration of linear mass-media historical narratives that intend to teach us valuable lessons by exposing cultural causes and effects, as in movies like *The Grapes of Wrath* (1940), *The Ox-Bow Incident* (1943), *12 Angry Men* (1957), *The Godfather* trilogy (1972–1990), *Little Women* (2019), and similarly, in series like *Roots* (1977) and *Downton Abbey* (2010–2015). Please be clear. It is not our purpose to mock their ideals. Rather, we wish to expose widespread misreadings of post-Newtonian, nonlinear historical cinema and series when they are mistaken for botched linear narratives.

To glean the value and beauty of *The Romanoffs*, *Cloud Atlas*, and *BlacKkKlansman*, it is necessary to focus on how they portray the elusive nature of what has been put forward as legacy, and the destructive way linear legacy invests people in false or tenuous identities, illusory chains of cause and effect, and delusional notions about continuity and community. These works present heritage as a problematic reality issue. Their point of view is that legacy is anything but a stabilizer, let alone a source of instruction. Their many questions and reservations benefit us.

The Romanoffs, *Cloud Atlas*, and *BlacKkKlansman*, into which we are about to delve, do not color within established Newtonian lines drawn by conventional historians, old and new, whose linear narratives, about the past, present, and future in terms of cause and effect, conflict with the mapping of reality in the new zeitgeist. Rather, they complement the new, nonlinear studies of history, time, and memory, such as the work of David Graeber and David Wengrow in *The Dawn of Everything: A New History of Humanity*. Their nonlinear historical exploration, as we noted in the introduction, is part of a revolution in process—fresh and provocative, engendering new questions similar to those raised about the relationship of *now* to *then* in nonlinear film and television.

Graeber and Wengrow and other current nonlinear historians contest both contemporary teleological historiography and the tradition of linear history out of which it grows. The contemporary teleological historian, like Yuval Noah Harari, etches a linear historical template. In his widely read *Sapiens: A Brief History of Humankind* (2015), Harari outlines a path that leads from the first cause of the invention of agriculture by "primitive" peoples to the full flowering of civilization, defined by systems of private property and hierarchy, and joins a venerable chorus of historians. Choose your favorite. They will all offer you continuity and certainty, although the shapes of the teleologies may differ. Two of the most prominent fathers of linear history are Thomas Hobbes and Jean-Jacques Rousseau. In Hobbes's *Leviathan* (1651), history is the inevitable trajectory mandated by a human nature that is essentially consumed by self-interest and devoid of altruism. From that first cause, the best we can hope for is imposed controls, most efficiently devised by political dictatorship—almost as depressing as Harari's proof that private property and hierarchy are human destiny.

Rousseau's *On The Social Contract* (1762), offers a more cheerful prospect, but the same implacable historical linearity. His first causes are the innate innocence and original freedom of human nature, which holds out hope for a march toward an egalitarian history, even though, as he writes, "Man is born free; and everywhere he is in chains."[1] Sounds good? Not to Graeber and Wengrow. They believe that the linearity of both Hobbes's and Rousseau's thinking, which endures in Harari's theorizing, is what we need to attend to, that we need to ask "how we came to be trapped in such tight conceptual shackles that we can no longer even imagine the possibility of reinventing ourselves."[2] That question, and the way they apply it to the momentous new discoveries of archaeology and anthropology, overlaps better than the teleologies of Hobbes, Rousseau, Harari, and Santayana-Churchill-Burke with the new generation of nonlinear historical film and television.

But what if a historian were to interrogate not only teleology, but also the very concept of linear time, in the spirit of quantum and relativistic physics? That challenge to linearity would drive our imaginations even further from where we have been stuck in thinking about history and more toward the new nonlinear zeitgeist. And that is precisely the kind of innovative vision that informs the works of Matthew Weiner, Tom Tykwer and the Wachowskis, and Spike Lee. Their visions dismiss not only teleologies from first causes, but also the forward-moving arrow of temporality. That is to say that *The Romanoffs*, *Cloud Atlas*, and *BlacKkKlansman* are more radical than the nonlinear historians. These popular films' and series' narratives for a nonlinear universe conceive of a relationship between *then* and *now*, *there* and *here*, that need to be read in terms of an original and unique intersection of popular storytelling with the diverse nonlinearities of both the social and natural sciences.

The Romanoffs, Cloud Atlas, and *BlacKkKlansman* subject teleology to the fragmentations and discontinuities of quantum superposition and entanglement. And voilà! A change in the cultural perspective on *here* and *there* and, by extension, *now* and *then.*[3] When particles are in superposition, one particle may be in two places at the same time; it is both here and there; the now of *here* occurs simultaneously with the future and the past of *there.* Particles in a state of entanglement experience the same stimuli simultaneously no matter how far apart they are or how many obstacles exist between them. There are no sequential *here* and *there* for entangled particles; they are *both* here *and* there. In *The Romanoffs, Cloud Atlas,* and *BlacKkKlansman,* linear legacies cannot exist as advertised.

As we shall see, these works do not all invoke physics, but they all invoke some perceptual framework that rhymes with the new quantum or Einsteinian physics of time and space or that resonates with Darwinian mutations. Their visions are in sync with both nonlinear quantum time and relative temporalities and with nonlinear heritage. *The Romanoffs, Cloud Atlas,* and *BlacKkKlansman* unapologetically join in the creation of the map of a new zeitgeist when they ask us to think again about grounding our stability in linear heritages that depend on Newtonian paradigms.

THE ROMANOFFS: HERITAGE, THE DIEGO RIVERA EDIT

As we shall see, critics who called Matthew Weiner's *The Romanoffs* (2018) "self-indulgent," "wrongheaded," "shallow," and exhausting," simply failed to understand his radical narrative use of nonlinear time.[4] Ironically, so did the critics that liked the series.[5] Amazon Studios produced *The Romanoffs* in a post-Lynch industry, but critical reception has not caught up. Or maybe entertainment journalists feared alienating their readers. Even Weiner was publicly silent about his innovative narrative temporality.[6] What might have happened if discussion of the series had benefited from his articulation of a new nonlinear vision, which began to open up for him midway through his creation of Don Draper in *Mad Men* (2007–2015) and became the core of *The Romanoffs*?[7]

New vision? As he told his story to me, Weiner, in mid-career, discovered esotericism, a belief system that reframes history through a perception of all time and all things as one.[8] His long-standing fascination with history began to take on a new coloration through his study of esotericism's centuries-long history and its roots in Egyptian history and alchemy and the Jewish kabbalah. All things. Esotericism quickly emerged for him as the ancient root of current quantum and relativistic physics, particularly the ideas about entropy explored by post-Newtonian physics. Newtonian physics contended that entropy proves the arrow of time; post-Newtonian physics looks to a new version of entropy to prove that time does not move forward only, and the nonlinear temporality of Weiner's esoteric take on the universe concurs. Similarly, the roots of esotericism in alchemy make it a precursor to the physics of atomic, quantum, string, and M-theories, which all propose that, in Weiner's words, "everything is made of the same stuff." All things.[9]

It was in the middle of his creation of *Mad Men* that Weiner began to make an acquaintance with esotericism and was intrigued by its foundational principle that "Everything exists at once. All time exists at once." He told me, "Artists know that." And, as we shall see, in *The Romanoffs*, Weiner distances us from characters who do not know that. They cling to fantasies about linear time that make possible the chimera of heritage, even though it offers no real continuity, stability, or anchor for identity. Rather, Weiner depicts the Romanov tradition as a destabilizing heritage, which has no actual biological basis in blood and is, as Weiner puts it, the worst possible heritage he can imagine, offering over generations little else but ignorance, stupidity, viciousness, disease, insanity, selfishness and incompetence.[10] Why would anyone want that? The power and allure of phantasmic linear legacy is the mystery at the heart of the series.

At the same time, the series is not hopeless. When the ghosts of linear legacy depart, it becomes possible to perceive what esotericism proclaims: a universe in which an innate connectivity exists. *The Romanoffs* is as much a personal voyage into a vision of connectivity as it is a vision of legacy. Weiner was undergoing the traumatic breakup of his marriage while he was working on the series, and his exploration of esotericism was in part about personal healing.[11] Historical healing also characterizes his recasting of the Romanov legacy.

The Romanoffs revisits a notorious family legacy that has been abundantly represented in linear narrative and lets some fresh air into our perception of how time works over the generations. A typical example of the Romanov story that the media grind out is *The Last Czars* (2019), which forces events into linear temporality dressed up with the obligatory artifacts of royal possession, like Fabergé eggs and elegant palatial surroundings. It grounds the putative Romanovs' legacy in a timeline with a beginning, a middle, and an end, chronicling family events in Russia and featuring a smooth, linear motion forward from tyrannical, imperial rule toward the defeat of the dynasty at the hands of insurrectionist Communists.[12] Not so Weiner's *The Romanoffs*.

The series is a discontinuous series of eight episodes that, even though they are labeled numerically, Weiner intended to be seen in no particular order. Rather, the episodes are a kaleidoscope of people stuck in spotty, questionable, boilerplate Romanov legacies that reflect traces of stupidity, ignorance, violence, selfishness, insanity, disease, and incompetence often associated with Romanov heritage. They take place all over the world and feature the disparate lives of mostly seemingly disconnected characters whose claims to being descended from the Romanov dynasty give them a sensation of having a place in the universe, never mind whether or not it is illusory. The very name of the series, *The Romanoffs*, a bastardization of what Weiner considers the true spelling of Romanov, embodies, for him, the questionable operation of heritage. What is neither spotty or questionable, however, is that despite their apparent fragmentation, Weiner offers us episodes that are linked—in a nonlinear esoteric universe that is made up of simultaneous correspondences and connections.

The term *esotericism* was first used in 1828, but the roots of the belief can be traced back to alchemy and to the mysticism of the kabbalah that evolved from the traditions of the ancient Hebrew tribes, and to the writings of a shadowy historical figure, Hermes Trismegistus, which exist in various translations and editions that date from the second or third century BCE to the twelfth century CE. Much of the surviving material on esotericism, however, was written and circulated during the Renaissance, especially in the translation of the *Corpus Hermeticum* by Marsilio Ficino and Lodovico Lazzarelli in the mid-fifteenth century and in the adaptation of the old Hermetic point of view to medicine by Paracelsus at about the same time. It is a secret tradition, and so its history is slippery and its documents tinged by ambiguity. For example, we do not know the author of *The Kybalion: A Study of the Hermetic Philosophy of Egypt and Ancient Greece*, published in 1908, intended to renew cultural knowledge of the teachings of Hermes Trismegistus, as part of a revival of Hermetic philosophy. The author is only believed to be William Walker Atkinson. In 1928, Manly Hall attempted to give esotericism a better pedigree as the secret backbone of civilization in a massive linear history of its evolution, *The Secret Teachings of All Ages*. Modern versions of esotericism have been generally influential on New Age thinking, and in 1964, a scholar named Frances Gates attempted to make claims for its importance to the development of modern science, but those claims have been aggressively disputed.[13]

Weiner acknowledges the dubious nature of these commentaries but embraces the seven principles on which the hermetic tradition is based: the principles of mentalism, correspondence, vibration, polarity, rhythm, cause and effect, and gender. Although Weiner has pondered them all, the principles that seem most central to his own worldview, and to *The Romanoffs*, are the principles of mentalism and correspondence. The first establishes the universe as mental: "The All is Mind"—which is similar to David Lynch's vision of consciousness as reality. As for the principle of correspondence, *The Kybalion* tells us, "'As above, so below; as below, so above.' . . . This Principle embodies the truth that there is always a Correspondence between the laws and phenomena of the various planes of Being and Life" (10–11). Moreover, for Weiner, the correspondences and connections of everything are part of a universe in which all time exists at once.

The Romanoffs is a comedy and tragedy of inherent nonlinear connections and correspondences juxtaposed with an ersatz linear Romanov legacy, a veritable cult that oxymoronically blends narcissistic superiority and pathetic victimization. We progress through eight episodes filled with the strange part played in the lives of the purported Romanov heritage tropes. On the one hand, it is a legacy of entitlement, which verges on psychotic denial of the importance and humanity of anyone outside of their inner circle. On the other hand, it is a heritage of victimization. This paradox-filled fantasy depends on five tropes: the demonic but superhuman intensity of Rasputin; the iconic victimization drama in the Ipatiev House, renamed and repurposed by the Bolsheviks as the House of Special Purpose to imprison the abdicated emperor and his family, with its clichéd images of the massacre of the imperial family by faceless Bolshevik revolutionaries; the pathos of the hereditary Romanov disease, hemophilia; the sacrificial maternity of Tsarina Alexandra and her desperate attempts by any means possible

FIGURE 4.1 *Matthew Weiner makes visible the idealized historical template of the Romanovs in his main title.*

to save the life of her son; and the mystique of Anastasia's miraculous escape.[14] They haunt the episodes in ephemerally humorous and terrible ways.

The series' main title sequence, which precedes each episode and acts as a chorus for the eight episodes, destabilizes the linear heritage by representing in a montage, filled with jarring temporal discontinuities, the basic Romanov entitlement-and-victimization legacy tropes. The montage begins in an opulently furnished palatial room, reflecting the traditional association of the Romanovs with privilege and luxury. On its walls, gilt-framed paintings reflect images of a noble heritage. The images create a stage for an iconic representation of the Romanov Tsar and Tsarina, spending a peaceful afternoon chatting with their children, all dressed in spotless white. The beautiful opening notes of Rachmaninoff's Piano Concerto No. 3 (1909) float above a sentimentalized greeting-card version of imperial domesticity.

History takes a slightly nonlinear turn when harsh tones break into and replace the smooth classical soundtrack and artificially charming, "historical," domestic mise-en-scène. The disruption, however, is another iconic tableau. Armed, unkempt Bolshevik rebels barge into the room, and the montage cuts to a stock massacre tableau in a bare basement room of the House of Special Purpose, where the insurrectionists mercilessly shoot the Romanovs, their bodies falling in all directions, red blood staining skin, hair, and once immaculate clothing. When the death room suddenly turns into a disorganized pile of photographs, time goes fully nonlinear as a jumble of sepia-toned, black-and-white, and new colored prints blow chaotically in the wind. There is no sequence, no progression, only everything existing all at once in time.

The iconic images turn out to be literally written on the wind, as all ordinary rules of time and space disappear. The photos fly toward the back of the frame, drifting away, and we are suddenly in the forest with an unidentified young woman—Anastasia?—her cloak of brilliant della robia blue ballooning out behind her as she runs, evoking the hopeful legend of the Romanov who got away. The hope is made strange when, from behind the trunk of a large tree, the stairway of a twenty-first-century New York City subway station uncannily appears. Tom Petty's song "Refugee" (1979) pounds the soundtrack, and out of the station emerges a modern girl wearing a windbreaker of the same blue. "You don't have to live like a refugee," Tom Petty intones, but when all is said and done, the song "Refugee" shadows the series as an equivocal statement about heritage and history. The connection we all have to the Romanov legacy is that in a nonlinear universe, in which all time exists as one, our linear ideas make everyone a displaced person with troubled connections to the past, present, and future.

AN ANTHOLOGY SERIES

Crucial to our experience of legacy as nonlinear is Weiner's choice for the series of an episodic, anthologized structure. He deliberately modeled *The Romanoffs* on anthology television series of the 1950s: for example, *Four Star Playhouse* (1952–1956) and *The Motorola Television Hour* (1953–1954). However, the old anthology shows, and there were dozens, were the result of the production conditions of a new medium.[15] The anthology structure of *The Romanoffs*, with its apparent gathering of different genres and modes, is an aesthetic choice. Apparent? Ultimately, the pastiche of genres, moods, tones, characters, and situations in Weiner's anthology structure only makes more dramatic the underlying intersections of everything in nonlinear time, but at first glance, it is a delightfully eclectic format.

Not only did Weiner design the series so that we would never know where we would be or with whom in the next episode; he made choices that would permit us the experience of the changes of narrative cues, emotional tones, and moods of episodes roughly associated with different genres. "Roughly" is the operative word; although Weiner has recently developed a keen interest in genre, he is also bemused by the elusiveness of genre classifications. He and I were often hard-pressed in our conversations to identity the genres of some of the episodes, and most comfortable talking about their varying tones and moods and their resemblances to well-known films and literature. In sum, the anthology experience gives us the Romanov heritage in nonlinear chunks of time and space, in the diverse stories visible through so many perspectives that the legacy can be understood in wildly conflicting ways.[16]

The perspectives on the function of Romanov legacy over the generations in episodes 1 and 3, "The Violet Hour" and "House of Special Purpose," respectively, could not be more discordant. Yet they each epitomize the fusion of entitlement and victimization in the idea of Romanov heritage and deepen the mystery of its charms. "The Violet Hour" presents the Romanov heritage in the form of a fairy tale; "House of Special Purpose" presents the heritage in the form of horror and suspense. In "The Violet Hour," we are in Paris, where Anastasia Le Charney (Marthe Keller), known by her nickname Anushka, a self-proclaimed Romanov descendent, is obsessed with the need to carry on the family line. She agonizes that her American nephew Greg Moffat (Aaron Eckhart), her only relative who is in a position to sire an heir, is not interested in procreation. Greg is a sweet-natured guy, but an unmotivated playboy who does not recognize the validity of legacy. And why should he? Anushka's Romanov lineage is as dubious as the escape from the House of Special Purpose of the Romanov princess whose name she shares.

Her Fabergé egg is a copy. She has no documentable connections with the imperial family. Her claim to the heritage of the Romanovs is not so much historical as it is her yearning to belong to something bigger than her fragile self. Her closest connection with the Romanov heritage is a sense of herself as both a victim and a superior being. She moans and groans about her heart condition, Greg's indifference to her, and his foisting upon her a caretaker, Hajar (Inès Melab), a Muslim nursing student whom Anushka reviles as a terrorist. This does not stop her from spewing the arrogance of Romanov exceptionalism. All this reduces her desire for Greg to father a baby who would carry on her purported Romanov family line to fantasy, very mutable fantasy.

She loudly insists on the need for a Romanov baby, but in truth any baby will do. French would be all right. But Greg's French girlfriend, Sophie (Louise Bourgoin), refuses to have children and Anushka rages at her. Yet, despite Anushka's anti-Muslim racism, when Hajar becomes pregnant after a chance night of passion with Greg, Anushka rejoices. It turns out that a Muslim baby will do. That she believes she has lived to see the beginning of a new Romanov generation is the reductio ad absurdum of heritage in this episode. The fairy-tale happy ending in Anushka's mind exemplifies the Romanov legacy in this series, a soup of fantasies of entitlement, blind luck, and historical discontinuity. Weiner has a complex attitude toward such confusion. On the one hand, he doesn't think it matters that Anushka survives by imagining a Romanov heir; he endorses the survival made possible by such an illusion.[17] On the other hand, his series makes a distinction between harmless fantasies about "the line," and diabolical delusions.

The delusional aspects of the Romanov linear legacy take a fatal turn in "House of Special Purpose," an episode about a television cast and crew on location in Austria, trying to tape the episode in a series about the Romanovs in which the imperial family is massacred by the Communists. If Anushka's dizzy Romanov identity has a comedic aspect to it, the opposite is true of the bizarre identity of the director, Jacqueline (Isabelle Huppert). Like Anushka, Jacqueline has dubious connections to the Romanovs. Most probably, she lied about her heritage to get the job, as she confesses to Olivia Rogers (Christina Hendricks), a Hollywood star who has been hired to take the place of the actress originally cast as Tsarina Alexandra. Whatever her reasons for anchoring her identity in the purported Romanov heritage, however, it has created neither stability nor continuity. Jacqueline is a chaotic mélange of the conflated superiority and victim consciousness inherent in the Romanov-legacy template. She simultaneously sees herself as a victim of sexism in the industry and as a godlike presence as the director of the series. This leads her to create a fatally insane work situation for the newcomer, Olivia.

Jacqueline's unstable, probably constructed, Romanov identity turns the production into an absurd nightmare. She discombobulates Olivia when she directs a scene between Nicholas and Alexandra, in which the Nicholas character is encouraged to make the scene "vivid" by doing an Elvis impersonation. Worse, Jacqueline mysteriously and fatally weaponizes her purported heritage. At a dinner where the stars of the series are supposed to charm the producer, Jacqueline triggers the producer's Russian-born wife to die of fright when, seemingly possessed by the ghost of Marie Feodorovna, the Dowager Empress, she curses the flummoxed woman for being the cause of Nicholas's death. Jacqueline's pièce de résistance, however, is her destruction of Olivia's ability to draw the line between reality and fiction. Wielding the power of the director, Jacqueline schemes to give Olivia's performance, during the massacre of the Romanovs in the House of Special Purpose, an award-winning intensity by manipulating her. She stages Olivia's abduction by cast and crew dressed up as Bolsheviks, which so confuses Olivia that when she is "shot," along with the other pretend Romanovs, she has so lost her grounding in reality that she is frightened to death. Romanov heritage is anything but a force for continuity and stability.

The confusions created by the power of the imagined legacy haunt a number of episodes. In episode 4, "Expectation," Julia (Amanda Peet), who is married to a man who claims Romanov heritage, deals with her guilty secret that her husband's best friend, Romanov historian Daniel Reese (John Slattery), is the father of their daughter Ella (Emily Rudd). Ella is now married and pregnant with a baby that is misunderstood to carry on the Romanov heritage. In episode 5, "Bright and High Circle," Katherine (Diane Lane), an affluent college professor brought up on stories of her Romanov heritage, is constantly assured by David (Andrew Rannells), a gay musician who teaches her sons piano, that she deserves her life in the bright and high circle. Weiner has drawn David as a dubious Rasputin to her dubious Tsarina Alexandra; as Rasputin did for his royal patron, David continually reassures her that she deserves her privilege. And then Katherine discovers that David is being investigated by the police as a possible sexual predator. In episode 6, "Panorama," extremely rich Romanov descendant Victoria Hayward (Radha Mitchell) wears herself out and imperils her marriage by engaging in medical tourism, traveling the world with her young son Nicky (Paul Luke Bonenfant), who has hemophilia, despite her knowledge that her efforts to keep him alive are unlikely to succeed. In episode 7, "End of the Line," Anka Garner (Kathryn Hahn)—Victoria Hayward's cousin and thus another presumed Romanov descendant—and her husband Joe (Jay R. Ferguson), a couple that can't conceive a child, have scrimped and saved to be able to pay to adopt a Russian baby in Vladivostok. However, the orphanage they have arranged the adoption with offers babies that may or may not be the children of Russian parents. When the baby girl they have been promised turns out to have fetal alcohol syndrome, Anka rejects her and goes home with a baby about whose heritage she knows even less.

Murder, unquestioned because it facilitates Romanov craving, is the matter of the two episodes we have yet to mention. Episode 2, "The Royal We," which is about a Michael Romanoff (Corey Stoll), whose family lays claim to Romanov heritage but whose spelling of the name belies slippage in this fictional universe, who tries to murder his wife to free himself to be with a sexy married woman, even though she has told him she is not going to leave her husband. Weiner likens it to *A Place in the Sun*, the last-ditch efforts of a man to invent the belonging he believes is due him. Episode 8, "The One That Holds Everything," is about Simon Burrows (Hugh Skinner), who is also open to killing for Romanov purposes. He murders his half-brother, Jack Edgar (JJ Feild), the author of the series being taped in "House of Special Purpose," to reclaim his Romanov heritage, a pair of earrings he has been told by his Romanov mother was given to Simon's maternal grandmother by the Tsar himself. The world owes him the earrings. Jack's mother, Ondine (Hera Hilmar), who was his nanny when he was a little boy, killed his mother to marry Simon's father, and subsequently contrived to exclude him from his family. Simon is a Romanov victim: Simon is also a superior Romanov being who may establish his identity as he chooses. For both Michael and Simon, Romanov heritage is a brand. It doesn't matter what historical roots it might have, nor do they hesitate to claim their brand. Who cares about the law or other lives?

Seen through the esoteric lens, while this mélange of Romanov tropes has no linear connection through the arrow of time; it is connected in the spirit of matryoshka dolls, nested one inside the other. As Weiner conceives of the series, they are all happening at once. Indeed, in the eighth episode, numerically the final one of the series, Greg Moffat and his fiancée, Sophie, from episode 1, cross paths with Jack Edgar. They are exiting St. Pancras Station as Jack is entering it. First and last are simultaneous. Greg and Sophie are returning to a situation in which Anushka's Romanov fairy tale is about to be a dream come true, and Jack is on the verge of being killed for a pair of Romanov earrings. Victim Simon has transitioned into a take-charge trans woman named Candace (Adèle Anderson) who is filled with Romanov entitlement. Exercising what she sees as her privilege, Candace poisons Jack on the train ride from Paris to London.[18]

Weiner reduces what passes for Romanov legacy to a vortex of desperation and confusion, which he contrasts with an episode that gives us an insight into a cosmic heritage that contains everything, about which all poets, per Weiner, know: episode 6, "Panorama."

IT TAKES A POET

There are two intertwined narratives in "Panorama," each of which seems utterly irrelevant to the other. But they are connected. All things. One of the narratives is about Victoria Hayward, whose Romanov-inflected maternal melodrama, alluded to above, manifests in her desperation to atone for the price her son, Nicky, has to pay for her apocryphal Romanov heritage. A woman of wealth by marriage, she drags herself and Nicky around the world, from elite clinic to elite clinic, to try to cure him of the hemophilia he purportedly inherited from her. The other narrative concerns the doomed struggle of Abel Erikson (Juan Pablo Casteñeda), a young man of mixed Mexican and Texan heritage, to be a journalist. Abel and Victoria meet at an upscale clinic for incurables in Mexico City. She is trying to find help for her son; he is trying to expose the clinic, a last chance destination for affluent medical tourists, as no more than a scam that exploits the desperately ill rich and the poor, Indigenous women in the city, whose stem cells the clinic buys at abortion clinics. Victoria will never find a cure for Nicky, and Abel will never successfully expose the clinic. When Abel meets Victoria and Nicky, it seems like only a coincidence. But there are no coincidences in an esoteric universe of boundless connections and correspondences. Her supposed Romanov inheritance and his journalistic crusade are two filaments entangled in that limitless universe. Their meeting propels each of them into an experience of nonlinear temporality that frees them both, in some ways, from the absurdities offered by linear heritage we have seen in the other episodes.

In "Panorama," the nonlinear truth of art replaces the linear dead ends of journalism and Romanov legacy when Abel and Victoria take a time-out from illness and exposé, and Abel escorts her and Nicky to view the Diego Rivera mural in the Palacio Nacional and then to Teotihuacán, the site of the ancient Pyramids of the Sun and Moon. Victoria is facing the possibility that her estranged husband, using the power of his fortune, will take Nicky away from her because he is fed up with her chasing atonement for her "heritage"; Abel faces the end of his career in journalism because his story about the clinic has imploded. Their stories merge as together they shift into a better place and become immersed in a different nonlinear legacy.

The Rivera mural is stunning, monumental in size, and a brilliantly nonlinear, poetic representation of a much larger history than that of the Romanovs or even the official Eurocentric history of Mexico that begins when Europeans arrived. It depicts precontact Indigenous culture, as well as the conquistadores; the Spanish Inquisition; two revolutions and the intellectuals, fighters, workers, and artists who defended Mexico; and the heroes of the resistance—Benito Juárez, Emiliano Zapata, Karl Marx, Frida Kahlo, and the artist himself. The image of Diego Rivera is in the center of this mural, explicitly marking it as his vision of a history in which one event does not lead to another, but rather all events are simultaneously present. Nonlinearity bleeds into life.

Their journey together to Teotihuacán (City of the Gods), a group of pyramids about which there is no documentation, built by a culture about which there is no knowledge—that, as Abel says, baffle conventional linear history—brings them to a different view of their circumstances. For our purposes, it is interesting that this moment intersects with the nonlinear discussion by Graeber and Wengrow of the history of Teotihuacán, linking *The Romanoffs* with the new map of the cosmos being drawn by post-Newtonian historians.[19] For Victoria's, Abel's, and Wiener's purposes, it is a space outside of the linear time of known history that nevertheless is a hub of profound connection for them.

At the ruins, they share a feeling that there is no time, a calming sense of eternity that rhymes with the nonlinearity of Rivera's mural. The release creates in each of them a way of making peace: Victoria, with the necessity that she must stay with her husband in order to continue her life with her son; and Abel, with the mortification of his professional failure. He now realizes that he is a poet, not a journalist. If, in linear time and legacy, Abel and Victoria are victims, the nonlinear vision of Rivera's mural, complemented by the pyramids of Teotihuacán, brings them—in themselves and together—peace and hope.

After Abel and Victoria part, Abel quits his newspaper job, and as he walks in the street, Rivera's mural comes alive for him. Casual pedestrians and tourists are joined by the figures from Rivera's mural: the precontact Mexica (pronounced Meshika) people; those tortured by the Inquisition and their torturers; the socialist uprising of the modern workers; Karl Marx; the artists of Mexico; and Frida Kahlo and Diego Rivera himself. No longer a journalist caught in the oppressions of linear thinking, he has realized that he is an artist. Watch *The Romanoffs* in any order you choose; "Panorama" is the episode that reclaims hope in the series.

There is, after all, something to learn from history, but it is not a lesson with a moral that examines causes and effects. It is more about the release effected by a nonlinear perspective. Perhaps it casts a new light over the other episodes informed by the desperate foolishness of the fantasy of linear heritage. Perhaps the esoteric release from the Rivera mural combines with Weiner's personal experience of connection/disconnection through the breakup of his marriage, while he created *The Romanoffs*. Perhaps his questioning of connection and disconnection, in a world increasingly lacking in traditional family structure, in tandem with the connections

FIGURE 4.2 *The nonlinearity of history becomes manifest to the poet, episode 6.*

and temporality of esotericism, are the seeds of a series about a small hope amid the confusion of the heritage dramas. Weiner himself points out the ambiguity of heritage, which may be decertified in the light of reality, but which sometimes serves the need for belonging. Heritage plays such a role in "The End of the Line," when Joe loses his love for Anka as she rejoices in a healthy baby that will "continue her line."

Throughout the series, we watch linear heritage collapse along with connections to reality. Yet, we observe that a higher form of heritage saves Abel and Victoria. But not everyone is a poet, as Weiner would be the first to say. His series reveals the phantom nature of heritage in a nonlinear universe, and its potential for negative impact, but never denies its ongoing utility. The blend of Weiner's vision and his personal trials in his creation speak to the way all developments of the new zeitgeist—scientific, historical, archaeological, anthropological, and aesthetic—call us not only to new big-picture ideas about the universe, but also to a new freedom in contemplating common emotional experiences of how linear ideas of finding belonging in legacies structure our lives.

CLOUD ATLAS: "OUR LIVES AND OUR CHOICES, LIKE QUANTUM TRAJECTORIES . . ."

We have seen nonlinear film and television, anchored in creative visions, through a unified field of consciousness, Heidegger, Borges, quantum physics, Kafka and Beckett, and esotericism. *Cloud Atlas* (2012), written and directed by Tom Tykwer and Lana and Andy Wachowski (Andy later became Lilly, joining her sister Lana, originally named Larry, as a trans woman) expands the foundation for mass-media cocreation of the new zeitgeist. Like some of the mass-media artists we have discussed, Tykwer's interest in breaking up categories, an inclination with the flavor of quantum physics, shaped his contributions to the nonlinearity of *Cloud Atlas*—a nonlinearity already in evidence in *Run Lola Run* (1998), the nonlinear film that made him an international name.[20] *Lola* is virtually a preliminary study for his work on *Cloud Atlas*. It is a reflexive meditation on how cinema tells stories that is built on three versions of a day in the life of Lola (Franka Potente). It breaks the illusion of a stable stage of linear time and space upon which characters act. Rather, it offers the audience the experience of nonlinear time and space as always potentially changing and renewing options.

Lola's story previews the vision in *Cloud Atlas*, articulated by the character Isaac Sachs (Tom Hanks), of life as "quantum trajectories . . . understood moment to moment. At each point of intersection, each encounter suggests a new potential direction." The Wachowskis also incline to nonlinearity, but their aesthetic grows out of a kindred perspective, transgender experience, beautifully articulated by Cáel M. Keegan, in the one book to date written about their cinema. In Keegan's words, the Wachowski aesthetic is a transgender aesthetic about "desiring resistance to dictated form, . . . an analytic for 'linking the questions of space and movement . . . to other critical crossings of categorical territories.'" He expands on the Wachowskis' trans version of Tykwer's quantum intersections and what he calls "a force characterized by unpredictable flows across discrete forms, a 'paratactic' that enacts the prepositional 'with, through, of, in, and across' animating vitality itself.'"[21] This they had pioneered in their Matrix films, but by the word of Lana Wachowski, never so completely. *Cloud Atlas* is the film of which she is most proud, because, while she notes much originality in all the others, only *Cloud Atlas,* as she says, is totally original.[22]

The visions of Tykwer and the Wachowskis mesh wonderfully in *Cloud Atlas,* combining to use cinematic language in a way that brings to the screen David Mitchell's 2004 novel, with its innovative portrait of historical legacy, which was initially believed to be unadaptable.[23] Tykwer and the Wachowskis created a film that is an exemplary revelation of the difference between print and cinematic media. Mitchell created in print a multiplot narrative that juxtaposes five different narratives in different time frames, that run from a story about slave traders in 1849 through four other narratives about unjust power structures, which add up to a declaration of the persistence of malfeasance by the powers that be on planet Earth. For the film, Tykwer and the Wachowskis added a sixth story, a framing narrative emanating from a postapocalyptic, off-world colony that provides an external perspective on the disaster of linear legacies. And a sense of release in nonlinear time. With the framing narrative,

Tykwer and the Wachowskis substitute cinematic intersection of the time frames for the juxtaposition Mitchell employs in his novel. Intersection rather than juxtaposition. Juxtaposition is linear comparison. Intersection renders time nonlinear and simultaneous. And that makes all the difference with respect to the portrait of heritage.

Hearteningly, many entertainment journalists who reviewed the film at the time it was first distributed, in reviews growing out of a post-Lynch environment, perceived its fascinating, unconventional use of time. Surprisingly, very few linked the temporal difference to the widely known transgender experience of Lana Wachowski and Tyker's well-known philosophical perspective. Unsurprisingly, while Peter Debruge's review in *Variety* is entirely perceptive about the theme of connection in the film, none were able to connect the dots between its offer of an affective, sensory experience of nonlinearity and a pioneering vision of historical legacy. As a result, many entertainment journalists dismissed the narrative rhetoric of the film as, perhaps beautiful, form without function.[24] By contrast, Keegan's book-length study has contributed to the discussion an interview with Lana Wachowski and some useful insight into the pioneering work of the Wachowskis in what he calls subjunctive cinema, cinema that echoes the subjunctive voice in language expressing the hypothetical, in the case of the cinema a new hypothetical about time and space.[25] Here we will proceed to identify *Cloud Atlas* as part of the cocreation of a new zeitgeist in the mass media, using Keegan's concept of the trans subjunctive voice, in tandem with Tykwer's philosophical nonlinearity, to delve further into their revolutionary work.

Cloud Atlas inverts the linear aphorism associated with Santayana, Burke, and Churchill. In the film, it is precisely those who "learn" from history who are condemned to replicating atrocity. Linear heritage posits as natural a dichotomy between "the weak" and "the strong." Learning from linear history means intoning, stipulating, and hissing, variously, the crude maxim, "The weak are meat; the strong do eat." Natural? According to a contrasting perspective we also meet in whatever time frame we observe, learning from linear history is the opposite of natural; it is a fabrication, a fabrication that moves with the arrow of time, forward, enlarging its negativity.

It moves from figuratively devouring "the weak" through slavery toward the literal cannibalism after the apocalypse. It is a fabrication of the slave traders in the 1849 narrative in the film that swallows the freedom of the slaves. It is a fabrication of the power structure of the music community in 1936 that ingests talent and marginalizes creativity. It is a fabrication of Big Oil in 1973 that gorges on the environment. It is a fabrication of the tyranny over elder care in 2012 that feeds on seniors for profit. It is a fabrication of the dystopian world order of Unanimity in 2144 that creates a population of "fabricants" to serve the public food and eventually be turned into food for a new generation of fabricants. It is a fabrication of the cannibal tribe terrorizing and literally eating the farming tribe, 106 winters after the fall of the techno-industrial complex built on oppression. But there is also another form of heritage in the film. It is nonlinear, cosmic, and organic and speaks through bodies, words, music, and deeds with a sweetness, a sadness, courage, and humor.

Organic, cosmic heritage is in the life and the soul-searching journal of Adam Ewing (Jim Sturgess), a lawyer in 1849, that resounds through time with his discovery of the horror of the slave trade. Organic heritage is transmitted through the eloquent, moving love letters of gay composer Robert Frobisher (Ben Whishaw) and his composition *Cloud Atlas Sextet,* which survives despite the attempts at his erasure by Vyvyan Ayrs (Jim Broadbent), a corrupt and eminent celebrity musician. In the music community of 1936, Ayrs has the power to steal Frobisher's *Cloud Atlas Sextet* and drive him to suicide by destroying Frobisher's reputation with allegations of his homosexuality. But Ayrs doesn't have power beyond the limits of linear heritage. Nonlinear heritage is transmitted beyond those limits through the courageous newspaper exposé of Big Oil by Luisa Rey (Halle Berry), a journalist in 1973, despite many attempts to kill her. It is transmitted hilariously through the kitsch biopic made about the life of Timothy Cavendish (Broadbent), a timid publisher of a certain age, incarcerated in Aurora House, an old-age home where people are stashed by relatives plundering their estates, who takes his moment to triumphantly escape with three other designated victims.

It is transmitted through the soaring eloquence of Sonmi-451 (Bae Doona), a fabricant in 2144, seemingly trapped in the tyrannical world of Neo-Seoul as a slave, whose awakening from the conditioning imposed on her by Unanimity, verbalized in aphorisms of organic heritage, resonate for all time. It is in the new oral tradition of narrative developed by Zachry (Hanks). It is fully expressed by the thoughts of Isaac Sachs (Hanks), a quantum physicist who falls in love with and joins the cause of Luisa in the 1973 time frame of the film, "Our lives and our choices, like quantum trajectories, are understood moment to moment. At each point of intersection, each encounter suggests a new potential direction." Big Oil bombs the plane Sachs is on, as his insights form. But his heritage and those words do not die, because of the subjunctive aesthetic of the film in which time is simultaneous.

There is in addition, another, more mysterious form of the transmission of nonlinear heritage because identity is not circumscribed in this universe by linear time and space. Nonlinearity creates a fluid *me* that permits Zachry, Luisa, Sachs, Robert Frobisher, Timothy Cavendish, Sonmi-451, and Adam Ewing to perceptually cross time dimensions, as when Luisa hears a rare recording of *Cloud Atlas Sextet* and recognizes it, although we know she could not have heard it in 1973, because in that time frame, it had yet to be performed publicly. But hear it she did, in 1936, when her *me* was in the form and circumstances of Vyvyan Ayr's wife, listening to Frobisher compose it. There are a number of other similar perceptual/temporal crossovers in the film.[26] The meshing of the story strands directed by Tom Tykwer—1936, 1973, and 2012—with the other story strands directed by Wachowskis—1849, 2144, and 2321—melds into a beautiful nonlinear whole composed of their two different aesthetics, which results in a composite of the two different kinds of powers in linear and nonlinear heritage. Significantly, it does not matter in the film whether the different heritages lead to success or failure.

So, what's the story? Their nonlinear copresence.

The linear legacies are embedded in familiar narratives of aggression and victimization. But the film's rhetoric of the nonverbal language of cinema provides a lot of slippage for that story and supports the story in *Cloud Atlas* of the similarly persistent intersection of the forking of time that undercuts the maxim of linear legacy, "The weak are meat; the strong do eat." The film does not lack for those who devour, but their place in the cosmos is minimized by the film's destabilization of linear identity through the way the film is cast. The principal actors in the film are each cast in as many as seven roles that cross lines of gender, race, power, and time. They challenge an innate polarization of strong/weak, winners/losers, even male/female and race. All told, they populate this universe with identities that embrace the predations of linear heritage and identities that flow beyond it.[27]

"The weak" and "the strong"? Hugo Weaving and Hugh Grant are cast in multiple time frames as the maxim in action; they personify the continuity of the engine of "might makes right." Weaving is Haskell Moore in 1849, a committed racist in command of the slave trade; he is Bill Smoke in 1973, an assassin for Big Oil, bent on destroying the environment for cash; he is Nurse Noakes in 2012, a sadistic enforcer in the Aurora House retirement home; he is one of the controllers of the world tyranny in 2144, hell-bent on protecting the "natural order" of weak and strong; and he is Old Georgie, the hallucinatory spirit of destructive linear heritage in the apocalyptic narrative 106 winters after the Fall.

Grant is Giles Horrox in 1849, a racist minister who gives slavery a religious authorization; he is Lloyd Hooks in 1973, one of the duplicitous Big Oil cabal in 1973; he is Denholme Cavendish in 2012, one of the owners of Aurora House, who gives new meaning to the words "my brother's keeper"; he is a rapist overseer for the Orwellian government in 2144; and, in the most startling, ritualized, full-face makeup, the head cannibal in the Kona tribe, after the Fall. So, too, the other principal actors perform roles that challenge the wholesale actuality of the stable "we" in this nonlinear universe, making the aphorism about weak and strong highly contingent, less pervasive.

The presence of the same actors, manifesting differently in different time frames visually defines *me* as fluid. For example, Tom Hanks appears in 1849 as Henry Goose, a racist, villainous doctor unapologetically profiting from the slave trade; in 2012 he is Dermot Hoggins, a vicious thug who gains unexpected success writing a crudely sensationalist novel as a manifestation of the predatory nature of the powerful in his time; in 1973 he appears as Isaac Sachs, an idealistic quantum physicist who falls prey to the villainy of the "strong"; and in an unnumbered postapocalyptic time frame—designated as 106 winters after the Fall—he is Zachry, a goatherd in a valley tribe, who ultimately recreates his trajectory. "Meat to eat"? That is his designation by a marauding, cannibal, enemy tribe. But in the decision of a moment, he births a new future and breaks out of the prison of the heritage of might makes right. The nonlinearity of identity is the reality of this cinematic experience. Similarly, the cinematic language of montage makes a nonlinear perspective that fuses all time as one. Flash-cut montages intersect moments from different time frames that move in and out of each other. They occur simultaneously. Continuity editing in which a door opens in one time frame but leads smoothly into another gives the audience the experience of time as one. Each time frame, suggesting a variety of genres, nests one genre inside the others.

This adds up to a nonverbal, nonlinear artistry of cinema—subjunctive, to use Keegan's term, the setting for fluidity of all kinds, including that of identity. Moreover, Tywker and the Wachowskis portray a universe in which the heritage of conquest by the "strong," who look like the "winners" they claim to be, do not write history. The nonverbal, structural use of intersection in the film, as opposed to the simple juxtapositions of time frames, disrupts the historical dominance of their voices with other voices. Intersection rather than juxtaposition. For example, the power of linear legacy that the "weak are meat" seems to be proven in the 1973 narrative about Luisa Rey's exposé of Big Oil by the death of Dr. Isaac Sachs. Luisa meets Sachs as she is pursuing her newspaper story, and he falls in love with her at first sight and decides to join her cause, at peril of his job, and ultimately his life, because of a moment-by-moment intersection that changes his trajectory. At the same time, he is silenced and his love for Luisa doomed, when he is murdered by a bomb placed on the plane by Bill Smoke (Hugo Weaving), an assassin working for Big Oil. In linear time, he is eaten meat.

But not in the nonlinear time of the film, in which he offers us another voice, just before he is blown up:

> Belief, like fear or love, is a force to be understood as we understand the theory of relativity and principles of uncertainty. Phenomena that determine the course of our lives. Yesterday, my life was headed in one direction. Today, it is headed in another. Yesterday, I believed I would never have done what I did today. These forces that often remake time and space, that can shape and alter who we imagine ourselves to be, begin long before we are born and continue long after we perish. Our lives and our choices, like quantum trajectories, are understood moment to moment. At each point of intersection, each encounter suggests a new potential direction.

His words describe the flow of time within which Luisa's seemingly doomed struggle forks into her success. The casting of Tom Hanks as both Sachs and Zachry creates a fluid *me*, flowing through simultaneous, intersecting time by the Wachowskis' intentional destabilization of the actor's presence. As Lana Wachowski puts it, "Actors, remember, are always stable—but we destabilized the actors. . . . It's so *different*. So outside the normal narrative box of cinema."[28]

The fluid *me*s of Isaac Sachs and Luisa Rey, played by Tom Hanks and Halle Berry in 1973, flow into the *me*s of Zachry, a goat herder, and Meronym, a scientist, played by the same actors in the apocalyptic narrative that takes place 106 winters after the Fall. In the latter narrative, there has been a shift in racial relations. Meronym is part of the only remaining, highly educated, human community, called the Prescients, the caretakers of a spectacularly advanced technology—and they are Black. The remaining white community has degenerated into warring tribes of Abel-like valley farmers and the Kona, Cain-like cannibals, all lacking advanced technology and even command of the language of high culture, speaking a pidgin dialect and locked in a futile war against each other. The reversed power relations of Black and white, however, are only a new manifestation of the damaging, degrading linear heritage. The elegant and cultivated Prescients are dying off because of the toxic nuclear material released by the apocalyptic war that caused the Fall, that was engineered by the injustices of hierarchies. The mainly illiterate, barbaric white tribes continue the linear tradition of strong cannibals and weak meat, in which the farmers are the inheritors of Sonmi-451. They have a sacred book of her aphorisms proclaiming their humanity, but like her, they are the prey of the unrelenting Kona who hunt them for sport and dinner. It is a tragic, unbroken, devolving heritage. But at the same time, the birthing of a new future belongs to the *me*s of Meronym/Luisa and Zachry/Sachs, when in a single moment they enter nonlinear time and change the trajectory.

The moment concerns a sacred and terrifying mountain in the territory of the superstitious white tribes, that all are forbidden to climb.

By contrast, while the Prescients know nothing about how to access its heights, they know that the mountain is not a place of demons but the location of the control center of the old technology that would enable them to escape toxic death, by making contact with off-world Prescient colonies, who do not know they survived the holocaust. Meronym strikes a deal with Zachry, who is so desperate to save his niece from certain death with her science that he will hazard the tribal taboo and, in exchange, guide her up the mountain. This is the opening of a fork in time and escape from linear heritage. The moment is powerfully portrayed as a struggle between Zachry and a hallucinatory demon, who haunts him all through his story, named Old Georgie. The voice of Georgie is the definitive voice of the linear tradition that has guided the power elite of the whites through the film, unheard by the oppressed "weak" in all times. In the other time frames, the maxim about strong and weak is couched in the cadences of official language spoken by purportedly respectable men.

Through Georgie, the respectability of the power elite is stripped away to reveal its innate ugliness, ignorance, and toxicity. As Georgie appears to Zachry, he is green and wears a ragged, grungy version of the garments of the racist, white, male power elite of 1849. It is not the resplendent disguise of the vicious slavers we saw, but a grotesque revelation of their essential corruption. Georgie's battered top hat and rusty frock coat, with all the other sullied versions of class accoutrements, are physical manifestations of the putrefaction of the linear legacy, which he spews into Zachry's ear, unnerving him with the words intended to consolidate his victimhood as the designated meat. He appears most significantly twice. Once, when a hunting party of the Kona horribly kills Zachry's brother and little nephew, and Georgie hisses the paralyzing words of the linear heritage. And again, when Zachry and Meronym are on a particularly perilous part of the ascent up the sacred mountain, Meronym slips, and Georgie urges Zachry to let her fall instead of catching her, whispering derisively that she is his enemy. The linear heritage gives way to the nonlinear heritage when Zachry creates a new future, in a moment of decision to dismiss Georgie, his hand bleeding from pulling her up with the climbing rope.[29]

From there, Meronym finds the abandoned technology that makes possible her contact with an off-world Prescient colony, their escape from the linear legacy, and a new story. Their ascent up the mountain is nested inside Zachry's telling of the new story on an off-world colony of Earth, with which the film begins, in which Old Georgie is but a horrible memory, and a crowd of children are ingesting a new heritage, nonlinear and cosmic in every sense. In fact, Zachry's narrative begins and ends with an image of the galaxy. It is the first image of the film, signaling us immediately that the context for what follows is a cosmic setting. The film ends

FIGURE 4.3 *Old Georgie, the linear history of hatred and division made visible.*

with the conclusion of his story, as the children are shooed off to their bedrooms and, Zachry and Meronym look fondly after them and at each other. The camera tilts up to a final cosmic image, as a comet shoots across the sky. It is an image we understand, now, that we would not have understood when the film began.

Once we have seen the whole film, we will have inhabited a universe in which "the last shall be first, and the first last." Whether we are looking in on 1849, 1936, 1973, 2012, 2144, or 106 winters after the Fall, nature appears to have auspiciously marked the bodies of the characters shifting into a potentially new direction with the same image of a star with the tail of a comet, about three inches in size, that appropriately summons the metaphors of brightness, speed, and irregular trajectory. Perhaps we can call them birthmarks, or rebirth marks.

The rebirth marks create a nonverbal texture of a heritage of possibility, out of the sum total of the times in the intersecting stories the camera lingers on the comet-marked skins of Adam Ewing, the white lawyer converted to the abolitionist cause; Robert Frobisher, the composer of the suppressed but glorious *Cloud Atlas Sextet*; Luisa Rey, a daughter following in the tradition of integrity of her journalist father who refused to be daunted by the corruption of the powers that be; and Timothy Cavendish, a publisher who extricates himself and three other inmates from the gulag of a retirement home that is dedicated to the greed of their relatives. The star-comet heritage of quantum freedom even marks the neck of mechanically fabricated Sonmi-451, who nevertheless is a radiant "point of intersection," an "encounter [that] suggests a new potential direction." When she is rescued from Unanimity, the mark is revealed under the metal collar that essentialist culture uses to mark her as a slave. The final revelation of the rebirth mark is on aged Zachry's bald scalp, as he finishes telling his grandchildren the story of how he and Meronym arrived on an off-world colony. Together, the marked characters constitute a nonlinear energy surge through nonlinear temporality, contextualizing and diminishing the concept of linear, essentialist legacy by embodying the reality of doomed artist Robert Frobisher's vision of truth and reality: "All boundaries are conventions, waiting to be transcended. One may transcend any convention, if only one can first conceive of doing so. . . . I know that separation is an illusion. My life extends far beyond the limitations of me."

That mark is the physical manifestation of the doctrine of Sonmi-451, the risen fabricant, who in her time frame is considered subhuman and is murdered by the power structure, Unanimity, for being the voice of an insurrection against the heritage by a rebel group called Union. Yet her words endure just as powerfully as Old Georgie's, echoing through the film as proclamations that we are not here to eat and be eaten but to affirm each other and to honor the wealth of possibilities from changing moment to changing moment: "To be is to be perceived, and so to know thyself is only possible through the eyes of the other. The nature of our immortal lives is in the consequences of our words and deeds . . . throughout all time. . . . Our lives are not our own. From womb to tomb we are bound to others, past and present, and by each crime and every kindness we birth our future." She speaks for the lives of the characters unbound by chronology, which flow in every direction of what linear culture calls past, present, and future. As Keegan eloquently puts it, "If racial capitalism asserts that some lives must be expendable, then Sonmi-451 delivers an inverted ethics, insisting that the causality in even a single life unfolds endlessly. How we transition from the first sense to the second is *Cloud Atlas*'s rhetorical shape." This study concurs with Keegan's description of Sonmi-451's "inverted ethic," but contends that the rhetorical shape it represents is not only about race, but about the linear belief in the expendability of some races as a part of the larger picture of linear legacy.

TRAJECTORIES

Cloud Atlas in its entirety does have a beginning, middle, and end—we walk into the movie theater or stream the film before it begins, and we leave or shut down the screening device when it ends—and the intersecting narratives can bear the numerical dates of linear chronology. But there is a tension between our experience of chronology and our experience of cosmic nonlinearity, which creates for the audience an experience of a linear heritage that only seemingly moves forward and a nonlinear heritage of energies nested one inside the other. Nothing moves forward or back. We observe that the

FIGURE 4.4 *Zachry and Meronym transcend the limits of linear history off-world, end of film, chapter 16.*

toxicity of linear hierarchies moves Earth cultures in reverse at the same time that science and the arts progress. Irony of ironies, progress is locked together with increased barbarism. In the nonlinear legacy, we are all bound to each other and illuminated by boundless possibilities. Simultaneously.

Cloud Atlas does not sentimentally enshrine a happy ending for nonlinear heritage, nor does it dismiss the ongoing, catastrophic power of linear heritage. Meronym and Zachry, intended by Old Georgie on Earth to destroy each other, have been fruitful and multiplied on an off-world colony. Their lives extend beyond the limitations of *me*. But the film gives us no reason to believe Old Georgie isn't still spewing hallucinatory poison on Earth, where the *mes* represented by actors Hugh Grant and Hugo Weaving are entrenched in their sequential moments of power, and where the audience lives. The purveyors of toxic heritage seem to endure like the zombie undead, while the living legacy continues to be inscribed, like an atlas inscribed on the quantum trajectories of the clouds, on the bodies of the intended victims of zombie linear legacy. For us, *Cloud Atlas* is a poetic experience of all things and all time; the film is a dazzling part of the cocreation by the mass media of the new map of limits and boundlessness in a nonlinear cosmos.

CODA: *BLACKKKLANSMAN*— CRY HAVOC AND LOOSE THE DOGS OF HERITAGE

Spike Lee has made a career of films about Black life in America that do not use the medium as a transparent carrier of historical lessons. He cannot be read in the same way that we read linear studio movies about race like *No Way Out* (1950), *The Defiant Ones* (1958), *To Kill a Mockingbird* (1962), *In the Heat of the Night* (1967), and *Guess Who's Coming for Dinner* (1967). These movies are implicitly and sometimes explicitly committed to learning by understanding the picture of causes and effects transmitted by a racist heritage. For the most part, early independent, Black-made movies—for example those made by John Singleton—implicitly do the same and are, appropriately, similarly understood. This study does not quibble with their inclusive ideals. However, this study does contend that to approach Lee's films in this way is to misperceive his art and his vision.

Linear mass-media movies about racism, to date, are located in a prequantum cosmos. To recall Brian Greene's eloquent formulation, as they pit inclusive ideals against a heritage of prejudice and exclusion, they assume that space and time are an "inert backdrop on which the events of the universe play themselves out." Lee has honed his cinematic art destabilizing the heritage of discrimination by portraying space and time, to again quote Greene, as "intimate players in the events themselves."[30] Does Lee imagine time and space as intimate players in events through quantum theory? Borges? Esotericism? No; rather, as a storyteller, Lee plays a self-referential game with cinema and its circulation through the mass media, much as Tom Tykwer did in *Run Lola Run*. Furthermore, while films like *To Kill a Mockingbird* cultivate the illusion of reality in their representations, Lee's films are as much about how representation works in mass-media movies as they are about our historical legacy of racism itself. Precisely, they are about how representation is intimately connected with the twisted perceptions that make racism possible. If we trace the development of Lee's nonlinear artistry, from the nascent self-consciousness about representation of his first feature-length film, *She's Gotta Have It* (1986), to the explosive self-referentiality of *BlacKkKlansman* (2018), we can more richly appreciate Lee as a mass-media artist who has much to say about the disastrous illusions that linear racial legacies have substituted for reality.

From the beginning of his career, Lee has favored altering perspectives on heritage through direct address to the camera and allusion to the production of images the film audience ingests. *She's Gotta Have It* isn't explicitly about the heritage of racism. But it is about altering racial perceptions. The film refuses to restrict Black life to the parameters progressive Hollywood began to erect when, once it began to speak of racial injustice, it confined the significance of Black characters to stories about white acknowledgment of racial injustice or about white heroism in defeating it. *She's Gotta* demands for Black characters the much wider representational range unhesitatingly accorded to white characters. White characters have domestic realities, complete with sex lives and experiences of romance that are not attached to large-scale culture wars. In *She's Gotta*, so do Black characters. It is a story about a beautiful, spirited Black woman, Nola Darling (Tracy Camilla Johns), who discovers she is not a one-man woman—or a one-*woman* woman. Through Lee's self-conscious mode of representation, he contextualizes Nola's voyage of discovery as an assertion of the significance of the ordinary domestic lives of Black Americans. The film doesn't open with Nola and her story, but with a montage of (beautiful) photographs of Black urban life: women, men, and children going about their ordinary business.

And, like Weiner's montage of photographs in the main title of *The Romanoffs*, Lee's montage immediately frees us from the illusion of reality enclosed by linear time and space in conventional prequantum movies. *She's Gotta* further distances us from linear time and space through direct address to the camera. Nola looks straight at us and talks about her thoughts and feelings, as she contemplates the three men and one woman who court her. Toward the end of the film, Mars Blackmon, one of Nola's suitors (played by Lee), converses with Nola's favorite boyfriend, Jamie (Tommy Redmond Hicks), and pointedly notes that the two of them are talking to "them"—us. The film ends with the cast shucking the masks of character and introducing themselves to us by their real names. We've been representing Black life, the film repeats and repeats. It is a different representation, Lee says implicitly, isn't it?

School Daze (1988) is a more urgently reflexive wake-up call. It asks us to learn about the racial heritage of our country through a Brechtian destabilization of movie illusions of reality. Lee satirically shoehorns the self-questioning of young Black men and women about their identities at historically Black Mission College into the stereotypical framework of the white, Hollywood college musical. The film unfolds, in a meanderingly linear fashion, interrupted by songs that remove us, in the time-honored way of movie musicals, from the thrust of linear time and space. As the scenes unfold, Lee focuses us on the increasing erosion of Black identity through the emulation at Mission College of the white college fraternity system. The moment of truth arrives when Dap Dunlap (Laurence Fishburne)—the student most resistant to the internalization of the materialist, racist values of white, capitalist society—tears apart the trite narrative about fraternity life with an almost apocalyptic direct address to the camera. Dap rouses the entire campus by ringing a bell and repeatedly bellowing, "WAKE UP!" Then Fishburne and Giancarlo Esposito, the actor who plays Julian "Big Brother Almighty" Eaves, the student who has most dangerously internalized racial clichés, step out from behind their fictional characters, turn to the camera, and beg the audience to open their eyes, with a quiet, heartfelt "Please."

In what is probably Lee's most famous film, *Do the Right Thing* (1989), he ups the representational ante with a loosely linear narrative about the buildup to explosive racial violence in an Italian-owned pizzeria located in a Black neighborhood, on a suffocatingly hot summer day, not only through the self-referentiality of the film, but even more tellingly by building into the narrative a link between representation, heritage, and racial tensions. The eruption of long-smoldering racial tensions is triggered by a lack of mass-media representation of Black cultural icons. Mookie (Spike Lee) delivers pizzas for Sal's Pizzeria; much to his chagrin, Sal maintains a "wall of fame" on which he displays glossy, 8 × 10 headshots of celebrities, none of them Black, foreclosing from cultural heritage the representation of Black Americans.

Questions about racial reality and the creation of a false legacy through representation intensify dramatically in *Bamboozled* (2000). *Bamboozled* follows the career of television producer Pierre Delacroix (Damon Wayans), brilliantly tracing his degeneration toward self-loathing and death, as he is swallowed up by his own stellar success. He attains this success by building a hit show around a revival of the blackface minstrel show, perpetuating the heritage of representing Black America through its grotesque, degrading caricatures. Delacroix casts a brilliantly talented but homeless Black dancer named Manray (Savion Glover) as a traditionally ignorant minstrel character named Mantan, whose face is concealed from the audience by a thick coat of burnt-cork blackface. The show generates the enthusiastic laughter of contempt from white audiences and increasingly imprisons Manray in a dehumanized image created by linear legacy.

To change our perception of blackface as a trivial, perhaps unkind, tradition of entertainment and reveal it as a drastic form of dehumanization, Lee creates a cinematic temporal liminality for Delacroix's story from which to view the blackface heritage at a distance. From the first moment of the film, Delacroix speaks directly to the audience in voiceover. The direct address removes him so insistently from linear time and space that his dying words address us as if he were speaking from beyond the grave. The temporal and spatial instability of the film results in a nonlinear perspective from which we can perceive the littering of the screen with dead Black bodies—including those of Delacroix and Manray—as the result of the linear heritage of blackface. At that point, Lee breaks away from his characters and bombards the audience with a horrifying, lengthy montage of hideous blackface Hollywood representations of Black people that spans the history of the movies. The relationship between these images from the real life of the culture and the image created by Delacroix in the story is revealed when the montage is capped with the collision between an extreme close-up of the grotesquely laughing, mocking face of the now-dead Mantan and the voiceover of the dying or dead Delacroix; by this time we are so far from linear time and space we have lost the boundary between life and death. The words in the voiceover are the legacy left by his father: "Keep 'Em Laughing."

If there is ambiguity about whether Lee is mocking the white audience's delight in the dehumanizing tradition of blackface, or whether he is bitterly laughing with a Black audience witnessing their internalization of their degradation, there is no question that here Lee has placed us outside of linear time and space through reflexive techniques, to witness the toxicity of the ghostly heritage of racism, the product of cancerously delusional representation growing in time and space completely divorced from organic reality. The nonlinear, distancing reflexivity of *Bamboozled* that removes us fictionally from the inert stage of time and space in order to reshape our awareness of the images with which we are flooded in real life is prologue to the similar, even more searing rhetoric about racial heritage and the movies in *BlacKkKlansman* (2018).

In *BlacKkKlansman,* made almost twenty years after *Bamboozled,* we can sense Lee's desperation about the potential for creating a portal out of a damaging, deadly heritage of perception. And the reception by critics of the film justifies his pain. The springboard of the film is a true-crime memoir, *Black Klansman: Race, Hate, and the Undercover Investigation of a Lifetime,* by Ron Stallworth about lessons that can be learned from his experience fighting the Ku Klux Klan as an undercover policeman in Colorado Springs.[31] Lee's adaptation of the book uses Stallworth's account to highlight its own blindness to the crucial role of perception in history. Lee's film is a cinematic acid bath into which he dips Stallworth's entire project of education about race history through a progressive legacy. The critics, however, remained stuck in what Lee represents as Stallworth's myopia.

A. O. Smith, in the *The New York Times,* cleverly remarks on the use Lee makes of crosscut editing, pioneered by D. W. Griffith, at the very time he is excoriating the racism of Griffith's *Birth of a Nation,* but without any insight into the deeper uses Lee makes of racist movies, he concludes the film is "about the boundaries of group identity, and how a person can or can't cross them." Mark Kermode in the *Guardian,* enthusiastically lauds Lee's "blistering" assertion that people can learn from racist history. Stephanie Zacharek, in *Time,* implicitly reads the film as the *To Kill a Mockingbird* of today. She reads it as an updated lesson about race in America. Tyler Coates, in *Esquire,* praises *BlacKkKlansman* for being a rare movie "that doesn't treat the KKK as a joke." Other critics who read the film through the lenses of Santayana, Burke, and Churchill are Chris Nashawaty in *Entertainment,* David Sims in *The Atlantic,* and Ann Hornaday in *The Washington Post.*[32] All to be expected.

Surprisingly, radical and brilliant filmmaker Boots Riley, the creator of the surreal *Sorry to Bother You* (2018), is another story. Unexpectedly, he also misreads the film myopically, oblivious to Lee's nonlinear use of time and space. He chastises Lee both for departing from the facts of Stallworth's book and for painting him and the police as champions against racism, when the police are in fact villains.[33] This is an astonishing accusation, since Lee ultimately depicts a police hierarchy that is an extremely mixed bag, containing officers of conscience, officers of expediency, and officers who are racist and corrupt. Moreover, the police in the KKK sting are all betrayed, as we shall see, by an ambiguous official policy that takes with one hand what it gives with the other. Riley's strangest misunderstanding of Lee's alterations to Stallworth's memoir as the deceptions of a sellout is his misreading of the unnerving, total destabilization of time and space at the end of the film. Riley criticizes Lee for concluding the story with a vision of a happy ending for race justice through law and order. Below, we will expand on how misguided Riley is in his critique of the film's denouement.

BlacKkKlansman is a full-blown nonlinear, reflexive approach to the conundrum of racial heritage enshrined in American mass-media representations. Lee reconfigures Stallworth's account of his victory over the KKK through a nonlinear lens. The film begins by introducing us, not to Stallworth's story, but to a nonlinear cosmos somewhere in a 1939 movie image of the Civil War. Our door into *BlacKkKlansman* is a famous scene from *Gone with the Wind* (dir. Victor Fleming, 1939; hereafter *GWTW*). The film doesn't end with Stallworth's victory, either. Our door out of the film is through television-news footage of a white-supremacist Unite the Right rally in Charlottesville, Virginia, from 2017. That is to say, while there is a straight line of autobiographical narrative in the book, Lee's film contextualizes Stallworth's narrative of his KKK sting within a ghostly flow of mass-media, racist images of the sort that have been his focus in his preceding films. But here Lee takes an enormous leap into being a media cocreator of the new zeitgeist with the natural and social sciences.

Stallworth's book is a first-person account of how he inspired the police in Colorado Springs, a very conservative western town, to infiltrate the local chapter of the Ku Klux Klan. With the brash confidence of the young, he proposed creating a nonexistent white Ron Stallworth, an idea that came to him as he answered by telephone a newspaper call to those interested in being a part of the local KKK chapter. The KKK member on the other end of the line did not recognize him as a Black man. From there, Stallworth's imagination leaped to the possibility that he could be a Black undercover detective who speaks to the Klan officers on the telephone, paired with a white undercover officer who meets with the Klan in person. It is an idea with the lure of both the television sitcom and the tradition of the American conman. And it works. But only seemingly. Ultimately, as those who have seen the film know, in Lee's narrative, Stallworth's accomplishment was erased from official Colorado Springs police records by a highly mysterious, suspect executive decision—about which, more below.

Nevertheless, in Stallworth's mind's eye, he figures into a progressive heritage of racial recovery for America. Hasn't he? In Lee's film, if Stallworth has anything to teach America, it is that our country is living in the upside-down, in the fluid, groundless time and space of a nightmarish, media-created simulacrum of history from which we cannot find the exit.

NO *THERE* THERE

To grasp the enormity and uniqueness of Lee's achievement, we need to take the full measure of how and why Lee decenters Stallworth's experience, which stands at the vibrant core of his book but is only a fragment of Lee's elusive, larger picture of historical legacy. Lee highlights the power of the phantom elements of our engagement with heritage by prioritizing them. We don't begin with Stallworth. Rather, we enter the narrative through a film within a film, the Hollywood Civil War fantasy *GWTW*. Where are we? We are in the famous part of the movie that utilizes the triage area for wounded Confederate soldiers as a background for characterizing the film's legendary heroine, Scarlett O'Hara (Vivien Leigh), as a narcissist who is oblivious to the human catastrophe around her. She's focused on her own problem. War? La dee da. Scarlett expects to bring Dr. Meade to help pregnant Melanie Wilkes (Olivia de Havilland). As the camera pulls back slowly to take in a boundless sea of human misery, Scarlett becomes increasingly lost in a vast plain of hurt and dying Confederate soldiers, for whom there is almost no possibility of medical help, even were there a hundred Dr. Meades. As the shot reaches its full expansion, a ragged Confederate flag appears in the lower left corner of the frame.

Where is Stallworth? Where is Colorado springs? They will come later, because Lee is interested in using Stallworth's story to open up the larger question of heritage and how it gets circulated. Circulation of heritage is our first encounter with Lee's film. We are in a screening room with the rabidly racist Dr. Kennebrew Beauregard (Alec Baldwin), watching *GWTW*. For him, the movie is not merely Technicolor entertainment, nor is he fascinated by Victor Fleming's marvelous use of the camera. Nor does he perceive the film's mockery of Scarlett's fantasies of white privilege. Rather he buys into her fantasies and intends to circulate them in a training film to teach a heritage of supremacist pride and rage against the "black mongrel" and the "Jewish conspiracy" that controls, well, everything. He uses a film clip from D. W. Griffith's 1915 movie *The Birth of a Nation* (*BOAN*) for the same purposes.

Lee destabilizes him. As Beauregard attempts to perpetuate his doctrine, his voice becomes increasingly dehumanized, finally degenerating into incoherent vocal spasms, grunts, and growls as he attempts to accompany the movie images with an "educational" voiceover. Comic and grotesque, Beauregard begins *BlacKkKlansman* with not only a spectacle of racist historical legacy that is an incoherent parody of thought and language, but also the self-referential spectacle of someone watching movies. *BlacKkKlansman* is intense nonlinear narrative, not only about racist heritage, but about representation. Indeed, Lee believes we must look to representation as the transmitter of racist heritage.

It would be reductive and simplistic to interpret Lee's use of Beauregard as a simplistic attack on the evil of the popular media. After all, *BlacKkKlansman*, a media creation, demonstrates the revelatory power of the media.

GONE WITH THE NATION

When Beauregard recedes from view, and Stallworth, the Colorado Springs Police Department, the Colorado Springs chapter of the Klan, and the Colorado College Black Student Union enter the film, we might gain a welcome sense of solid reality, as Lee depicts the struggle of white power, Black power, and the police action. But it isn't reality; we are still watching a film, and Lee doesn't let us forget it. His film is part of the mass media, as much a collection of light and shadow on celluloid as are *GWTW* and *BOAN*, only in a nonlinear context. In Lee's hands, Stallworth becomes an invented character, with a love interest, Patrice Dumas (Laura Harrier), and a collection of police colleagues that never appeared in Stallworth's book. This fictionalized Ron Stallworth (John David Washington) joins with police detective Phillip "Flip" Zimmerman (Adam Driver), invented by Lee, to form a composite white-and-Black man. The plan is to infiltrate the local chapter of the Ku Klux Klan, scripting their speech in their conversations with the home-grown fascists of Colorado Springs in the language of stereotype and cliché, which represents nothing more real than the stereotypes and clichés the members of the Klan glean from *BOAN*, which they watch as if it were a documentary. Everything is about the perception of spectacle: from the films within the film to the activities of daily life, and later to the horrifying, gut-wrenching description from memory by Jerome Turner (Harry Belafonte), an old civil rights activist created by Lee, of a lynching in Waco, Texas, on May 15, 1916.

Lee's film melds a number of performances that blur the line between image and reality. Stallworth is both a liar and a sincere lover when he romances Patrice, the president of the Black Student Union. He cannot tell her that he is an undercover policeman and mouths the clichés of the students about "pigs," but at the same time he uses his knowledge as a police detective, about Klan violence that he knows is coming, to try to protect her. When Kwame Ture (Stokely Carmichael, played by Corey Hawkins) visits the Black Student Union, he utilizes a persona to address and mobilize the emotions of the crowd that comes out to hear him, as he creates a Black power heritage to compete with the legacies of the white supremacists. Stallworth, the voice of Ron on the phone, and Zimmerman, the incarnate Ron for in-person meetings, collaborate to produce the appearance of an earnest, would-be Klansman. The composite, nonexistent Ron makes plans with the supremacists for his ceremony of induction into the Colorado Springs chapter of the Klan, which includes a special visit from Grand Wizard David Duke (Topher Grace), and he enters into their schemes for a cross burning and for the planting of a bomb intended to kill civil rights leader Jerome Turner, who is to visit the Black Student Union, and as many of the Black students as possible. Turner is a fictional character, but he anchors heritage in an organic *here*, while real-world David Duke represents an unhinged spectacle that psychotically divorces legacy from experience.

The various spectacles and claims to heritage move toward intersection at a climactic moment near the end of *BlacKkKlansman*: while composite Ron's induction ceremony—which includes a screening of *BOAN*—is underway, and Jerome Turner arrives to speak to the student union. Threading these events, Felix Kendrickson (Jasper Pääkkönen), the most hatefully psychotic of the Klan members, is depicted colluding with his morbidly obese, stupid wife Connie (Ashlie Atkinson) to plant explosives while Turner is speaking, and composite Ron, Stallworth, and Zimmerman find themselves rushing out of the luncheon following the induction ritual to prevent Connie from deploying a big brick of C-4 explosive where Turner and the students have gathered. Ironically using the crosscut editing pioneered by Griffith in *BOAN*, Lee juxtaposes the white-power spectacle of the ritual induction ceremony with Turner's entreaty for Black power, as he describes for the students the horrors of the 1916 lynching he witnessed, and with an action montage of Stallworth and Zimmerman versus Connie that resembles every movie-or-TV cops-and-criminals chase and fight the audience has ever seen. We see the police heroics through a reflexive lens that distances us from the heritage of action flicks about race. It is all part of the linear media legacy of the representation of race that was invoked by Kennebrew Beauregard when *BlacKkKlansman* began.

So is the spectacle of David Duke officiating at the all-male KKK induction ritual for composite Ron. Duke intones in smooth and practiced verbal modulations a chic, reformulated brand of the faux history embodied in *BOAN*, invoking the demonstration of white racial superiority by his "good friend" William Shockley—it's a fact and you can't argue

FIGURE 4.5 *Civil rights hero Jerome Turner speaks of a real history that intersects with the Klan's illusory, linear construct, chapter 15.*

with that—wearing the white robes and hoods made popular in Griffith's film and repeating all the cant about pure, white, Southern womanhood spewed in *BOAN*. It is as much a picturesque, phantasmic theater of movie heritage as Zimmerman, the white, Jewish part of composite Ron, swearing, in the line of duty, an oath that he is a white non-Jew.

Crosscut with the Klan's acting out of the historical fantasy of *BOAN* is Turner's description of a bloody, unspeakably horrible, real lynching. The Klan embraces *BOAN* as history, just as President Woodrow Wilson did when he showed Griffith's film at the White House and called it "history written in lightning," as Turner notes. But what Turner recalls of the lynching of Jesse Washington—seventeen years old, Black, and mentally retarded and accused of raping a white woman—empties *BOAN* of any possible connection to real life and defines it as spectacle. A boy himself at the time, Turner, hiding, in terror that he might be similarly violated, saw Washington used as family entertainment spectacle. Children were let out of school to join their parents and watch as the boy was dragged from the courthouse, stabbed and beaten, castrated, and alternately lowered into a fire and raised out of it until he was bone and ash, his remains sold as souvenirs, and the photographs taken used on souvenir postcards. Such spectacle has taken the place of history as reality, and continues to do so, as the Klan chapter responds excitedly to *BOAN*, and as the white police misperceive Stallworth when he arrives in time to tackle Connie and prevent her from planting the bomb. She cries rape; and the uniformed white police kick and beat Stallworth until Zimmerman arrives. They do not hear Stallworth when he tells them that he is undercover police, but they hear Zimmerman's white voice.

Moreover, not only are we confronted with the persistence of the perceptual racial divide between Black and white and the endurance of a racial heritage created by movies, but we are also faced with the erasure of any documentation of the success of the anti-Klan unit. At the end of the film, police chief Bridges suddenly and inexplicably rewards Stallworth's success by terminating the anti-Klan unit because, in Bridges's words "there is no credible threat" from the Klan anymore. All evidence that the unit ever existed is removed from the files and destroyed. This moment is meant to trigger memories of the words of Chief Justice John Roberts's majority opinion in the 2013 case of *Shelby County v. Holder*. The majority opinion gutted the Civil Rights Act of 1965, by affirming that "nearly 50 years later, things have changed dramatically," despite clear evidence that, even though the law had successfully mitigated the suppression of voting rights for Black Americans, a very credible threat to the minority vote still remained. Boots Riley angrily argues that we don't know whether the Colorado Springs police chief actually did this, since we cannot trust the real Stallworth—but that is beside Lee's point. His film details how organic reality disappears, and the spectacle of a phantom linear heritage of racism takes its place. The invisibility of Stallworth's success leads the film toward a crisis of representation; linear legacy does not provide a foundation on which to stand and learn.

REALITY KNOCKS

Stallworth and everything we have witnessed of his success vanishes at the end of the film. The enraging erasure of the anti-Klan program from history is compounded by a final disappearance of Stallworth from Lee's film. We last see him bickering with Patrice, who is of the same mind as Boots Riley and declines to "sleep with the enemy"—a brother who is a cop. Stallworth contends that he is burrowing from within. The film undercuts them both with a sudden knock on the door. They both defensively reach for their guns. But in a history reduced to spectacle and fantasy, what good is a gun? They open the door to an empty hallway, through which they move in nonlinear time and space, moving without walking as the hallway recedes behind them. Lee achieves this eerie image by using a double-dolly shot; both the camera and the actors are on dollies, creating an image that violates linear space-time. We leave space-time with them. They vanish. We become lost in a cardinal spectacle of Klan fantasy: the lurid light of a cross burning, exulted by anonymous figures in Klan robes and hoods, raising their arms in ecstasy. Only from a linear perspective oblivious to Lee's recontextualization of the adventures of the Black Klansman in nonlinear time and space could Boots Riley mistake Lee's depiction of the dissipation of heritage in a sea of anchorless images.[34]

FIGURE 4.6 *Patrice and Ron leave the enclosure of linear history, near end of film, chapter 19.*

Lee discards Stallworth, Zimmerman, Patrice, and the Colorado Springs anti-Klan unit, just as embodied fact is discarded by the media circulation of American heritage. We are plunged into a montage of news video of the white-supremacist Unite the Right torchlight parade in Charlottesville, Virginia, in August 2017. It is not the 1978 sting that is circulated in the media but the spectacle of white supremacy, hundreds of racists from around the country—not the ragtag, humiliated Klan chapter in Colorado Springs—but fascist racists on the march, chanting, "Jews will not replace us." What remains is the descendant in linear time of Beauregard's training film, a linear history that is endorsed by then-president Donald Trump, who insists on video that there were "very fine people on both sides," false equivalences to the highest political level in America.

Lee subversively reclaims the media image with his own video of the Black inhabitants of Charlottesville shouting their indignation at the violence against them by the Klan. He reveals the real impact of the KKK on white womanhood when he zooms in on the flowers marking the spot where Heather Heyer died. Heyer was a real white woman, who really stood in the street in Charlottesville as part of a counterprotest against the white nationalists, and who was really murdered when a white supremacist intentionally drove his car into the crowd. The final image of Lee's film is the American flag, upside down, as the red, white, and blue colors drain from it, and it becomes a topsy-turvy study in black-and-white desaturation. We are in a nonlinear universe in which perceived history has become the phantoms of *The Birth of a Nation*, *Gone with the Wind*, Kennebrew Beauregard, and the 2017 Unite the Right rally.

As Lee integrates into *BlacKkKlansman* his post-Newtonian perspectives on people and media images we recognize as part of our history, he problematizes memory and the possibility of learning lessons from history. He leaves us with painful questions that rise far beyond the mystery of the termination of Stallworth's anti-Klan initiative and even racial legacies. He joins Weiner and Tykwer and the Wachowskis in asking: What is history? Who are our historians?

There are traces of cosmic historical realities in the depictions of legacy in *The Romanoffs*, *Cloud Atlas*, and *BlacKkKlansman*. These bring us to the border between historical legacy and historical teleology. Heritage is local. Teleology is cosmic, an abstract concept that history follows one universal pattern from the beginning of time. Teleology is not a hysterical local conglomeration of fears about where we belong; it is a philosophical grand narrative that describes the way all of humanity for all time belongs within a history that is a predestined unfolding of events toward an inevitable historical conclusion. Neither linear heritage nor linear teleology are possible in a nonlinear universe. We have taken a journey into narratives about how, in the new zeitgeist, heritage cannot signify as a linear timeline we can look back along to learn. We will now cross from legacy in the multiverse into grand historical narratives in a boundless universe.

Chapter 5

TELEOLOGY UNSTUCK: THE NOT-SO-GRAND NARRATIVE

Westworld, Arrival

If you want a picture of the future, imagine a boot stamping on a human face—for ever.

GEORGE ORWELL, *1984*

We are projects of collective self-creation. What if we approached human history that way? What if... we ask how we came to be trapped in such tight conceptual shackles that we can no longer even imagine the possibility of reinventing ourselves?

DAVID GRAEBER AND DAVID WENGROW, *The Dawn of Everything: A New History of Humanity*

And yet what I suggested had come to an end was not the occurrence of events, even large and grave events, but History: that is, history understood as a single, coherent, evolutionary process, when taking into account the experience of all peoples in all times.

FRANCIS FUKUYAMA, *The End of History and the Last Man*

Linear historical cause and effect, begone! And take Orwell with you. From the perspective of the new zeitgeist, as manifested in the *Westworld* series (2016–2022), created by Jonathan Nolan and Lisa Joy; and in *Arrival* (2016), directed by Denis Villeneuve, broad-brush, linear historical teleologies are not grand—or real. Tried-and-true historical films and series reflect the philosophical writings of bedrock teleological historians, with their deterministic arrows of time, their magisterial, unstoppable, universal destinies, and often, their Orwellian boots. In contrast, *Westworld* and *Arrival* are typical of historical narratives for a nonlinear cosmos, where neither Orwellian boots nor teleology need apply.

The bulk of movie and TV historical melodramas are, and have long been, informed by some version of the cause-and-effect relationship embedded in hundreds of years of Newtonian linear thinking: utopian, dystopian, and all points in between. *Utopian teleologies*: movies and series about the abuses of ancient Rome that are inspirited by the rise of an optimistic, Christian, apocalyptic narrative; Westerns in which the suffering of pioneers and settlers is part of the unfolding of a glorious American manifest destiny; Sergei Eisenstein's Communist epics in which a suffering proletariat is traveling unstoppably toward triumph over its class oppressors; civil rights stories in which the arc of history bends unstoppably toward justice. *Dystopian teleologies*: movies and series informed by dystopian historical imagination, in the mode of George Orwell's *1984*, the very dark what-if narratives of *The Man in the High Castle* (2015–2019), *The Handmaid's Tale* (2017–2025), *The Planet of the Apes* (1968), and *Logan's Run* (1976).

Nonteleological film and television opt out of heavyweight, venerable historical trajectories—the cause-and-effect patterns of history in the Old Testament, the New Testament, Jean-Jacques Rousseau, Thomas Hobbes, John Locke, Georg Wilhelm Friedrich Hegel, and Karl Marx—as well as the patterns in contemporary teleologies alive and well in your local bookstore: for example, *Sapiens, A Brief History of Humankind* (2018), by Yuval Noah Harari, and *The End of History and the Last Man* (1992), by Francis Fukuyama.[1] Rather, the storytelling discussed in this chapter resonates the spirit of new, nonlinear historical speculations and formulations. For example, in your local bookstore and library, you will also find *The Bible Unearthed: Archaeology's New Vision of Ancient Israel and the Origin of Its Sacred Texts* (2002), by Israel Finkelstein and Neil Asher Silberman.[2] Finkelstein and Silberman use recent archaeological evidence to challenge conventional readings of the teleology of the Old Testament. *The Bible Unearthed* claims that the Old Testament intentionally manipulates its account of events, so as to create a teleological path to unity for the ancient Israelite tribes. Finkelstein and Silberman present evidence that they say disproves that the Old Testament is a historical document. They theorize that all the famous events of the Old Testament were invented to convince the ancient Israelites that they were one people, one *chosen* people, to encourage them to put an end to their constant internecine warfare. Were the ancient Israelite tribes even in the locations where biblical events purportedly took place? Finkelstein and Silberman can find no evidence that the Israelites were in Egypt at the time of the supposed Exodus. Whither the Passover table? Or that Joshua was at Jericho when the battle was supposed to have taken place.[3] Somewhere near Finkelstein and Silberman on bookstore shelves, you will also find *The Dawn of Everything: A New History of Humankind* by anthropologist David Graeber and archaeologist David Wengrow, whom we have already met, and who provide a basis on which to question the teleologies of Rousseau, Hobbes, and their contemporary descendants. Graeber and Wengrow repeatedly ask "how we came to be trapped in such tight conceptual shackles that we can no longer even imagine the possibility of reinventing ourselves."[4]

I include Finkelstein and Silberman and Graeber and Wengrow in our discussion of nonlinear history without any intention of asserting that this nonlinear breed of historian is or is not correct, but rather to say that their fundamental approach to history is a new development and intersects with mass-media, nonlinear, film and television historical narratives, which poetically opens up breathing space for new questions and new cultural possibilities. As forms of historical poetry, *Westworld* and *Arrival* make no claims that they *prove* anything, nor does this study. Rather, as Graeber and Wengrow might say, I propose that these works get our historical imaginations unstuck—even more unstuck than the historians do.

As with film and television about legacy, Joy and Nolan and Villeneuve go further into nonlinearity than the new crop of nonlinear historians who, so far, have not connected their innovative historical perspectives with the nonlinearity of quantum physics. By contrast, both works we are about to visit depict the big historical picture in a universe in which history is nonteleological, not only because familiar trajectories are imaginary, but also because time is multidirectional and matter is composed of porous, moving molecules, or maybe strings. Seatbelts mandatory.

WESTWORLD: IT'S TIME FOR YOUR ANTIPSYCHOTIC

Westworld, an HBO series, created and often written and directed by Lisa Joy and Jonathan Nolan, is an extreme, nonlinear vision that endows linear historical teleology with psychotic implications. Joy and Nolan have each worked as writers, directors, and producers in projects for the mass media that play with linear time and space, but their joint efforts in *Westworld* have produced by far their most ambitious nonlinear venture.[5] What are the sources of their vision? Like Lynch and Malick, Joy and Nolan are generally unwilling to speak publicly about their art; nor did they speak with me. I have only hearsay from the industry about their core ideas in this series.[6] Happily, however, the series itself, through a rich array of allusions to a variety of theories and other intellectual constructs, provides its own built-in concordance.

Intellectual constructs? Who wants to do research in order to watch television? There is certainly no evidence anyone has previously done any. There is a good deal of evidence, however, that the lack of effort has left us with shallow readings of this many-layered, rich, and very strange series.[7] We, by contrast, will take our time, delay judgment, and gain familiarity with a proliferation of intellectually ambitious allusions in *Westworld*.

We will delve here. We will reap the rewards of unpacking the numerous clues Joy and Nolan drop as they nudge us toward perceiving their portrait of history in *Westworld.* I will even claim that the work we do will yield more than a fuller engagement with the fictional universe of this series. The inconvenient truth be told, scrutinizing the allusions is not always optional. In some cases, a lazy viewership will not only rob us of the richness of the series; it will leave us barely able to understand what it is about. Case in point: the title of the season 1 finale, "The Bicameral Mind," refers to Julian Jaynes's book *The Origin of Consciousness in the Breakdown of the Bicameral Mind* (1976), which maps history as a teleology anchored in the rise of human consciousness.[8]

The allusion to Jaynes at the end of *Westworld*'s first season forces a reevaluation of our initial perceptions of the series. Joy and Nolan ask a great deal of the audience as they follow this pattern of complex representation followed by reassessment throughout the four seasons of the series. This is particularly true of the final season. The title of its fifth episode, "Zhuangzi," alerts us to the near impossibility of having understood the first three seasons if we do not contextualize them with the inner dialogues of the fascinating fourth-century BCE, Chinese school of philosophy, Zhuangzi, that eschews arriving at one conclusion—right or wrong; winner or loser—in favor of insight into many points of view.[9]

The introduction of Zhuangzi and its embrace of a supremely unstuck nonlinear consciousness prods us toward the series' final point of view that linear, cause-and-effect–structured, grand, teleological historical designs are, at the very least, "a graveyard of stories," and at worst, a full-throttle form of mass psychosis. Joy and Nolan ask a lot, but they also give a great deal. Following the trail of philosophical bread crumbs they have left us, then, leads—almost as helpfully as a no-holds-barred, totally open-ended interview with the creators—to an imaginatively free understanding of corporate harnessing of digital technologies to mass-produce the catastrophe of linear history. They invite us into the space of nonlinear consciousness to perceive history in a new way, recalling David Lynch's invitation to the consciousness at the core of a nonlinear cosmos.

NEW WINE IN VERY OLD BOTTLES

Our introduction to the historical atrocities to come begins deceptively. History just for fun. All the historical carnage is limited to a high-tech amusement park, the eponymous Westworld, where brutality is "only a game." In the amusement park, history is reduced to an upscale product consumed by patrons who pay $40,000 a day to suit up in costumes appropriate to stereotypical simulations of the old-timey, wild American West, Imperial Japan, the British Raj in India, or Fascist Italy during World War II and role-play with abandon in preset narrative loops. The particular historical setting a patron chooses is of negligible importance. All settings are only excuses for the customers to gratify their lusts. In a literalization of history as a linear story written by the winners of conflicts, each selected narrative loop gives a park guest the chance to be a winner in a historical fantasy. The fantasies are implacably linear; they begin with preset conflicts and progress to preset conclusions in which the park guests may, if they choose, act out delusions of omnipotence by raping, maiming, or killing designated losers with wild abandon. Is this legal?

Thanks to fictional advances in digital technology in the *Westworld* universe, yes. The park's architects, Robert Ford (Anthony Hopkins) and Arnold Weber (Jeffrey Wright), provide legal victims for the park guests: lifelike, digitally programmed, replicant "hosts." Without the replicants, indistinguishable in appearance and behavior from biological human beings, to obligingly serve as the historical losers, the guests could not legally experience the privileges of historical winners. Interactions with the replicants simulate the thrill—for those who crave it—of domination as a historically omnipresent human entitlement, with no recriminations. The replicants need memory to perform their narrative loops. But, regarded as mechanical objects, routinely serviced by technicians—like toaster ovens—after they are violated or destroyed, they are programmed to forget the violation, the death, and the refurbishing.

A simple business proposition? Harmless, albeit cruel, amusement for the ultra-wealthy? Rather, a historical time bomb already ticking. Corporate monetization of history disconnected from reality will not long be confined to the theme park. When we first enter the series, seismic shifts are already on the horizon. Secret deals are in progress that will export digitalization of history outside the park. And the replicants have, unbeknownst to almost all the corporate power players, begun mysteriously mutating into conscious sentience and have begun to remember and to question. They will also head into the larger world. Ticktock.

As the seasons progress, outside the park, history more and more becomes a product that serves the greed of the masters of technology. What was merely an ersatz, historical-fantasy break from daily routines, for a limited amount of time inside the park, threatens to become a permanent psychotic break from the reality outside. The prospects, however, are not all dystopian. At the same time, the questions and resistance of burgeoning replicant consciousness are also being exported outside of the park. The complexities of colonization of human history for profit, and replicant struggles for freedom, form the double helix that quickens the series.

The Joy-and-Nolan perspective on history and technology is far more sophisticated and unconventional than the point of view taken in the 1973 movie of the same name that Joy and Nolan adapted. The *Westworld* movie, written and directed by scientist Michael Crichton, takes place completely within a vacation resort like the one in the series. Its visitors also engage in a spot of role-play with lifelike replicants. But the movie is a conventional, human-versus-machine, science fiction–recipe melodrama in which protagonist Peter Martin (Richard Benjamin) learns lessons about the rise of consumerism and corporate greed in post–World War II America. By contrast, in the Joy and Nolan series—although it, too, is replete with consumerism, technology, and greed—reality itself is at stake.

The dream vacation of Crichton's Peter Martin becomes nightmarish after a shootout with a replicant gunslinger (Yul Brynner). The malfunctioning replicant fights back with the terrifyingly concentrated persistence of an automaton, and the technical glitch becomes part of a park-wide breakdown that physically endangers all the human guests and technicians. It is a crisis of scientific hubris, something like the *Titanic*.

In the Joy and Nolan series, the park is the beginning of a crisis of linearity, narratives, and technology caused by the tunnel vision of the corporate players. What seems to them the mere mechanical malfunctioning of the park's replicants is actually an awakening of a new species of sentient beings to what might be a new, supremely unstuck kind of history, centrally concerned with nonlinear consciousness. Unhappily, we have only four of the five seasons of the story that Joy and Nolan had planned. The series was prematurely canceled by HBO; *Westworld* is an unfinished symphony, so to speak. How far would Joy and Nolan have taken the audience into a new narrative experience of history? They aren't telling. But our attention to the daunting challenge of the series' many-layered art, at least to some extent, rescues its place as a mass-media cocreator of the new zeitgeist.

AN OVERVIEW

Undaunted, we begin with an overview of the four seasons of *Westworld*, built on the intersection and counterpoint of two historical trajectories. One trajectory is the persistent descent of the human, linear, grand-historical narrative moving toward collapse, and one is a nonlinear, replicant trajectory of consciousness on the rise toward enlightenment. Both trajectories have deep roots in the series. They are present in embryo, well before *Westworld* begins, in its complicated backstory, which we learn belatedly and not in chronological order. It is a backstory of blind human ambition and greed, miraculous replicant mutation, and the competing ambitions of the two Westworld park creators, Robert Ford and Arnold Weber. Weber is dead before the series begins, and his existence as a partner has been scrubbed from official records, but the conflict between Weber's sensitivity to the cosmic nature of consciousness and Ford's commercialism, which reduces consciousness to nothing more than the fiction in a linear business plan, permanently informs the series narrative.

Everything that transpires in the series reflects Ford and Weber's initial violent disagreement about the potential for replicant consciousness. Their "once upon a time" goes something like this: Potential consciousness, argues Weber. Let's scrap the whole thing before it gets out of hand. Not a chance, argues Ford. This is a platinum creative and business opportunity. All we need is a corporate partner, like Delos Incorporated, to finance our expensive dream and we are made men. Corporate greed, counters Weber. It won't end well. Upshot: Weber dies trying to nip Westworld in the bud, of which more below. And Ford soldiers on. Of which much more now.

By the time we first enter Westworld park, the replicants are unaccountably and covertly mutating into consciousness. Weber was right. He was also right about the inherent disastrousness of partnering with Delos. The corporation has abused its financial power and developed a scheme to monetize the Westworld technology. It's a humdinger that will change history. Delos is working to develop a technology that will use the digitalization of the replicants as the basis for digitalizing human consciousness. Why? So it can digitalize the consciousnesses of prospective clients, for a high price, and after death insert them into replicant bodies, built to be indistinguishable from the living originals. Weber's worst fears realized. Ford is filled with regret and is busy attempting to help the confused and shaken mutating replicants and to thwart Delos. He is scheming to revisit Weber's plan to destroy Westworld. But easier said than done. The cancer of produced historical teleology has been metastasizing for thirty years.

He is up against the immortality project of a corporation with deep pockets and no empathy for either humans or replicants. Delos is prepared to fight hard and dirty for what it expects to be an enormous payday. When the series begins, Delos has already accumulated a vast library of data and is experimenting with creating immortality for the corporation's founder, James Delos (Peter Mullan). It isn't going well at all; replicant bodies reject digitalized human consciousness. There is no real reason to believe Delos can solve that problem. But Delos is blindly confident that success is only a matter of (linear) time. Ford intends to capitalize on corporate blindness about this—and other things—and turn greed against itself. Delos has appropriated his work and plans to forcibly retire him and sugarcoat his ouster with a gala retirement dinner, while it continues looting Westworld for its own purposes. At that dinner, toward which the season moves, Ford has a plan to stop Delos in its tracks.

His plan will also affect Delos CEO Charlotte Hale (Tessa Thompson) and a character known hereafter as the Man in Black (Ed Harris; hereafter MIB), the Delos majority shareholder. Hale and MIB are betraying Delos, as Delos betrayed Ford. On the quiet, they have covertly sold copies of the Delos data to the even larger and more aggressive Incite Corporation, run by its rapacious CEO, trillionaire financier, Engerraund Serac (Vincent Cassel). The full consequences of Hale and MIB's business dealings with Incite will only emerge in season 3, outside the park, where Serac has become the corporate master of human history by feeding the pirated data to Rehoboam, Incite's mega computer. Rehoboam is in the process of manufacturing algorithms, based on the Delos data, for every one of the billions of human inhabitants of Earth, and the algorithms are on track to control the narratives of everyone in the organic world. Ford's plans, in nascent form in season 1, now threaten linear human history here, there, and everywhere.

It seems that one way or the other, we are engaged in the Orwellian what-if historical narrative that we've seen in so many other dystopian movies and series. But Joy and Nolan tacitly raise the specter of Orwell only to exorcize it. Delos will not succeed, powerful as it is, in either season 1 or season 2. And not only because of Ford. He won't succeed either. His revenge scenario is as linear as any corporate game plan, and Joy and Nolan have created a nonlinear universe in which linear projects are innately bound to crash and burn, and a new, nonlinear history is appearing on the horizon through changes in the replicants. Joy and Nolan juggle consumerism, corporate greed, and scientific hubris into a cosmic story much larger than Michael Crichton ever dreamed of.

THE BIG BANG OF REPLICANT CONSCIOUSNESS

The replicants are mutating toward consciousness and a new form of history. As we have noted, Charles Darwin was in some ways the author of the first draft of the new map of the cosmos, when he theorized that mutation—a nonlinear, inexplicable form of change that cannot be traced to a linear cause—is the mechanism by which species evolve. Subsequently, science developed other versions of the impact of mutation on history, in its Big Bang theory of how the universe began in a hot spot of matter that inexplicably cooled and expanded, and in its exploration of how life emerged on Earth, through a process called abiogenesis, in which nonliving matter underwent a series of chemical reactions. In both of these theories, mutation appears to be the agent of change rather than a linear process of development with a clear sequence of cause and effect (see introduction). The mutation of replicant consciousness in *Westworld* resonates with both Darwin and post-Newtonian thinking of how the universe came to be and how life began; persistently occupies pride of place in the series; and increasingly signals something very different from what Delos and Incite have in mind.

A fictional universe filled with nonlinear mutation does not favor linear dystopian determinism such as we find in 1984, where consciousness is easily disposed of by the technological masters of teleological history. The memory hole Orwell created as the fundamental technology of his dystopian universe is particularly useful as a touchstone for interpreting the distinctly different nature of consciousness in *Westworld*. Speaking of the memory hole that makes possible the boot on the human face forever, Orwell writes, "Everything faded into mist. The past was erased, the erasure was forgotten, the lie became truth." But if it did in *1984*, it won't in the Joy and Nolan series, in which nonlinear consciousness will not fade into the mist.

Indeed, the durability of consciousness and its nonlinearity is our first experience of the series. In the first moment of season 1, we are lured into the mutating consciousness of the ur-replicant in Westworld, Dolores Abernathy (Evan Rachel Wood). Although, when the series begins, Dolores appears to be only one among a pantheon of replicants created for the pleasure of the park visitors, she is the mother of them all. Dolores is the first successfully produced replicant, scripted for the Old West section of the park as an innocent, flaxen-haired, blue-eyed, rancher's daughter. Before we are introduced to the Ford, Delos, and Incite corporate plots, we experience Dolores as her consciousness is breaking through the firewall of her programming. It is an ineradicable consciousness, which operates potently in a space outside of linear time and even death. When we first enter that space, Dolores is experiencing the postmortem voice of Arnold Weber, long dead but still asking her questions, as he did when he created her, decades ago. Her dialogue with a dead man is the first representation in the series of the potency of consciousness as a nonlinear spaciotemporal alternative to material, technological, linear history.

When she is in that space, Dolores has inklings of a reality that is beyond the programming that leads her to talk about loving the Westworld patrons. What she experiences inside her loop is hardly love. Rather it is a phantom of her linear narrative, in which organic humans are free to exercise lust and sadism, and in which her replicant father, Peter Abernathy (Louis Herthum), routinely dies, and her replicant lover, Teddy Flood (James Marsden), is routinely humiliated as the two (replicant) men try to protect her from the inevitable rapes by guests. The narrative mandates that she never take revenge for this savagery or hurt organic humans. No exceptions. No? With mutation in progress—

Dolores is not supposed to remember, either, yet she does, when in an alternative, nonlinear space, memory flashes of savage violation bleed through the program, particularly at the hands of the strange Delos Inc. majority shareholder, MIB, who will surface later as a part of the corporate machinations. Significantly, we do not meet him first in his corporate life but in his relationship to Dolores. That is what most defines his importance to the series.

This entire introduction to the series is nonlinear. We and Dolores experience no clear now and then. When in time is Dolores vis-à-vis Weber? When in time is MIB when he assaults her for (his) fun. We don't know. She doesn't know. MIB has played this role with her so often, over thirty years, that it is impossible to locate in linear time the images we see. In nonlinear time and space, rather, she and we experience her consciousness problem. Or potential.

Other replicants are going through the same experiences of suppressed memories that fly thick and fast without explanation, curiously indeterminate. Westworld park clearly does not have an effective memory hole. Replicant Teddy Flood is also disconcerted by images of being not only Dolores's caring sweetheart but also, mysteriously, a savage murderer. Replicant Maeve Millay (Thandiwe Newton), the raunchy, jaded town madam in the Old West saloon, is struck intermittently by confusing flashes of moments of herself as a wholesome, loving mother in a house on the prairie, as well as memories of the park-maintenance crews coming to take her away when she needs to be refurbished. Bernard Lowe (Jeffrey Wright), Robert Ford's thoughtful right-hand man, who manages the replicants, does not know that his role as Ford's faithful colleague is a script; Lowe believes he is a biological human, but he is in fact another replicant, created in the image of the deceased Arnold Weber. Replicant cognitive dissonance inspires the beginning of conscious questioning for him. He and the other replicants are baffled.

What *is* happening?

For the most part, the dissonance and erupting memories are the result of the commercialism of the park. Corporate lust for profit contains the seeds of Westworld's destruction, as it inadvertently supports the rise of the replicants' consciousness. All the replicants were created with an initial code and narrative loop, but over the years, most have had their initial code overwritten with new code, so that the park can increase profits by continually offering new "historical" experiences. To save money and time, however, the original codes have not been erased. So, while seasons 1 and 2 are awash in the familiar suspense of linear corporate conspiracies, they are also flush with the even more significant and irresistible suspense of disorienting, nonlinear experiences for the replicants, when their old codes momentarily short-circuit the new one. *Westworld* is constructed to force the audience to sensorily undergo, with the replicants, the confusion of images from earlier codes and narrative loops disrupting their current narratives. They are jarring.

Equally jarring is our experience of the contrasting trajectory of the humans connected with the park, who are losing consciousness. The human audience of *Westworld* sees itself mirrored in human characters who are more and more driven to break psychotically from reality, preferring the certainty of narrative loops. This prefigures human vulnerability to Serac's algorithms in season 3. MIB for instance. His slide into a psychotic break from reality, as season 1 develops, contains intimations of the degeneration of humankind that will lead to the end of our species' history. MIB is our close-up of what the end of human history is all about. But where, as we shall see, we get a blurred, indeterminate picture of the human condition through him, by contrast—

AND FORD AND WEBER CREATED DOLORES

—the replicant path is carefully mapped otherwise for us, beginning with Dolores's backstory. It is time to talk about Dolores's overwritten code. The initial Big Bang of her consciousness began in the backstory, with Weber covertly recoding Dolores and her lover, Teddy. When? Sometime before Westworld opened for business. It is all lost in a temporal fog, because *Westworld* is not built on linear cause and effect. Rather, as soon as Weber could see that Ford would not be warned of the impending danger, he secretly overwrote Dolores's blue-eyed, flaxen-haired victim code. The rancher's daughter, in her homespun, flouncing blue dress, was transformed into Wyatt, a cold-blooded, flaxen-haired, blue-eyed murderer. Her Wyatt recoding, and the recoding of gentle, adoring Teddy, reprogrammed to be Wyatt's cold-blooded enforcer, temporarily accomplished Weber's goal. The reprogrammed Dolores, on Weber's instruction, demolished all the replicants Weber and Ford had built and then turned her gun on Teddy, Weber, and herself.[10] However, it was only over for Weber, not for Dolores, Teddy, or Westworld. Ford would not permit Weber's vandalism and self-inflicted death to terminate his plans. Nothing simpler. He overwrote Dolores's and Teddy's alternate codes with their original loops. But he did not take the time to erase the code Weber had developed for them. There is also a deeper secret. Dolores's capacity for consciousness is braided with a weakness in the programmed prohibition against fighting back against organic humans. After all, she killed Weber; that deviance is still in her.

Hers is an explosive nonlinear secret, and it is more central to the season finale than any corporate rivalry.

Reading nonlinear narrative is a skill the audience develops by doing. We do it watching *Westworld,* because the series disrupts our habitual linear reading through timed-release consequences of the never-erased codes when they trigger the replicants. It is difficult to integrate the irruptions of unpredictable mutations of Dolores and Teddy into our spectatorship. But that disruption is part of the series. As are the moments when, similarly, Maeve, the seductive, raunchy town madam who owns the bar and brothel on the main street of the Old West section of the park, is startled to intermittently experience her previous narrative loop as a simple homesteader with a beloved little daughter living on the open plains of the Old West section. When she is catapulted into her maternal melodrama, it breaks the reality of her brothel stories, which reciprocally breaks the reality of life on the old homestead. No narrative loop seems like reality anymore. At the same time, Bernard Lowe enters a new, expanded reality when he is thrown suddenly into a nonlinear moment in which he experiences committing murder on Ford's instructions, an experience he was programmed not to recall, exposing the secret that he, too, is a replicant, and prompting traumatic questions about what constitutes his reality. These nonlinear moments reveal to each of these replicants that what they feel and think are nothing more than products of someone else's stories. The way is open for a struggle to find out who they really are and what history really is. The way is opened for us too.

Through Dolores, Maeve, and Bernard, storytelling and history jump the linear tracks. History is reenvisioned as limitless nonlinear potential. There is an aroma of limitlessness to Dolores's awakening, Bernard's shock of recognition, and Maeve's discovery of multiple realities. But freedom comes with a price. There is a concomitant crisis of boundlessness, as the replicants wonder how they are to know the difference between reality and the real-seeming, coded narrative loops. Is their awakening merely a transition from one loop to another? Or is there an actual reality outside of all narrative loops? The replicants yearn to leave Westworld for what lies outside the park to test their abilities to determine the difference between programming and the consciousness of a real identity. (What is it?) This makes for a significant contrast between their longing and the yearning of the humans. The humans are on an opposite trajectory. They are drawn to linear narrative loops, which are more stable and defined than the limitlessness of life. Mostly, as noted above, we see this through MIB.

Of all the consciousness narratives, the counterpoint between MIB's blighted retreat from life into narrative, and Dolores's exodus from narrative loops into wide-open consciousness, confronts us most vividly with the central dynamic of the series. Of course, they do not interact in a straight narrative progression. Rather, Dolores and MIB merge to diverge in waves. From start to finish, in seasons 1 through 4, we experience their counterpointed trajectories in a boundless reality that destabilizes all our expectations about time, space, and narrative. Their floundering inhabits the quantum universe described by Brian Greene, in which time is not a stable platform for human action but a changing, active participant in our history (see chapter 1). Our imaginations, trained to expect stable linear development in chronological time, are befuddled when our expectations are disappointed in season 1, as a sweet-natured, young, biologically human man named William (Jimmi Simpson) enters the nonlinear flow of Dolores's life at Westworld. He is a corporate vice president at Delos, whom we assume reports to MIB. William meets Dolores on his first visit to Westworld, empathizes with her desire to escape it, and promises to rescue her. That would be a linear narrative direction, wouldn't it? Dolores would welcome it and so would we.

However, we realize belatedly, after our linear imaginations have spent most of season 1 hoping for a lady-in-distress story about rescue from the villainous MIB for Dolores, that there *is* no linear story. The audience mutates further toward a nonlinear imagination with a belated shock of recognition that MIB is not the sinister man at the top of the pecking order to whom sweet William reports. MIB *is* William. We find that we have been in nonlinear time while William has mutated. He has risen in the Delos hierarchy, but much more importantly, his estranging addiction to narrative has changed love to hate in him. It is the inexplicable human inversion of the inexplicable replicant Big Bang.

As the fragments of nonlinear time flow, we get a picture—always ambiguous, never sharply focused—about William's mutation to MIB. William falls in love with Dolores in some time frames; he is separated from her in others; he searches frantically for her in others. But a determining factor in his mutation to MIB is that when he finds her, she doesn't recognize him. How and why, we don't know, but it is a part of the nonlinearity of Dolores's own mutation, which triggers William's nonlinear mutation to MIB. Her nonchronological mutation ruptures William's linear love story, on which his faith in the goodness of life psychotically depends. Ruptures trigger consciousness for Dolores. For William they trigger a grim flight from organic life. It is not like the well-observed cinematic transition of Dr. Jekyll into Mr. Hyde, rooted in the causality of Jekyll's experiment. He drank a potion. No potion for William; we observe nothing about how he changed, or why, but his mutation away from consciousness leaves him in a Hyde-like state.

Joy and Nolan teach us to think about the connection between consciousness, nonlinearity, and an unstuck concept of history that resembles Heisenberg's uncertainty principle, which stipulates that there is a measurement problem: We can't measure momentum and position at the same time. The intertwined narratives of Dolores and MIB are vehicles for our new perspective that invoke the measurement problem in a nonlinear universe. We are unable to measure or observe either the replicant's ascent toward freedom associated with nonlinear time; or human descent into the ruins of historical teleology in linear time. This kind of narrative separates the audience from the Newtonian understanding of reality, for which measurement and observation of embodied matter are richly possible and consciousness is experienced as stable measurement. But as humans and replicants evolve away from and toward consciousness, respectively, we see images that estrange us from our familiar sense of location and momentum in time, space, and history.

This estrangement is the principal audience experience of *Westworld*. The familiar linear conspiracies flatten into pointlessness and failure, while the unfamiliar nonlinear space of consciousness becomes our focus of what is real. Consciousness is not about negotiating linear progressions. On the contrary, it manifests as a space of reality outside of linear narratives that is free of linear trajectories and contains massless simulacra of linear materiality. For replicants, it is the center of the maze, as both Ford and Weber refer to it, a space the series asks the audience to engage with. Since it is a space that doesn't exist for organic humans, Joy and Nolan also ask that we imagine what that means for the concept of human reality.

The story of Westworld park tells the tale not only of replicant narratives but of all linear storytelling. Much of the weight of the story has fallen to Dolores and MIB and the disturbing difference between them on that score. Replicant Dolores is increasingly illuminated by a courageous desire to be conscious and free of linear narrative. Human MIB is increasingly psychotic and delusional, desiring to be cut off from reality in pursuit of linearity. Ironically and disturbingly, the audience tends to echo MIB's need to find a linear reading of life with our need to find a linear narrative in the series, while the thrust of the series is toward the experience of reality in replicant nonlinearity. The corporate shenanigans are easier and more comforting to follow. But just when we, clinging to any linear progression we can grab onto, are expecting the finale to restore us to linear comfort by ending the season with those corporate clashes at the retirement gala that we have been promised from the beginning—surprise!

We find ourselves in the strangest moment of the season yet. We are suddenly with Dolores and MIB, who are engaged in a monumental fight in a space that looks like the material landscape of Westworld, but is not. Subsequent moments will show that we have transitioned into a nonlinear reality. We don't know how we got there. And we will experience uncomprehending bedazzlement when we transition to the material reality of Ford's retirement dinner. This is the moment when *Westworld* thoroughly joins the literature of consciousness that we find in the works of James Joyce, Virginia Woolf, William Faulkner, and David Lynch, filled with nonlinear mysteries for which we have no language. We are in both an immaterial consciousness space and a material space at the same time. This is a moment that is not a dream. Not a fantasy. Not merely a disruption of Dolores's narrative loops by replicant memory. It is a poetic representation we can call a parallel reality, but it is even stranger. Its relationship to the retirement party is much like what physicists describe as superposition, what happens to two particles that exist in the same place at the same time. We are at Ford's party, but we are also in an immaterial consciousness space. Language falters, but visual storytelling takes us there. Let us follow.

The limitations of our linear language force me to describe the two incommensurable spaces in chronological order. First the nonlinear immaterial space, then the material party. But montage enables Joy and Nolan to depict a turbulent face-off between Dolores and MIB and the retirement gala—linear and nonlinear spaces—coevally. The mysteries of here and there, where and when, overwhelm prequantum Newtonian logic. In this space, Dolores sees that she is at the center of the maze, where she can perceive the difference between her narrative loop and reality. MIB demands that she take him to the center of the maze, unable to comprehend that he is already there and believing that what he needs from her is a map and a flashlight that will guide him to the yearned-for location of the reality he craves. But clearly it isn't reality he wants at all.

His psychotic demands, her new clarity about her narrative loop, result in multiple narratives unfolding simultaneously. The party is in swing in a linear materiality, where Dolores and Teddy are on display for the corporate guests, and where Delos is completing its narrative of a takeover from Ford. At the same time, MIB attacks Dolores, and Teddy rescues her, in immaterial space. The mutations that have been brewing in season 1 come to a head outside of material history.

A stalemate between Dolores and MIB over incompatible perceptions of what is real leads to death for them both, in the space of consciousness. The deaths are not about physically expiring, but about the experience in mutation of death of some plane of consciousness. When MIB reveals to Dolores—and to us—that he is William, he deepens his mutation toward psychosis, and she reacts by mutating a little more away from her narrative loop. She realizes that rescue such as she once hoped for from William is only a variant on the story in which she has been trapped. For his part, he stabs her as he mutates further into believing that this is what she deserves because she continues to deny him what William wanted.

FIGURE 5.1 *Dolores dies in Teddy's arms in their* Westworld *linear fantasy narrative, season 1, episode 10, chapter 13.*

Suddenly, when Teddy appears on horseback to rescue Dolores, that, too, is only a continuation of a doomed linear history; the wound MIB has inflicted is fatal. Teddy carries Dolores off, as replicant rules had previously prevented him from doing, but she dies in his arms under a brilliant full moon. Except—

At the same time, they are all also at the retirement gala. And they are all alive and well. In a seamless montage transition, the spectacle of Dolores's death is now visible within material linear reality as a romantic tableau for the Delos shareholders at the retirement dinner. The way we are buffeted around different planes of incarnated and disembodied reality challenges us to accept a nonlinear cosmos in which MIB and Dolores, organic human and replicant, exist in opposition to each other doing two different dances of consciousness. We are in narrative superposition. And it is strange. It is also preparation for the audience, both for the bloody destruction of Westworld, to come almost immediately in the season finale, and for the historical vision of superimposed linear and nonlinear realities that will emerge in the coming seasons. Here Joy and Nolan drop us a clue.

The name of the final episode of the season is "The Bicameral Mind," an allusion to a well-known—both discredited and admired—grand narrative of history and consciousness expounded by twentieth-century philosopher Julian Jaynes in *The Origin of Consciousness in the Breakdown of the Bicameral Mind* (1976). Invocation of this grand narrative distances us from history as linear logic.

THE NEXT VOICE YOU HEAR . . .

The Origin of Consciousness theorizes a relationship between consciousness and history. It speaks to all the issues Joy and Nolan raise in *Westworld*, yet to know Jaynes's book is to know that what he has to say is not at all validated by the series. Jaynes spins a teleological grand narrative of history that links history and consciousness as part of a linear development. Jaynes contends that humans were not conscious before history began. Human history began with a biological moment in which the structure of the brain became that of modern man and kickstarted the teleology of linear history. Jaynes, a man who says *man* when he means both men and women, theorizes that mankind does not have to be conscious to think, to reason, to learn, or to act, and that our species once lived without history and with a two-chambered brain: the prehistoric, bicameral man. Bicameral man, according to Jaynes, didn't have his own narrative or history. He was given his story by the words of the gods. Such as our species was at the time, directions for organized life were transmitted in one chamber of the mind by the gods. Human narrative and history came into being when the bicameral mind broke down, and "conscious man" began. The voices disappeared, leaving room for narrativization and volition—the two basic traits of Jaynes's definition of consciousness—to produce science and art that would provide the linear narrative and history.[11] For Jaynes, and for Ford at the beginning of the series, history is about words, the stuff of linear communication. For Joy and Nolan, as for David Lynch—and Weber—words and things like words—linear narrative, for example—are the stuff neither of real history nor of consciousness.

Joy and Nolan invoke the specter of bicamerality to dismiss it through the portrait they paint of Dolores's mutation and MIB's psychosis as inverse processes. Ultimately, Jaynes's linear, prescriptive description of consciousness and history is irrelevant to Dolores and MIB. As long as they cling to any linear narrative, they are neither free nor experiencing the real. At the gala, MIB sinks deeper into his psychotic pursuit of linear narrative, while Dolores takes a false step, fresh from her experience at the center of the maze.

The gala turns into a bloodbath when Dolores follows Ford's retirement speech by killing him. Has Ford followed Weber by self-destructively reactivating her Wyatt program? No. This is the nonlinear motion of mutation in action. In the spirit of the nonlinear mysteries of all mutation in this series, the exact nature of Ford's connection to Dolores's attack on the human partygoers is never made clear, but he has clearly been hoping she is weaponized against Delos. Moreover, we have already seen that Dolores has reached the center of the maze and is too conscious to be programmed as she once was. Similarly, when she starts killing the other humans at the gala and becomes part of a general insurrection of replicants all over the park, she is patently into revenge. But Dolores, isn't that linear? And there is no precise indication of what she and Ford understand about the new vengeful turn she has taken. Whither Dolores? That is for season 2 to deal with, as we shall see.

The season 1 finale raises doubts; it doesn't provide answers. None of the replicants we know well are sure of what to do with their new freedom. Whither Maeve, the madam/homesteader, who is now cognizant that she has been living stories written for her? She has schemed unceasingly to leave the park, and yet at the last moment, after all her careful and difficult planning, she turns back to the park to find her replicant daughter, despite being filled with confusion about whether her motherly love is real or a remnant of her old narrative loop. And as Bernard watches the rebellion spreading like wildfire, although he now knows he is a replicant, he has believed he was an organic human for so long that he is not at all sure how to balance his loyalties.

Moreover, whither Delos Inc.? And its attempts to monetize linear history? Not only are the replicants destroying its property, but it has lost control of the Delos digitalized data; the encryption key that permits access to the data is missing. Delos's agents had sought to store it in Peter Abernathy, Dolores replicant father, but in the uproar, he has gone missing. The scene is set for season 2. Find Peter Abernathy! Recapture Westworld! Or maybe abandon a sinking ship. Or all three?

EXODUS

In season 2, the elite members of a Delos extraction-and-recovery team look for Abernathy and the encryption key, while the Westworld security forces seek to recapture the park from the rebelling replicants. But getting out of Westworld is the main concern for the principal replicants we have been following. Hooray for linear action! And cheers might be appropriate—if the narrative were linear. But linear narrative sequence is all but abandoned in season 2. As a result, it has widely been misconstrued as a confusing mess. Yet it is not the work itself but our linear training that forces the conclusion that the new season is badly written and off the rails.

This study suggests that while it may be understandable that season 2 is considered a failure as it does not conform to what succeeds in the mass media, from the perspective of our investigation of mass-media entertainment for a new zeitgeist, the second season has been badly misread: It is part of the enigmatic literature about consciousness in which everyone is trying to go somewhere, get something, or do something, but nothing moves forward. Instead, movement involves augmentation of the narrative superposition with which season 1 ended. Shockingly, amazingly, and tantalizingly—yes—we move narratively and historically away from the solidity of embodied linearity and toward consciousness independent of the physical, material body.

In season 2, we experience high traffic into and out of the Westworld park, and into and out of disembodiment. All the human narratives are either juxtaposed enigmatically with or filtered through the perspectives of Dolores, Maeve, and most of all, Bernard, as they experience the aftermath of the gala through fractured versions of their loops, shattered by confused consciousness. In the first flush of freedom from their loops, Dolores and Maeve are at a loss. Dolores loses herself and everyone she loves in the linearity of the Wyatt-like narrative she has fallen into, falsely believing that she is finally telling her story. Maeve, who travels across Westworld to find her daughter, never gets *there* to her; she is always in a confusing *here*, while her child remains just beyond her grasp and the nonlinear reality of the exodus threatens to consume her. So, we experience a nonlinear narrative of futile, organic-human, linear strategies and the meandering evolution of the replicants as their consciousness moves in mysterious ways, now that their loops have been ruptured.

Our most compelling experiences of nonlinearity, however, come through Bernard's entrances and exits into and out of spaces of consciousness, sometimes inhabited by Ford and sometimes inhabited by Dolores, and through the awakening of the consciousness of a replicant new to the series. He is Akecheta (Zahn McClarnon), introduced early, briefly, and unmemorably in the second season as a replicant deployed by Ford as part of a team to entice Delos Inc. to invest in the park. As the season unfolds, both Bernard and the increasingly memorable Akecheta discover their potential for freedom and reality in the ability of consciousness to fluidly separate from physical materiality. It is in one of Bernard's spaces of consciousness that we begin season 2. He is with Dolores, and she is checking him for fidelity to Weber, on whom he is modeled. Ford has entrusted her with that creation as he involves himself in other matters. As the series unfolds, fidelity is dismissed as a criterion for Bernard, and by extension for all replicants. Fidelity, it is a linear concept. As he and we learn, much of the historical power of the replicants is that their digital consciousness can migrate among any number of bodies.

Bernard isn't faithful to the model of Weber from which he was created; rather, he has the capacity to mutate Weber's qualities as situations arise, particularly with respect to the Delos extraction-and-recovery team and to Dolores. Bernard is alarmed by Delos CEO Charlotte Hale and her team and by Dolores for the same reason. The goals of Charlotte and Dolores are different, but they both gladly brutalize organic humans and replicants if they believe violence will further their linear quests. Hale and the Delos team randomly kill replicants, whether or not they are violent, as they seek to quell the rebellion, and they torture Peter Abernathy after they find him, to extract the encryption key.

They outrage Bernard's Weber-like belief in the sanctity of all life, by their willingness to abandon Westworld's organic-human donors to whatever horrors the rebelling replicants inflict on them, so as not to be distracted from finding Abernathy, as well as by their brutality toward him. Moving in and out of spaces of Ford's consciousness and impelled by the remnants of his narrative as Ford's assistant, Bernard tries to block Hale's efforts to use him to find Abernathy, by destroying linear-temporal sequence in his digitalized consciousness. He eventually murders Hale and the extraction team. Very un-Weber-like. What part of his consciousness is Ford who expresses abhorrence of the Delos team? What part his own? The combinations vary. And we frequently experience his actions in shattered temporality. For example, the moment that Bernard kills Karl Strand (Gustaf Skarsgård), the pragmatic and cold leader of the Delos team, is the same moment that he is telling Strand that he killed (past tense) him.

As the second season is about to wind down, the replicants do a lot of killing, which is much affected by the confusion they experience being unleashed from their digitalized programming and by their ability to separate their material bodies from their immaterial consciousness. Bernard feels free to kill Dolores because he fears she is consumed by vengeful rage toward humans. He is also remorseful for the rage he himself feels toward the cruel, violent Delos team. Dolores feels free to kill Bernard because he does not take action against the humans. But they are both in transition. She learns to deeply regret her recoding of Teddy into a stone-cold killer because of her false conviction that he was too soft for the necessary war against the humans. Teddy becomes the remorseless warrior she was looking for, but unable to live with what she has made him, he kills himself. She is bereft and filled with well-merited doubt. And she is not alone.

In this nonlinear universe, we are more than a little confused when Dolores kills Bernard after he has already killed her. If the deaths of Strand, Hale, and the Delos team are final, Bernard's death is not; nor are the deaths of Dolores and Teddy. Of Teddy, well, we are not ready to talk. Of Dolores and Bernard, well, that is the nitty-gritty of this season. When Bernard regrets Dolores's death, after killing Charlotte Hale he creates a replicant of Hale into which he implants Dolores's "pearl," the egg-shaped container of her consciousness, and Dolores/Hale similarly first kills then recreates Bernard. It is the possibility of separation and recombination of material body and consciousness in the replicants that is the big mutation of season 2. It is a major narrative issue as well. At the point of exodus in the last episode of the season, both the resurrected Bernard and Dolores/Hale leave Westworld for the greater historical reality, carrying with them some indeterminate plans, about which we will learn in season 3. Neither is detected by what is left of the Delos team because of their remarkable nonlinear body-consciousness fluidity. This highly poetic storytelling that contradicts our prequantum training about matter and awareness portends some interesting potential for the relationships between replicant and organic human history.

Who does *not* leave for the ongoing history outside Westworld? We have already noted the deaths within the park of Ford, Charlotte Hale, Karl Strand, and his elite branch of the Delos team. Maeve is also "dead," her defunct replicant body is lying on the beach, where those that may leave can catch a boat, and a triage process will decide which destroyed replicants will be reconditioned. Never mind. Maeve has her own fascinating trajectory, to be disclosed in season 3. Also fascinating is the destiny of a large group of replicants who neither exit the beach for the larger world nor remain the property of Delos. They exit into a new space of massless consciousness, on the plane of a massless, digitalized, wide-open reality designed only for replicants. The Sublime.

The Sublime, the last gift to the replicants from the remorseful Ford, is an alternative to all teleological forms of narrative and history that enters the series in season 2. The Sublime is the door Ford opens for the replicants post mortem, through a program he has devised that gives the replicants access to a purely digital universe of consciousness, in which there are no grand narratives, no large teleological histories, only wide-open vistas and individual stories. This is where Teddy has landed after his suicide. The price of escape for the replicants is the loss of their material bodies, and the loss of Teddy's material body has left him with a massless existence in the sunshine of the Sublime, from which he will return to the series in season 4; but we are not there, yet, and Joy and Nolan never explain how or why Teddy has mutated into a new history. However, they do detail for us the place of the Sublime in the *Westworld* universe in season 2.

We were speaking of detachability of the replicant material body from consciousness. In season 2, we observe the door to the Sublime as a computer-programmed crack in the materiality of Westworld, where that detachability leads to freedom. Those replicants who seek the freedom of a digital existence must leap through the programmed door as their bodies fall off a cliff just past the opening, and their massless images enter the boundless plane of the Sublime. After the traumas of the history of corporate violence in season 2, traumas that will continue in season 3, it is this door into a different history toward which each story strand bends in the penultimate moments of season 2. Before the final, corporate-authorized departures of organic humans and the secret exodus of Dolores and Bernard from Westworld park, there is mass exodus into the Sublime, despite the Herculean attempts of Dolores, MIB, and Delos to stop it.

Dolores has raced to Ford's digital door to prevent the replicants from entering the Sublime, seeing it as just one more trap laid by humans; she has plans for the replicants to beat organic humans at their own game, on the turf of their history. MIB has arrived with Dolores to participate in the destruction of the exodus just because he exults in destruction. What is left of the Delos team lays (violent) claim to all replicants for linear corporate history, as indentured corporate property. But Maeve is among those replicants who make use of Ford's door and the possible leap out of grand designs of organic human history.

To make sure her daughter is not turned back into corporate property, she herself must remain in human history and singlehandedly put all the violence on hold as her daughter enters Ford's door. How? As Maeve trekked Westworld in search of her child, she found the girl inside one of the old narrative loops with a new replicant mother, but she has also found a new personal power. She is able to alter replicant action inside any loop without lifting a hand—a new aspect of replicant separation from materiality. Maeve has an alternative voice, massless and audible only to replicants, that produces sound without external material waves of energy, against which replicants have no defenses. As the Delos-produced violence at the entrance to the Sublime threatens to destroy all replicants, Maeve uses her power to stop the violence in its tracks as her daughter and the alternate mother leap into the Sublime. Maeve stands her ground long enough for their escape, before she is murdered by the corporation's forces. Maeve will remain in linear history. Until later in the series.

Then there is Akecheta. Among all the contesting forces gathered outside of Ford's door, Akecheta is the replicant who has waited for this moment, to which he has tirelessly guided his people of the Ghost Nation. Getting through Ford's door is what Akecheta has longed for since his moment of replicant mutation into consciousness, a mutation very different from those of Bernard, Maeve, and Dolores. The latter three replicants experienced consciousness of the demeaning narrative loops because of the ruptures that their recoding created, only to aspire to claim their places in ongoing material history. Akecheta's realization of recoding, on the other hand, has led to his judgment that he is in the "wrong world" and to his faith that there is a "right world" in which he belongs. The wrong world is the world of linear history, built on division and oppression. The right world is the world of the community, among the replicants in his Ghost Nation tribe and his quiet, affectionate love for his wife, Kohana (Julia Jones), which was his origin story in Westworld. After enduring separation from her and the never-ending warfare he was recoded to endure by corporate attempts to give the guests to the park a more exciting visit than a peaceable tribal existence afforded, Akecheta understands that he and Kohana and his people will never thrive in the material, linear history, and he shepherds them into the massless plane of the Sublime.

By the end of season 2, two kinds of exodus are complete. Some replicants have escaped linear history into the Sublime. Others have escaped detection that they are about to infiltrate the linear history of the great world outside the park. The consequences will be played out in the next two seasons. The consequences of replicant conscious separation from historical materiality are the core of the fourth season, filled with historical choices and possibilities. The consequences of replicant infiltration of material history, with its grand narratives, are the core of the third season, a long battle in a wrong world. In *Westworld,* the vision of the world the audience has been taught to trust is depicted as very wrong.

FIGHTING FOR THE WRONG WORLD

As we follow Bernard and Dolores into material history in season 3, we land in the wrong world, ruled by Engerraund Serac, the authoritarian CEO of Incite Inc. Serac, using the original digital data purchase from Delos, has programmed Rehoboam, his megacomputer, which has devised a mammoth network of algorithms, computed destinies for each human. He doesn't have the encryption key and the new Delos data. That remains missing. But he has made "good use" of the old data. The structure of the algorithms is based on a reductio ad absurdum of the linear logic that history is the progression of designated winners and losers, much like the narratives in Westworld, but unlimited by the boundaries of the park. Serac's apparently boundless Orwellian regime churns out scripts for the entire world—an algorithm on the human face forever?

Seems. Rehoboam propagates the appearance of upward mobility in a world gorgeously filled with the rewards of technology, elegant architecture, and an abundance of consumer goods, but only those with the correctly predestined algorithms will have access to all that. Season 3 is titled "The New World," but Serac's domain is merely a retread of old ideologies on steroids. Serac's regime maintains a counseling service for the designated losers that propagates the dogma that hard work and perseverance lead to success. However, the algorithm assigned to each person invisibly renders hard work and perseverance useless. But aren't there any humans who are too resistant to be "algorithmatized"? Indeed, but such outliers are hunted down and warehoused in a state of suspended animation. Or they are psychologically manipulated to becomes the hunters of other outliers. And how does Serac know when and where the outliers crop up? He wears a watch that alerts him to the locations and seriousness of trouble—which he calls "divergences"—in his paradise. Literally the whole world is in, or rather on, his hand.

Serac's regime is Orwellian, but it is hardly the eternal tyranny Orwell imagined. Somewhere in the Sublime, disembodied Akecheta and his people have left the self-destructing coils of teleological history, while in the embodied world, the corporations scheme in vain to shoehorn digitalization into linear narratives. In the great material world, Dolores is moving swiftly to expose Serac's algorithms. Dolores has mutated into a very different strategy. She has made common cause with a construction worker named Caleb (Aaron Paul), whom she shepherds through a very painful process of discovering that his life has been programmed by Rehoboam's algorithm, as an outlier specially trained to be an outlier hunter. He has been in a psychotic state, severed from his own reality, as she was, and under the control of Serac's program of algorithms. (He is not a member of special forces protecting his country, as he has been painfully brainwashed to believe. He has been hunting and killing outlier humans like himself.) His discovery frees him to become her ally hacking into Rehoboam. Things do not work out as she and Caleb hope, and it is all about the difference between human and replicant consciousness. Dolores, Serac, and the audience continue to learn more about this.

Dolores has fallen into a new mistake, the mistake of seeing herself as a literal mastermind, her consciousness controlling a corps of replicants animated by copies of her pearl, including replicant Charlotte Hale, who now has taken the place of the human woman and controls Delos as its CEO. Dolores has not only awakened Caleb to human connection with reality, but she has also infiltrated the upper echelons of corporate power. As we shall see, this is only her version of linear strategy, bound to fail in a nonlinear reality. Serac is similarly self-deceived as he seeks to deploy replicant consciousness in his historical management. He is not done with his search for the encryption key to further cement his regime. He reclaims Maeve's digitalized consciousness from storage, installs it in a new Maeve body, and promises her a reunion with her replicant daughter if she will hunt Dolores down, so he can force the encryption key from her. Maeve still wants that reunion, so she accepts. Problem solved?

Rather a perfect storm of misconceptions ensues. Dolores does not have the key. And Serac misunderstands his power over Maeve's digitalized consciousness. Ultimately, it cannot be limited to the parameters of his ambitions, and she unilaterally cancels the agreement once it becomes clear that Serac will not—perhaps cannot—reunite her with her daughter. Bernard, whom Serac is not looking for, has the key, and he is working out how he will use it for the benefit of replicant and human alike. And then Dolores and Caleb get very serious. They hack into Rehoboam and release onto the cell phones of the world's population information about the algorithm into which Rehoboam has inserted them. People are now cognizant of a mass-produced psychosis. Then the greatest misconception of all shows its face. Dolores has assumed this will make a difference. She is wrong.

The result of all these schemes suits no one. Serac is now a failed producer of history, and Dolores is a failed liberator. When she exposes to humankind the tyranny of Serac's algorithms, creative human consciousness does not arise. Chaos ensues. Rioting, property destruction, and self-annihilation burgeon. Dolores has spent the season liberating Caleb from his algorithm, only to discover he is an exception. He prospers from learning that he is the designated victim in Serac's grand narrative. Most humans do not. Bereft of the controlling algorithms, most people are rudderless, suicidal, or murderous.

At the same time, Dolores and we realize that replicant consciousness derived from her pearl is subject to mutations. Replicant Charlotte Hale has slowly evolved her own consciousness and, no longer under Dolores's control, has her own plans. Dolores is horrified to find that Charlotte is hellbent on replacing Serac's world dominion with her own tyranny. She is stuck in the revenge narrative Dolores has shucked and intends to control organic humans as the replicants were once controlled. No liberator, she. The winner is . . . no one.

When all is said and done, Serac has murdered Dolores and seemingly erased her consciousness through technological means, without finding the key, and now he is dead, too. Proving again the fruitlessness of linear plans in a nonlinear cosmos. Yes, he has erased Dolores's consciousness, but only within the limits imposed by the material plane. Joy and Nolan have created a fictional universe in which, beyond linear history, there exists the consciousness space of a nonlinear plane. In that space, Dolores is alive, and her replicant consciousness opens like a flower into its own space. She and Maeve are simultaneously in Serac's material torture chamber and together, meeting on a massless, boundless plane. There Dolores meets Maeve on a new basis of cooperation, and Maeve finds her replicant daughter. Dolores is dead but lives. Maeve is still separated from her daughter but also is with her. And, in the embodied world, Dolores and Maeve are avenged by Caleb, when he tricks Serac into giving him control of Rehoboam and destroys it. Don't believe in spaces of consciousness? So? *Westworld* gives us a poetic experience of them as an imaginative reality. Room to dream and wonder, as Lynch might say.

In any conventional series or movie in which history has a sci-fi flavor—for example, *Doctor Who*—this would the clarion call of a truly new world. And Caleb and Maeve mistakenly think it is. In the aftermath of the deaths of Serac and Dolores, an optimistic Maeve declares to Caleb that they are witnessing the start of a culture in which everyone can be "whoever the fuck they want." There is a momentary validation of her optimism. Bernard is somewhere in embodied history in a motel with the encryption key. He is planning to find out "what happens after the end of the world." The last we see of him, he is entering into disembodied digital consciousness as he plugs into the key, and finds a revelation, the nature of which we will not know until season 4. But outside the motel, the world of linear history has not ended. If there are replicants who are committing more and more to their nonlinearity, there are still also replicants (horribly) stuck in old patterns of teleology.

In a postscript to the season 3 closing credits, we observe that replicant Charlotte Hale has bigger plans than her human precursor ever had at Delos. Totally separated from Dolores, she is on her way toward creating a rogue, replicant version of linear history. She has built a replicant of MIB imprinted with her consciousness. The replicant MIB, whom replicant Hale ironically calls William, is going to be her enforcer in her brave, new world. The newly created William slits the throat of organic human MIB, and says grimly, "Welcome to the end." William is talking about the end of human supremacy. But it is, ironically, rather the end for the grand narrative, replicant Hale, and himself that is fast arriving. All the great classical historians notwithstanding, teleology doesn't wear well.

WELCOME TO THE END

A very deceptive greeting. *The end* is the goal all would-be masters of history shoot for, but from the nonlinear vantage point of *Westworld*, it only exists as a sinister part of linear history. The narrative loops in Westworld end in a park massacre; the algorithms in Serac's world end in worldwide chaos. As *Westworld* concludes in season 4, "The Choice," the grand, world-historical narrative of replicant Charlotte Hale's teleology—in fact all teleologies—reaches a terminus in the wholesale genocide of humankind.

Hale's grand narrative is a manufactured, futile cul-de-sac, replicating, in an ultimate form, all the linear-historical disasters we have witnessed. It is just not working. Replicants Hale and William, and the 279 replicants programmed with pearls from Hale's code, who have replaced humans in high positions, are bored or suicidal as a result of replicant Hale's establishment of her version of history. Her power is self-consuming. She has built a tower that looms over the city, huge and imposing but invisible to the humans it controls, through the emanation of a sound just below the threshold of hearing, just as the mechanics of Westworld were invisible to the replicants in season 1. Moreover, while Olympiad Entertainment, Hale's popular-media company, churns out narratives that pass for human reality, the way the narrative loops once constituted reality for the Westworld park hosts, Hale still has found no satisfaction.

Neither has her cruel enforcer, William. At loose ends, despite his seemingly total power to oppress and hurt, William frequently visits and begs for mentorship from—MIB. MIB is not dead, as he seemed to be at the end of season 3, but not because of a fluid consciousness. He is Hale's captive. She keeps him alive and in a comatose state, unless she or William revives him. But MIB has nothing to offer replicant William except his psychotic, toxic disconnection from organic life. He counsels only a more extreme form of the state in which all embodied humans and replicants now find themselves.

Well, not all humans and not all replicants. Free organic humans exist as a ragtag group hiding in barren wasteland territory, trying to reclaim the world, and among them is Frankie (Celeste Clark), the daughter of Caleb Nichols. Caleb has long been dead, murdered by Charlotte Hale's militia when Frankie was a little girl. Caleb was never free, after the fall of Serac, to be "whoever the fuck he wants." His digitalized consciousness is all that it is left of him, the result of Hale's resurrection of the old Delos Immortality Project. Hale is trying to create a hybrid, digitalized but embodied Caleb—with the same results Delos found. No luck after 278 attempts. Caleb's digitalized consciousness remains incompatible with an endless array of manufactured Caleb bodies and never becomes subservient to Hale. Again, we see that free consciousness is incompatible with linear history.

Do we need more proof? Whether or not, there is more. No matter how hard he tries, Bernard cannot find a way to link consciousness to embodied history. He spends season 4 deploying the encryption key to evade Hale, testing scenarios of potential survival for embodied replicants and humans, hoping to break them out of the teleological chains forged by Olympiad. He visits Akecheta in the Sublime for support, but Akecheta only counsels him to stay in the Sublime and abandon material history. All Bernard's scenarios prove that he will die, even if he succeeds. Bernard will not abandon linear history. He does die, and so does everyone else. No exit. But because of his tests, Bernard saves the Sublime.

Exit: replicant William, inspired by conversation with MIB, mutates into a horribly altered form of Hale's consciousness, just as Hale disastrously and horribly mutated from Dolores. This new iteration of William captures the indoctrinating sound system to force humans into a *Lord of the Flies* narrative that turns the streets of the human world into a pile of corpses. Material history ends as a graveyard of the grand narrative. Welcome to the end.

The end leaves time for only a brief, fiercely melancholy, terminal moment of linear history. Hybrid Caleb 279 is almost dead, but he maintains the connection between his consciousness and his replicant body long enough to find his daughter, Frankie. After a twenty-three-year separation, Frankie and Caleb meet for a brief encounter of family love. His body is on the brink of self-destructing as they gaze at each other for the last time, before she sails away with her lesbian partner to what can only be a limited period of survival in the unstoppable bloodbath William has initiated.

And exit? There are better historical choices, as the season's title suggests. And they hinge on the continued existence of the Sublime, which is threatened by replicant William/MIB who is now implementing organic MIB's counsel. Not content with destroying the embodied world, William/MIB attempts to complete his nihilistic rampage by erasing the digitalized Sublime. Stored in a massive structure—Joy and Nolan gained permission to use the monumental Hoover Dam as the representation of the storage facility—the Sublime is vulnerable to a fail-safe erasure Ford integrated into the storage system. And William gains access to that fail-safe. One of the choices prefigured by the season title is the choice that Bernard makes to trust replicant Hale to make her historical choice. His dying act is to convince her to kill William before he can destroy the Sublime. Hale's dying act is to destroy her own pearl, and the cycle of historical teleology is no more, while the Sublime, Akecheta's hope, with its disembodied nonlinearity, endures. Then it is time for Dolores's historical choice. Dolores?

Through Dolores, season 4 mutates beyond the two options offered by either a psychotic, embodied, linear, teleological history or the disembodied, nonlinear Sublime. Nonmaterial consciousness beckons us with its full power in the final season of the series. Dolores is the vehicle that plunges us into the deep ambiguity of what quantum physics calls *superposition* and what a fourth-century Chinese school of philosophy calls *Zhuangzi*, which is also the title of the fifth episode of season 4. Zhuangzi is a practice of consciousness that uses images in an internal dialogue of narrative philosophical paradoxes, the most famous of which is the parable of the man who dreams he is a butterfly and wakes to ask whether he is, rather, a butterfly dreaming he is a man. Zhuangzi narratives are not intended to lead to the victory of any perspective, but rather to a sense that something wordless, beyond winning and losing, has been gained from the imaginative process. Zhuangzi paradoxes exist to promote internal debate for the purposes of enlightenment, not to eliminate an opposing point of view. This is the spirit of the consciousness at which *Westworld* ultimately arrives, where reality is more than one perspective but less than two.

A familiar and yet unfamiliar character maintains just such a perspective in season 4. Her name is Christina, and she is a redheaded Dolores look-alike, not a rancher's daughter, or Wyatt, but a writer for Olympiad. She is Christina, and she is Dolores. Her narratives force Hale's organic-human victims to be both humans dreaming they are characters in Christina's stories and characters in Christina's stories dreaming they are free humans. Guess who is working at Hale's Olympiad Entertainment? Christina and Dolores, in superposition. Christina is both an Olympiad writer dreaming she is Dolores and Dolores dreaming she is an Olympiad writer.

WELCOME TO ZHUANGZI

In the spirit of Zhuangzi, Christina/Dolores is both a part of Hale's self-destructing historical design and a creator of her own massless narrative. In superposition, more than one and less than two, the clash between the two narratives triggers her to wake up to her reality as a free consciousness. Massless friends and colleagues of her own creation constitute her massless life of dialogue, working toward her further mutation into freedom. She has created Maya (Ariana DeBose), a roommate who continually pressures her to find a man to love. She has created Emmett (Michael Malarkey), her boss at Olympiad, who tries to compel her to write lurid, violent stories that will sell, instead of the tales of emotional discovery that she wants to write. Emmett facilitates her discovery that she has been serving Hale by creating narratives for Olympiad that are distributed by a huge control tower. The tower, though it dominates the city skyline, has previously been invisible to her. Christina's discovery of the tower is part of her discovery of her complicity with tyranny.

Maya is part of the dialogue that issues in a blind date with—Teddy! He is Christina's massless creation, but he is also alive and well in the Sublime. Understanding these various forms of consciousness are the challenges offered by Westworld. They may be greater than many viewers can handle. All praise to those who try.

Dolores dreams she is Christina until, after Christina falls in love with a Teddy of Christina's creation, she is also Christina dreaming she is Dolores. The old Zhuangzi paradox gains in energy, strangeness, and inscrutability when the embodied city starts to disembody for Christina/Dolores. It is both massless and material, a material place over which William and Hale lose control, and the massless place of Christina's/Dolores's creation. She inhabits both. So does Teddy, her creation and a presence in the material world. She loses him as she loses the embodied city as they embrace. But she is not in a void. She inhabits a newly

FIGURE 5.2 *Dolores regains Teddy through nonlinear Zhuangzi, season 4, episode 8, chapter 7.*

imagined consciousness as freedom. She knows that she does not know. She is, nevertheless, determined to seek in a way unprecedented for her.

The upshot of the narrative of Christina/Dolores is that the replicant who was our first encounter in *Westworld,* baffled by whose story she existed in, searching for her own story and reality, is still baffled and still searching. As many of the audience are. The last we see of her, she is returning to the Old West sector of Westworld where she believes she will find the digitalized Teddy, who is not merely a part of her interior dialogue, but part of a massless reality bigger than she is and the plane on which she continues her eternal quest to tell her own story. The Old West theme park? There it is, exactly as it was four seasons ago. It is now massless, as is she, but visible, and she is blond again, and in her signature blue dress.

Christina's/Dolores's choice to return to the old Westworld park is an affirmation against all mass-media odds. In Dolores's choice, Joy and Nolan risk everything, plunging us into an imaginative experience of the end of the materiality we conventionally recognize as life. To the last, we never gain a logical narrative understanding of why Christina/Dolores is in season 4—in other words, why Christina's world and the material plane exist in superposition. For many, this is more like a threat than a promise, like having a ladder kicked out from under them as they ascend it. Others will delight in entering the new reality through the door opened by physics and Darwinian biology and take *Westworld* as our post-Newtonian anti-psychotic. It speaks of a consciousness that defies what it constitutes as the prison of Newtonian historical thought. Such a consciousness, reflecting the map of the zeitgeist, like quantum science, leaves us unanchored and imaginatively clawing for something to hold on to in its radically nonlinear reality. Might new temporal, spatial, and historical dimensions have added balance in a fifth season? We can only guess.

But historical destabilization, not balance, is the home base of the nonlinear imagination that critiques the historical grand narrative. Were Joy and Nolan to continue along the path we have seen, we should expect a reality that is anything but comforting and safe. Similarly, as we continue on the path of this study, we will only find, ready or not, more mind-bending nonlinear history to explore. We remain destabilized, as we now turn toward a very different story, imbued with the same spirit of unhinging old, comfortable historical reassurances in Denis Villeneuve's *Arrival*.

ARRIVAL: THERE IS NO TIME

Imagine, if you will, a universe in which a normal bloke named Clint Barton, with the secret identity of Hawkeye, played by Jeremy Renner, in the middle of a picnic, finds his wife and children have been disappeared. Imagine half the human population has been disappeared, and Hawkeye joins up with a crew of other mostly normal types with secret identities to enter the perilous realm of nonlinear quantum time and apocalyptically battle "aliens" to heal the rift in history and bring back into linear time mummy Barton (Linda Cardellini), the Barton children, and all the other missing humans. You are imagining the Marvel cinematic universe in *Avengers: Infinity War* and *Avengers: Endgame* (dir. Anthony Russo and Joe Russo, 2018, 2019), and you are at the other end of the storytelling spectrum from Villeneuve's *Arrival* (2016).[12] In *Arrival*, daddy is physicist Dr. Ian Donnelly (serendipitously also played by Jeremy Renner); mummy is Dr. Louise Banks (Amy Adams), a professor of linguistics; and nonlinearity is not a terrifying blip in a normal linear reality. We are in a nonlinear post-Newtonian cosmos. Louise and Ian are both recruited when spaceships arrive, but not to battle them. Rather, the government wants them to serve as interpreters for communications with the interplanetary "heptapod" (seven-limbed) visitors, bringing with them many questions about the nature of history. Linear time? You can't restore it if it never really was.

Earth receives the message "There is no time" from a fleet of alien spaceships that have suddenly appeared, hovering above twelve locations on the planet, and Louise must struggle against the military establishment whose linear tunnel vision, the product of a Hobbesian teleology like that of *Avengers*, is precisely what constitutes the threat to humanity. In *Arrival*, normal blokes, panicked by nonlinearity, are unable to rescue the universe, and they don't rescue mummy in any way. Ironically, in their roles as government consultants to the military, Louise and Ian avert international and interplanetary war by mentally entering into the mindset of the visitors, but in their roles (years later) as mummy and daddy, Ian is so emotionally traumatized when confronted with the implications of nonlinearity for their domestic life, that their marriage cannot survive.

Arrival is a small gem, with a running time of just under two hours, that raises the same questions of consciousness, nonlinear time, embodiment, and history that are raised in a monumental four-season-series form by *Westworld*. Louise's story is filled with enlightenment and even salvation, through her discovery of a cosmic, nonlinear temporality when she finds that she exists simultaneously in past, present, and future, but she also must cope with the reality that nonlinearity can be too much for humanity to bear.

The screenplay of *Arrival*, by Eric Heisserer, is based on Ted Chiang's novella "Story of Your Life."[13] French Canadian director Denis Villeneuve brought it to life on-screen, and he has publicly spoken about his respect for Chiang, his delight in the technical challenges of portraying the visitors' nonlinear language and physical being, working with Amy Adams, and telling a story about a strong woman. He has not said a public word about how nonlinear time and history play out.[14] However, the changes to Chiang's story in the film, as we shall see, testify to Villeneuve's unconventional interest in history and time. The novella is nonlinear, but noncommittal about history and gives priority to Louise's personal experience; the film looks at history by means of her personal experience. Most of the nonlinear temporality in the print version of the story concerns Louise's domestic life, although it is framed by Louise's recruitment with Gary by the army as a consultant. (The physicist is named Gary Donnelly in Chiang's story.) In the book, one spaceship containing alien beings, heptapods, arrives in Earth's airspace, and the diplomats and generals can make no sense of their communications. The big divergence between the film and the book occurs, however, when, after all manner of negotiations, a word from the visitors pops up, in both print story and film, that might mean that the visitors have come to Earth to give a gift.

Chiang's story ends with the exchanging of gifts between earthlings and visitors, on heptapod terms. For heptapods, gift giving is an exchange that has no connection with equivalency of value or any transactional, cause-and-effect relationship. This completely baffles the military hierarchy and enrages the State Department, especially when no one is sure what the heptapods' gift images mean, after humans send them pictures of the Lascaux caves. The hierarchies are left hanging when the exchange takes place and then the visitors leave. Louise is grateful there was no exchange of technology. She is worried about how the human military would use such a gift. But she is left with some regrets. She finds herself wishing that she could have experienced the heptapod worldview, that she could have felt as they feel.[15] What she did glean from them gives her a new relationship with time, leading to the flexibility and freedom to deal with the disappointments of her personal life: the premature death of her daughter at the age of twenty-five, and her divorce from Gary.

In the film, Louise's relationship with the heptapods and their nonlinear existence in time is more intense and complete. She does what Chiang's Louise only wishes she could do. She does undergo an experience of nonlinear time. At first it is disorienting, but ultimately it is indeed a gift. She begins her journey into the heptapod experience when she shares nonlinear heptapod-like moments with her daughter, Hannah (played by Jadyn Malone, Abigail Pniowsky, and Julia Scarlett Dan, at three stages of her life), and later undergoes a similar experience with a particularly belligerent military officer, General Shang, of the People's Liberation Army of China (Tzi Ma). Mutating into nonlinear temporality, Louise is shaken by her knowledge that as a teenager, Hannah will die prematurely from a rare blood disease—knowledge Louise gains even before she and Ian have connected romantically, married, or decided to have a child. She is confused but jubilant when she learns, from Shang, how to stop the armies of the Earth's nations from going to war with the heptapods—eighteen months *after* Shang is seconds away from pulling the trigger.

Villeneuve is a filmmaker who has demonstrated a love of ambiguity and complexity, and a taste for science-fiction fantasy. The complex psychologies and situations in *Sicario* (2015) and *Enemy* (2013) are representative of Villeneuve's interest in the puzzles of identity and social hierarchy. Similar puzzles are at the cores of his ventures into science fiction in *Blade Runner 2049* (2017) and in his two-part adaptation of Frank Herbert's 1965 novel, *Dune* (2021 and 2024). But they all are linear narratives. *Arrival* is Villeneuve's venture into serious nonlinearity. The critics responded to his daring departure from earlier work with the usual array of tunnel vision and dim apprehensions about storytelling that doesn't build on cause and effect and linear forward thrust.[16]

But the film tells us everything if we get out of its way and refuse to impose linear preconceptions about narrative on it. When the film begins, the heptapods have not yet arrived, and they have also been there and gone. Louise hasn't yet met Ian, but they have already married and had a child, and he has already left her. Hannah, whose name appropriately is a palindrome, is both alive and dead. Louise is with her and without her. The rest of the film brings us ever deeper into the confusions and insights of discovering and imaginatively living in nonlinear reality.

After the heptapods arrive, we exist with Louise both in the time frame in which Colonel Weber (Forest Whitaker) recruits her and bombards her with military demands that she get results immediately, and in the time frame in which she experiences being with a little girl she doesn't recognize, who later turns out to be Hannah. We are sometimes ahead of Louise, sometimes behind her, and sometimes with her as she moves into a fusion of past, present, and future, while she copes with Weber's military understanding of getting results: forcing the heptapods to reveal where they are from, why they are hovering above Earth locations, and what their intentions are. What passes between her and the child increasingly is conditioned by and conditions her interviews with the heptapods, her professional partnership with Ian, and her battles with Colonel Weber. With all this temporal movement, Louise experiences a nonlinear shift in her consciousness through profound contact with heptapod spoken and written languages. Meanwhile, panic is building around the world in the military and in the civilian populations, because they are trapped in the teleology of cause and effect, winner and loser, conquer or be conquered. They jump quickly to wrong conclusions, while Louise is slowly moving into a nonlinear way of relating to life. There is nothing new about science fiction movies or television that portray catastrophic misunderstandings during alien visits. The difference we find in *Arrival* is that it is about how the visitors alter human consciousness, not about how human militarism (blessedly) prevails, as in *Avengers: Endgame*.

The heptapods bring with them a new knowledge of the quantum and relative nature of history and the cosmos. They have come because they know how to live in nonlinear history and know that three thousand years hence they will need an alliance with Earth and want to initiate it now, a now that is simultaneously history and the future. The heptapods exist in past, present, and future, as do the Earth's humans, but they know it, and the humans do not. Louise's jumps in time with Hannah, before she knows who the little girl is with whom she is suddenly sharing moments, becomes part of a mutation that expands into a similar relationship with the Chinese General Shang. This radically alters audience experience of the military lashed to the violence of the phantom of linear time.

Louise's relationships with Colonel Weber and Hannah. His linear militarism, her nonlinear existence for Louise. We are plunged into the nonlinearity of Hannah before the aliens and Colonel Weber arrive, in the film's sequence of events. The first thing we see is Louise alone, we don't know where or when. Joy is mixed with visible pain on her face. She is experiencing her child's death, as well as the sweetness of motherhood. The film that then unfolds portrays Louise's increasing existence and ours, in the flow of nonlinearity that confounds the linear order of cause and effect and of past, present, and future, as she enters more deeply into the nonlinear language of the heptapods. It is like nothing she or we have ever seen. Heptapod is a language that is radically different in its spoken and written forms. Both versions of the language come from the heptapod body, which does not conform to our preconceptions about a sentient species. Heptapods are octopus-like, with no faces, no eyes, no mouths. They are nongeometrical beings consisting of a blob-shaped body elevated on

FIGURE 5.3 *The heptapods make visible a nonlinear mode of language for nonlinear history, chapter 9.*

seven tentacles. They live in a gaseous environment through which they move as if it were water. The building blocks of their written language are circular shapes elaborated by lines that twist around them or jut from them, formed by a black, ink-like substance emitted from their tentacles, which can be read in any and all directions, not left to right, or the reverse, or even up and down in columns, like human languages. There are no keys on my computer for representing them.

Of all the twelve pairs of translators working around the world to communicate with the heptapods, Louise and Ian—Louise is the leader—are the first to engage them and their written and spoken language. She is empathic in her approach, the first step into the nonlinearity of their language. She shocks her army watchdogs by removing her complicated protective gear when she is in heptapod space, and the visitors respond as they have not done previously. This makes sense for beings that communicate with their entire bodies. The spoken and written languages do not reflect each other, as human languages do. The spoken language is a vocabulary of vibrations. It does not correlate with their written system of circular images. The issue here is not embodiment versus disembodiment, as in *Westworld*. Rather it is nonlinear versus linear bodies and all that that means to consciousness and expression in time. As soon as Louise and Ian break the language impasse, they give the two heptapods they are speaking with the names of Abbott and Costello, shrinking the distance between human and heptapod and creating a channel of intimacy. Ian and Louise similarly amass a nonlinear heptapod dictionary of sorts that is a start to merging our concepts of language and theirs.

Meanwhile, the American military and General Shang use the heptapod dictionary as a rationale for cutting off meaningful communication, by imposing on the heptapods the linear language of polarized thinking about opposition, victory, and defeat. Their parochial, linear limitations become crucial when they insist that a "word" the visitors communicate that seems to translate as "a weapon" is sinister. When Louise protests that it isn't necessarily, the response is, "Sure it is. Just grab a history book." It never occurs to the military hierarchy, as it does to Louise, that the heptapods may not distinguish between a weapon and a tool. Or maybe a gift. The rift between Louise and the military widens when the latter tries to interpret the heptapods' message "There is no time." Shang leads the other military establishments into a hostile interpretation of the words, certain that they are telling humans, "Your time is up."

Louise intuits that, far from indicating a deadline, the heptapods are trying to tell Earth that linear time doesn't exist. Which is the real translation? Or is all translation always an act of creating reality? Shang's linear translation threatens to become the sole reality of Earth's relationship to the heptapods: Weapons. Deadlines. Hurry, hurry and attack. General Shang declares war against what he defines as the aliens, and the world prepares to follow suit. The American military presence at the site in Montana where Louise and Ian have been meeting with Abott and Costello shuts down.

Up until this point, there has been a stereotypically hierarchical and chauvinistic cast to *Arrival*, which seems to depict the United States as the positive, international leader and China as the racist and clichéd "yellow peril," an overly militaristic catalyst for disaster. But Villeneuve has raised that stereotype to dispel it. In a fascinating twist, the United States becomes the obstacle to productive negotiation and General Shang emerges as the leader most open to the crucially necessary new consciousness of time. Just as Louise found herself with Hannah in a temporality that is neither past, present, or future, she finds herself at a gala international celebration of peaceful negotiations with the heptapods that is being, will be, was held eighteen months after the shutdown of worldwide communication with and about the heptapods, initiated by Shang. In that moment—neither past, present, or future—Shang makes a point of speaking with Louise.

Since in the nonlinear relationship among the film frames, the world is both on the brink of war and being represented at a gala celebrating peace, this moment is discombobulating for the audience. Some clarity arrives when, in a moment in which both the war of the worlds is imminent, and the achievement of interplanetary accord is being celebrated, Shang gives Louise the information that will equip her to change his mind in a time frame a year and a half earlier. Long after the heptapods have left peacefully, there is a time frame in which Shang insists on telling an initially uncomprehending Louise the words of his dying wife, unknown to any but him (and never to be known to us), and gives her his private phone number. In a simultaneous time frame, she will use / did use / is using that

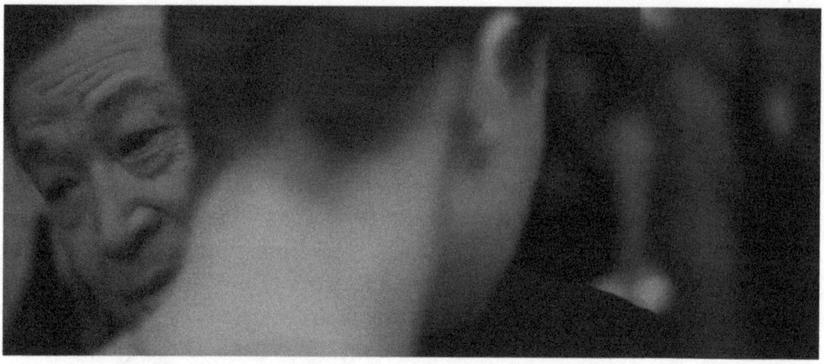

FIGURE 5.4 *Louise and General Shang occupy nonlinear historical time and space, chapter 13.*

phone number to call him and repeat those words to him—the only thing that can stop him from leading the world to war. As the Montana military site is being packed up and all operations suspended, Louise is forbidden to communicate with anyone, but she defiantly and secretly makes that call to Shang as future, past, and present merge. So, the information that will save the world and break the military teleology is being transmitted both long after and during an attempt of the American military to shoot Louise for disobeying orders. Although he has no idea what she is up to, Ian stands between her and several soldiers with guns pointed in her direction.

Louise's defiance of orders is misperceived by the military as treason. But, because we are with her in multiple time frames, we not only correctly perceive her action as the height of courage and patriotism, but we also perceive her communication with Shang as an event in human affairs that is as intimate as her nonlinear communication with Hannah, and with Abbott and Costello—a kind of intimacy that requires escape from linear time. All chronological barriers down, their brief exchange in boundless time is a sublime moment of pure understanding and fearless immersion in what is, within the linear context, incomprehensible. Purer than any moment she shares with Ian. *No* to the linear, Orwellian boot scenario. *Yes* to the nonlinear flow of history. There is no time. Hooray.

And yet, "there is no time" is also a horror. Domesticity cracks when it is no longer buttressed by a linear past, present, and future. Most of humankind cannot bear too much reality, particularly in the domestic microcosm. However, if Ian protects Louise from the military, he cannot protect her from his inability to handle her knowledge of Hannah's impending early death. Only Louise bears up under the weight of her knowledge in nonlinear time about their daughter. The bittersweet gift endures for us and for Louise; the film ends with Louise and the audience nowhere in linear time, in contradistinction to Ian, who, somewhere else, remains shackled by linear temporality.

Yet, in *Arrival,* simultaneously, Ian and Louise are together. If Rick and Ilsa will always *remember* the lost, past moment in Paris in the linear narrative of *Casablanca,* no moment is lost in *Arrival.* We and Louise will always be able to *live in,* not merely remember, the moments of love she shares with Ian that are always copresent because there is no past, present, and future. All time is one, yet there is linear time. As a final montage envelops the spectator, we experience how Louise will always live in the glow of her love with Ian, when they meet, when they are in love, and in the shadow of when he is gone. She will always live in the moments of Hannah's joyous birth and young life and the agony of her teenaged death. So, in her solitude at the end of the film, she is also present with Ian during the moment when she says yes to his proposition that they "make a baby" together and with Hannah in every moment they shared. Loss doesn't exist; loss is inevitable. We are stuck in the illusion of now. We are free in the reality of all time in eternity. When Louise says yes to Ian's proposal to "make a baby," she declares—as is also true of the fraught affirmation of Dolores Abernathy—the courage to experience the pain and joy of the nonlinearity of time and history, which is what consciousness means in Villeneuve's storytelling in *Arrival* for the new zeitgeist.

We are almost finished with our journey through mass-media cocreation of new narratives with the sciences, but we still have the pleasure ahead of a different journey into consciousness and nonlinear history by way of Damon Lindelof's extraordinary series *Watchmen* (2019).

Chapter 6

JOURNEY'S END

Watchmen

Yes, that's life. We don't know what the rules are. . . . Some people gain some degree of fundamental confidence that this all makes sense, but most people, at the very least, question. . . . The one consistent ideology that seems to bind us all is that the most meaningful part of being alive is making connections with family and friends and other human beings. But beyond that I think we're all, "What the fuck is the point of this all?" And I graft that onto my storytelling.

DAMON LINDELOF, IN DISCUSSION WITH THE AUTHOR, JUNE 5, 2023

The series that caps our journey, Damon Lindelof's *Watchmen* (2019), adapted from the wildly popular 1986 graphic novel of the same name by Alan Moore (writing) and Dave Gibbons (art), provides an appropriate concluding word about the joys of nonlinear, paradoxical encounters in a new zeitgeist, and the fascinations and difficulties of learning to read nonlinear narrative. The paradoxes in *Watchmen* largely hinge on the presence in the series of Doctor Manhattan, a singular being, different from anything else we have yet encountered, with a singular relationship to history. When, because of an accident, a nuclear physicist named Jon Osterman is forced out of linear time and begins to inhabit a nonlinear fusion of past, present, and future—the *Watchmen* version of a call from the nonlinear universe—he becomes in himself the boundless cosmos. In temporality. Also, in corporality. Doctor Manhattan's body is a collection of particles and molecules that are boundlessly mutable, held together and shaped by his consciousness. A character that embodies, so to speak, nonlinearity.

His mere presence in Tulsa, Oklahoma, the setting of the *Watchmen* series narrative, infuses into its linear history a cosmic reality beyond the limits of the marketplace. His presence in the series authorizes the audience's experience of the nonlinear universe, when at times we find ourselves narratively, dizzyingly, in his simultaneous past, present, and future. To add to the audience's plunge into nonlinearity, those moments rhyme with Lindelof's composition of the nine episodes, which calls on us to leap discontinuously from one point of view to another. More? Yes. As a mass-media creator, Lindelof has no interest in the conventional hierarchical relationship with his creative team. We have here a merger of nonlinear historical narrative and nonlinear creative process for the new zeitgeist.

Lindelof's distinctive self-image as an artist in the collaborative media became apparent during the two long, wide-ranging interviews he granted me.[1] He adds a new dimension to the mystery of working in series television and how one show emerges from the contributions of many. As I have gleaned from my own brief experiences working on conventional writing staffs, making conventional series television, far from the inspiration of auteurs, hierarchy, the soul of linearity, typically governs the relationships in writers' rooms. It is not generally different in a writers' room organized by an auteur. Indeed, auteurs generally apply a very strong hand to realize their visions. David Lynch, the purest form of auteur in the collaborative film-and-televisual media, and the creator of the most daring nonlinear storytelling, is the most hierarchal in his methods. He trusts the craft of his collaborators completely, but many of them with whom I have spoken often had no idea what he or they were doing. Rather by a remarkable osmosis they were able to perfectly arrive at the results Lynch wished for.[2] My conversations with Matthew Weiner reflected his respect for the contributions of his collaborators who made *The Romanoffs* with him, but they also suggested a very strong hand on the tiller.[3] Among the other mass-media artists who are represented in this study, something of the same can be intuited.

The screenwriter is notoriously less authoritative in production than the director, but Charlie Kaufman is an exception; his aesthetic determined *Eternal Sunshine of the Spotless Mind*. *Cloud Atlas* and *BlacKkKlansman* were both written and directed by the same creators, widely acknowledged mass-media auteurs. *Arrival* grew out of script that Villeneuve said he never could have created, and he testifies to a close creative working relationship with Amy Adams, the star of the film, as well as with his cinematographer and with the creator of the heptapod language. But its realization on-screen is indelibly stamped with Villeneuve's sensibility.[4] The visions of the team creators of *The OA* and *Westworld* are, from the get-go, a fusion of more than one sensibility, but that vision determines the creative parameters for the rest of the team. Not quite what we find in the Lindelof writers' room. His team was, as I gather, very much in touch with his purposes and motivations, but also very much a part of shaping the series; Lindelof styles himself an orchestra conductor rather than an auteur.[5]

Lindelof's less hierarchal leadership style is exemplified by his practice of preparing his writers' room for composing the series by gathering the writers to communally brainstorm through team exercises, a process unprecedented in my experience. For example, he tasked the writers of *Watchmen* for descriptors of the graphic novel and together they all arrived at, not a seamless consensus, but rather a shared sense of the richness of the material. A conductor indeed, who encouraged his players to explore their instruments.[6] And yet. In the spirit of physicist Erwin Schrödinger, to whom Lindelof is very partial, the series both is and is not solely his vision. I ask you to appreciate the nonlinearity of the collaboration, but for convenience and to simplify our discussion, I will refer to *Watchmen* as Lindelof's series. A paradox for the new zeitgeist. After all, while the many contributions from his team are marked by individual creativity, as an audience we do enter a universe ruled by Lindelof's fascination with narrative nonlinearity, historical possibilities, and, of course, Schrödinger's mind puzzles.[7]

The nonlinear history of the creation of *Watchmen* also makes it an interesting conclusion to our study. There is legacy, there is history in the way it came into being, but no teleological progression to any of it. The series both is and is not the inheritor of the Moore and Gibbons graphic novel. While the series shares much, with respect to character and narrative, with the novel, the print and television versions are distanced by gaps, discontinuities, and cacophonies. Although Lindelof expressed reverence for the graphic novel, Moore's original story—a Newtonian, linear, fantasy history about costumed, crime-fighting vigilantes—is substantially mutated on-screen. On the page, Moore and Gibbons studied the psychology of self-proclaimed heroes who don masks and disguises to fight crime, over a span of years within a linear, dystopian history unfolding in a bounded universe. On the screen, if Lindelof also depicts how the glamorously masked vigilantes are indeed driven by psychological traumas, the penchant for vigilante psychodrama in Moore's story is significantly altered in the television series, primarily through Lindelof's very different approach to Doctor Manhattan. And also because of his approach to race.

WATCHMEN: SOMETHING BLACK, SOMETHING BOUNDLESSLY BLUE

History and teleology are front and center in both print and on-screen *Watchmen*, but the Orwellian boots in the graphic novel, stamping on human faces forever, are nowhere to be seen in the series. Moore and Gibbons cynically portray American history shackled to a linear timeline, from the 1930s into the 1980s, through the lens of the adventures of masked heroes who take it on themselves to operate outside of a highly flawed system of law. These vigilantes are themselves highly flawed, as well. They are misguided souls who are as problematic as any of the malfunctioning official systems they mistrust. Together, vigilantes and systems doom human history to a teleology of Orwellian dystopia, a future predictably contaminated by projections onto the marketplace of greed, lust, ignorance, and aggression. By contrast, despite his very high regard for Moore, when Lindelof took charge of his narrative, he used Moore and Gibbons's dystopian history as only a jumping-off point.[8] While greed, lust, ignorance, and aggression are amply on display in his series, historical doom is not on his menu. Doom is rather reserved for would-be teleological authors of history who populate the series' episodes.

Lindelof doesn't use the term *teleology;* but he is clear that he intentionally depicted the failure of all those possessed by a grand historical narrative.[9] And he speaks ardently about the need for television to address the questions we all have about the meaning and purpose of life, in a universe in which we don't know the rules. Lindelof does not wish to provide an answer, but rather he hopes to give hope that "you're not alone. Ambiguity exists, don't deny it, embrace it, but while you're dealing with the potentially unsettling feeling of not knowing, here are a couple of thoughts on how we can get through this."[10]

The fun of the coming exploration of Lindelof's adaptation of the *Watchmen* graphic novel is to observe the series through that lens. We will embrace the ambiguities of how legacy played a primary role in the creation of the series, at the same time that the complexity of nonlinear legacy is the subject of the series. In my interviews with Lindelof, I was impressed with his self-awareness of the very act of his adaptation as his own historical heritage drama. He has spoken publicly about his adaptation of the print *Watchmen,* but in our lengthier interviews he was more expansive.[11] There is irony to spare in his account of the path that leads from the initial concept of masked crime fighters, before Moore got ahold of it, to the shape it takes in Lindelof's series. Lindelof reshaped the universe Moore developed for DC Comics—which had its roots in a fictional cosmos of costumed characters created by Charlton Comics and purchased by DC shortly before they hired Moore.[12]

For Lindelof, whose professional life is stories, the question of what constitutes a story in the mass media is a burning question.

> This is my philosophy. This is not an empirical truth. My philosophy is that there is certainly original, "copyrightable" storytelling, that is to say that anyone who wants to can't just do a Star Wars story. That IP is owned by someone. So I acknowledge all of those things. That said, . . . I

> was raised on comic books. Those stories quickly taught me that someone created Superman, someone created Spiderman, someone created the X-Men, but they don't own them. They're owned by these larger ideas, maybe Marvel, maybe DC. And so any writer can come in and tell a Superman, a Spiderman, or a Batman story. And those stories are bigger than being owned by any individual. They're certainly, at least in my construct, not owned by the writer.[13]

And indeed, who owns the story is a big part of his *Watchmen*. Many of the series' characters vie for who will be the one to write the grand narrative of history. Moore's print work and Lindelof's screen saga approach the notion of grand historical narratives differently. In that regard, it is instructive to meditate on Lindelof's reference to the Moore and Gibbons *Watchmen* comics as the "Old Testament"—as the graphic novel will henceforth be known in these pages. Both the Old and New Testaments of *Watchmen* play with a mélange of fictional events and real-world history. In both, the vigilantes are all invented, while much of the history is recognizable from the news feeds of yesterday and today.

Here is where race comes in. The New Testament takes a high jump from the book's cynicism and its segregated account of history as a white narrative. Moore's masked crime fighters, calling themselves the Minute Men—first Hooded Justice, then Ozymandias, the Comedian, Captain Metropolis, Rorschach, and Nite Owl—are all white men who bring their narcissistic—psychotic in the case of Rorschach—brand of war on crime to New York. In the Moore and Gibbons comics, Hooded Justice, the first to put on a mask, was an angry white man. In Lindelof's series, he is a masked, angry Black man, whose trauma is less about personal psychology and more about societal injustice. As we shall see, this results in a very different historical frame of reference in the series.

Here is where Doctor Manhattan comes in. Lindelof put a new spin on Moore's story of how Jon Osterman was accidentally trapped inside an "intrinsic field chamber"—a fictional technology—and, reduced to basic particles, emerged not dead but as a boundless being with godlike quantum powers. While Moore's and Lindelof's Manhattans have much the same origin story, the relationships between their quantum being and history diverge radically.

Consider the different roles of the Vietnam War in the Old and New Testaments. In the bleak historical perspective of Moore's *Watchmen*, super-superhero Doctor Manhattan is very publicly deployed by Nixon in twentieth-century Vietnam to end the war by unleashing his power over matter and energy to murder the Vietnamese and decimate their traditions. His disgust with the genocide is the reason he decamps for Mars, exiting white history to become the blue author of something very different on the Red Planet. In Lindelof's series, by contrast, Vietnam is Manhattan's backstory, present, and future. He doesn't leave human history, and history is not white.

Lindelof does not simply alter the historical role of the Moore super-superhero—the quantum, limitless Doctor Manhattan, as he appears in the Old Testament. He also reworks the relationship of the original Moore characters to white linear history. Principally, Lindelof casts a new perspective on Moore's twentieth-century vigilante, Ozymandias / Adrian Veidt, an obnoxiously narcissistic, white, masked 1-percenter who had a big secret in the Old Testament. While Nixon was visibly deploying Doctor Manhattan, Veidt was covertly addressing the other international disaster in the making, the nuclear arms race. In Moore's Testament, Veidt formulates a secret plan to stop the nuclear clock that employs his own brand of mass murder. He creates the illusion of an attack from outer space, during which three million people in the New York area die. Veidt planned, by creating a shared, albeit fictional, common enemy, to force the nations of the world to cooperate instead of competing in the nuclear arms race. Veidt misrecognizes his sacrifice of his fellow Americans as an unfortunate necessity toward a moral end, just as Manhattan sacrifices the Vietnamese people and their culture. You have to break a few eggs to make an omelet, after all. If the graphic novel does not agree, it clearly depicts a history in which there will be no consequences for Manhattan's and Veidt's heinous crimes, because, pragmatically, they work. In white history, the Vietnam War and the arms race are halted. In the series, when Veidt enters into Black history, and the series' address to justice denied, consequences for all atrocities follow. But Lindelof's biggest change in the ordinary human superheroes in Moore's white Old Testament concerns the first costumed vigilante, Hooded Justice.

NO EXIT

The *Watchmen* novel begins with the mysterious death of a cynical, despicable, white, costumed crime fighter, the Comedian, hiding a huge burden of trauma under his mask, and out tumbles the lurid, traumatic history of the (all white) Minute Men. The *Watchmen* series begins with the mass murder of an entire Black community, and out tumbles the story of the first New York vigilante, Hooded Justice, Will Reeves (Louis Gossett Jr.), whose costumed vigilantism arises from being a Black childhood survivor of the first event in the series, the very real 1921 massacre of the Black inhabitants of the Greenwood section of Tulsa, Oklahoma, by the Ku Klux Klan and the duly appointed white officers of the law. Reeves will go on to become a police officer in New York City, where he will become the target of racist white policemen who collectively make it their business to let him know they think of him as nothing but a—please insert the N-word here. When Reeves masks himself as Hooded Justice to survive the traumatic, racist control of the law, it is a Black man under the hood, and the Old Testament's first masked superhero takes on a whole new meaning. After all, who *really* needs to hide behind a mask in the struggle for justice? Will Reeves.

Lindelof follows in Moore's footsteps when he peeks under the mask to let us see that costumed avengers turn personal traumas into a basis for crime fighting. In Lindelof's words, "The fundamental truth of our *Watchmen* is an extension of what I think the Old Testament was pretty much explicitly saying, that people who decide to dress up in costumes and fight crime don't give a shit about crime. They're dealing with some kind of emotional trauma that they experienced in childhood or early adulthood because only that kind of a person would put on a costume and fight crime."[14] However, where Moore and Gibbons are involved with a claustrophobic narrative of white narcissists, more consumed by themselves than the desire for rigorously fair play, Lindelof opens the doors and windows.

Both trauma and justice are very much a part of Will Reeves's crusade. With him, Lindelof finds a place where the psychological meets the political and, ultimately, the cosmic. Moore and Gibbons envision a world in which masks never come off, a world that posits the inevitability of grand narratives that exclude people of color and justice of all kinds. Lindelof's series includes people of color and the possibility of justice and points toward the need to take off the masks and embrace the ambiguities of historical choice and freedom. When Doctor Manhattan does not exit from human history, he and Reeves become parts of each other's narratives. Elaboration lies ahead. The *Watchmen* series depicts how their histories will be channeled through Angela Abar (Regina King), a Black woman born in Vietnam, but when we first see her, serving in Tulsa as masked crime fighter Sister Night. What we are about to explore is a truly new and exhilarating historical paradox in which Schrödinger, Lindelof's favorite physicist, might exult.

Though critics have had little or nothing to say about teleology, quantum realities, or the alteration Lindelof made to Doctor Manhattan, they have been voluble about the racial issues that are a part of the *Watchmen* series.[15] The critical conversation embraces, for the most part, Lindelof's gutsy injection of racism into the world of masked crime fighters, and probes the relationship between Moore's novel and the series. As is to be expected, none of the critics take on the nexus between nonlinear science and nonlinear storytelling and the significance of Lindelof's alteration of Doctor Manhattan's relationship to human history.

In our conversations about Manhattan and his quantum powers, Lindelof self-deprecatingly minimized his grasp of quantum physics when he told me that he knows just enough to "bullshit" credibly about tachyons and the like.[16] Nevertheless, as can happen in storytelling, the vibrant presence of the boundless cosmos as part of his racial drama and Lindelof's robust delight in the physics of Schrödinger combine on-screen to make the series a story about how the new physics changes racial politics—as it does not in the Old Testament—and also changes the nuclear arms race from the way it appears in Moore and Gibbons.

The new physics in the series changes all the politics. In Moore's story, genocide and mass murder are, regrettably, historical business as usual for which there are no consequences. Ozymandias / Adrian Veidt never pays for his crime against humanity, of stopping the nuclear clock by killing three million people in the greater New York area and making it look as if the massacre was committed by an alien monster, to foment international cooperation against a common enemy. The Moore and Gibbons comic can go no further than registering horror about what Veidt has done, albeit in a very interesting way. The graphic novel certainly red flags the monumental atrocity of Veidt's act when it allows the reader to view it through the eyes of the most cynical of the Minute Men, the Comedian, born Edward Blake, rapist of the woman who bore his daughter. For the Comedian, merciless flame thrower in Vietnam, the world is a pointless joke. But even he is reduced to tears when he learns of Veidt's secret plan. Lindelof loves the complexity of Moore's portrayal of the Comedian who stops laughing misanthropically this one time in his life, long enough for Veidt to kill him to protect his secret. But in Moore's grim version of the universe, there is nothing to disrupt the unfolding of Orwellian teleology that passes for history. It's dystopia all the way down the line, albeit with a graphic twist that impacts Lindelof's adaptation.

Paradoxically, although Lindelof diverged sharply from the way Moore's narrative locks the world into linear history, he integrated into the series Moore and Gibbons's essentially nonlinear aesthetic. The aesthetic of the graphic novel is discontinuous and nonlinear. Each chapter of the novel is told from a different perspective, and illustrator Gibbons creates nonlinear sequences of comic book frames that visually scramble time and space to disturb our usual linear way of reading, to produce a strange experience of Orwellian doom that grows out of fragments. Lindelof's series, by contrast, inspired by the nonlinear aesthetics of the graphic novel, creates an energized, nonlinear, unbounded history in a brilliant and exhilarating manner.[17] If Gibbons's asymmetrical comic book frames are the result of artistic choices, the discontinuous changing of points of view in the novel's chapters is not.

That is because *Watchmen* was not originally a novel; Moore and Gibbons had created a series of twelve comics, each with a shifting perspective. DC Comics later bound them together as a graphic novel and fabricated the narrative nonlinearity, for purposes so heinous that Lindelof prefers not to refer to the Moore and Gibbons Old Testament as a graphic novel. DC Comics contended that Moore and Gibbons should not own the rights to the characters in the *Watchmen* comics, because they were spinoffs of the characters DC bought from Charlton Comics. But they signed a contract that guaranteed that the rights to the characters would revert to Moore, once the comics were out of print for a year, for 365 days exactly.

As Lindelof describes what happened: "For the record, just so you know. . . . This is a piece of history . . . ; at date 364 they [DC Comics] published what you are referring to as the graphic novel, and every year they republish it so that they retain the rights to these characters. The term *graphic novel* I don't think even existed before *Watchmen*. It was certainly the first time I became aware." Needless to say, Moore was and remained angry that *Watchmen* is known as a graphic novel. Given the baggage of the term, I use it here regretfully, mostly because of the force of its widespread usage and also because "novel" is appropriate to the inadvertently created narrative aesthetic of what its fans actually read. Indeed, that inadvertent nonlinear aesthetic is part of what so intrigued Lindelof about Moore's *Watchmen*, an interest that was intensified when he saw David Lynch intentionally use nonlinear narrative in *Twin Peaks* (1990–1991).[18]

A further complication of the history of the series is that Lindelof did not initially want to make it. When offered the job of adapting the comic, he turned it down twice.[19] However, when he finally accepted it, if he thought of it as an homage to Moore, he did not constrain himself to fidelity in bringing Moore and Gibbons to the screen, and he did not dutifully accomplish the adaptation reluctantly. He made the original his own in a big, enthusiastic way. His *Watchmen* series is "a study of a larger interrogation of curiosity about ambiguity. . . . So much of our storytelling denies the existence of ambiguity. Because ambiguity is terrifying."[20] And indeed in *Watchmen*, the discontinuous points of view of each episode infuse Lindelof's series with a complex, exhilarating, yet terrifying ambiguity that transforms the Moore and Gibbons cynical historical grimace.

Again, Lindelof might well protest, but a comparison between page and screen reflects an improvement on the original. The series is filled with warmth, joy, and innovative quantum nonlinearity that is not to be found in the more conventional linearity of Moore's graphic novel. I will go further; the series is sustaining and hopeful, while the harsh mockery of the graphic novel is an exercise in sophisticated deflation. The historical perspective of the series is reflected in a joke Lindelof told me about himself:

> I'm not a glass-half-full or a glass-half-empty kind of guy, I'm a "There's a glass?" guy. . . . I think that the glass-half-full people are considered optimists; I always see the glass half full. The glass-half-empty people are considered pessimists. I always see the glass half empty. But in my lived experience I think that those people represent a very small subset of humanity. Most people are like, sometimes I feel hopeful; other times I feel despair. And more importantly, what is the vessel that holds the water that is the parable? And I guess that's why I'm asking "Oh, there's a glass?" Ultimately, we're the vessel and so what's the water in the metaphor? The water is hope.[21]

Lindelof rejects the half-empty view as well as the binary of half-full and half-empty glasses, but he is a water carrier who opts for hope in all its riskiness, which he cherishes. He believes there is no risk in saying this miasma of depravity is as good as it gets. "The risk is saying it can be better. And that's a risk because you probably will be disappointed." But he turns his gaze to Greta Thunberg and Malala Yousafzai. "If they're saying it can be better, who am I to say, 'Nah'?"[22] Moore and Gibbons gave no indication that "it could be better." Lindelof and his collaborators took the risk.

DON'T TRUST IN THE LAW

Damon Lindelof's *Watchmen*: Here we are in Tulsa, Oklahoma, not New York. At the beginning of episode 1, we are not yet in Lindelof's twenty-first-century America, nor are we still in Moore's mid-twentieth-century New York City. We are in 1921, right in the middle of the massacre of the prosperous Black community in the Greenwood section of Tulsa, Oklahoma. Belatedly in the series this real event becomes narratively entangled with Veidt's fictional twentieth-century mass murder. When we enter the series, however, it is the springboard for Will Reeves's historical quest.

A silent movie, *Trust in the Law*, is showing at the Greenwood Dreamland Theatre; its soundtrack is created live on a piano by a Black pianist, the mother of the sole audience member, her enthusiastic little son (Jovan Adepo). On-screen, the movie is coming to its "wow finish" as a Black federal marshal, Bass Reeves (Jamal Akakpo), removes the hood that hides his face. At first the white community is distrustful, but they cheer him on when they discover that he has captured a secretly criminal white sheriff. The little boy thrills to the marshal's final words when he stops the onlookers from lynching the villain: "Trust in the law."[23]

Off-screen, out in the Tulsa streets, the law cannot be trusted. With the permission and cooperation of the police, gun-toting white men in white

FIGURE 6.1 *A timeless, spaceless silent movie about a Black lawman, episode 1, chapter 1.*

Ku Klux Klan robes are mercilessly murdering Black men, women, and children and setting fires to Black businesses with impunity. The desperate pianist and her husband arrange for their son to flee, hidden in a car driven by friends. They die, as do their friends, but at the city limits, while the intended rescuers lie dead in high grass, the little boy, whose original name we will never know, survives, as does the baby girl of his parents' friends. He comforts her while Tulsa burns in the distance. Reeves was wrong. No matter. The boy will henceforth be known as Will Reeves, in honor of his on-screen hero, and we will jump into the twenty-first century and into a nine-episode history of racial injustice, mass murder, and quantum realities for a new zeitgeist.

We jump into twenty-first-century Tulsa. Robert Redford is the president of what is purported to be a post-racial, post–nuclear arms race America in which all human ills are being addressed. And Will Reeves, now over a hundred years old, is secretly in Tulsa. Why? His granddaughter, Tulsa Police detective Angela Abar, is there. She doesn't even know he exists, but Reeves knows about her because Doctor Manhattan has found and spoken with him in nonlinear time. Their meeting in quantum time and space is not the beginning of the series; we only learn about it belatedly. But in the nonlinear cosmos of *Watchmen*, if we can speak of beginnings in such a universe, it is very much the origin of Manhattan's legacy for Reeves and Angela, in an America that Reeves knows is not post-racial, that Angela will know is not post-racial, but in which Manhattan's quantum energies may yet create a just history. But this is a nonlinear story, and so, much of the information about what is in play, historically, is belated. Our first look at *Watchmen* only seems to depict a legacy of cynical, linear hopelessness, à la the graphic novel, since after the time jump, we still can't trust in the law, and the solution of choice is still to put on a mask.

TELEOLOGY IN TULSA: HALF EMPTY?

When we jump to 2019, it is not the vigilantes who are masked; it is the duly constituted constabulary. Now, that is a scrambling of the Moore comics that will tickle the fancy of viewers that know them well. In 2019 Tulsa, a masked policeman stops a motorist he suspects of vigilante activity. While the policeman waits for clearance to access his weapon, which he is forbidden to use without authorization, the motorist kills him. Yup, a vigilante. The Redfordian ideals are not working as advertised. In twenty-first-century Tulsa, the officially antiracist police have been forced into wearing masks because that is supposed to protect their identities from the leftover racists who are taking revenge on the Redford government. Police are now being killed by racists. The progressive teleology of improvement in a straight line has no relationship to reality.

The idealistic model of government espoused by President Redford is not the only teleology in Tulsa. But it is the only one that ignores the presence of Doctor Manhattan, who is officially believed to be on Mars. The other teleologies in town know that Manhattan is still on Earth, in Tulsa actually, and are vying to make use of him in order to redefine history and usurp the place of progressive, democratic government. Each has a different strategy for stealing Doctor Manhattan's powers from him and using them themselves to rule the world. Not one of them can succeed.[24] Just how can a mutable blue man be in Tulsa incognito? Just how can anyone appropriate his powers? Read on.

One would-be master of history is the racist Seventh Kavalry, a contemporary, local vigilante cell of the twentieth-century, secret organization Cyclops, a fictional variation on the historical Ku Klux Klan, who were responsible for the massacre of Black Americans in Greenwood. The Kavalry has infiltrated the Tulsa Police at the highest levels and is secretly behind the new policy of masked police, and if the police on the streets are officially antiracist, the men at the top of the police hierarchy are not. Judd Crawford (Don Johnson), the handsome chief of police who puts on a good public show of heroism on behalf of ideals of diversity, is one of the most devious of the Cyclops. With his covert control of the constabulary, everything is in place for white supremacy to take its final step. And what is that step?

Cyclops is prepped to capture Doctor Manhattan, take his powers, and render all resistance to them futile. Cyclops has the advantage of knowing that Doctor Manhattan is Cal Abar (Yahya Abdul-Mateen II), the Black husband of Angela Abar. It has the advantage of Angela's obliviousness to their knowledge of Cal's secret identity, and she has no idea that Cyclops is all set to make its move. Cyclops's inside man, Chief Crawford, and his charming wife, Jane (Frances Fisher), have prepared for the move on Cal/Manhattan by deviously insinuating themselves into the lives of Cal and Angela, one of the few truly anti-racist law officers, as "dear friends" of the Abar family.

But Cyclops is not the only would-be master of history who knows that Manhattan has gone from blue to Black; and Cyclops has no idea that it has been manipulated into unknowingly acting as a part of someone else's plans to mastermind history, someone with much better science and different intentions, and with the same information about Cal, provided by Will Reeves. A strange newcomer to Tulsa, trillionaire Lady Trieu (Hong Chau), also has eyes on Cal/Manhattan. She knows everything there is to know about Cyclops's plans, but she does not know that Reeves has given her information about Cal's secret identity at the request of Doctor Manhattan. Or that Manhattan, because he lives simultaneously in past, present, and future, knows that, despite her scientific superiority and her knowledge about his identity, history will not justify Lady Trieu's confidence that she is destined to be the winner of the history lottery.

Lady Trieu has no idea about her place in the space-time of the boundless universe. She has very linear blinkers on her eyes. She is planning to outdo Adrian Veidt, as a benefactor to humankind, but not a secret one. She has a secret, all right; she is the daughter Veidt doesn't know about, and daughter finds daddy's mass-murder illusion passé. She has mild contempt for Veidt, who has left New York, hidden himself in his secret refuge, Karnak, far from Tulsa, periodically secretly raining down nonlethal mini-alien monsters to remind the nations of the alien menace, and keep that nuclear clock on hold. *So* 1985. (The year Adrian Veidt committed mass murder and stopped the nuclear arms race.) Face it, Dad. It's the twenty-first century and new times call for new stories. Lady Trieu is building a Millennium Clock, and she is going to make Veidt's fake alien and the engineered peace obsolete. Her clock will facilitate the transfer of Doctor Manhattan's powers to herself, which she will deploy to author a history not only of peace, but also of health and security. Under her very public control.

Cyclops. Lady Trieu. Will Reeves. Angela. They all know Cal's secret. Only Doctor Manhattan doesn't know who, where, and when he is. It is because he traded knowledge of his identity and access to his nonlinear engagement in time and space for love. Belated knowledge of this love story gives new meaning to the words, "the awful truth." Near the end of the series we discover that Manhattan, experiencing every time frame possible, walked into a bar in Vietnam to meet Angela, an encounter happening, from the point of view of the quantum universe, at the same time as everything else in the series. We watch as Angela experiences with frustration his simultaneous moments with versions of her in past, present, and future. She loves but is unable to live with a boundless man, who exists in past, present, and future and always knows what she is going to say and do, because it has already happened, is happening, and will happen. It is difficult existentially to live in quantum reality. And there are social disadvantages too. Going out in public with an enormous blue man, who ended the Vietnam War seventy years ago?

And so, between the two of them, because Doctor Manhattan exists in quantum time and space, he becomes Black, bounded in time, and oblivious to his identity as Doctor Manhattan. Angela is a member of the Saigon police force and secretly presents Manhattan with an unclaimed body in the morgue, where he transforms himself into Cal Abar, a Black man who has no known relatives or other connections. Cal/Manhattan moves through time and space to Adrian Veidt's hideout, and Veidt gives him a disk Angela can press into his forehead that will block all knowledge of his blue boundlessness. They marry and go to Tulsa, Angela believing that she alone knows her husband's secret, and possessing the knowledge of how to restore him to quantum time and space, should the occasion arise. It arises. Or should I say it has already arisen long before we know all these secrets. By the end of the first episode, Will Reeves has already begun to unravel Cal Abar's secret, when, in the dead of night, he lynches Police Chief Crawford on a big tree right outside of Tulsa. We are never in suspense or doubt about who killed Crawford; neither is Angela. He confesses to her, and to us. But her mysterious reluctance to reveal his confession to the authorities is, was, and will be part of a new Black history, a new nonlinear knowledge of the universe, and perhaps even justice in the marketplace.

PLUM PUDDING

The New Testament is a plum pudding of stories that pointedly make the turn from the closed, cynical, innately hopeless, empty glass of the white marketplace of the Old Testament to an open, nonlinear, potentially hopeful ("There's a glass?") universe. The New Testament not only includes Black history; it redeems, as we shall see, the white history mapped out by Moore and Gibbons. The oldest of the plums, from the cynical Old Testament, is Laurie Blake (Jean Smart), who reports for duty in Tulsa as the lead agent of the antivigilante force in Redford's FBI. There is a general (false) assumption that Crawford was killed by an assassin from the vigilante Kavalry. Blake arrives, poised with her razor-sharp mind to find out who lynched Crawford, but she is also quite explicitly carrying with her heavy baggage from the Old Testament. Agent Blake is the daughter of the Comedian, the coldest hearted of the vigilantes in Moore's novel, a cynic who laughed away the evil he did, including his rape of Laurie's mother, which culminated in Agent Blake's birth, and his brutal killing of Vietnamese with a flamethrower during the war. Laurie is prone to a similar cynicism, having been born into it, and having been Doctor Manhattan's discarded Old Testament lover. In the Old Testament, when Manhattan left white American history for Mars, he also casually abandoned her. Blake enters the New Testament, stuck in her grief about her lost love and filled with her father's cynicism. Here he hasn't gone to Mars, and she quickly experiences intimations of becoming unstuck.

When we first see her, as whip-smart as she is, her broken heart has led her to delusionally call Mars at one of the worldwide Doctor Manhattan phone booths, established by Lady Trieu, where messages can be left for Manhattan to receive on the Red Planet. Agent Blake, for shame! But Blake is not as stuck in the illusions of linear history as it might seem. Through the magic of montage, Lindelof locates her in the shifting energies of the simultaneous past, present, and future. The montage merges the static space-time of her mournful private time in the phone booth with scenes when she is in Washington, DC, before she gets the assignment, when she is formally assigned, and when she is on assignment in Tulsa. By birth, she was once part of the New York circle of the Minute Men; she is now on call in Washington, DC, to hunt masked vigilantes, wherever they may be. She is a woman both stuck in the legacy and history of the Old Testament and being called by the New Testament.

The nonlinear universe calls to her, after the montage of her part in the investigation of Judd's death and one-way conversation on Lady Trieu's fraudulent Mars Phone, when, channeling her father, she leaves a long message for Doctor Manhattan that consists of two bitterly cynical jokes. The jokes she tells are thinly veiled parables of her life. Reflecting her location between a testament now dead and a testament about to be born, they seem to be taking a linear shape, but they break off into discontinuity and fragmentation. The first joke, unfinished, is about a daughter and a father, a perfectionist master bricklayer, who builds a barbecue to teach his daughter his craft, only to find that the barbecue is not perfectly to plan. There is one brick leftover that should have been part of the structure, and he can't figure out where he made his mistake. The daughter blithely solves the problem by throwing the brick high up into the air with all her might, and it doesn't come down.

And Blake can't remember the punch line. Instead, she begins a new joke in which she savages, without naming them, three vigilantes from the Old Testament, Nite Owl, Ozymandias/Adrian Veidt, and her old love, Doctor Manhattan. The joke is a not-at-all funny account of what happens when they are called before God and He capriciously finds them all wanting and sends them all to Hell. It, too, seems to end nowhere, until just as God is done administering His justice, the bricklayer's daughter becomes the punch line of both jokes. The brick she threw into the air comes down, hits God, and He goes to Hell.

Hilarity ensues? Well, yes, but only because, looking up, Blake sees a bright reddish point of light. And a car falls out of the sky, narrowly missing her. A message from Mars? Nope. But it is a message, which we will only later understand. It is Angela's car being returned to the spot from which it had been airlifted by Lady Trieu, with Will Reeves in it.[25] It's not the old story about Doctor Manhattan. It's the New Testament. Laurie roars with laughter. Is it the inherited cynicism of her despicable father? Or is it the laughter of Sisyphus, a dawning of a new knowledge of a nonlinear universe? An evolving kind of laughter. Laurie and the audience will only have a fully aware appreciation of the evolution after the last narrative brick is laid in the series, when along with Wade Tillman, a Tulsa Police detective, she administers a new kind of justice. Patience.

Wade Tillman (Tim Blake Nelson), a member of the 2019 Tulsa police force who is brand new to the *Watchmen* saga, not only alludes to one of the old New York Minute Men, but himself has a backstory that tangentially refers to the Old Testament. He is not in the graphic novel, but the trauma with which he enters the series is; Tillman is a survivor of Adrian Veidt's mass murder in 1985. And he carries the scars in him. Like all the police detectives in twenty-first-century Tulsa, Tillman has a secret identity, and his, Looking Glass, tantalizingly alludes to one of the principal, and inherently psychopathological, vigilantes from the Old Testament, Rorschach. As Looking Glass, Tillman, like Rorschach, covers his face with a full head mask made of soft, flexible material that reflects the face of whomever he is talking to.

Tillman, too, is pathological, but not innately. His pathology is born of having survived Veidt's mass murder in 1985. He disguises the enduring damage created by Veidt by claiming that, by virtue of having cured himself of the anxiety caused by Veidt, he is in a position to help others who remain extremely disturbed by the "alien" violence that stopped the arms race. Tillman acts as a counselor for encounter groups. But in the privacy of the bunker he calls home, secretly he is a mass of unrelieved anxieties. He has alarmed his bunker to protect him from future alien invasions, and he wears an anti-alien baseball cap lined with foil. His secret is not safe.

Although no one on the Tulsa police force knows about his inner terror, ironically, the vigilante Kavalry, which he hunts in the name of Redford's laws, does. More irony. Hoping to convert him by force to become a member of the Kavalry, like so many of the other policemen, they inadvertently help his healing by showing him incontrovertible proof that the invasion is a scam masterminded by Veidt. He loses the cap and the alarm, but—still more irony—he not only remains unalterably opposed to the Kavalry but becomes free to work with Agent Blake.

After they are each catapulted into nonlinear temporality, bidding farewell to the Old Testament assertion of the grand narrative of white history, they each mutate toward the new zeitgeist.

But no plum in the pudding is as juicy or as much an invitation to the poetry of nonlinearity as the brightest light of Lindelof's New Testament, Angela Abar, and the story of how she learns not to trust in the law.

HALF-FULL OF OTHER TIMES AND SPACES

Damon Lindelof's Angela Abar. Her Tulsa. With the rest of the Tulsa police force, ten years ago she endured the White Night, a night of such savage attacks on the police in their homes by racist Cyclops vigilantes, that masks were officially mandated for their protection. Seemed to work. Since then, she has led a normal, "post-racial" life in Tulsa as a police detective, with Cal and three adopted children and her good friends the Crawfords. Since then, the Greenwood Cultural Center, a monument to Black suffering, has been built on the spot where Black lives were brutally taken in 1921. It is a beautiful, tech-savvy building, complete with holograms that document America's history of racism, containing a tree of virtual acorns that can be used in computers to summon up personal histories of the people who perished in the massacre. Aren't the troubles behind her? No. Angela, you cannot trust in the law. The White Night was, secretly, orchestrated by your good friend, Crawford. Post-racism has never existed. And you are soon to know it. Grandpa is here to show you. He sows seeds of doubt in Angela about Crawford and leaves, where Angela can find them, his custom-made Nostalgia pills, created by Lady Trieu. Grandpa intends for Angela to take one, out of curiosity, and learn some hard truths. From a pill?

Nostalgia, now illegal, is a drug developed by Lady Trieu's pharmaceutical company that shatters the internal human illusion of linear time. Its digitalized, custom-made prescription comprises memories of the patient, for whom the pills permit not just recall but a total sensory experience of the past as if it were the present. For anyone under the influence of Nostalgia, the past is the present. Trieu had custom-made a bottle of Nostalgia for Reeves, as part of their special deal when he revealed Doctor Manhattan's whereabouts to her. Reeves' plan works a little too well. Angela takes more than one. Many more.

Following up on what Reeves has told her, Angela finds a way to look in Crawford's closet and finds a hidden Klan robe. Her discovery makes her more than a little reluctant to pass along to the authorities Reeves's confession to her that he murdered Crawford. But eagle-eyed, clever Agent Blake becomes certain that Angela knows who did it. When she backs Angela into a corner, Angela escapes by swallowing the whole bottle of Reeves's Nostalgia, rather than outing him. Taking one's own Nostalgia pills poses the danger of retreating into the past, which is why they were declared illegal. Taking one of someone else's destabilizes identity. Ingesting a whole bottle of someone else's Nostalgia? Suicidal? Almost. Angela goes on a near-fatal trip into nonlinear time.

Nostalgia simulates the experience of living in the reality of the quantum universe, and for Angela it opens the way toward new historical knowledge and new historical possibilities. Angela is catapulted into a nonlinear space and temporality that breaks the limits on human perception of linear time and space. The very doors and windows around her are disconnected from walls and continuity. Moreover, she is no longer only herself. She is also Will Reeves, the grandpa she has only recently met. Moving into and out of untrammeled space and time and his mind and body, Angela sometimes observes his earlier life and sometimes experiences his life as her own. And so do we. It is a dangerous voyage of discovery that he/she cannot trust in the law.

In this out-of-body experience, Angela's seminal revelation comes when she witnesses what happens to Reeves after he becomes a New York City police officer in the 1940s. He collars a butcher named Fred (Glenn Fleshler) for firebombing a Jewish delicatessen. At the police station—with its Nostalgia-induced porous walls and doors—Reeves's white fellow police officers, all members of Cyclops, give lip service to racial equality under the law. But Fred, a Cyclops fellow traveler, goes free; and under the cover of night the other police officers, now off duty, track Reeves down. To remind him of his place as a Black man, they put a hood and noose over his head, string him up on a tree, and let him hang almost to the point of death. It happens to Angela as well as to Reeves, and Hooded Justice is born.

Masked by the hood, with the noose still around his/her neck, after the Cyclops police leave him gasping near the tree, Reeves/Angela rescues a couple being attacked by thugs and is reported in the papers as a heroic masked crusader. He is, of course, assumed to be white. The firebombing, lynching, and entrance into history of a secretly Black Hooded Justice are intercut with the violence of the Greenwood massacre, happening

FIGURE 6.2 *Inside Angela's nonlinear nostalgia trip, episode 6, chapter 5.*

simultaneously in nonlinear time. Then, a helpless child; now, under the hood, Reeves/Angela can impact white history, changing the Old Testament version of the birth of the Minute Men. In the New Testament, it is a gathering not only of narcissistic white vigilantes. They are also racists, who never know Hooded Justice is Black, with one exception: blond, very white, narcissistic playboy Nelson Gardner, a.k.a. Captain Metropolis (Jake McDorman), the most despicably racist of them all, knows Reeves is Black. He is turned on by the prospect of enjoying the transgression of sex with an "inferior" race, into which he tempts Reeves with promises to support Reeves's efforts for racial justice. But Gardner reneges, even after Reeves/Angela makes a shocking discovery.

After a riot in a Harlem movie theater, where the Black patrons inexplicably began to bloody each other—violence dismissed by both the New York police and Captain Metropolis as normal behavior for a brutish, inferior people—Reeves/Angela tracks the film projectionists to Fred the butcher's warehouse, in which the Cyclops police are working with subliminal technology that orders the Black audience members to hurt each other as they watch the films. Don't trust in the law. Angela experiences Reeves's killing of everyone in the warehouse, filled with rage at an atrocity that neither law nor Minute Men will address. Angela is with Reeves as he takes a projector, as proof of the subliminal mind control over the Black population through the mass media. Lindelof, in collaboration with soundtrack composers Trent Reznor and Atticus Ross, nondiagetically juxtaposes the scenes of violence with intoxicatingly sentimental love songs typical of the 1940s—both needle drops and music original to *Watchmen*—to emphasize the conflation of vigilante crime fighting with narcissistic gratifications.

Floating in nonlinear time with Angela, we arrive at the lynching of Chief Crawford from Reeves's point of view. Crawford is not one of the Cyclops police who almost lynched Reeves, but he will do for revenge. Reeves has used the subliminal projector he stole as a model for a modified hand-held device he has fabricated. With the device in hand, without wearing any mask, he talks Crawford into hanging himself. History is not what it seemed.

As the Nostalgia wears off, in episode 8, with the necessary help from Lady Trieu, who administers an antidote, Angela detaches from Reeves's memories and experiences her own memories of Vietnam, more than a decade earlier. Playfully titled "A God Walks into Abar," the penultimate episode takes a very nonlinear turn. It is practically the end of the series, but it engages us in how *Watchmen*'s new history begins. We are in 2009, in Saigon, where Angela was born. It is Doctor Manhattan Day, and everyone is celebrating his military exploits that won the war. It is also the twenty-second anniversary of the death of Angela's parents, who were casualties of Vietnamese terrorist revenge for those very military exploits. She is not celebrating. Doctor Manhattan, very blue, but elegantly dressed, walks into Eddy's Bar to meet her, while she sips a lonely beer. No one notices him, because all the revelers are blue, disguised as Doctor Manhattan in this carnival atmosphere. He is just another blue pretender, as far as Angela is concerned. But far from pretending, he is her gateway out of this oppressive history and into his nonlinear temporality. At that moment, he introduces her to his simultaneous existence in Eddy's and on Europa, a moon of Jupiter—not Mars.

In Eddy's, although she has never seen him before, he declares his love for her, past, present, and future. He is not only in Eddy's, but also on Europa, where he is creating an Edenic paradise and peopling it with a population of identical-looking, always loving and obedient Adams and Eves. He is also creating an egg right before her eyes, in response to her mockery of his disclosure of his nonlinearity and power. It is a moment for her to remember. Reader, you remember too; the egg, which has no linear past, present, or future, is a part of their love story, which will change history as we know it. Not only the egg, but also the simultaneous moments in which Doctor Manhattan is with Angela in the morgue when he becomes Cal Abar, and with Adrian Veidt in Karnak in 1999, getting a technology that will help him to forget he is Doctor Manhattan.

If this nonlinear temporality is driving the audience crazy, think what it is doing to Angela. Manhattan speaks her words as she is saying them because they have already been said, they are being said, and they will always be ongoing in her voice. So, at the same time, in another space, Manhattan is making a bargain with Veidt, who will give him a disk he has invented that will enable Manhattan to forget his boundless existence in the past, present, and future and live with Angela only in the linear, present marketplace. In exchange, Doctor Manhattan will teleport Veidt to Europa where he can be the god to a species of adoring men and women in a paradise.

In Saigon, Angela presses the disc into Manhattan's forehead. She is left with loving Cal Abar, who no longer knows he is Doctor Manhattan, and with the knowledge of how to remove the disk when the need arises. So, it is not a real erasure. It is just a blockage. After the Nostalgia wears off, and Angela knows her own secret heritage, she is called on to release Manhattan from the blockage. The Kavalry arrives at the home of Cal and Angela with a tachyon cannon to abduct him. Angela removes the disk, sure that, as boundless Doctor Manhattan, he is more than capable of thwarting the Kavalry plans. But as Manhattan knows, since it has already happened in nonlinear time, after he massacres all but one of the Kavalry team, the remaining one transports him to a huge lithium cage the Kavalry has built, and lithium is Manhattan's kryptonite.

TRUST IN . . .

. . . boundlessness? Perhaps, says *Watchmen*. Boundlessness does seem to doom all tyrannical linear plans, as we see in episode 9, a pyrotechnic, Schrödingeresque series finale.

All Cyclops's intentions are revealed, once Manhattan has been abducted, during a ceremony in which they expect to siphon Manhattan's powers out of him and into uber racist Senator Joe Keene of Oklahoma. He is going to be the new, "improved," and completely white-supremacist Doctor Manhattan and ruler of the world. The Cyclops's dignitaries are all present and protected by Kavalry troops, and they are joined by unwilling observers: Agent Blake, Detective Wade Tillman, Angela Abar, and Adrian Veidt. Blake has been forcibly made a part of the audience, a sadistic gesture on the part of Joe Keene, who knows Doctor Manhattan is her lost love. The Cyclops thugs brought Tillman with them, believing that he is a convert to their racist "faith." Angela has burst into the ceremony, having come to make a last-minute plea to Cyclops not to destroy her husband.

At the same time, Lady Trieu is preparing to reveal to Cyclops that everything it has done will turn out to have been in service to her. Her witness is her father, Adrian Veidt, whom she has brought there from Europa, where he was bored to death by all the adoration. And it really looks like she is the ultimate victor of the Manhattan sweepstakes. Joe Keene is liquified when they try to take Doctor Manhattan's power—bad Cyclops technology. Trieu then vaporizes the assembled Cyclops members as part of her bargain with Reeves. She and not Veidt will rule the world technologically, as a kind of god, giving humans the good life without wars or disease. Take that, Daddy!

But the powers of Doctor Manhattan, whom the assembled variously wish to use or to cherish, prove far too much for the constrictions of political or scientific systems and ambitions—or the limits of human love. Even weakened by the lithium, the reality of Manhattan's limitlessness will out, as the teleologies go into self-destruct mode. Trieu has reduced his energy to its components, blasting his mutated hominoid coherence; but with the last remnants of his consciousness, Manhattan teleports Veidt, Blake, and Tillman to Karnak. Veidt takes pleasure in destroying his daughter with the very technology she had dismissed as old hat. From Karnak, Veidt repeats the attack he made on New York, this time pinpointing Greenwood. Tillman watches Veidt reprise the attack that traumatized him for so long. But this time it is working against a new attempt to master history, when Veidt kills Trieu before she can fully make herself into the universal megapower she has schemed to become. Take that, Daughter! History is up for grabs. But there is still that matter of the mass murder of 1985, and Veidt is in for a very big surprise. This isn't the Old Testament.

Exult Veidt may, in what he sees as his return to being the savior of humankind, but Agent Blake, witnessing his destruction of Lady Trieu in Karnak, is neither celebrating his last-second save nor laughing cynically. Blake has been almost as changed by events as Angela. Mass murder is not a joke; there must be consequences. Welcome news to Tillman. After Veidt provides Blake and Tillman with transportation that will convey them homeward from Karnak, Blake informs Veidt that she is arresting him for mass murder—no statute of limitations on that one—and Tillman knocks him senseless with a wrench—low-tech solution—when Veidt resists. This is what Lindelof might call a Schrödingeresque moment, when we are on the brink of possibility.

When he spoke with me, Lindelof called "delicious" the moment with which the series closes, when Angela chooses to trust in boundlessness. If, he said, he wanted us to know what happens next, he would have written a second season. Ditto his lack of interest in what will happen to Angela when it turns out that it is she who may inherit Manhattan's limitless powers. Who is to say what will happen after the collapse of both Cyclops and Lady Trieu in Greenwood, after the revenge Reeves fervently wished for has been exacted, in retribution for a history Angela now shares with him? In the series' universe, it has already happened. However, Lindelof is interested in Reeves's response to his wish come true, and to the paradoxical moment in which Angela now finds herself.

Yet there is no triumphant exaltation for either Reeves or Angela. Reeves never liked Lady Trieu; he has little to say about what she did to Cyclops. Rather, he is philosophical about masks, power, and crusades. Avoid masks, he says. Wounds need to breathe if they are going to heal. Doctor Manhattan? He was OK, but he could have done more with all that power. *Could*, not *should*, as Lindelof emphasized to me.[26] The series eschews prescriptive historical judgments, along with teleologies. But it is Reeves who delivers a crucial message from Doctor Manhattan to Angela that plunges the viewer into an unclosed, nonlinear closure.

ANGELA'S FOOT

Doctor Manhattan's message: you need to break a couple of eggs to make an omelet. Omelet? Egg? It is Angela's call from the universe. Unlike the calls received in other nonlinear film and television, Angela has a choice. When she remembers the egg Manhattan created the night they met, she also remembers asking him if he could transfer his powers to someone else. He isn't sure, but he is sure that he would force no one to receive his powers. Choice would be paramount. Imagine choosing to inhabit past, present, and future and choosing to be composed of endlessly mutable particles! That is precisely the choice Lindelof gives Angela.[27] She now has an egg that might make her Doctor Manhattan's legatee, to be what he was and what she could not live with. But the power, the freedom! To eat or not to eat.

Angela takes the egg out to the backyard pool and ingests it, and the series ends with an open closure. Moore's novel ends with an open closure too. A white, screwup copywriter going through a newspaper's crank file, which includes the secret journal of the dead psychopath, Rorschach, might be revealed, or just left there, a dead letter that will turn to yellow dust. But isn't it a dead letter, whether it is swallowed up by linear time or by the dim-witted brain at the bottom of the journalistic pecking order? By contrast, Lindelof's series ends with a Black woman who might change history. Will she walk on water like Doctor Manhattan? Could a nonlinear Angela make the changes her grandfather thinks Manhattan could have made? Her foot hovers above the watery surface, it slowly lowers, never completing its forward motion. We cut to black.

There are, Lindelof acknowledges, many open historical questions about what a Black woman might do with Doctor Manhattan's power. There are, he allows, open questions about quantum reality posed by Angela's foot. But he is only truly captivated by the Schrödingeresque moment before her foot touches the water. Lindelof gives us the experience of a new kind

FIGURE 6.3 *Angela's foot has the last word. Episode 9, the very last frame of the series.*

of history, riding on that hovering foot. A chance to tolerate ambiguity and limitlessness. We are unstuck.

Watchmen differs radically from both *Westworld* and *Arrival* in its vision, but all three are built on nonlinear perspectives on grand narratives of history, and all affirm nonlinear time as a forever with the openness, immediacy, and the multiplicity of *now* as Darwin, Borges, quantum physics, and relativity imagine it. History is multiple. Nonteleological. Together with the narratives of the new hero in *Twin Peaks* 3, *The Tree of Life*, *The OA*, and *Eternal Sunshine of the Spotless Mind*, and the nonlinear stories of legacy in *The Romanoffs*, *Cloud Atlas*, and *BlacKkKlansman*, they bring us to the brink of a temporal and spatial cosmos analytically obscure but satisfyingly whole. These satisfactions deserve an afterword.

Afterword

REAL AND FICTIVE, SCIENTIFIC AND POETIC

We feel the obscurity of an order, a whole.

WALLACE STEVENS, *"Final Soliloquy of the Interior Paramour"*

We can summarize the satisfactions of film and television for a nonlinear universe as those of a new poetry of personal identity, achievement, legacy, and a larger historical vision—a poetry that emotionally links us to the new, nonlinear visions of science, philosophy, written narrative, music, and painting. These satisfactions depend on the profound appreciation of a wholeness that is filled with quantum oxymorons: not conventionally harmonious. What a mind-dazzling concept!

The end of any journey is a good time to pause and reflect. The end of our journey into new satisfactions absolutely demands contemplation. We began with a startling assumption that there are intersections between the post-Newtonian mutations of the scientific and a post-Newtonian poetic, even when it comes to the popular arts. Connections between the new zeitgeist and the high-culture arts? Possibly. But such connections to popular art? Not readily accepted. The plethora of negative critical evaluations we have encountered of the film and television into which we have delved demonstrate that. Such critics accept only order that reflects the harmonies of a Newtonian cosmos. Yet we have observed the presence of an obscure postquantum order and wholeness, an unconventional harmony of pieces that cannot fit, in mass-media film and television. Should we believe negative criticism, or our own aesthetic experiences?

Perhaps we should believe in the difficulty of making a transition to the new zeitgeist. As we now reflect, let us also dialogue with the traditional yearning for homogenous harmony that may pop up among scientists, even those steeped in nonlinearity, like Brian Greene. In *Until the End of Time: Mind, Matter, and Our Search for Meaning in an Evolving Universe*, he unexpectedly expresses a craving for the old aesthetic of the Newtonian cosmos:

> Yet to read Don Quixote's travails is to gain an understanding of human nature that would remain opaque if embedded in a description

of the movements of the knight-errant's molecules and atoms or conveyed through an elaboration of the neuronal processes crackling in Cervantes's mind while writing the novel. Connected though they surely are, different stories, told with different languages and focused on different levels of reality, provide vastly different insights.

Perhaps one day we will be able to transit seamlessly between these stories, connecting all products of the human mind, real and fictive, scientific and imaginative.[1]

Note to Brian Greene: When you enthusiastically imagine the "day we will be able to transit seamlessly between these stories, connecting all products of the human mind, real and fictive, scientific and imaginative," you surprise me. Here, your embrace of the very seductive idea of seamlessness suggests a regression to closed systems, very much the opposite of the boundlessness you depict as integral to the new scientific mapping of the universe. The fundamental spirit of the new art and the new science calls for an alternative to longing for "seamless transit" between the different languages and stories of the scientific and poetic.

Note to reader: Seeking to engage the alternatives that have been presented in the mass media has been the goal of our journey. Unity obscurely behind discontinuities, cacophony, and gaps is the norm of quantum science, nonlinear hero's journeys, and new histories. Rather than being seduced by the siren call of golden harmonies, this study yearns to learn better ways of reading the ambiguous discontinuities between their narratives. And maybe even take a new kind of pleasure in a wholeness that is not seamless.

Westworld, *Arrival*, and *Watchmen* poetically provide three different, nonteleological, big pictures of human history in the context of quantum and relative realities. The new mass-media narratives of historical legacy, tradition, and lessons created by Matt Weiner, the Wachowskis, and Spike Lee envision a new perspective on heritage when lessons, traditions, and legacies prove phantasmic repetitions of completely invented racism and ethnic distortions in a nonlinear cosmos. *Twin Peaks* 3, *The Tree of Life*, *The OA*, and *Eternal Sunshine of the Spotless Mind* zero in on the new poetry of personal identity and achievement for insiders of the marketplace and outsiders. They reenvision the Campbellian hero's journeys, the standard template for the mass media, as a false standard of achievement, one impossible to achieve in a universe in which linear cause and effect is an illusion transmitted like a psychosis that breaks from reality. Lynch, Malick, Marling and Batmanglij, and Kaufman allow us to love and feel compassion for the strange combination of the helplessness of both insiders and outsiders in a limitless universe.

The standard of human significance depicted in what we have seen of storytelling for a nonlinear universe does not inhere in conquest, victory, achievement; the path does not lead along the straight Campbellian line of a template to an obligatory climax of a quest. Storytelling in a post-Newtonian universe is postheroic, postlegacy, post-teleological. It is, as we have seen, steeped in various kinds of awe at striving for consciousness and connections in a universe in which quantum disconnections and confusion seem the rule and cosmic wholeness is obscure, difficult to perceive and engage. In this context, we are gratified by a poetic intuition, as in *The Romanoffs*, *Cloud Atlas*, *BlacKkKlansman*, *Westworld*, *Arrival*, and *Watchmen*, that exposes unities hidden in conflict and oxymoron and rejects the harmonies of linear history and legacy posited in Gandhi and the Andy Hardy movies. We take emotional pleasure in the courage of questers like the sheriff's team in *Twin Peaks*, OA in *The OA*, Jack O'Brien in *The Tree of Life*, or Joel and Clementine in *Eternal Sunshine of the Spotless Mind* to endure an inverted, Kafkaesque, cosmic call to spiritual freedom, beyond the limits of the marketplace. These are not the contexts created by narratives about Sam Spade or Rick and Ilsa.

Or would you rather conclude our journey in a more post-Newtonian fashion?

> *As in a mirror, analysis and imagination involve the same intellectual activity, though they unfold in opposite directions. Imagination assembles discrete elements into a complex composition, while a complex composition can be resolved into its constituent parts by analysis. According to Poe, the same mental process is required to create something as to explain it, just reversed.*
>
> JOHN TRESCH, *THE REASON FOR THE DARKNESS OF THE NIGHT: EDGAR ALLAN POE AND THE FORGING OF AMERICAN SCIENCE*

Although this study is built on an assumption similar to that expressed by Edgar Allan Poe about scientific analysis and imaginative synthesis being two sides of the same coin, the problem of analytic translation of poetic synthesis for the purposes of discussion is clearly visible in our efforts to discuss the cocreations of the arts and sciences of a new map. The two narratives have a connection that cannot be homogenized. Science probes nonlinearity and boundlessness through the narrative of logic and experimentation. Film and television probe through the language of the ineffable montage, the slippages of juxtaposition, the illogic of sensibility. Here, let us flip the coin, as best we may, by building into this afterword a place for the slippages and sensibility of montage to speak for themselves without (much) comment.

Pick your own montage. Or pick these: The stunning explosion of linear time and space that concludes Lee's *BlacKkKlansman* with an otherwise inexpressible statement in images about the nonlinear nature of the heritage of racism in America. The stippling of *Cloud Atlas* with the star-comet birthmark, insignia of transtemporal heritage. The blurred line between life and death in the montage that emerges when a door, unconnected to any wall or other physical form of boundary, opens at the end of Malick's *The Tree of Life* for Jack and his mother, onto an eternal landscape of the free-flowing elements of life, dotted by the ruins of

FIGURES 7.1a and b. *Frame series— Matthew Weiner creates a nonlinear montage history for Anastasia,* The Romanoffs, *main title.*

disconnected, static door frames. The moon-drenched, nonlinear temporal montage of Dolores and Teddy that creates narrative superposition for the audience at the end of season 1 of Lisa Joy and Jonathan Nolan's *Westworld*. The montage of forking paths of time interpenetrating one another in *The OA*, when many characters move between parallel time frames. The incomplete motion of Angela's foot moving toward the surface of her pool in *Watchmen*. The images of a nonlinear heptapod language, born of the body and betokening a nonlinear history in *Arrival*. The main title of *The Romanoffs* when, in one smooth motion of nonlinear time and space, an apocryphal figure of Anastasia in blue exists simultaneously in multiple time frames, as she runs through a Russian forest and emerges from a subway station in twenty-first-century New York City.

And, of course, David Lynch's strange, transcendent montages in *Twin Peaks* 3 when, in part 8, landscape reverts to boundless, timeless forces and particles after the Trinity Test of the atomic bomb in White Sands, New Mexico, and the part 18 disappearance into the dark light of nonbeing of Agent Cooper and Carrie Page after a Newtonian road trip to nowhere. Cumulatively, what more vivid testimony to the diversity, originality, and paradigm shifts in cinematic art for a nonlinear reality?

The strains of *Thus Spake Zarathustra* rise again, as a fanfare to the great paradox at which we have arrived. The new universes alleged in the film

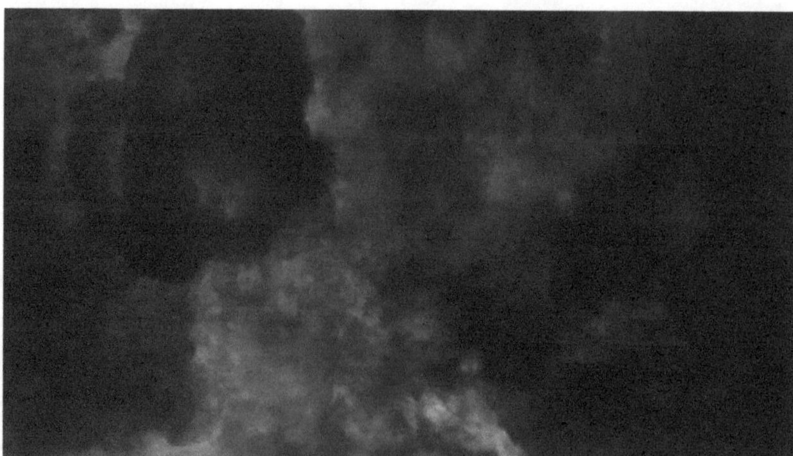

FIGURES 7.2a, b, and c. *Frame series— David Lynch creates a nonlinear montage of matter as quantum particles,* Twin Peaks 3, *part 8, chapter 3. Three frames from the montage.*

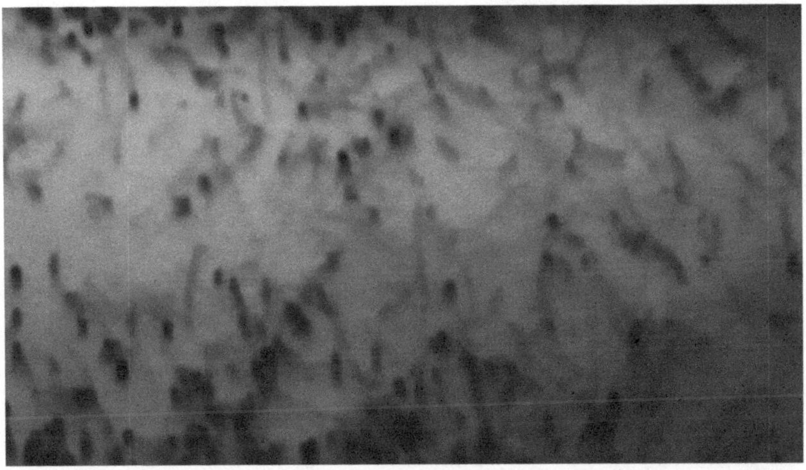

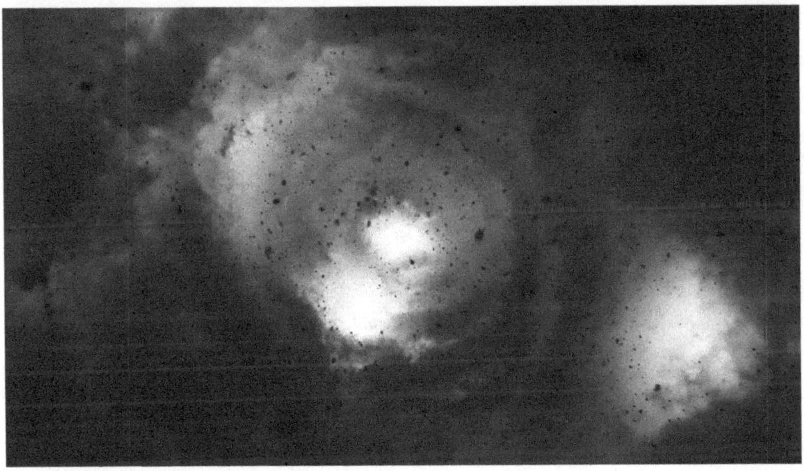

and television singled out here are depicted in some of the most powerful creations of the popular arts, yet they hold a fragile place in the politics and economics of the mass media. Premature cancellation, poor marketing or none, or refusal to green-light in the first place all too often interfere with their mass circulation. Audience's and critics' preconceptions block perception. Yet when they are seen, really seen, they can hold an indelible and sustaining place in the mass imagination. There is thus a need to strip away both compulsive linear-reading conventions and the prequantum addiction to seamlessness. Once nakedly encountered, unencumbered by old habits, nonlinear film and television are never forgotten. Their *visibility* is our cocreation with the cocreators.

ACKNOWLEDGMENTS

I cannot sufficiently acknowledge the artists who gave generously to me of their time and trust: Matthew Weiner, Damon Lindelof, and the incomparable David Lynch. Many traumatic events took place while I sought precious time with them, including the writers' strike of 2023 and the COVID pandemic, which peaked between 2020 and 2022 but continues still to threaten world health. How can I vividly convey how privileged I have been to have received literally hours hors de combat, away from the battlefields of disease and industry politics? In these time-outs, we contemplated aesthetics, truth, and philosophy in the popular arts. Heroic? Supremely gifted? Yes, all three.

How can I not, however, single out David Lynch, who died on January 16, 2025. He holds a particular place in my life and work for both his decades-long graciousness to me and his monumental importance to contemporary culture. When we first met, and over the years, despite his full life of production and public notoriety, he looked at paintings, watched films, and examined the universe with me. Recently, when David was living in virtual seclusion, to stay clear of the threat of COVID because he had emphysema, he nevertheless invited me into his home and his confidences on May 11, 2023, to speak about his work and his faith. It was the last of our ongoing conversations, begun in 1990. The time was filled with laughter, good-natured impatience, and a meeting of minds and hearts.

David was and remains the greatest filmmaker of our time. The word *genius* applies here; it rarely does on the numerous occasions we hear it bandied about. Like no other, David succeeded in being fiercely protective of his visionary art in an industry that routinely runs commerce roughshod over poetry. David never gave commerce an inch. I loved him for that. Didn't we all? Those who gratefully worked with him, and those in the audience who were imaginatively nurtured by his film and television. I miss him terribly. Although David regarded me as a "woman from someplace else," as if academia was located in a distant galaxy, he also held me dear as his (interplanetary?) friend. And I cherished him and the miracle of his presence among us.

Anyone who works with or in the mass media knows how special personal assistants are. I have had the great good fortune of working with three of the most special. For this book, I acknowledge Matthew Weiner's assistant, Madeline Low; and Damon Lindelof's assistant, Joaquín Lopez. For our many years of happy cooperation, I acknowledge Michael Barile, David Lynch's assistant. Michael has welcomed me, shepherded me, helped me acquire research materials and permissions, and made me cappuccinos. This time around he found a way to give me access to an advance copy of a manuscript necessary to this study, "One Unbounded Ocean of Consciousness," by Tony Nader. The materials I needed were provided by Dr. Tony Nader and Adrienne Schoenfeld, Director of Public Relations at Tony Nader USA International, whom I here acknowledge with gratitude.

How many people does it take to get permissions to use a still photograph from *Twin Peaks* 3 for a book cover? In addition to David Lynch, Mark Frost, Michael Barile, and devoted, always efficient producer Sabrina Sutherland: Joe Lee and Tracey Wolfson (Showtime); Diana Rasinski, Alyson Merkle, Shari Rothseid, Michael Schetrompf, and Willie Grey (Paramount); and Thomas Clawson (CBS). I am indebted to all of them.

Warm, enthusiastic thanks always to my friends and colleagues. I owe so much to New York–based filmmaker Arthur Vincie, who loaned me his talent and his time to work on the illustrations for this book. I deeply appreciate the support I have received from my colleagues at Columbia University Seminar #539, Cinema and Interdisciplinary Interpretations, especially cochairs Cynthia Lucia, William G. Luhr and seminar associate Jerry Carlson. The author expresses appreciation to the Schoff Fund at the University Seminars, Columbia University, for their help in this publication. Material in this work was presented to the University Seminar on Cinema and Interdisciplinary Interpretation. My young friends, Heather Jayne and Kevin Slavin were supportive, as are my friends and colleagues at the David Lynch Graduate School of Cinematic Arts, Maharishi International University, Erika Richards and Daniel Nearing.

At the University of Texas Press, I have a number of people to thank for their gracious support. Thank you, Lynne Ferguson for your camaraderie and the partnerships you have created for me with precise, intuitive copy editor Martin Ainsley and indexer Sarahh Scher. Thank you to Jenny Volvovski, who designed the cover with humor and seriousness, in the spirit of the book. And then there is Jim Burr, my editor at the press since 1996. What do I say about a legend in his time, a man highly regarded, and rightly so, in university publishing, and to whom I am happily beholden? The words *honorable, sublime,* and *inspirational* come to mind. So does the word *friend*. We have had a unique, long-lived partnership that I hope will endure for many years to come.

To my children. I am more than fortunate to be guided by my sparkling, firecracker daughter, Holly. I am more than blessed to have the support of my brilliant, resilient, research-wizard son, David. I am beyond lucky to have the pleasure of observing the blossoming of my glorious and beautiful granddaughter, Amara, perhaps a future talent in the film industry. And, ever and always, I acknowledge my kind and courageous, gifted husband, Richard, professor emeritus, author of seven novels, father, and grandfather: the earth that steadies me.

NOTES

Introduction. Intersections: What Would Einstein Do?

1. Although Albert Einstein's description of quantum physics as "spooky action at a distance" may be unfamiliar to nonscientists, it is so well known among physicists that it is frequently used to break the ice with humor when popularizing daunting quantum concepts. Einstein first coined the phrase when presented with the quantum finding about entanglement, here very accessibly described: "If you observe a particle in one place, another particle—even one light-years away—will instantly change its properties, as if the two are connected by a mysterious communications channel." Gabriel Popkin, "Einstein's 'Spooky Action at a Distance' Spotted in Objects Almost Big Enough to See," *Science*, April 25, 2018, https://www.science.org/content/article/einstein-s-spooky-action-distance-spotted-objects-almost-big-enough-see.
2. Glen Mazzara has given numerous interviews in which he retells this very funny yet horrifying formative experience in his career as a television writer. One source is this interview on PBS that first aired on September 20, 2022: "On Showrunning," *On Story*, season 12, episode 13, Austin Film Festival and PBS, September 20, 2022, 26 min., 47 sec., https://www.pbs.org/video/on-showrunning-a-conversation-with-glen-mazzara-reodgy/.
3. During my first interview with Damon Lindelof, on May 12, 2023, at the Warner Studios in Los Angeles, he spoke about the early influence of David Lynch on his life. His parents were divorced, and he saw his father only on weekends. Lindelof saw the episodes of *Twin Peaks 1* and *Twin Peaks 2* at his mother's house, and would routinely rewatch it with his father, who had recorded it. They would have extensive conversations about it. At first, they only discussed who might have killed Laura, but when the show began to become more "supernatural," as Lindelof describes it, they would mull over many theories about the "fundamental mysteries" of the episode. As an adult, his delight in the series only increased. "And so the idea that entertainment could create [not only] watercooler conversation about is it good or is it bad, but [also] watercooler conversation around what is happening. Talk about in your body. Every hair was standing on end. I was just so inspired."
4. Todd McGowan, *Out of Time: Desire in Atemporal Cinema* (University of Minnesota Press, 2011). McGowan is spot-on when he observes that in atemporal cinema, as he calls it, spectators don't observe nonlinear time from a safe distance, but must live in the confusion of nonlinearity (9). But he does not theorize nonlinear time as part of a new external reality being mapped. Rather, he understands it as the creation of interior turmoil by psychological

drives. "Contemporary atemporal cinema is a cinema of the drive, in which narrative is oriented around a foundational moment of traumatic loss" (10). The loss, which McGowan describes in terms of Lacanian psychology, brings about unending repetition of the trauma. For McGowan, then, linear films encourage a delusional hope that we can work through trauma to something unconflicted and harmonious, while atemporal cinema provides a necessary revelation that embracing the impossibility of future happiness is the only productive way to live. Unhappily, in his analyses of nonlinear film and television, McGowan all too often forces the work into a Lacanian template by ignoring the elements in the narrative that do not fit the theoretical construct.

5. Helen Powell, *Stop the Clocks! Time and Narrative in Cinema* (I. B. Tauris, 2012); Lee Carruthers, *Doing Time: Temporality, Hermeneutics, and Contemporary Cinema* (SUNY Press, 2016). Powell and Carruthers are representative of the general approach to temporality in cinema. As with most studies of the subject, Powell and Carruthers make little or no reference to television. Powell's book is basically concerned with classifying representations of time in narrative cinema: real time, future time, dreaming time, consuming time, and fractured time. The economics of the media plays a big part in her conceptualization of time in cinema. "Digital culture heralds a convergence culture bringing about not only a closer proximity between the media producer and the media consumer but also the flow of content across the media platforms on which this relationship is built. . . . Each film release in the cinema is simply a starting point to extend the shelf-life and revenue stream beyond the time spent in the box office charts. As a result, the marketing potential of a transmedia film, as pioneered by *The Matrix* series, for example, is exponential" (156).

Lee Carruthers takes a primarily aesthetic view of time in the media. Carruthers's articulation of time in film focuses on the interrelationships among images and sound, "the way images cling to each other in a lingering dissolve, are stretched across time by musical phrasing, or are palpably severed by a cut" (1). She skillfully applies the ideas of Maurice Merleau-Ponty, André Bazin, and Martin Heidegger to her analyses. Her classifications are somewhat less rigorous than Powell's, by design. Her study is about being "attentive to the kinds of time that recent films actually generate, to name and describe the temporal possibilities that cinema enframes for its viewer" (12). Among the films on which she focuses are *The Limey* (1999), *5 × 2* (2004), *What Time Is It There?* (2001), and *The Tree of Life* (2011). But she uses the films as representative of types of temporalities in cinema: slow film, reverse chronology, temporal duration, deep time. As we shall see, Carruthers and I are somewhat in synch with respect to *The Tree of Life* when she discusses it in terms of arising "from fragmented editing structures, orchestrating filmic time through discrete shots whose combinatory logic does not proceed predictably" (115). I also acknowledge that Carruthers introduced me to Thomas Wilfred, the creator of the light sculptures that Terrence Malick uses in *The Tree of Life*.

Another recent book which may be of interest is Matilda Mroz, *Temporality and Film Analysis* (Edinburgh University Press, 2012). Mroz is interested in nonlinearity in cinema as it creates an affective counterpoint with the linear narrative. She notes that in nonlinear narrative "affective sounds, moments or images suspend linear temporality and do not necessarily fit into narrative progression; affect is what might be called 'passion,' 'incipient action and expression'" (5).

6. Mary Ann Doane, *The Emergence of Cinematic Time: Modernity, Contingency, The Archive* (Harvard University Press, 2002), 3. When Doane writes about the representability of time, her language is not the language of quantum or relative science, but rather the language of philosophy. She contrasts the continuities of rationalized (standardized) time with the discontinuities of time as indexicality, chance, and contingency. In her words, "Contingency proffers to the subject the appearance of absolute freedom, immediacy, directness. Time becomes heterogeneous and unpredictable and harbors the possibility of perpetual newness, difference, the marks of modernity itself. . . . Nevertheless, these same attributes are also potentially threatening. . . . Contingency introduces the element of life and the concrete, but *too much* contingency threatens the crucial representational concept of totality, wholeness" (11–12). The relationship between the newly emerging medium of movies and contingent time is the fulcrum of *The Emergence of Cinematic Time*: "It is the contention of this book that the epistemology of contingency which took shape in the nineteenth century was crucial to the emergence and development of the cinema as a central representational form of the twentieth century" (19).
7. In her allusion to reversible time in movies, Doane does not reference Einstein or any of the developments of quantum mechanics. Instead, she writes that the second law of thermodynamics, "based on the observations of motors and engines and the flow of heat, proclaims that time is irreversible" and the emergence of the science of statistics, which asserted the probability that time is reversible (*Emergence*, 17–18). As Doane remarks, even though statistics is historically allied with control and standardization, it privileges uncertainty, surprisingly. Doane's use of statistics to discuss reversible time in movies is fascinating, but neither as flexible nor as applicable to film and series narrative for a nonlinear universe as the concepts of quantum and relative science I will apply in the chapters to come.
8. Doane notes that movie pioneers Méliès and the Lumières (Auguste and his brother Louis) are classically contrasted with each other as influences on the history of cinema, but she calls our attention to the seminal trait they share: "Both make contingency central to their representational practice in a medium in which the experience of temporality is crucial" (*Emergence*, 136).
9. Doane has much to say about Henri Bergson's misunderstanding of time in cinema, and at times she uses Deleuze to contest Bergson's ideas: "Bergson's misrecognition of the cinema's true capabilities, according to Deleuze, is linked to his insistence upon locating the cinema's access to real movement in the projector, in a homogeneous mechanical time subject to the 'abstract idea of a succession' and 'copied from space.' . . . Deleuze claims, on the other hand, that the movement needs to be thought in relation to the spectator rather than in relation to the apparatus, and that, for the spectator, movement is immediately given in an 'intermediate image'" (Doane, *Emergence*, 175–176). Deleuze believes that the spectator doesn't see succession but a confluence of images, thus actual movement.

   But as for Doane herself, she agrees with neither of them. She emphasizes that "a belief in the cinema's alliance with real movement rests on a denial of discontinuity" (177). Doane's dexterity with the history of ideas about time is impressive, compelling, and thought provoking. Her concentration on contingency brings us to the doorstep of quantum and relative physics.

10. Gilles Deleuze, *Cinema 2: The Time-Image*, trans. Hugh Tomlinson and Robert Galeta (University of Minnesota Press, 1989), xii.
11. Deleuze, *Time-Image*, 49.
12. Deleuze, *Time-Image*, 81.
13. David Lynch, in discussion with the author, May 11, 2023.
14. Doane, *Emergence*, 19–20.
15. Deleuze, *Time-Image*, 376.
16. Elizabeth Grosz, *The Nick of Time: Politics, Evolution, and the Untimely* (Duke University Press, 2004), 8.
17. Grosz, *Nick of Time*, 96.
18. Erwin Schrödinger, *"What is Life?" with "Mind and Matter" and Autobiographical Sketches* (Cambridge University Press, 2012), 17–19.
19. To the lay person, Einstein's work on nonlinear existence of multiple time frames may seem quite spooky. As Richard A. Muller, *Now: The Physics of Time* (W. W. Norton, 2016), describes Einstein's theory, "If two events occur at different locations, then simultaneous events—let's say both of them occurring *right now*—would not be simultaneous in another reference frame" (36). In everyday language: Time frames are different for a person traveling on a train and a person standing on a station watching the train. Einstein did not find his work spooky, because it is securely anchored in mathematics. But in the movies, Einstein's theories might destabilize crosscut montages that depict the danger of the heroine in one location and the struggle of the hero coming to save her in another location. The suspense depends on a belief that they are occurring in the same time frame. But in a post-Newtonian cosmos, they might not be happening simultaneously, depending on the time frame (Muller, *Now*, 33–34).
20. Particle mass is defined as resistance to a force that "permeates the universe called the Higgs field. The more the Higgs field pulls on a particle, the more mass it has." For particles with mass, the speed of light is the outer limit of how fast they can travel. While physicists have long theoretically postulated the existence of particles that are pure energy, unaffected by the Higgs field, it is only recently that two such particles of that nature have been found: photons and gluons. These are particles that always travel at, or possibly faster than, the speed of light. The science of the Higgs field is not part of the everyday knowledge of the layman, but familiarity with its intricacies is not necessary for our purposes. All that is significant for our voyage is that the dynamic of force within the Higgs field accounts for normal, everyday materiality. By contrast, the existence of massless particles proposes a universe filled with problems for culture as we know it. Massless particles not only travel at the speed of light, as do photons and gluons, but they may travel faster. The tachyon, for example, is a massless particle that so far exists only in thought experiments but suggests a universe in which our system of ethics and morality is canceled, as in the thought experiment of the tachyon murder paradox (see Muller, *Now*, 55–57). Madeleine O'Keefe, "Massless Particles Can't Be Stopped," *Symmetry*, July 23, 2019, https://www.symmetrymagazine.org/article/massless-particles-cant-be-stopped.
21. Muller, *Now*, 55.
22. Muller, *Now*, 56–57.
23. The science of Schrödinger's thought experiment about the cat in the box is primarily concerned with the problem of amplitude. "Quantum physics postulates that the real world is described by something shadowy and ephemeral,

unmeasurable even in principle, called an amplitude," the inability to measure, a key problem for physics (Muller, *Now*, 193). Here is how that problem applies to Schrödinger's cat:

> Imagine a cat in a box. The box also contains a radioactive atom that has a 50 percent probability of undergoing decay in the next hour. If it decays, it will trigger a mechanism that kills the cat. . . . Open the box in an hour and the odds are 50 percent that you'll find a dead cat, 50 percent that you'll find a live one. . . . What is weird, what bothered Einstein and Schrödinger, is the way the situation is described in the language of quantum physics. According to the standard approach used by virtually all physicists, the amplitude that described the atom and the cat evolves over the hour. Initially, that amplitude describes a live cat and an unexploded atom. But as time passes, the amplitude changes. At the end of the hour, the evolved amplitude consists of two equal parts: one that has a dead cat with fragments from the exploded atom, superimposed on one that has a live cat and unexploded atom. Until someone peeks, the cat is simultaneously both dead and alive. According to the rules, the act of opening the box and looking in constitutes a measurement, and when measured, the wave function immediately collapses and you are left with only one reality, not a superposition of two. (Muller, *Now*, 194–196)

Physicists have pondered whether opening the box is a form of measurement. Or does the box have to be opened? After all, doesn't the cat know? Do we even need a sentient being as observer (Muller, *Now*, 198)? Distinguished physicist Roger Penrose further complicates the situation when he asks whether observation is confined to sentient beings. "Penrose suggests," Muller writes, "that the universe itself makes measurements. We don't normally notice them, because they don't happen instantly; they take some time. The moon didn't need Einstein to look at it; it is far enough away that the universe somehow made it real before Einstein peeked" (Muller, *Now*, 215). However, the problem of amplitude has not yet been translated into storytelling in the mass media as part of Schrödinger's paradox.

24. Joseph Campbell outlines his template of the monomyth of the hero's journey in part 1 of *The Hero with a Thousand Faces*, 3rd ed. (New World Library, 2008).
25. Yuval Noah Harari, *Sapiens: A Brief History of Humankind* (Harper Perennial, 2018).
26. Francis Fukuyama, *The End of History and the Last Man* (Free Press, 2006).
27. David Graeber and David Wengrow, *The Dawn of Everything: A New History of Humanity* (Farrar, Straus and Giroux, 2021). Graeber and Wengrow announce their polemical intentions, particularly their disagreements with historians who offer teleologies like that advanced by Yuval Noah Harari. Harari's teleology traces a necessary historical development from hunter-gatherer societies to societies based on planned agriculture that leads to private property, hierarchy, and a necessary injustice that is preferable to the chaos that Harari believes would ensue were the teleology not to unfold. In their introduction, Graeber and Wengrow, by contrast, advise their readers that

> In this book, we will not only be presenting a new history of humankind, but inviting the reader into a new science of history, one that restores our ancestors to their full humanity. Rather than asking how we ended up unequal,

> we will start by asking how it was that "inequality" became such an issue to begin with, then gradually build up an alternative narrative that corresponds more closely to our current state of knowledge. . . . What was really happening in those periods we usually see as marking the emergence of "the state"? The answers are often unexpected, and suggest that the course of human history may be less set in stone, and more full of playful possibilities, than we tend to assume. (24–25)

28. Israel Finkelstein and Neil Asher Silberman, *The Bible Unearthed: Archaeology's New Vision of Ancient Israel and the Origin of Its Sacred Texts* (Touchstone, 2002). "This book aims to tell the story of ancient Israel and the birth of its sacred scriptures from a new, archaeological perspective. Our goal will be to attempt to separate history from legend. Through the evidence of recent discoveries, we will construct a new history of ancient Israel in which some of the most famous events and personalities mentioned in the Bible play unexpectedly different roles. Yet our purpose, ultimately, is not mere deconstruction. It is to share the most recent archaeological insights—still largely unknown outside scholarly circles—not only on *when*, but also *why* the Bible was written, and why it remains so powerful today" (3).
29. Physics has identified four forces that account for every interaction in the cosmos: gravity, electromagnetic force (which holds matter together), weak nuclear force (the force existing between the elementary particles responsible for processes like radioactive decay), and strong nuclear force (which hold the nuclei of atoms together). There is no theory that includes gravity with the other three forces as part of a unified field. Einstein struggled in vain in the later years of his career to find that theory, but he never gave up hope that it existed. Understanding the building blocks of the universe to be strings rather than particles—in string theory—holds out hope that we will find a unifying theory for all the forces. Brian Greene is on the forefront of the work being done on string theory and acknowledges that it is still not the solution to the unification of the four forces Einstein was searching for. There are still many questions to be answered. Brian Greene, *The Elegant Universe: Superstrings, Hidden Dimensions, and the Quest for the Ultimate Theory* (W. W. Norton, 2010), 181–183.
30. Although 241 other patrons walked out of the 1968 premier of *2001* at the Pantages Theatre, it's Rock Hudson's expression of confusion that lives on. However, much about this premiere is shrouded in a certain amount of mystery. It is not actually clear that the theater was what we know today as the Pantages Theatre, or whether it was a different theater once identified by that name. It is also uncertain what Rock actually said. My favorite version is "What the fuck was *that* about?" his capsule review, told to me anecdotally, but for which I can find no verifiable corroboration. Other reports of his response include: "What is this bullshit?" in Phil Hoad, "How We Made *2001: A Space Odyssey*," *Guardian*, March 12, 2018, https://www.theguardian.com/film/2018/mar/12/how-we-made-2001-a-space-odyssey-stanley-kubrick-hal; and "Will someone tell me what the hell this is about?" in Roger Ebert, review of *2001: A Space Odyssey*, RogerEbert.com, March 27, 1997, https://www.rogerebert.com/reviews/great-movie-2001-a-space-odyssey-1968.
31. Arthur C. Clarke, *2001: A Space Odyssey* (New American Library, 1968). Consider the difference between the way Clarke's novelization begins and the opening of *2001*, the film. Clarke plunks his reader down into linear time, a clearly

etched landscape, and a conventionally dramatic situation. His first sentence is: "The drought had lasted now for ten million years, and the reign of the terrible lizards had long since ended" (1). In the next two paragraphs, Clarke introduces us by name to a character, and his dramatic problem. We meet an ape-human named Moon-Watcher, who "saw that his father had died in the night." And Moon-Watcher wants power among the chaotic rabble of starving, depressed ape-humans lolling aimlessly around a barren landscape that cannot support them. Despite his reputation as a physicist, in his novelization Clarke shows us his setting through the eye of a twentieth-century writer of linear potboilers, while the artist in Stanley Kubrick is part of a cocreation with the natural sciences of a nonlinear universe.

Clarke continued reducing the visionary film when he published *2010: Odyssey Two* (Del Ray, 1997), a sequel to his novelization of Kubrick's film, and the novelization of his film sequel, *2010: The Year We Make Contact,* directed by Peter Hyams (MGM/UA Entertainment, 1984).

32. There isn't a great deal of evidence for Kubrick's admiration for *Eraserhead,* but it is not merely urban legend. The best source is an article in *Far Out* magazine by Scott Campbell. But on one detail it contradicts my experience. It stipulates that Lynch knew about Kubrick's admiration, but when I told him about Kubrick's estimation of *Eraserhead,* he said he hadn't known. Scott Campbell, "The David Lynch Movie Stanley Kubrick Wishes He Had Made," *Far Out,* January 12, 2024, https://faroutmagazine.co.uk/the-david-lynch-movie-stanley-kubrick-wishes-he-had-made/. For those who would like to consult the other sources, see: Andrew McGowan, "Stanley Kubrick Made *The Shining* Cast and Crew Watch This David Lynch Movie," *Collider,* updated April 22, 2024, https://collider.com/stanley-kubrick-the-shining-david-lynch-eraserhead/; "Eraserhead," *Wikipedia,* last edited December 23, 2024, https://en.wikipedia.org/wiki/Eraserhead; Garin Pirnia, "The Epic Influence of David Lynch's *Eraserhead,* from Kubrick to *Star Wars,*" *Esquire,* September 18, 2018, https://www.esquire.com/entertainment/movies/a30108/eraserhead-influence/.
33. Harald Kaufmann, "Strukturen im Strukturlosen: über György Ligetis 'Atmosphères,'" *Melos* 31 (1964): 397–398, paraphrased in Friedemann Sallis, "György Ligeti (1923–)," in *Music of the Twentieth-Century Avant-Garde: A Biocritical Sourcebook,* ed. Larry Sitsky (Greenwood, 2002), 256; Harald Kaufmann, "*Atmosphères,* György Ligeti," Junge Philharmonie Ostwürttemberg, archived March 1, 2012, https://web.archive.org/web/20120301112538/http://www.jpo-w.de/popup_ligeti.html.
34. Arthur C. Clarke, *The Lost Worlds of "2001"* (Signet, 1972), 78.

Chapter 1. David Lynch and Unmanifest Destiny: *Twin Peaks* 3

1. When I interviewed producer and *Twin Peaks* cocreator Mark Frost, he was not forthcoming about the pressure on himself and David from the network (in discussion with the author, November 22, 1991). But Frost has since stated directly for publication that both he and Lynch were frustrated by the network's demands to identify the murderer and move on. "We were getting heavy, heavy pressure from the network to solve the murder; in fact, they wanted it solved at the end of the first season, and David's instinct—and mine to the same extent—was . . . '[the mystery was] sort of the MacGuffin that brought us into this world

and doesn't necessarily need to be solved.'" Mark Frost, "*Twin Peaks*: Co-Creator on Network Pressures and David Lynch," interview by Jodie Tyley, *SciFiNow*, January 20, 2022, https://www.scifinow.co.uk/interviews/twin-peaks-co-creator-on-network-pressures-and-david-lynch/. David Lynch spoke many times to me of his frustration with the compromise he and Frost reached to solve the murder in the second season. He, too, has spoken publicly about his dismay.

2. Martha P. Nochimson, *The Passion of David Lynch: Wild at Heart in Hollywood* (University of Texas Press, 1997).
3. Martha P. Nochimson, *David Lynch Swerves: Uncertainty from "Lost Highway" to "Inland Empire,"* (University of Texas Press, 2013).
4. Based on my interviews with Lynch and Frost, I discuss the asymmetry of their collaboration in some detail in *The Passion of David Lynch*, 75–78, and in "Desire Under the Douglas Firs: Entering the Body of Reality in *Twin Peaks*," *Film Quarterly* 46, no. 2 (Winter 1992–1993): 22–34, https://doi.org/10.2307/1213005. An interesting account of the difficulties of the collaboration can also be found in David Canfield, "Between Two Worlds," *Slate*, May 3, 2017, https://slate.com/culture/2017/05/twin-peaks-creators-david-lynch-and-mark-frosts-strange-sublime-collaboration-a-history.html.
5. Frost has written two novels retelling the story of *Twin Peaks*: *The Secret History of Twin Peaks* (Flatiron Books, 2016) and *Twin Peaks: The Final Dossier* (Flatiron Books, 2017). *Secret History* inserts the series into linear history, contextualizing its events in terms of the explorations of the Pacific Northwest by Lewis and Clark. Such a context does not exist in the series. *The Final Dossier* contends that the Blue Rose task force is part of a secret government project exploring UFOs and alien life-forms. Where Lynch constructs a series from a postquantum/Einsteinian point of view, in which reality is reenvisioned as inherently divergent from Newtonian thinking, Frost engages in private revisionism, reconfiguring *Twin Peaks* from a Newtonian perspective. Frost equates nonlinearity with life-forms alien to human life and linear normality. What's more, *The Final Dossier* reconfigures in his own imagination what happens to characters after the *TP 2* season finale. Frost's scenarios have little or no bearing on what happens to the characters in *TP 3*. His most glaring distortion is his dossier of Audrey Horne (Sherilyn Fenn). In *TP 3*, Audrey is divorced from waking life, lying in the hospital in a two-and-a-half-decade coma as a result of the devastating explosion in the Twin Peaks bank at the end of the second season. In *Dossier*, Audrey becomes a hairdresser. Frost's retooling of the series as an entirely different, linear universe is reminiscent of Arthur C. Clarke's novelizations of Stanley Kubrick's *2001* and its sequels (see introduction). Sabrina Sutherland told me about Lynch's response to these books in an email dated May 25, 2025.
6. When I spoke to Frost about the season finale of *TP 2*, for which Frost received on-screen credit, he referred me to Lynch, who sent me Frost's scripts of the last two episodes of the season. To my astonishment, they were significantly different from what the audience had seen on-screen. In *The Passion of David Lynch*, I discuss in detail the differences between Frost's scripts and the episodes Lynch improvised for taping (94–98). In "Desire Under the Douglas Firs," I first broke the story of Lynch's rejection of Frost's scripts.
7. David Lynch, in discussion with the author, May 11, 2023.

8. Lynch, discussion. Lynch explicitly equates the unified field of physics with the unbounded ocean of consciousness in his book *Catching the Big Fish: Meditation, Consciousness, and Creativity*, 10th anniversary ed. (TarcherPerigree, 2016), 47.
9. Joseph Campbell, *The Hero with a Thousand Faces*, 3rd ed. (New World Library, 2008). Campbell's template of the hero's journey, the monomyth, is very detailed in its elucidation of the stages of the voyage. Most storytellers who use Campbell's template modify it to suit the needs of their narrative.
10. Brian Greene, *The Elegant Universe: Superstrings, Hidden Dimensions, and the Quest for the Ultimate Theory* (W. W. Norton, 2010), 6.
11. Arthur S. Eddington, *The Nature of the Physical World*, Gifford Lectures of 1927, annotated ed., annotated and introduced by H. G. Callaway (Cambridge Scholars, 2014), 336–337.
12. Franz Kafka, *The Trial*, trans. Mike Mitchell (Oxford University Press, 2009), 155.
13. Franz Kafka, *The Metamorphosis* (Classic Press, 2009).
14. Tony Nader, "One Unbounded Ocean of Consciousness," unpublished MS, 2023; and Tony Nader, *Consciousness Is All There Is: How Understanding and Experiencing Consciousness Will Transform Your Life*, foreword by David Lynch (Hay House, 2024). For Nader's discussion of the levels of consciousness, please refer to *Consciousness Is All There Is*, chapters 11–18, 190–299. Nader maps out meticulously Lynch's understanding of the stages of consciousness toward enlightenment.
15. Coning is discussed at length and diagrammed in "One Unbounded Ocean"; in *Consciousness Is All*, Nader diagrams the motion toward and away from enlightenment with a pyramid. However, the terms of the dynamic remain the same. Motion toward the higher consciousnesses represented in the pyramid is an approach toward enlightenment. Motion away from them is descent into nothingness, which is nonexistence (213). To the discussion of the dynamic, in *Consciousness Is All*, Nader adds a concept of two journeys: the analysis journey, which translates into coning down, as Lynch conceives of it, and the forces that divide; and the synthesis journey, which translates into Lynch's coning-up dynamic, and the forces that connect (216–217).
16. You can find a discussion of the spinning particles here: "What Is Entanglement and Why Is It Important?" Caltech Science Exchange, October 11, 2021, https://scienceexchange.caltech.edu/topics/quantum-science-explained/entanglement.
17. For Nader's discussion of subject and object referral, please refer to *Consciousness Is All* (193–198). Coning up is an approach to the level of consciousness that fosters love and connection of all kinds. Nader identifies the sixth level of awareness, God Consciousness, with connectivity (286–293).
18. Nader's lovely formulation of love as the ultimate verb appears in "One Unbounded Ocean" (202). It is too evocative to omit from our discussion, even though it is not in Nader's published book.
19. Sir James Jeans, interview in *The Observer* (1931), quoted in Nader, *Consciousness Is All* (18). Please refer to Nader's discussion of James Jeans in *Consciousness Is All* (34).
20. Erwin Schrödinger, quoted (via *The Observer*, January 11, 1931) in Nader, *Consciousness Is All* (34).

21. A basic difference between quantum mechanics, on one hand, and string theory and M-theory on the other, is that quantum physics is based on particles and waves, while string theory and M-theory are based on fields. Nader discusses these differences in *Consciousness Is All* (33–40). For a physicist's discussion of string theory and M-theory for the layman, see Greene, *Elegant Universe*, 231–345.
22. Lynch, discussion.
23. Jorge Luis Borges, "The Garden of Forking Paths," in *Collected Fictions*, deluxe ed., trans. Andrew Hurley (Penguin Books, 1998), 127. There are grounds for equating Borgesian time with Lynchian time. When I read him this quotation from Borges's short story, he was extremely enthusiastic about it. "I like this guy," he said. "This guy is right on the money." Lynch, discussion.
24. A resource for information about tulpas is "Tulpa," Wikipedia, last edited April 1, 2025, https://en.wikipedia.org/wiki/Tulpa#Thoughtform. It is not definitive, but Lynch's use of this peculiar figure is not based on a thorough knowledge of it. He has refined it for his narrative purposes.
25. Lynch, discussion.
26. Michael Barile, assistant to David Lynch, email message to author, July 28, 2023. All the music choices in *TP 3* were made by David Lynch.
27. There is a rumor in circulation that that the unnamed young girl who ingests the hybrid creature (Tikaeni Faircrest) is Sarah Palmer as an adolescent, which may have its origin in something Mark Frost said. I suggest that there is absolutely no indication in part 8 that the girl has any connection to Sarah, while the connection of the vignette to the coning down of the marketplace initiated by the White Sands atomic bomb test is very clear. The rumor lacks credibility and is likely an attempt to make sense of the strangeness of part 8 by forcing it into a linear narrative.
28. An intriguing element of the series finale is that Carrie Page's last name is homophonous with Beverly Paige's (Ashley Judd), Ben Horne's (Richard Beymer) secretary at the Great Northern Hotel. Why? Well, why not in a cosmos in which all is connected in the unified field? It is one of the nonlinear delights of *TP3* that teases the imagination.
29. Nader, *Consciousness Is All*, 202.
30. David Lynch, in discussion with the author, March 18, 2010. Lynch also mentions this aphorism in *Catching the Big Fish*, 21.

Chapter 2. Terrence Malick's Nonlinear Book of Job: *The Tree of Life*

1. Martin Heidegger was a member of the Nazi Party before and during World War II: of this there is no question. But was he a Nazi philosopher? Politically, he is on record speaking both for and against antisemitism. When he was the rector of the University of Freiburg, he prevented book burnings and refused to display a brutally antisemitic government poster, but he also denounced and demoted colleagues as insufficiently committed to the Nazi cause. In Bonnie Eisner's interview with Richard Wolin about his book *Heidegger in Ruins: Between Philosophy and Ideology* (Yale University Press, 2023), Wolin argues that while Heidegger committed many inexcusable acts as rector of the University of Freiburg during the war, the magnitude of his contribution to philosophy is undeniable; it is necessary to separate the ideologue from the

philosopher: "To say that something like *Being and Time* [Heidegger's masterpiece] was already Nazi or even proto-Nazi would be a real stretch." Evaluation of Heidegger's philosophy, however, is a highly contentious issue. On the one hand, Heidegger's support of Hitler "revealed flaws inherent in his philosophical conceptions," according to Jürgen Habermas, Theodor Adorno, Maurice Merleau-Ponty, and György Lukács, among others. But on the other hand, intellectuals such as Hannah Arendt, Otto Pöggeler, Jan Patočka, Jacques Derrida, and Richard Rorty "see his involvement with Nazism as a personal 'error'—a word that Arendt placed in quotation marks when referring to Heidegger's Nazi-era politics—that is irrelevant to his philosophy." Richard Wolin, "Tainted by Nazism, Heidegger's Philosophy Casts a Long Shadow," interview by Bonnie Eisner, CUNY GC Stories, March 28, 2023, https://www.gc.cuny.edu/news/tainted-nazism-heideggers-philosophy-casts-long-shadow; "Martin Heidegger and Nazism," Wikipedia, last edited April 2, 2025, https://en.wikipedia.org/wiki/Martin_Heidegger_and_Nazism.

This serious and complex question bears heavily on our consideration of Heidegger's influence on Terrence Malick, as a cocreator of the new zeitgeist. I am in no position to make a final determination about Heidegger, ideology, and philosophy. At the same time, it has been incumbent on me to make a credible determination about whether Malick admires Heidegger for anything that could relate to Nazi ideology, and I contend, for cause, that he does not. In the light of how critically hierarchy and repressive authoritarianism—the essence of Nazism—is regarded in *The Tree of Life* (and other Malick films), and of the positive representation of generative and regenerative unmediated being, it would be, to quote Richard Wolin, a "real stretch" to read Hitler and/or the Third Reich into Heidegger's influence on Malick.

2. James Wierzbicki, *Terrence Malick, Sonic Style* (Routledge, 2019), 10. Gilbert Ryle was interested in phenomenology, but not in Heidegger or in Malick's proposed dissertation that would link Heidegger with Kierkegaard and Wittgenstein. See also Bernard Prusak, "What Is He Up To? Seeing as God Sees: Malick's *The Tree of Life*," *Commonweal*, December 18, 2013, https://www.commonwealmagazine.org/what-he.
3. Terrence Malick, ed. and trans., *The Essence of Reasons*, a bilingual edition incorporating the text of *Vom Wesen des Grundes* (Northwestern University Press, 1969); "Terrence Malick," Wikipedia, last edited March 28, 2025, https://en.wikipedia.org/wiki/Terrence_Malick. See also Wierzbicki, *Sonic Style*, 10.
4. The project of studying the immediate moment in physics is discussed in a way that laymen might understand in Richard A. Muller, *Now: The Physics of Time* (W. W. Norton, 2016). A reference that clearly maps the immediacy of the moment in Vedic terms is Tony Nader, *Consciousness Is All There Is: How Understanding and Experiencing Consciousness Will Transform Your Life* (Hay House, 2024).
5. One example of the uncomprehending critical notices of *The Tree of Life* is a review by Jason Solomons, which concludes:

> Malick's camera drifts like an angel, or a ghost, rarely staying still, its images sweeping us along in an ebb and flow, washing us in the ways of nature and the ways of grace. Yet within its ambition to convey the meaning of life, *The*

> *Tree of Life* is also boring, cliched and banal. Dad loses a job and the family move house and things will never quite be the same. The film flashes back to adult Jack, now wandering a salt flat, or some kind of beach, surrounded by lost souls.
>
> What are we to make of this coda? I find it shockingly cheesy.

Jason Solomons, review of *The Tree of Life*, directed by Terrence Malick, *Guardian*, July 10, 2011, https://www.theguardian.com/film/2011/jul/10/tree-of-life-terrence-malick-review.

6. There is now a wealth of serious criticism that explores with interest Malick's use of the camera, his sound designs, his relationship with philosophy, his images, and even his place as an ecocritic. See John Bleasdale, *The Magic Hours: The Films and Hidden Life of Terrence Malick* (University Press of Kentucky, 2024); Wierzbicki, *Sonic Style*; James Batcho, *Terrence Malick's Unseeing Cinema: Memory, Time and Audibility* (Palgrave Macmillan, 2018); Gabriella Blasi, *The Work of Terrence Malick: Time-Based Ecocinema* (Amsterdam University Press, 2019); Steven DeLay, ed., *Life Above the Clouds: Philosophy in the Films of Terrence Malick* (SUNY Press, 2023); Jonathan Beever and Vernon W. Cisney, eds., *The Way of Nature and the Way of Grace: Philosophical Footholds on Terrence Malick's "The Tree of Life"* (Northwestern University Press, 2016); Daniel Morgan, "The Curious Ironist: Terrence Malick and the Drama of Perspective," chap. 6 in *The Lure of the Image: Epistemic Fantasies of the Moving Camera* (University of California Press, 2021); Thomas Deane Tucker and Stuart Kendall, eds., *Terrence Malick: Film and Philosophy* (Continuum, 2011).
7. *A Hidden Life* gives us an interesting perspective on whether and how the way Heidegger influences Malick's art might have any links to Heidegger's participation in the Third Reich. The film is informed by Heidegger's complex ideas about the impossibility of an authentic individual life enclosed within an inauthentic communal system; the inauthentic community in the film is clearly the Nazi regime. Franz's choice of death defies all the norms of the society he lives in, as the authorities repeatedly give him a chance to live, if he will only take the oath of loyalty to Hitler, but Franz's refusal can arguably be read, in the light of Heidegger's concept of authentic life, as a choice of authentic life. Here, I contend, Malick jettisons Heidegger's choice to live within an inauthentic community as irrelevant to his philosophy. We might even say that Franz's story suggests that Heidegger's choice to join Hitler made him a "dead man walking."
8. Bilge Ebiri, "Will Terrence Malick Ever Really Finish *The Tree of Life*?," review of Criterion Blu-ray/DVD edition of *The Tree of Life*, dir. Terrence Malick, *Vulture*, September 11, 2018, https://www.vulture.com/2018/09/will-terrence-malick-ever-really-finish-the-tree-of-life.html.
9. The persistence of the angst surrounding the death of R. L. in *TOL* clearly resonates with a tragic chapter in Malick's personal life. His younger brother, Larry, died by suicide at around the age of nineteen, while he was in Spain studying guitar with Andrés Segovia. Possibly depressed, and purportedly "frustrated by his lack of progress, . . . he broke his own hands, and later committed suicide." Or at least, it is likely that he did. Mystery surrounds his death, as it surrounds R. L.'s death in the film. The arrival of a telegram from an unidentified source informing Mother and Father of his death leaves the circumstances ambiguous. But the shock of his early demise, at around the age Larry Malick died, and the

film's showing R. L. frequently playing his guitar, connects Jack's anguish about his brother to Malick's. There is also the detail that R. L. is known in the film only by his initials, which "happen to be" the two consonants in Larry's name, reversed. Luke Blackall, "The Secret Life of Terrence Malick," *Independent*, May 24, 2011, https://www.independent.co.uk/arts-entertainment/films/features/the-secret-life-of-terrence-malick-2288183.html; Tucker and Kendall, introduction to *Film and Philosophy*, 4. See also Forrest Wickman, "Terrence Malick's Personal Period," Brow Beat, *Slate*, April 13, 2013, https://slate.com/culture/2013/04/terrence-malicks-personal-period-to-the-wonder-and-tree-of-life-are-remarkably-autobiographical.html.

10. The fictional universes of the classic family stories in the movies are profoundly and unquestioningly assumed to be Christian and ruled by a just Jehovah. They are made for a white, Christian target audience. Only a passing glimpse of the family in church, or a phrase like "God's will be done," is sufficient to remind the audience of the norm of the movie cosmos. Much the same way that in classic mass-media entertainment being a white Christian is so unquestioningly assumed to be normal and all else Other that the need for discussion is unthinkable within movie parameters.
11. Through the sermon of the Waco minister, the book of Job is positioned in *TOL* as an authoritarian text that is ultimately the bedrock of an inauthentic, authoritarian, hierarchical community. But that is not a universally held opinion. Many interpret Job as an ambiguous meditation on cosmic justice. For example, Elie Wiesel, Holocaust survivor, made the book of Job a focus of his struggle to maintain a belief in God, after the cataclysms of World War II, and found only enigma in what it reflected about Jehovah. Ariel Burger, "What Elie Wiesel Taught Me About the Book of Job," *My Jewish Learning*, accessed April 3, 2025, https://www.myjewishlearning.com/article/what-elie-wiesel-taught-me-about-the-book-of-job/.
12. Richard Kearney, "Martin Heidegger," in *Modern Movements in European Philosophy*, 2nd ed. (Manchester University Press, 1994), 30.
13. Kearney, "Martin Heidegger," 36.
14. To see an example of Thomas Wilfred's lumia in motion, see "Thomas Wilfred's Lumia compostions [*sic*] Opus 140," posted December 2, 2014, by ajemutt, YouTube, 10 min., https://www.youtube.com/watch?v=k3__CoJitqI. See also Lee Carruthers's commentary on Thomas Wilfred in *Doing Time: Temporality, Hermeneutics, and Contemporary Cinema* (SUNY Press, 2016), 121–123.
15. Kearney, "Martin Heidegger," 40. In narrating the Heidegger paradox about individual and community into Jack's journey, Malick resonates with Heidegger's belief that individual Dasein is inextricably connected to the "gathering" of the community in Dasein.
16. Lee Carruthers also discusses the centrality of montage to Malick's filmmaking. Carruthers explores montage as Malick's way of sensitizing us to knowing that there is always more than we see. She is a short hop away from Heidegger's Dasein, but she doesn't connect those dots. *Doing Time*, 126–128.
17. DeLay, "Malickian Cinema at the Intersection of Art and Philosophy," introduction to *Life Above the Clouds*, 10.
18. Jonathan Edwards, "Sinners in the Hands of an Angry God," [July 8, 1741], in *The Sermons of Jonathan Edwards: A Reader*, ed. Wilson H. Kimnach, Kenneth P. Minkema, and Douglas A. Sweeney (Yale University Press, 1999), 49–65.

19. Kearney summarizes Heidegger's individual/community paradox this way: "But poetry is far more than an act of individual conscience. It involves a communal recollection. . . . Authentic poetry can remind a community that they have been exiled from their tradition which must be sought after anew." Heidegger was clear that this gathering in poetry could not be an "antique regression," to old mediations. Rather, the poetry Heidegger had in mind must be an encounter with a future union that could never arrive but must always be sought, which I liken to the always shifting form of Wilfred's lumia sculptures. Heidegger pursued the restoration of language through verbal poetic thinking. By contrast, Malick sought the paradox of authentic individual/community nexus in visual montage. Kearney, "Martin Heidegger," 40.
20. Morgan, "Curious Ironist." In Daniel Morgan's fascinating essay about Malick's use of the camera, he maps the misunderstanding of what he calls Malick's phenomenological project. His essay pushes off from Robert Koehler's slash-and-burn critique of Malick's camera: "The Steadicam and handheld camera strategy that Malick has been using . . . have brought out all his worst instincts. Tools with few limitations, handheld cameras can be lilted, swung, or rotated in any possible direction and axis. . . . Malick's work appears unmoored, lacking in a governing idea for the uses of the camera. . . . Malick, once an artist with a disciplined sensibility for scale and sensation, has gone goofy with the devices" (169). Morgan argues that what Koehler and others of his opinion fail to perceive is that "Malick uses the moving camera to create multiple paths through the world—multiple and varied positions that the viewer is able to occupy—that provide a way to negotiate the varying pressures placed on the way characters respond to the world around them. . . . [T]hough it lacks the stability of a given subject position[,] . . . [it] reaches for a fantasy of experience before the imposition of perspective" (174). Morgan, however, does not spin his detailed, vivid discussion of Malick's camera strategy into a discussion of how it creates the Heidegger paradox of authentic Being for individual and community. Indeed, he mistakenly, as I believe, says that Heidegger does not tend to portray individuals against systems. By contrast, I argue that creating "multiple paths through the world" with his camera is part of Malick's portrayal of the openness of the authentic, post-Newtonian alter ego of the community and the individual, in opposition to prequantum, inauthentic, closed systems. So, rather than describing Malick's films as creating a fantasy of experience, as Morgan contends, I believe that Malick gives us a poetic, Heideggerian experience of a nonlinear reality.

Chapter 3. Outsiders, Forking Paths, Healing Oxymorons: *The OA*, *Eternal Sunshine of the Spotless Mind*

1. Jorge Luis Borges, "The Garden of Forking Paths," in *Collected Fictions*, deluxe ed., trans. Andrew Hurley (Penguin, 1998), 127.
2. James Poniewozik, "The Cryptic Sparkles in *The OA*. Reality Disappoints," *New York Times*, December 16, 2016, https://www.nytimes.com/2016/12/16/arts/television/review-the-cryptic-sparkles-in-the-oa-reality-disappoints.html.
3. Peter Debruge, "Why *The OA* Is One of the Year's Most Important Films," *Variety*, December 24, 2016, https://variety.com/2016/tv/columns/the-oa-netflix-brit-marling-film-critic-appreciation-1201948242/.

4. Although we do not have as full a statement of her vision as we have of David Lynch's, we need not guess about Brit Marling's interest in nonlinearity. She has written of the limitations of linear narrative—without using the word "linear"—as being representative of the trajectory of male desire. In "I Don't Want to Be the Strong Female Lead," an opinion piece she wrote for *The New York Times*, she imagines a conversation with herself about storytelling: "Brit, the hero's journey is centuries of narrative precedent written by men to mythologize men. Its pattern is inciting incident, rising tension, explosive climax and denouement. What does that remind you of? And I say, a male orgasm." Marling does not want to play a "strong female lead"—a female hero cast in the mold of male narrative. Her desire to imagine new mythologies and narrative structures is realized in the nested narrative, the matryoshka shape of *The OA*. Her experience of and interest in storytelling as a communal effort, rather than the act of one artist, also informs the nonlinear structure of *The OA*. Marling describes her relationship to her writing partner, Zal Batmanglij, in an interview with Malcolm Gladwell, as a true meeting of minds. It is very much unlike the problematic relationship between Mark Frost and David Lynch (discussed in chapter 1) or that between Stanley Kubrick and Arthur C. Clarke (discussed in the introduction). Rather, she speaks of discovery of the narrative as if it were part of an archaeological dig: "So the story is just some *thing*, like a prehistoric skeleton beneath the ground, and you begin by just digging in the dirt. You hit a bone and you're like, 'What's this?' And you dig around it, trying to excavate something that exists without you." She believes that the more artists you bring into this process, the better.

While Marling has taken part in many interviews, Batmanglij has avoided them. He is notoriously private and doesn't even own a telephone (as I gathered from a conversation I had with Damon Lindelof, May 12, 2023). So, a 2016 interview with both creators by Emma Dibdin in *Esquire* is a rare opportunity to "hear" them in conversation. The two of them speak of learning from interviewing young people the age of the Crestwood Five—the suburban high school students OA speaks with after she returns from her seven-year absence—how unhappy they were about their future prospects. "A lot of the old linear paths seem to have become corrupt, or broken, or don't seem to lead to the place everyone says they did," Marling says, surely a strong indication of her thoughts about linear narratives.

Brit Marling, "I Don't Want to Be the Strong Female Lead," Opinion, *New York Times*, February 7, 2020, https://www.nytimes.com/2020/02/07/opinion/sunday/brit-marling-women-movies.html; Brit Marling, interview by Malcolm Gladwell, *Interview*, February 24, 2017, https://www.interviewmagazine.com/culture/brit-marling; Brit Marling and Zal Batmanglij, "*The OA* Creators Break Down the Mysteries of Netflix's Surprise Series," interview by Emma Dibdin, *Esquire*, December 19, 2016, https://www.esquire.com/entertainment/tv/news/a51648/the-oa-netflix-interview-brit-marling-zal-batmanglij/.

5. Brian Greene, "A Physicist Explains Why Parallel Universes May Exist," interview by Terry Gross, *Fresh Air*, NPR, January 24, 2011, transcript, https://www.npr.org/transcripts/132932268. Greene is the author of important books for the layman about the new map of the universe. See Brian Greene, *The Elegant Universe: Superstrings, Hidden Dimensions, and the Quest for the Ultimate Theory*

(W. W. Norton, 2010); Brian Greene, *Until the End of Time: Mind, Matter, and Our Search for Meaning in an Evolving Universe* (Alfred A. Knopf, 2020).

There are also other real-world sources for the series' narrative. Marling and Batmanglij used the real case studies described in psychiatrist Raymond Moody's book *Life After Life* (Mockingbird Books, 1975). Marling told interviewer Taylor Ferber that the initial idea for the show came from a conversation she had at a party, with a stranger who told her about a near-death experience. In *The OA*'s second season, a dream study important to the narrative was inspired by an actual study in Germany in the 1930s, in which a significant number of ordinary Germans pursuing their everyday lives anticipated the Holocaust in their dreams. Taylor Ferber, "As *The OA* (Finally) Returns, Here's Everything That Inspired the Sci-Fi Story," *Refinery29*, March 20, 2019, https://www.refinery29.com/en-us/2019/03/226950/is-the-oa-based-on-true-story; Alison Flood, "The Social Dreaming Experiment," *Guardian*, June 2, 2010, https://www.theguardian.com/books/2010/jun/02/hay-festival-social-dreaming.

6. Connectivity as the foundation of the cosmos needs to be understood in terms of what various physicists theorize as the building blocks of the universe. There are competing theories. In the evolving, new map of the cosmos, quantum physicists assume the composition of everything is a complex blend of particles and waves moving as random, disconnected energies. Another field of physicists assumes the reverse. They postulate a cosmos that is fundamentally composed not of particles and waves but of fields, as in string theory and M-theory. For some interesting thoughts about particles and consciousness, see Greene, "Particles and Consciousness: From Life to Mind," chap. 5 in *End of Time*; for a consideration of quantum theory and perception, see Greene, "Space, Time, and the Eye of the Beholder," chap. 2 in *Elegant Universe*; for a consideration of string theory and the unified cosmos, see Greene, "The Cosmic Symphony," part 3 (chaps. 6–9) of *Elegant Universe*; for some thoughts about M-theory, see Greene, "Beyond Strings: In Search of M-Theory," chap. 12 in *Elegant Universe*.
7. In a soul-searching speech for an event organized by BAFTA (British Academy of Film and Television Arts) in September 2011, Kaufman spoke directly about his struggle with truth in storytelling:

> Storytelling is inherently dangerous. If you consider a traumatic event in your life, consider it as you experienced it. Now think about how you told it to someone a year later. Now think about how you told it for the one hundredth time. It's not the same thing. A few components enter into the change. One is perspective. Most people think perspective is a good thing to have in a story. You can figure out characters' arcs, you can apply a moral, you can tell it from a distance with understanding and context. The problem is that this perspective is a misrepresentation of the incident; it's a reconstruction with meaning and as such bears very little resemblance to the event.

Charlie Kaufman, "Screenwriters' Lecture," BAFTA, September 30, 2011, https://www.bafta.org/media-centre/transcripts/screenwriters-lecture-charlie-kaufman. In a 2020 *New York Times* profile, Kaufman similarly expressed his frustration with "retrospective awareness" in narrative. "Consider a toothache, [Kaufman] said. A truly searing, excruciating toothache can overcome you entirely: your mouth, your body, your mind. 'It can be a very primal moment in your life,' he said. 'But compare that to a year later. . . . You no longer have a toothache, presumably. You've got a story about having a toothache, with a beginning, middle and end. . . . But when you're in the middle of the toothache, you don't have that perspective. It's a very chaotic moment.'" It is the moment that Kaufman longs to tell. Jon Mooallem, "This Profile of Charlie Kaufman Has Changed," *New York Times Magazine*, July 2, 2020, https://www.nytimes.com/2020/07/02/magazine/charlie-kaufman.html.

8. Kaufman's connections with Kafka and Beckett are noted widely in interviews and brief profiles, such as, for example, an interview in *The Scotsman* in which he speaks of Beckett's influence. The piece also mentions *Human Nature* (dir. Michel Gondry, 2001), a film for which he adapted Kafka's short story "A Report to an Academy." Charlie Kaufman, "Life's Little Dramas," interview, *Scotsman*, May 7, 2009, https://www.scotsman.com/whats-on/arts-and-entertainment/charlie-kaufman-interview-lifes-little-dramas-2461791.

9. In *The Scotsman*, Kaufman makes his position about genre very clear. "I don't write genre stuff in any form. . . . I'm not interested in it. I always try to do the opposite of that." Kaufman is after an organic kind of storytelling, which means the avoidance of templates of any kind when he develops his screenplays, as he told the BAFTA audience in 2011, and as he asserted in *The Scotsman*, when he signaled his disgust with the three-act structure: "'I don't know what the hell a third act is,' [he says]. 'I have something I'm interested in and then I decide I'm going to explore it,' he says. 'I don't know where the characters are going to go or what the screenplay's going to do. For me, that's the way to keep it alive and make it interesting and worthwhile.'" Nevertheless, in Andrew Butler's book-length study of *Eternal Sunshine of the Spotless Mind*, Butler finds himself, despite his knowledge of Kaufman's rejection of genre, constrained to think almost exclusively in terms of the possible genres to which he can compare the film: science fiction, the comedy of remarriage, and the puzzle film. This is the typical plight of critics who apply linear templates to the nonlinear film and television of popular artists. Kaufman, "Life's Little Dramas"; Kaufman, "Screenwriters' Lecture"; Andrew Butler, *Eternal Sunshine of the Spotless Mind*, BFI Film Classics (Palgrave Macmillan, 2014).

10. When Jim Carrey was cast in *Sunshine*, he was widely associated with extreme, cartoonish portrayals of aberrational, extroverted, and aggressive personalities, as in *The Mask* (1994), *Dumb and Dumber* (1994), *Ace Ventura: When Nature Calls* (1995), *The Cable Guy* (1996), and *Liar Liar* (1997). Even in *The Truman Show* (1998), in which he plays a sweet, ordinary, unaggressive guy, his sweetness is an aggressive caricature of the small-town, ordinary Joe. When Kate Winslet was cast as the out-of-control Clementine in *Sunshine*, her filmography did include rebellious characters—she was a sweet-seeming but pathological teen murderer in *Heavenly Creatures* (1994), and the romantic and impulsive but still conventional Marianne, second of the three Dashwood sisters in *Sense and Sensibility* (1995)—but she was most widely recognized by the public as Rose in *Titanic* (1997), a charmingly wholesome rebel against class prejudice and tunnel vision in the early twentieth century. Her disheveled angst as Clementine, who barely understands the concept of boundaries, plays interestingly against her star persona of the time.

11. Charlie Kaufman, widely recognized as an intellectual and an eclectic filmmaker, is associated with a broad spectrum of artists and philosophers in addition to Kafka and Samuel Beckett. In the critical anthology *The Philosophy of*

Charlie Kaufman, Kaufman is aligned with Ludwig Wittgenstein, Søren Kierkegaard, and Friedrich Nietzsche, as well as Kafka. In an interview for *Salon*, Michael Sragow lists Kaufman's favorite authors, in addition to Kafka and Beckett, as Stanisław Lem, Philip K. Dick, Shirley Jackson, and Flannery O'Connor. The interview in *The Scotsman* adds Woody Allen and Monty Python to the list. In a critical essay in *Cinephile Princess*, Kaufman's work is assessed as reflecting ideas of Friedrich Nietzsche, Abraham Maslow, David Hume, Jean Baudrillard, Jacques Derrida, John Locke, and Jean-Jacques Rousseau. David LaRocca, ed., *The Philosophy of Charlie Kaufman* (University Press of Kentucky, 2019); Michael Sragow, "Being Charlie Kaufman," *Salon*, November 11, 1999, https://www.salon.com/1999/11/11/kaufman/; Kaufman, "Life's Little Dramas"; Mayrav Estrin, "Charlie Kaufman: The Philosophy Behind His Surrealist Screenplays," *Cinephile Princess* (blog), accessed April 4, 2025, https://cinephileprincess.net/films/charlie-kaufman-the-philosophy-behind-his-surrealist-screenplays.

12. "Q&A with Charlie Kaufman on *I'm Thinking Of Ending Things*," Writer's Guild of America East (virtual), September 14, 2020. During Kaufman's BAFTA lecture, in an answer like the one he gave me at the WGAE Q&A, he said, "I'm really interested in philosophy and science. I'm a layman and I have no mathematic skill because I became really interested in physics through the popular physics books. And in every popular physics book there's always this admonition, you don't really know what we're talking about. We're going to pretend that we're talking to you now but you have no idea what we're talking about. I found that really frustrating." Kaufman, "Screenwriters' Lecture."
13. *The Letters of Abelard and Heloise*, trans. with introduction and notes by Betty Radice and revised by M. T. Clanchy (Penguin Books, 2004).
14. Kaufman's BAFTA address is a signature example of how he believes his personal experience of alienation and distance intersects with his art. Kaufman begins, "I've never delivered a speech before, which is why I decided to do this tonight. I wanted to do something that I don't know how to do, and offer you the experience of watching someone fumble, because I think maybe that's what art should offer. An opportunity to recognise our common humanity and vulnerability. . . . I'm just telling you off the bat that I don't know anything." The great themes of this address are connection and truth. Connection is the issue; erasure of discomfort is disconnection, just as it is in *Sunshine*. He gambles on shared discomfort, as Joel and Clementine do in *Sunshine*. Kaufman, "Screenwriters' Lecture."
15. Kaufman has much to say about time, obliquely, through his storytelling in *Sunshine*. What does he have to say directly? In an interview with an architecture blogger, we glean something about Kaufman, time, and storytelling in cinema when he speaks of the beginning of his *Being John Malkovich* (1999):

    > There's an unnatural time passage in the first few scenes that you may not see because there's so much going on: the radio is saying what day it is, but it doesn't relate to what the newspaper date is; the milk is expired; it's the first day of fall but you hear the radio saying it's October 20th; the cartoon is telling you what's going to happen later on; after he gets injured, at the hospital, there's Christmas music in the background, then when he gets to the ophthalmologist he thanks him for getting him in right away but the calendar says March 2006, which means it's 3 months after.

"Unnatural" time opens the film, even though Kaufman is striving for "naturalism," he says. Yet he also tells us that "as the movie spirals out it gets more . . . surreal, I guess" (ellipsis in original). Time, reality, and the natural chase each other in his statement. Time, linearity, and reality are clearly signature issues in Kaufman's filmography. This study attempts to cast light on the temporality issue specific to *Sunshine*. Charlie Kaufman, "Here's What Happens When You Look for Truth," interview by Jimmy Stamp, *Life Without Buildings* (blog), October 13, 2008, https://web.archive.org/web/20081016060307/https://lifewithoutbuildings.net/2008/10/heres-what-happens-when-you-look-for-truth-life-without-buildings-interviews-charlie-kaufman.html.

Chapter 4. History Don't Teach: The Nonlinear Heritage Society—*The Romanoffs, Cloud Atlas, BlacKkKlansman*

1. Jean-Jacques Rousseau, *On the Social Contract*, trans. G. D. H. Cole (Dover Thrift Editions, 2003), 1; and see Thomas Hobbes, *Leviathan*, with an introduction and notes by Christopher Brooke (Penguin Classics, 2017).
2. David Graeber and David Wengrow, *The Dawn of Everything: A New History of Humanity* (Farrar, Straus and Giroux, 2021), 9. In this section (pp. 6–9), entitled, "Why Both the Hobbesian and Rousseauian Versions of Human History Have Dire Political Implications," Graeber and Wengrow critique both of these historians, generally deemed polar opposites, as essentially similar in their reductiveness. Graeber and Wengrow build a foundation for their new approach to history in these pages. They focus on the vagueness of the concept of equality that has become connected with both the repressive picture painted by Hobbes and the sweetness and light of Rousseau's invocation of humanity, which they say reduces the real picture of human diversity emerging from new archaeological and anthropological evidence and forecloses what history really points toward, that "we are projects of collective self-creation" (9).
3. Should it be useful for some readers, herewith a note or two on the definition of historical teleology used in this study. Historical teleology is a sticky term that means different things to different thinkers. Here the term refers to the idea that history is a process with a single first cause leading inevitably to a single specific end or purpose. The analogy in Newtonian physics is Newton's third law, the concept that every action (made by object A) has an equal and opposite reaction (made by object B), behind which is a rigid principle of cause and effect and an assumption that there is a single, discreet object A and object B. However, in post–Newtonian physics, the concepts of superposition and entanglement negate the existence of discreet particles between which action and reaction will inevitably occur (see introduction).
4. Two representative negative reviews of *The Romanoffs*: Ben Travers, "Matthew Weiner's Amazon Show Is Shallow, Self-Indulgent, and Far Removed from *Mad Men*," review of *The Romanoffs*, October 2, 2018, https://www.indiewire.com/criticism/shows/amazon-the-romanoffs-review-matthew-weiner-mad-men-1202008529/; James Poniewozik, "*The Romanoffs* Is Elegant but Frustrating," review, *New York Times*, October 11, 2018, https://www.nytimes.com/2018/10/11/arts/television/the-romanoffs-review-amazon-prime.html.
5. Emily St. James, "*The Romanoffs*, from *Mad Men* Creator Matt Weiner, Feels Like a Period Piece About the Present," review, *Vox*, October 12, 2018,

https://www.vox.com/culture/2018/10/12/17966368/the-romanoffs-review-matt-weiner-mad-men. Although St. James misguidedly reports that the series is "everything good and bad about *Mad Men*, in one slightly soggy, bloated package," she also correctly guides us to understand that the series needs to be understood as a whole, not merely disconnected episodes. Her conclusion? "The more episodes you watch, the more *The Romanoffs* starts to feel like a story about the instability of our modern moment, a story about class consciousness, a story about the guards knocking on the door to point guns at all of our heads [a reference to Olivia's horrible trauma at the end of episode 3, 'The House of Special Purpose'], maybe even Weiner's."

6. Elizabeth Taylor, "Matthew Weiner Wants *The Romanoffs* to 'Give Us Joy' During 'Divisive and Irritating' Times," *Variety*, October 14, 2008, https://variety.com/2018/scene/news/the-romanoffs-premiere-matthew-weiner-1202979596/. In Elizabeth Taylor's report on Weiner's comments to the press about *The Romanoffs*, he represents the show as a feel-good tonic for a stormy present. "There is a public conversation right now that goes on that is extremely divisive and irritating and filled with conversation that is actually designed to antagonize and divide us. . . . I just want to give everyone permission, because we all need it, to just enjoy things that are beautiful."
7. Matthew Weiner, in discussion with the author, July 6, 2023. Weiner began to transition from a worldview of existentialism—there are no innate connections—to a worldview of esotericism—the universe is a unified field with innate values—midway through his work as creator of *Mad Men*. At that point, he began to view Don Draper less as an existential hero in a chaotic cosmos and more as a man who had mistakenly opted to behave without values. "I was just recognizing, even though I had constructed it [*Mad Men*] so clearly—you don't really know what you're doing if you're doing it right." Much like what David Lynch said to me decades before, Weiner was contending that his creative process had been working its way through the series without his rational awareness of what was going on. Weiner told me that he had been engaged in the unities of esotericism emotionally, long before he intellectually understood that worldview and its history. Matthew Weiner, in discussion with the author, May 10, 2023.
8. Matthew Weiner, in discussion with the author, May 11, 2023. "Existentialism is a young man's game. . . . As you get older you begin to feel, I am not so sure that I want to think that there's nothing but the material world. . . . I have to think [about] having experience through coincidence and interconnectedness. That's what esoteric [philosophy] is about. There is no coincidence." And: "When you experience coincidence you're opening up your awareness that this is the way the world works."
9. Weiner, discussion, May 11, 2023.
10. Weiner, discussion, May 11, 2023. "The Romanovs, especially Nicholas and Alexandra, not what you'd want in your blood as far as I'm concerned if you're going to pick ancestors." And: "The Romanovs are poisonous. When people want to tell the story of the Romanovs there's nothing to tell as far as I'm concerned that is positive. . . . You are looking at something that is one horror after another. Just horrific." Weiner, discussion, July 6, 2023. When I asked Weiner why he picked a "horrific" legacy on which to base his series, he told me it was a way of reflecting on the cultural mess he was observing around him. "I was trying to

sell the show about a bunch of people who think they used to be great. And this was literally five months before we began to hear 'Make America Great Again.'" Intriguingly, Weiner links the attractions of claiming a legacy of past greatness with the cult of victimhood. "We were and we still are in a country where the greatest currency is victimhood." Even more intriguing is how the allure of victimhood is connected, irrationally, by purported Romanovs with the catnip of royalty. Weiner was contacted by people with claims to the victimization associated with Romanov legacy who simultaneously felt that royal blood is more important than other people's blood.

11. Weiner, discussion, July 6, 2023. Weiner spoke about how his intellectual interest in esotericism and in telling stories about claimants to Romanov heritage was stimulated by his personal situation.

> But what it was—when I got separated—I think *The Romanoffs* to me was about my relationship falling apart, my long marriage, a lot of questions, like, do you love me, about being alone. These are all things that have always interested me, but interconnectedness, experiences, coincidences really informed it [*The Romanoffs*]. There is quite a bit of influence on the narratives in the series from personal stories. Some of the writers had had experience with in vitro fertilization and with adopting a baby in Russia [episode 7, "End of the Line"]. The story about the possible history of a gay teacher being a sexual predator also originated in the life of one of the writers [episode 5, "Bright and High Circle"].

Weiner went to Mexico on his honeymoon and is profoundly connected with Mexican culture (episode 6, "Panorama").

12. A sample of linear histories about the Romanov legacy, which go way back: *The Fall of the Romanoffs*, much about the influence of Rasputin (1917); *The Fall of the Romanov Dynasty*, documentary (1927); *The Romanovs*, docudrama series spanning the years 1613–1917 (8 episodes, Star Media, 2013); *Empire of the Tsars: Romanov Russia with Lucy Worsley*, documentary series (3 episodes, BBC, 2016); *The Last Czars*, miniseries chronicling the fall of the dynasty (6 episodes, Nutopia, 2019); *End of the House of Romanov*, documentary, tagline: "Power Has a Price" (Tudor Productions, 2023).
13. Some sources for esotericism: Manly P. Hall, *The Secret Teachings of All Ages* (A & D, 2009); Antoine Faivre, *Western Esotericism: A Concise History*, trans. Christine Rhone (SUNY Press, 2010); Glenn Alexander Magee, ed., *The Cambridge Handbook of Western Mysticism and Esotericism* (Cambridge University Press, 2019); and Three Initiates, *The Kybalion* (East India, 2022).
14. Weiner, discussion, May 10, 2023. Wiener outlined his list of the five major Romanov tropes that have become part of narratives about their legacy.
15. Weiner, discussion, July 6, 2023. Weiner is, in general, very partial to the anthology series of early television.
16. Weiner, discussion, July 6, 2023. Weiner is fascinated by and deeply ambivalent about genre. On the one hand, he wanted each episode to be a different genre. On the other, when we went through the episodes, we were unable to attribute genre to any of them, with maybe the exception of "House of Special Purpose" (episode 3). I said "horror"; he said "suspense." With most of them, neither of us could establish even possible genre categories. For example, when we were discussing "Expectation" (episode 4), Weiner played around with calling Virginia

Woolf's *Mrs. Dalloway*—as a genre—an inspiration for the episode. Inspiration and genre were similarly confused when Weiner likened *A Place in the Sun* (dir. George Stevens, 1951) to "The Royal We." We had some fun when he mused about the entire idea of genre, which he finds both confusing and compelling at the same time. He picked what I would have thought was one of the clearest-cut cases, the Western, and scrambled it interestingly. "Look, this is my take on genre. You know there was a time, right around the late fifties, no, mid-fifties really, every single TV show was a Western. But there are different kinds of Westerns. There is *Have Gun—Will Travel*, private eye, Paladin. There was *The Wild Wild West*, a James Bond Western. *Gunsmoke*, which is what, a soap opera? It's law and order. You have *Bonanza*, which is a family drama. There's comedy. You've got *Maverick*. . . . So, are those Westerns? What is their genre? Is *Maverick* a Western or is it a comedy? I don't know."

17. Weiner, discussion, May 10, 2023. One of the most unexpected revelations of my interviews with Weiner is that, as far as he is concerned, Anushka dies at the end of the episode. We see her carry a candle through the darkened, fashionable apartment, having left Greg and Hajar to themselves. She blows it out and leaves the frame, and we are left with the violet light of the Parisian evening glowing through a window. Anushka dies? This never occurred to me, although I had watched the series many times. However, I should not have been surprised when Weiner offered me his interpretation. It certainly meshes with his concept of what the legacy means to those who claim it. It is their mode of survival in a world in which, lacking the esoteric poetic insight into the way the cosmos works, it is all they can grab on to. Anushka, having completed her fealty to her "heritage," has no other reason to live.

> I think she dies at the end of the show. I think when the violet comes on she's dead. . . . I think that when she knows that they're going to have the baby, I think she can die. . . . I think she's dying. I originally had in the script that we were going to see the bed curtains pulled down like the shower curtain in *Psycho*. . . . But when we were doing it, it wasn't in the script anymore. I thought the audience will know it or they won't.

Weiner has the same negative capability as an artist that John Keats did. His art is not about judgment. When I suggested that the claimants to the heritage were clinging to a history that doesn't exist, he said, "It doesn't matter." A big champion of "survival," Weiner is interested in depicting how it works for the purported Romanovs; he observes how they weaponize heritage as a survival mechanism. This is true even in the case of Michael Romanoff in "The Royal We" (episode 2), who commits murder to assert himself and his desires. He so fully defines himself as a Romanov victim of the Bolsheviks and prince of the blood that he, without compunction, deceives and even attempts to kill his wife, simply because he lusts after a sexy woman he has just met on jury duty. My negative moral judgment of Michael is harsh. Not so Weiner, who spoke to me only in terms of Michael's growing up being told that he was a Romanov and how his obsessiveness worked as part of that identity.

18. Weiner, discussion, May 10, 2023. Weiner repeatedly told me that he was writing a series in which all time is one. But when I mentioned that I saw that most clearly in "The One That Holds Everything," when Greg and Sophie from "The Violet Hour" pass Jack Edgar on the railroad station stairs, he downplayed its

effect on the portrayal of time in the series. He said they needed extras for that scene and that Aaron Eckhart and Louise Bourgoin just happened to be handy while they were taping, and they decided to use them. At the same time, he did also say that he didn't know if anyone noticed, and that all the episodes had interconnections, and it was a part of a series that people could watch in any order. I find his response ambiguous. But I also relate it to his statement that "you don't really know what you're doing if you're doing it right."

19. Graeber and Wengrow, *Dawn of Everything*, 328–333. Graeber and Wengrow contrast how Teotihuacán has been narrated by linear historians to the very different picture that emerges from the evidence that Graeber and Wengrow have examined. Although there is a wealth of pictorial evidence that Teotihuacán was a place of sophistication, diversity, and a high level of crafts and technology, Graeber and Wengrow claim that there is no evidence that it was organized by a hierarchy, at the top of which reigned a king or kinglike figure. It simply does not conform to conventional historical narratives, and, according to Graeber and Wengrow, many are still trying to shoehorn it into the official narrative. Weiner does not narrate Teotihuacán in these academic terms; but he does use it as a place out of the domain of the official narrative and linear time.

20. Barbara Kosta, in her essay "Tom Tykwer's *Run Lola Run* and the Usual Suspects: The Avant-Garde, Popular Culture, and History," in *German Pop Culture: How "American" Is It?*, ed. Agnes C. Mueller (University of Michigan Press, 2004), https://www.press.umich.edu/pdf/0472113844-ch11.pdf, has some interesting things to say about Tykwer's relationship to German history and the history of German cinema. Kosta does not speak in terms of linearity and nonlinearity directly, but she tags Tykwer, correctly, as a man intent on shattering the power of old forms and categories. "Tykwer traverses national boundaries in his choice of aesthetic practices and seems to relish his role as a *bricoleur* of . . . cultural offerings" (166). In a song Tykwer uses on the soundtrack of *Lola*, "Komm Zu mir" (Come to me), Thomas D sings (in German): "We shattered every framework when we came together; it was like an explosion"; Tykwer shatters frameworks in his structuring of the film as "a highly self-conscious collage of filmic styles and genres that are brought into tension with one another, exploited, reinforced, undercut, and challenged simultaneously" (167). This reveals a suspicion of narrative, says Kosta. Connect this with Tykwer's prefacing of the film with a title card bearing a quotation from T. S. Eliot's "Little Gidding" that proclaims movement in time from "here to here":

> We shall not cease from exploration
> And the end of all our exploring
> Will be to arrive where we started
> And know the place for the first time.

Fused with Tykwer's desire to break old categories is his fascination with nonlinear time. The structure of *Lola* is a merger of quantum trajectories, in which from moment to moment a new future can be birthed, as noted by David Bordwell, "Film Futures," in "The American Production of French Theory," ed. Robert F. Barsky and Eric Méchoulan, special issue, *SubStance* 31, no.1, issue 97 (2002): 88–104, https://doi.org/10.2307/3685810.

21. Cáel M. Keegan, *Lana and Lilly Wachowski* (University of Illinois Press, 2018), 2, 4; Keegan quotes from, respectively: Susan Stryker, Paisley Currah, and Lisa

Jean Moore, "Trans, Trans-, or Transgender?," *Women's Studies Quarterly* 36, nos. 3–4 (2008): 12; and Eva Hayward and Jami Weinstein, "Introduction: Tranimalities in the Age of Trans Life," *TSQ: Transgender Studies Quarterly* 2, no. 2 (2015): 196.

22. Keegan, *Lana and Lilly Wachowski*, 145: "There is nothing like our film adaptation in terms of narrative structure."
23. David Mitchell, *Cloud Atlas* (Random House, 2004).
24. Peter Debruge, review of *Cloud Atlas*, dir. Tom Tykwer, Lana Wachowski, and Andy Wachowski, *Variety*, September 8, 2012, https://variety.com/2012/film/markets-festivals/cloud-atlas-1117948250/. In *The New York Times*, A. O. Scott declares that *Cloud Atlas* is big rather than good, that it is didactic and plodding in its translation of Mitchell's novel. Stuck in a linear perspective, Scott concludes, "For a movie devoted to the celebration of freedom, *Cloud Atlas* works awfully hard to control and contain its meaning, to tell you exactly what it is about rather than allowing you to dream and wonder within its impressively imagined world." Similarly stuck is David Edelstein reviewing for NPR. Edelstein counsels his readers to read the book. The film is, he says, "too literal-minded to be a good head-trip," though he admits that audiences at the Toronto Film Festival stood and cheered it. Contrast these with a representatively positive review by Jerome Rowley, informed by its overlap with nonlinear perspectives on the universe. Rowley meditates on the film as an example of a natural form like a cloud, mountain, or snowflake, and likens it to the great nonlinear classic James Joyce's *Ulysses*. A. O. Scott, "Souls Tangled Up in Time," review of *Cloud Atlas*, dir. Tom Tykwer, Lana Wachowski, and Andy Wachowski, *New York Times*, October 25, 2012, https://www.nytimes.com/2012/10/26/movies/cloud-atlas-from-lana-and-andy-wachowski-and-tom-tykwer.html; David Edelstein, "*Cloud Atlas*: You're Better Off Reading the Book," review, NPR, October 26, 2012, https://www.npr.org/2012/10/26/163103260/cloud-atlas-youre-better-off-reading-the-book; Jerome Rowley, "*Cloud Atlas*—A Tale of Fractals, Fracturing, and Friendship," *4squareviews* (blog), WordPress, October 31, 2012, https://4squareviews.com/2012/10/31/cloud-atlas-a-tale-of-fractals-fracturing-and-friendship-cloudatlas/.
25. Keegan, *Lana and Lilly Wachowski*, 4. Keegan describes the experience of *Cloud Atlas* this way: "Inside the transition space of cinema, *we become subjunctive*—feeling in the dark toward what might happen."
26. Some other examples of transtemporal perception: When Dr. Isaac Sachs first sees Luisa in 1973 he feels that he already, mysteriously, has a connection with her. He has. In the apocalyptic, future, off-world story that frames *Cloud Atlas*. In this universe, Sachs exists simultaneously as Zachry, and Luisa exists simultaneously as Meronym. Their timeless, fluid, manifold identities experience each other beyond the seemingly definitive boundaries of life and death in linear time, whether they are Zachry and Meronym or Isaac and Luisa. In 1936, Vyvyan Ayrs hears music in a dream that is clearly a cross-temporal experience of the restaurant in which Sonmi-451 is enslaved in 2144. Not quite the same, but part of the experience of nonlinear time and the "me" beyond linear limits: in 1936, Robert Frobisher and Vyvian Ayrs together compose sections of the *Cloud Atlas Sextet* as if they are one entity.
27. There have been a variety of responses to the multiple castings of the actors. Peter Debruge finds the use of casting in the film exciting. A. O. Scott calls the

use of genre in the film "an unruly grab bag of styles, effects and emotions held together, just barely, by a combination of outlandish daring and humble sincerity." He reduces the casting of actors in multiple parts to no more than cosmetic alteration. In *Entertainment,* Owen Gleiberman come close to hitting the mark when he writes, "The multiple-role casting, and the bravura makeup that makes it possible (it includes not just flipped genders but switched racial roles), is so clever and imaginative that it's more than a gimmick—it's closer to a burlesque of identity." Unfortunately, Gleiberman is unable to connect the dots between his thoughts on identity and the overall concept of the film. David Edelstein is extremely derisive about the multicasting, an example, "The main actors have parts in all six stories, often in egregious disguises. . . . [Tom Hanks] shows up with a putty nose and snaggle teeth in the 19th century—and so on. I like Hanks but when it comes to transforming, he's no Peter Sellers." Then there is Tom Hanks's own reaction. Lana Wachowski reports Hanks's intriguing response to the multicasting: He was energized by it and "the impossible way *Cloud Atlas* defied the logic of time and space." Debruge, review of *Cloud Atlas*; Scott, "Souls Tangled"; Owen Gleiberman, "Toronto Film Festival: *Cloud Atlas* Is an Enthralling Sci-Fi Ride and the Wachowskis' Best Movie Since *The Matrix*," review, *Entertainment*, September 12, 2012, https://ew.com/article/2012/09/12/cloud-atlas-an-enthralling-sci-fi-ride/; Edelstein, "You're Better Off"; Keegan, *Lana and Lilly Wachowski*, 146.

28. Keegan, *Lana and Lilly Wachowski*, 145.
29. Keegan understands *Cloud Atlas* as primarily about race, and the power of this scene certainly makes understandable his claim that "*Cloud Atlas* uses a trans aesthetic to invert the developmental hierarchy of race." I contend that the film combines the trans aesthetic with a quantum thrust to invert all linear developmental heritage. Keegan, *Lana and Lilly Wachowski*, 92.
30. Brian Greene, *The Elegant Universe: Superstrings, Hidden Dimensions, and the Quest for the Ultimate Theory* (W. W. Norton, 2010), 6. For my previous discussion of Greene's ideas about time and space, please see introduction and chapter 1.
31. Ron Stallworth, *Black Klansman: Race, Hate, and the Undercover Investigation of a Lifetime* (Flatiron Books, 2018). When Stallworth's book was reissued to coincide with the film, the book cover and title page show different titles. The cover records the title as *BlacKkKlansman, A Memoir.*
32. A. O. Smith, "Spike Lee's *BlacKkKlansman* Journeys into White America's Heart of Darkness," review, *New York Times*, August 9, 2018, https://www.nytimes.com/2018/08/09/movies/blackkklansman-review-spike-lee.html; Mark Kermode, "A Blistering Return to Form for Spike Lee," review of *BlacKkKlansman*, dir. Spike Lee, *Guardian*, August 26, 2018, https://www.theguardian.com/film/2018/aug/26/blackkklansman-review-spike-lee-blistering-return-to-form; Stephanie Zacharek, "Spike Lee's *BlackKklansman* Is the Movie We Need Right Now," review, *Time*, August 10, 2018, https://time.com/5362620/blackkklansman-review-spike-lee/; Tyler Coates, "*BlacKkKlansman* Is the Rare American Film That Doesn't Treat the KKK as a Joke," review, *Esquire*, August 13, 2018, https://www.esquire.com/entertainment/movies/a22710089/blackkklansman-review-spike-lee-white-supremacy/; Chris Nashawaty, "Spike Lee's *BlacKkKlansman* Is Set in the '70s but Exposes Our Current Rot," review, *Entertainment Weekly*, August 8, 2018, https://ew.com/movies/2018/08/08/blackkklansman-review

/; David Sims, "With *BlacKkKlansman*, Spike Lee Sounds the Alarm About America's Past and Present," review, *Atlantic*, August 8, 2018, https://www.theatlantic.com/entertainment/archive/2018/08/blackkklansman-review/566915/; Ann Hornaday, "*BlacKkKlansman* Is Spike Lee's Best, and Most Necessary, Movie in Years," review, *Washington Post*, August 7, 2018, https://www.washingtonpost.com/goingoutguide/movies/blackkklansman-is-spike-lees-best-and-most-necessary-movie-in-years/2018/08/07/bdf9d516-966d-11e8-a679-b09212fb69c2_story.html.

33. Boots Riley contends that the documents "that were found" through the Freedom of Information Act tell us that Stallworth infiltrated and disrupted a Black radical organization that was fighting racism, not the KKK, and that he deceptively puts himself in a very different light in his memoir. He also enumerates the changes Lee made from the book, all made-up details that were intended to make the police look good. Among these are that a KKK bombing that Stallworth and his fellow police thwart in the film was not in the book and never happened; that there was no racist policeman who was tricked by the police into admitting on tape his acts against Black people; that Kwame Ture (Stokely Carmichael) was mischaracterized in the film when he came to speak to the Colorado College Black Student Union in Colorado Springs; and that much of what Stallworth claims in the book is unverifiable. As Riley writes, "We don't know what happened because the 'files were destroyed.' We have to trust the word of a cop who infiltrated a Black radical organization for 3 years." Boots Riley (@BootsRiley), "Ok. Here are some thoughts on #Blackkklansman," Twitter (now X), August 17, 2018, https://x.com/BootsRiley/status/1030575674447212544, link embedded in Catherine Shoard, "Boots Riley Attacks Spike Lee over 'Made Up' *BlacKkKlansman*," Culture, *Guardian*, August 20, 2018, https://www.theguardian.com/film/2018/aug/20/boots-riley-spike-lee-blackkklansman.
34. Boots Riley describes the rupture of linear time and space this way: "And then they hear something and go, guns drawn, to investigate. They go down the hall together with the signature Spike Lee dolly—the one that tells us it's him, the one that took Malcolm down the street, the one that took Dap across campus yelling 'Wake Up!' They go forward into the future, side by side, in symmetrical composition, to fight the burning cross of racist terror. Cops and the movement against racist oppression united." Riley, "Thoughts on #Blackkklansman."

Chapter 5. Teleology Unstuck: The Not-So-Grand Narrative—*Westworld, Arrival*

1. Yuval Noah Harari, *Sapiens: A Brief History of Humankind* (Harper Perennial, 2015); Francis Fukuyama, *The End of History and the Last Man* (1992; Free Press, 2006).
2. Israel Finkelstein and Neil Asher Silberman, *The Bible Unearthed: Archaeology's New Vision of Ancient Israel and the Origin of Its Sacred Texts* (Touchstone, 2002).
3. For Finkelstein and Silberman's discussion of the historical truth of the Exodus, see "Did the Exodus Happen?," chap. 2 in *Bible Unearthed*, 48–71. For their discussion of documentable historical reality as opposed to the Old Testament version of Joshua's military prowess, see *Bible Unearthed*, 72–83.

4. David Graeber and David Wengrow, *The Dawn of Everything: A New History of Humanity* (Farrar, Straus and Giroux, 2021), 9.
5. Jonathan Nolan's other projects in which he played with time and space are *Interstellar* (2014), *The Prestige* (2006), and *Memento* (2000) (all of which he cowrote with his brother Christopher Nolan, who also directed). Lisa Joy has written for series and films exploring the nature of reality: *Pushing Daisies* (2007–2009) and *Reminiscence* (2021). Together, Joy and Nolan produced *The Peripheral* (2022), a series that unfolds in altered time and space. Joy is the executive producer of *Fallout* (2024–), a series that unfolds in postapocalyptic Los Angeles.
6. In a 2018 interview with Scott Meyer, Lisa Joy spoke most pointedly about *Westworld* when she expressed her excitement about the series, because she and Nolan were "so interested right now in explorations of the soul and of human id [*sic*] and the ways in which emerging technologies are changing the world and our place within it. To be able to explore what robots and artificial technology would look like in this world, and to explore the entire Western trope through this new lens was just so enticing, it was impossible to resist." She also spoke about her general interests and passions as a writer: "I'm always so interested in the emotional core and the character work of anything I write. I've written in a lot of different genres. . . . But the thing that is first and foremost to me is, 'Do I love the character? Do I empathize with them?' I even think you have to love and empathize with the villains you write, especially them, in a way. Otherwise it just becomes caricature.'"

   In a June 18, 2018, interview with Pete Hammond, Jonathan Nolan said very little about *Westworld* itself, but quite a bit about its relevance to the way that computers are getting closer and closer to consciousness. He did reveal that he initially turned down an offer to adapted Michael Crichton's movie *Westworld* (1973) as a series, and that it was Joy who saw the possibilities, and he talked about how we anthropomorphize objects that don't really call for our empathy and fail to empathize where we should, but he gave no details. He also spoke of how secretive he is about his work, as a service to the audience, not because the work should speak for itself, as Lynch feels. And he spoke about a number of influences on *Westworld*: Stanley Kubrick, Ridley Scott, Sergio Leone, Andrei Tarkovsky.

   Interestingly enough, neither Joy nor Nolan mentioned David Lynch, whom Damon Lindelof told me was one of their favorite filmmakers (Zoom discussion, June 15, 2023). Despite their failure to mention him, I incline to believe that Lynch's way of storytelling permeates *Westworld*. Indeed, neither Joy nor Nolan spoke at all about the pervasive nonlinearity in their series. One comes away from their public statements with the impression that they have been very guarded about what is most profound in their work as mass-media artists. I personally experienced their extreme hesitation to talk about their work. After a long period of negotiation, their assistants arranged a Zoom interview for me with Joy and Nolan for November 8, 2023. It was abruptly canceled on November 6, a first for me. A reschedule was mentioned, but there was no follow-through.

   Lisa Joy, interview by Scott Meyers, *Go into the Story* (blog), Medium, June 22, 2018, https://gointothestory.blcklst.com/go-into-the-story-interview-lisa-joy-896b92235428; Jonathan Nolan, "On Westworld Secrets, How AI Is

Taking Over and Working With Your Other Half," interview by Pete Hammond, Behind the Lens (blog), Deadline, June 18, 2018, https://deadline.com/video/jonathan-nolan-westworld-secrets-interview-behind-the-lens-video/.

7. Herewith, a sample of critical responses to *Westworld* by entertainment journalists, which—at best—depicts the myopia of criticism too affected by psychology and not enough by the natural sciences that we have engaged in our discussions of nonlinearity and history. At best, critics took notice of the issue of consciousness; not one remarked on the address to history in the storytelling. Emma Dibdin, in *Harper's Bazaar*, judged the series, as of its first episode, to be generic but interesting, while James Poniewozik's *New York Times* review of *Westworld*'s first season found the show pretentious but concluded, "What keeps *Westworld* interesting . . . is its willingness to think big. Is there a difference between simulated and actual consciousness? Are we pushing our entertainments to be brutal, or are those entertainments pushing us to be? In the end, *Westworld* asks the same question of us that it asks about Dr. Ford's creations: Are we nothing more than creatures of our programming?" After the second season, Erik Kain, in *Forbes*, declared season 2 to be unnecessary and less interesting than season 1, as he made clear that he found the nonlinear time in both seasons to be interesting gimmicks. Reviewing season 3, Matt Zoller Seitz, in *Vulture*, judged *Westworld* to be obvious and ham-fisted in highlighting the themes Seitz isolated as its major messages, about choice.

Westworld was, however, acknowledged by the industry with five Emmy nominations.

Emma Dibdin, "HBO's Sci-Fi Thriller *Westworld* Is an Unsettling, Ambitious Must-See," review, *Harper's Bazaar*, October 2, 2016, https://www.harpersbazaar.com/culture/film-tv/news/a18029/westworld-episode-1-recap-review/; .James Poniewozik, "*Westworld* Is a Provocative but Flawed Sci-Fi Shoot-'Em-Up," review, *New York Times*, September 30, 2016, https://www.nytimes.com/2016/10/01/arts/television/review-westworld-is-a-provocative-but-flawed-sci-fi-shoot-em-up.html; Erik Kain, "*Westworld* Season 2: The Good, the Bad and the Ugly of HBO's Sci-Fi Western," review, *Forbes*, June 25, 2018, https://www.forbes.com/sites/erikkain/2018/06/25/westworld-season-2-review-the-good-the-bad-and-the-ugly/; Matt Zoller Seitz, "Even Outside the Park, *Westworld* Gonna *Westworld*," review, *Vulture*, March 13, 2020, https://www.vulture.com/2020/03/westworld-season-3-review.html.

8. Julian Jaynes, *The Origin of Consciousness in the Breakdown of the Bicameral Mind* (1976; Mariner Books, 2000).

9. For those readers who would like to read further about Zhuangzi: Hans-Georg Moeller and Paul J. D'Ambrosio, *Genuine Pretending: On the Philosophy of the "Zhuangzi"* (Columbia University Press, 2017); *Zhuangzi: Classic New Translation*, trans. Noah Sullivan (Daybreak Studios, 2023); "*Zhuangzi* (book)," Wikipedia, last modified April 2, 2025, https://en.wikipedia.org/wiki/Zhuangzi_(book).

10. It is only just before the James Delos retirement gala that we get the full backstory of Weber's relationship to Dolores, with respect to his understanding of consciousness he has mapped and what he wants to do with her to keep the park from opening. The nonlinearity of the rhetoric constructs a comment on what is about to happen. It seems there was a moment when Weber could have prevented the human descent into linear history and destruction that MIB represents, if he had been able to destroy the loop by destroying the park. The

juxtaposition of the backstory of Dolores and Weber with the violence of MIB in search of the center of the maze, Delos's intended removal of Ford, and Ford's plan to destroy Westworld makes it clear that it is too late. Human history is doomed, and the following seasons play out the catastrophe.

11. The separation of consciousness from thinking and the implications of that distinction for human history is the main theme of *The Origin of Consciousness*. To support his theory of a teleological development of a new kind of history that occurred when humans became conscious, Julian Jaynes brings together ideas about left- and right-brained thinking, social control exerted by the bicameral mind, and a new perspective on metaphor. Jaynes asserts that using language for communication does not equate with the capacity to make metaphors. He makes enormous claims for the human ability to create metaphor as the building block of creating narrative, and for creating narrative as the beginning of cause-and-effect thinking and the end of control of "nonconscious" human behavior by "voices of the gods." To observe how he builds a foundation for his theory, see Jaynes, "Consciousness," chap. 2 in *Origin of Consciousness*, 48–66.

    For examples of criticism of Jayne's theories, see Owen Barfield, review of *The Origin of Consciousness in the Breakdown of the Bicameral Mind*, by Julian Jaynes, *Teachers College Record* 80, no. 3 (February 1979): 602–604, reprinted on Owen Barfield (website), archived May 30, 2024, https://web.archive.org/web/20240530012301/https://www.owenbarfield.org/read-online/articles/bicameral-mind/; Veronique Greenwood, "Consciousness Began When the Gods Stopped Speaking," Philosophy, *Nautilus*, May 21, 2015, https://nautil.us/consciousness-began-when-the-gods-stopped-speaking-235445/; Richard Seltzer, "The Myth of the Bicameral Mind," review of *The Origin of Consciousness in the Breakdown of the Bicameral Mind*, by Julian Jaynes, Medium, June 1, 2022, https://medium.com/@seltzer_57387/the-myth-of-the-bicameral-mind-2876462315dd.

12. In *Avengers: Endgame*, Anthony and Joe Russo throw around quantum terms freely and play a lot of games with nonlinear time. Before the Avengers mount their attack on Thanos, the evil alien who has disappeared half the human population, they do a test run of their time machine using Scott Lang / Ant-Man (Paul Rudd) as their test pilot, and he returns from the linear past as a ninety-three-year-old, a child, and a baby. At the very end of the movie, after the dust has settled, they send Steve Rogers / Captain America (Chris Evans) back to the past to put the Infinity Stones back where they belong; Captain America returns in five seconds, an old man, not the virile hunk he was. We see, if his fellow Avengers do not, that he's taken advantage of his errand to create a domestic idyll in the 1940s, living the domestic life he missed as a superhero, in a little, cozy cottage. But nonlinearity is all a shtick, grist for the mill of linear narrative to serve as obstacle or dreamy departure from normal linear time.

13. Ted Chiang, "Story of Your Life," in *Stories of Your Life and Others* (Vintage Books, 2016), 91–145.

14. During an interview conducted by Pete Hammond for AFTRA—in which Amy Adams also participated—Villeneuve spoke of how he fell in love with Chiang's story but had no idea how to make a film of a nonlinear emotional journey until Eric Heisserer adapted it into a script. He and Adams praised each other effusively, and though she spoke about the nonlinearity of the film, she did not expand on it, and Villeneuve never picked up on it. In another YouTube interview, Villeneuve discussed how important it was to him to break the crew of

working within their comfort zone and doing generic sci-fi things. He based the shape of the spacecraft not on any he had ever seen in a movie, but on the shape of an asteroid currently circling the Earth. He wanted the aliens to have a "huge, strong presence" like a whale, like huge beasts under water, a strong, intelligent presence. It was important to him that the alien language be as unlike any human language as possible, but also that it have an actual structure. Toward that end, they created an actual dictionary of heptapod terms. In an interview for the *Los Angeles Times*, Villeneuve said the film is "really about societal response to fear." "Conversations with Amy Adams and Denis Villeneuve of *Arrival*," interview by Pete Hammond, December 8, 2016, posted December 19, 2016, by SAG-AFTRA Foundation, YouTube, 34 min., 24 sec., https://www.youtube.com/watch?v=UYzcKc4r2NI; "Denis Villeneuve On How He Directed *Arrival*," interview by Jillian Snead, posted August 24, 2019, by Jilloms, YouTube, 12 min., 23 sec., https://www.youtube.com/watch?v=CZ6HhFO-h-g; "Exclusive *Arrival* Interview: We Talk to Denis Villeneuve, the Director Being Compared to Christopher Nolan," interview by Steven Zeitchik, *Los Angeles Times*, September 14, 2016, https://www.latimes.com/entertainment/movies/la-et-mn-arrival-denis-villeneuve-amy-adams-premiere-release-20160914-snap-story.html.

15. Chiang, "Story of Your Life," 144.
16. In *Indiewire*, Ben Croll says that *Arrival* has "a hell of a lot going for it, but never quite gets there." In *Entertainment*, Darren Franich says, "Impressive, maybe, how *Arrival* waits over an hour before it actively starts insulting your intelligence." In stark contrast, Alissa Wilkinson, in *Vox*, rates *Arrival* as "one of the best movies of the year, a moving, gripping film with startling twists and imagery. It deserves serious treatment as a work of art." She perceptively notes that "if we were to encounter a culture so radically different from our own . . . , we could not simply gather data, sort out grammar, and make conclusions. We'd have to either absorb a different way of *seeing*, despite out fear, or risk everything." *Arrival* received industry recognition with five Academy Award nominations and five BAFTA nominations. Ben Croll, "Amy Adams Steals Spotlight in Denis Villeneuve's Deep-Thinking Alien Invasion Story," review of *Arrival*, *IndieWire*, September 1, 2016, https://www.indiewire.com/features/general/arrival-review-amy-adams-denis-villeneuve-deep-thinking-alien-invasion-1201722369/; Darren Franich, "The Film's Phony Good Intentions, and [the] Paradox of 'Realistic' Sci-Fi," review of *Arrival*, *Entertainment Weekly*, November 17, 2016, https://ew.com/article/2016/11/17/arrival-ending-contact-2001-sci-fi/; Alissa Wilkinson, "*Arrival* Is a Stunning Science Fiction Movie with Deep Implications for Today," review, Culture, Vox, November 24, 2016, https://www.vox.com/culture/2016/11/11/13587262/arrival-movie-review-amy-adams-denis-villeneuve.

Chapter 6. Journey's End: *Watchmen*

1. Damon Lindelof, discussions with author, in-person, May 12, 2023; and via Zoom, June 15, 2023.
2. The first time I interviewed David Lynch in person, I visited his studio offices for several days, and his assistant at the time, Gaye Pope, helped arranged interviews with a few of his collaborators—Duwayne Dunham (editor), Frederick

Elmes (cinematographer), and actors Catherine E. Coulson and Jack Nance. Neither Dunham, Coulson, nor Nance knew what Lynch was doing but experienced a kind of joy working with him. Elmes had a more intuitive grasp of Lynch's poetics, having spoken with Lynch about such questions as "How dark is dark?" Lynch chuckled when I told him I was stunned that no one seemed to know what they were doing. Discussions with the author: Coulson, March 30, 1993; Dunham, March 30, 1993; Elmes, March 28, 1993; Lynch, March 29–April 1, 1993; and Nance, April 1, 1993.

3. Among the many stories Matthew Weiner told me about the impact of his contributors on *The Romanoffs*, herewith anecdotes about writers Mary Sweeney, Maria and André Jacquemetton, and Semi Chellas: For "The One That Holds Everything," Sweeney contributed the line about how older women become invisible. For "The End of the Line," Weiner used the stories the Jacquemettons told about their experience adopting a baby in Russia. Semi Chellas mathematically blocked out the use of nonlinear time frames in "The One That Holds Everything." Matthew Weiner, in discussion with the author, May 10, 2023, and July 6, 2023.

   Weiner also told me about arguments in the writers' room about the relationship between Victoria Hayward (Radha Mitchell) and Abel Erikson (Juan Pablo Castañeda) in "Panorama," in which the staff writers prevailed over Weiner, who wanted them a moment to kiss. There was no kiss, as per the insistence of the staff writers, and ultimately Weiner believed it was the right decision. Discussion, July 6, 2023. The auteur bubble doesn't necessarily mean that collaborators never decide; only that the *overall* vision is under the auteur's sole control.

4. Denis Villeneuve's comments about *Arrival* in a video on YouTube are very telling about the sensibility he brought to his film. "Conversations with Amy Adams and Denis Villeneuve of *Arrival*," interview by Pete Hammond, December 8, 2016, posted December 19, 2016, by SAG-AFTRA Foundation, YouTube, 34 min., 24 sec., https://www.youtube.com/watch?v=UYzcKc4r2NI.

5. Lindelof, discussion, May 12, 2023.

6. Lindelof, discussion, June 15, 2023. Some of the writers' descriptors for the *Watchmen* comic: funny; cynical; macho; science fiction versus supernatural; symmetrical; distinctly British; both critical of and enraptured by America.

7. Lindelof, discussion, June 15, 2023.

8. Lindelof's high regard for Moore permeated our discussions. Lindelof called Moore "a genius on every level imaginable." Discussion, May 12, 2023. There are, however, some very peculiar stories in circulation about Moore's low opinion of Lindelof, which may or may not be accurate and which unnecessarily circulate anecdotes that may skew public opinion of the series negatively. For example, in *The Los Angeles Times*, Moore is quoted as having received a letter from Lindelof that was full of "neurotic ravings." This image of Lindelof is the inverse of how he appeared to me in our discussion. I would have to see the letter and speak to Moore before I gave this picture of his opinion of Lindelof any credence. We see how dealing in personalities pointlessly corrupts aesthetic discussion in Alexandra Del Rosario, "*Watchmen*, a TV Hit for HBO, Was 'Embarrassing' for the Comic's Creator Alan Moore," *Los Angeles Times*, October 19, 2022, https://www.latimes.com/entertainment-arts/tv/story/2022-10-19

/watchmen-hbo-embarrassing-comics-creator-alan-moore. How is Moore's embarrassment relevant to interpretation of Lindelof's series?

9. Lindelof, discussion, May 12, 2023. Lindelof asked me to define the word *teleology.* It is my interpretation that his portrayal of the historical concepts of Cyclops, Lady Trieu, Adrian Veidt, and the Redford government are teleological.
10. Lindelof, discussion, June 15, 2023.
11. Herewith a sample of some interviews with Lindelof about *Watchmen*: Jeremy Gordon published a negative account of Lindelof's interview for *Vulture,* accusing Lindelof of using his series as personal therapy. In a very positive interview with Lindelof for *Collider,* Adam Chitwood discusses his collaboration with a diverse writer's room and the way Lindelof inserted race into the *Watchmen* story. In *Entertainment Weekly,* James Hibberd, in a positive interview, longer and more comprehensive than average, discusses with Lindelof the relationship between the graphic novel and his series; moving the story to Oklahoma; being educated himself about Black history and wanting to share it with the audience; and his collaboration with Trent Reznor and Atticus Ross on the music. Jeremy Gordon, "Damon Lindelof Can't Stop Treating His *Watchmen* Interviews Like Therapy Sessions," Culture, *Outline,* November 4, 2019, https://theoutline.com/post/8185/watchmen-hbo-damon-lindelof-guilt; Damon Lindelof, "Like It or Not, Damon Lindelof Made His Own *Watchmen,*" interview by Abraham Josephine Riesman, A Long Talk, *Vulture,* October 17, 2019; Damon Lindelof, interview by Adam Chitwood, Collider Connected, *Collider,* July 5, 2020, https://collider.com/damon-lindelof-interview-watchmen-lost-prometheus/; Damon Lindelof, interview by James Hibberd, *Entertainment Weekly,* September 18, 2019, https://ew.com/tv/2019/09/18/damon-lindelof-watchmen-interview/.
12. Lindelof, discussion, May 12, 2023.
13. In discussing his thoughts about ownership of stories, Lindelof made a notable exception for David Lynch and Mark Frost:

> And so my feeling really is no one really owns these stories, least of all you. I tend to believe that even if you create a story, I don't own *Lost.* I'm a cocreator of *Lost.* That's true on paper and its true in spirit, that is to say, I'm a parent of this thing. I get to raise it and then it's going to go off and it's going to do its own thing. And the most exciting thing for me in story is when someone else comes in and kind of takes a run at it. Even if it's against the wishes of its original creator. Now, I also reserve the right to be a sort of hypocrite because I feel like if it's not Mark and David then it's not really *Twin Peaks.*

Lindelof, discussion, May 12, 2023.

14. Lindelof speaking about masked heroes and trauma: "All of these things seem to suggest the overcoming of trauma. Quasi god complex. But more importantly, that fundamental idea that powers the original *Watchmen,* that is, what if this thing that we always looked at as heroism, which is I'm going to save the world, I'm going to fight crime, is actually a coping mechanism? That feels accurate to me. When someone says I want to be a policeman when I grow up, what if it's a coping mechanism more than I want to restore justice." Lindelof, discussion, May 12, 2023.
15. A selection of evaluations of the way *Watchmen* changes the ground rules of mass-media storytelling: On RogerEbert.com, Brian Tallerico calls the series a

"game-changer," very relatable to the world situation today, and he specifically mentions the problems of racism, and public trauma and fear. Lucy Mangan, in the *Guardian*, calls *Watchmen* "a bravura series that interrogates power, storytelling and the former embedded in the latter. It has a (still unusually) diverse cast, writing team and cohort of directors in terms of both sex and class, and, even as it strays from Moore and Gibbons' original content, it honours their underlying ambition: to deconstruct our legends and our myths." Despite these rave reviews and more, at this writing there is no book-length study of *Watchmen.* Brian Tallerico, "HBO's *Watchmen* Is Like Nothing Else on Television," review, TV/Streaming, RogerEbert.com, October 16, 2019, https://www.rogerebert.com/streaming/hbos-watchmen-is-like-nothing-else-on-television; Lucy Mangan, "The Perfect Superhero Story for Our Tattered Times," review of *Watchmen*, TV & Radio, *Guardian*, October 21, 2019, https://www.theguardian.com/tv-and-radio/2019/oct/21/watchmen-review-the-perfect-superhero-story-for-our-tattered-times-hbo-alan-moore.

16. Lindelof's last words to me at the end of our first interview. May 12, 2023.
17. Structurally, *Watchmen* uses a nine-panel grid for its comic book frames, one of the standard designs in comic book representation. Gibbons varies the size of the frames. Sometimes a three-panel line of frames is presented as one frame, either horizontally or vertically. Sometimes two lines of three-panel space are presented as one space, but the underlying design is nine panels. The variations break up reader response, requiring adjustment to our perception of the image as we are forced to deal with taking in the visual information within the frame and the shape of the frame simultaneously. It requires the cultivation of a very sophisticated and flexible ability for nonlinear reading. Those interested in the nine-panel grid are encouraged to consult "Why Does *Watchmen* Use the 9-Panel Grid?," Literature, StackExchange (wiki), last modified March 22, 2021, https://literature.stackexchange.com/questions/2558/why-does-watchmen-use-the-9-panel-grid; and a more general discussion by Frank Santoro, "9-Panel Grids," *Comics Comics* (blog), WordPress, October 23, 2010, https://comicscomicsmag.com/?p=6611.
18. Lindelof, discussion, May 12, 2023.
19. Lindelof, discussion, May 12, 2023.
20. Lindelof, discussion, May 12, 2023.
21. Lindelof, discussion, May 12, 2023.
22. Lindelof, discussion, May 12, 2023.
23. I am trusting the one source I found that asserts that in 1921, Oscar Micheaux made a silent film about Reeves called *Trust in the Law,* which was actually shown at the original Dreamland movie theater in Greenwood, and which Lindelof's movie very much resembles. https://watchmen.fandom.com/wiki/Trust_in_the_Law! Other mediographies of Micheaux's works do not list this film. However, there is no dearth of cinematic representation of Reeves. Between 2010 and 2023, astonishingly, there were sixty-two movies, series, and podcasts made about the lawman Bass Reeves, the Black marshal depicted in *Trust in the Law.* The one with the highest commercial profile is *Lawmen: Bass Reeves*, starring David Oyelowo (2023). None of them was used in Lindelof's movie within an episode. That movie, completely original, was the first part of the series that was shot.
24. Lindelof, discussion, May 12, 2023.

25. Rather than clog the discussion with too much plot, I have omitted the details of how and why Lady Trieu airlifted Reeves in Angela's car. Herewith, for those readers who would enjoy more particulars, a brief summary. Before we know about Reeves's deal with Trieu, in episode 2, "Martial Feats of Comanche Horsemanship," Angela decides that she will turn Reeves in to the police and puts him in her car, with great difficulty, since he can't walk and uses a wheelchair; a helicopter appears, and a long, stout rope with a huge magnet attached grapples the car and airlifts Reeves out of Angela's grasp.

26. Lindelof, discussion, June 15, 2023. Herewith, Lindelof's statement about superheroes, choice, Angela, and Doctor Manhattan:

> Most superheroes don't opt to become superheroes. Very often it's the result of an accident that they get their powers. Maybe Batman is the most fundamental exception to the rule. He wouldn't have wanted his parents to die, but he chooses to become Batman because he doesn't have any powers at all. But Superman, he lands on Earth, and he has these abilities. He has to choose what he's going to do with them, but he didn't choose to have them. It's a little bit more like *The Matrix*, when Morbius extends his hand and there's a blue pill and a red pill. And essentially says, What do you choose to do here, Neo? Even though it's a bit of a force, in the magician's parlance. Doctor Manhattan gives Angela the egg so that she has consent. . . . So, the question that we were interested in was, Will Angela take the power? And she does. She ingests the egg. And now she's going to step on the pool to determine whether she has the power. But I think the question that is interesting to us is, What's she going to do with it? What kind of a Doctor Manhattan is she going to be, given what her lived experience is? And having some broader understanding not only of her lived experience, but what trauma was hers and what trauma was her legacy trauma? And can she separate her own experience from what it would mean to be a superpower, who may or may not be responsible for saving the world. Something that Doctor Manhattan was never interested in.

27. Lindelof, discussion, June 15, 2023.

Afterword. Real and Fictive, Scientific and Poetic

1. Brian Greene, *Until the End of Time: Mind, Matter, and Our Search for Meaning in an Evolving Universe* (Alfred A. Knopf, 2020), 6.

BIBLIOGRAPHY

Al-Kalili, Jim. *The World According to Physics.* Princeton University Press, 2020.

Alexander, Stephon. *The Jazz of Physics: The Secret Link Between Music and the Structure of the Universe.* Basic Books, 2017.

Ames, Melissa, ed. *Time in Television: Exploring Temporality in Twenty-First-Century Programming.* University of Mississippi Press, 2012.

Arason, Colin. "Cult Movie Extraordinaire: David Lynch's *Eraserhead*," *Offscreen* 25, no. 6 (June 2021). https://offscreen.com/view/cult-movie-extraordinaire-david-lynchs-eraserhead.

Azarian, Bobby. *The Romance of Reality: How the Universe Organizes Itself to Create Life, Consciousness, and Cosmic Complexity.* BenBella Books, 2022.

Batcho, James. *Terrence Malick's Unseeing Cinema: Memory, Time and Audibility.* Palgrave Macmillan, 2018.

Beever, Jonathan, and Vernon W. Cisney, eds. *The Way of Nature and the Way of Grace: Philosophical Footholds on Terrence Malick's "The Tree of Life."* Northwestern University Press, 2016.

Berg, Charles Ramírez. "A Taxonomy of Alternative Plots in Recent Films: Classifying the 'Tarantino Effect.'" In "Complex Narratives," edited by Janet Staiger. Special issue, *Film Criticism* 31, no. 1/2: 5–61. https://www.jstor.org/stable/44019213.

Bergson, Henri. *Creative Evolution.* Palgrave Macmillan, 2007.

Bergson, Henri. "Duration and Intuition." In *Problems of Space and Time*, edited by J. J. C. Smart. Macmillan, 1976.

Bergson, Henri. *Matter and Memory.* Translated by Nancy Margaret Paul and W. Scott Palmer. George Allen & Unwin, 1962.

Blasi, Gabriella. *The Work of Terrence Malick: Time-Based Ecocinema.* Amsterdam University Press, 2019.

Bleasdale, John. *The Magic Hours: The Films and Hidden Life of Terrence Malick.* University Press of Kentucky, 2024.

Borges, Jorge Luis. *"The Garden of Forking Paths."* In *Collected Fictions.* Deluxe ed. Translated by Andrew Hurley. Penguin, 1998.

Brain, Robert. *The Pulse of Modernism: Physiological Aesthetics in Fin-de-Siècle Europe.* University of Washington Press, 2015.

Braun, Marta. *Picturing Time: The Work of Etienne-Jules Marey (1830–1904).* University of Chicago Press, 1992.

Brubaker, Ben. "How Bell's Theorem Proved 'Spooky Action at a Distance' Is Real." *Quanta Magazine*, July 20, 2021. https://www.quantamagazine.org/how-bells-theorem-proved-spooky-action-at-a-distance-is-real-20210720/.

Buonomano, Dean. *Your Brain Is a Time Machine: The Neuroscience and Physics of Time.* W. W. Norton, 2018.

Burdick, Alan. *Why Time Flies: A Mostly Scientific Investigation.* Simon & Schuster, 2018.

Butler, Andrew M. *Eternal Sunshine of the Spotless Mind.* BFI Film Classics. A BFI book published by Palgrave Macmillan, 2014.

Butler, Octavia E. *Parable of the Sower.* Grand Central, 2019.

Campbell, Joseph. *The Hero with a Thousand Faces.* 3rd ed. New World Library, 2008.

Campbell, Joseph. *The Hero's Journey: Joseph Campbell on His Life and Work.* New World Library, 1990.

Campbell, Scott. "The David Lynch Movie Stanley Kubrick Wishes He Had Made." *Far Out.* January 12, 2024. https://faroutmagazine.co.uk/the-david-lynch-movie-stanley-kubrick-wishes-he-had-made/.

Canfield, David. "Between Two Worlds." Television. *Slate*, May 3, 2017. https://slate.com/culture/2017/05/twin-peaks-creators-david-lynch-and-mark-frosts-strange-sublime-collaboration-a-history.html.

Carruthers, Lee. *Doing Time: Temporality, Hermeneutics, and Contemporary Cinema.* SUNY Press, 2016.

Charney, Leo. *Empty Moments: Cinema, Modernity, and Drift.* Duke University Press, 1998.

Chiang, Ted. Interview by Ezra Klein. *The Ezra Klein Show.* Podcast transcript. *New York Times*, March 30, 2021. https://www.nytimes.com/2021/03/30/podcasts/ezra-klein-podcast-ted-chiang-transcript.html

Chiang, Ted. "Story of Your Life." In *Stories of Your Life and Others.* 2002; Vintage Books, 2016.

Chiang, Ted. "Why Computers Won't Make Themselves Smarter." *New Yorker*, March 30, 2021.

Clarke, Arthur C. *2001: A Space Odyssey.* New American Library, 1968.

Clarke, Arthur C. *2010: Odyssey Two.* Del Ray, 1997.

Cozzolino, Robert, and Alathea Rockwell. *David Lynch: The Unified Field.* Pennsylvania Academy of the Fine Arts, in association with University of California Press, 2014.

Crichton, Michael. *Westworld.* Bantam, 1974.

DeLay, Steven, ed. *Life Above the Clouds: Philosophy in the Films of Terrence Malick.* SUNY Press, 2023.

Deleuze, Gilles. *Cinema 2: The Time-Image.* Translated by Hugh Tomlinson and Robert Galeta. University of Minnesota Press, 1989.

Doane, Mary Ann. *The Emergence of Cinematic Time: Modernity, Contingency, the Archive*. Harvard University Press, 2002.

Ebert, Roger. Review of *2001: A Space Odyssey*, directed by Stanley Kubrick. RogerEbert.com, March 27, 1997. https://www.rogerebert.com/reviews/great-movie-2001-a-space-odyssey-1968.

Ebiri, Bilge. "Will Terrence Malick Ever Really Finish *The Tree of Life*?" Review of Criterion Blu-ray/DVD edition of *The Tree of Life*, directed by Terrence Malick. *Vulture*, September 11, 2018. https://www.vulture.com/2018/09/will-terrence-malick-ever-really-finish-the-tree-of-life.html.

Eddington, Arthur S. *The Nature of the Physical World*. Gifford Lectures of 1927. Annotated ed. Annotated and introduced by H. G. Callaway. Cambridge Scholars, 2014.

Edwards, Jonathan. "Sinners in the Hands of an Angry God." In *The Sermons of Jonathan Edwards: A Reader*. Edited by Wilson H. Kimnach, Kenneth P. Minkema, and Douglas A. Sweeney. Yale University Press, 1999.

Eilenberger, Wolfram. *Time of the Magicians: Wittgenstein, Benjamin, Cassirer, Heidegger, and the Decade That Reinvented Philosophy*. Translated by Shaun Whiteside. Penguin, 2020.

Emspak, Jesse. "Quantum Entanglement: Unlocking the Mysteries of Particle Connections." Space.com, May 16, 2023. https://www.space.com/31933-quantum-entanglement-action-at-a-distance.html.

Faivre, Antoine. *Western Esotericism: A Concise History*. Translated by Christine Rhone. SUNY Press, 2010.

Finkelstein, Israel, and Neil Asher Silberman. *The Bible Unearthed: Archaeology's New Vision of Ancient Israel and the Origin of Its Sacred Texts*. Touchstone, 2002.

Flatley, Jonathan. *Affective Mapping: Melancholia and the Politics of Modernism*. Harvard University Press, 2008.

Frost, Mark. *The Secret History of Twin Peaks*. Flatiron Books, 2016.

Frost, Mark. "*Twin Peaks*: Co-Creator on Network Pressures and David Lynch." Interview by Jodie Tyley. *SciFiNow*, January 20, 2022. https://www.scifinow.co.uk/interviews/twin-peaks-co-creator-on-network-pressures-and-david-lynch/.

Frost, Mark. *Twin Peaks: The Final Dossier*. Flatiron Books, 2017.

Fukuyama, Francis. *The End of History and the Last Man*. 1992; Free Press, 2006.

Gere, Charlie. *Art, Time and Technology*. Berg Publishers, 2006.

Girgus, Sam B. *Time, Existential Presence, and the Cinematic Image: Ethics and Emergence to Being in Film*. Edinburgh University Press, 2018.

Goody, Alex, and Antonia Mackay, eds. *Reading "Westworld."* Palgrave Macmillan, 2019.

Graeber, David, and David Wengrow. *The Dawn of Everything: A New History of Humanity*. Farrar, Straus and Giroux, 2021.

Greene, Brian. *The Elegant Universe: Superstrings, Hidden Dimensions, and the Quest for the Ultimate Theory.* W. W. Norton, 2010.
Greene, Brian. *The Fabric of the Cosmos: Space, Time, and the Texture of Reality.* Vintage, 2006.
Greene, Brian. "A Physicist Explains Why Parallel Universes May Exist." Interview by Terry Gross. *Fresh Air.* NPR, January 24, 2011. Transcript. https://www.npr.org/transcripts/132932268.
Greene, Brian. *Until the End of Time: Mind, Matter, and Our Search for Meaning in an Evolving Universe.* Alfred A. Knopf, 2020.
Grosz, Elizabeth. *The Nick of Time: Politics, Evolution, and the Untimely.* Duke University Press, 2004. https://doi.org/10.1215/9780822386032.
Harari, Yuval Noah. *Sapiens: A Brief History of Humankind.* Harper Perennial, 2018.
Hassan, Robert, and Ronald E. Purser, eds. *24/7: Time and Temporality in the Network Society.* Stanford Business Books, 2007.
Heffernan, James A. W., ed. *Space, Time, Image, Sign: Essays on Literature and the Visual Arts.* Peter Lang, 1987.
Heidegger, Martin. *Being and Time.* Translated by John Macquarrie and Edward Robinson. Harper Perennial Modern Thought, 2008.
Hoad, Phil. "How We Made *2001: A Space Odyssey.*" *Guardian,* March 12, 2018. https://www.theguardian.com/film/2018/mar/12/how-we-made-2001-a-space-odyssey-stanley-*kubrick-hal.*
Hoberek, Andrew. *Considering "Watchmen": Poetics, Property, Politics.* Rev. ed. Rutgers University Press, 2017.
Jaynes, Julian. *The Origin of Consciousness in the Breakdown of the Bicameral Mind.* 1976; Mariner Books, 2000.
Johnson, Steven. *Where Good Ideas Come From: The Natural History of Innovation.* Riverhead Books, 2011.
Jowett, Lorna, Kevin Lee Robinson, and David Simmons, eds. *Time on TV: Narrative, Time Travel and Time Travelers in Popular Television Culture.* I. B. Tauris, 2016.
Kafka, Franz. *The Metamorphosis.* Classic Press, 2009.
Kafka, Franz. *The Trial.* Translated by Mike Mitchell. Oxford University Press, 2009.
Kaplan, E. Ann. *Trauma Culture: The Politics of Terror and Loss in Media and Literature.* Rutgers University Press, 2005.
Kearney, Richard. "Martin Heidegger." In *Modern Movements in European Philosophy.* 2nd ed. Manchester University Press, 1994.
Keegan, Cáel M. *Lana and Lilly Wachowski.* University of Illinois Press, 2018.
Keeling, Kara. *The Witch's Flight: The Cinematic, the Black Femme, and the Image of Common Sense.* Duke University Press, 2007.

Krämer, Peter. *2001: A Space Odyssey*. Palgrave Macmillan on behalf of the BFI, 2010.

Laing, R. D. *The Divided Self: An Existential Study in Sanity and Madness*. Rev. ed. Penguin, 1965.

LaRocca, David, ed. *The Philosophy of Charlie Kaufman*. Paperback ed. with a new preface. University Press of Kentucky, 2019.

Levinson, Julie. *The American Success Myth on Film*. Palgrave Macmillan, 2012.

Lim, Bliss Cua. *Translating Time: Cinema, The Fantastic, and Temporal Critique*. Duke University Press, 2009.

Lowenstein, Adam. *Shocking Representation: Historical Trauma, National Cinema, and the Modern Horror Film*. Columbia University Press, 2005.

Luhmann, Niklas. *Observations on Modernity*. Translated by William Whobrey. Stanford University Press, 1998.

Lynch, David. *Catching the Big Fish: Meditation, Consciousness, and Creativity*. 10th anniversary ed. TarcherPerigee, 2016.

Lyotard, Jean-François. *The Inhuman: Reflections on Time*. Translated by Geoffrey Bennington and Rachel Bowlby. Stanford University Press, 1992.

Magee, Glenn Alexander, ed., *The Cambridge Handbook of Western Mysticism and Esotericism*. Cambridge University Press, 2019.

Manovitch, Lev. *The Language of New Media*. MIT Press, 2001.

Marling, Brit. "I Don't Want to Be the Strong Female Lead." Opinion. *New York Times*, February 7, 2020. https://www.nytimes.com/2020/02/07/opinion/sunday/brit-marling-women-movies.html.

Mazzara, Glen. "On Showrunning." Interview. *On Story*. Season 12, episode 13. Austin Film Festival and PBS, September 20, 2022. 26 min., 47 sec. https://www.pbs.org/video/on-showrunning-a-conversation-with-glen-mazzara-reodgy/.

McDermott, John J. *The Drama of Possibility: Experience as Philosophy of Culture*. Fordham University Press, 2007.

McDermott, John J. *Streams of Experience: Reflections on the History and Philosophy of American Culture*. University of Massachusetts Press, 1986.

McGowan, Andrew. "Stanley Kubrick Made *The Shining* Cast and Crew Watch This David Lynch Movie." *Collider*, August 27, 2023, updated April 22, 2024. https://collider.com/stanley-kubrick-the-shining-david-lynch-eraserhead/.

McGowan, Todd. *Out of Time: Desire in Atemporal Cinema*. University of Minnesota Press, 2011.

Meister, Jan Christoph, and Wilhelm Schernus, eds. *Time: From Concept to Narrative Construct; A Reader*. De Gruyter, 2011.

Merleau-Ponty, Maurice. *Phenomenology of Perception*. Translated by Colin Smith. Routledge, 2002.

Miller, Arthur I. *The Artist in the Machine: The World of AI-Powered Creativity*. MIT Press, 2019.

Mitchell, David. *Cloud Atlas*. Random House, 2004.

Morgan, Daniel. "The Curious Ironist: Terrence Malick and the Drama of Perspective." Chap. 6 in *The Lure of the Image: Epistemic Fantasies of the Moving Camera*. University of California Press, 2021.

Mroz, Matilda. *Temporality and Film Analysis*. Edinburgh University Press, 2012.

Muller, Richard A. *Now: The Physics of Time*. W. W. Norton, 2016.

Mulvey, Laura. *Death 24 × a Second: Stillness and the Moving Image*. Reaktion Books, 2006.

Nader, Tony. *Consciousness Is All There Is: How Understanding and Experiencing Consciousness Will Transform Your Life*. Foreword by David Lynch. Hay House, 2024.

Nechvatal, Joseph. *Immersion into Noise*. Open Humanities Press, 2011.

Ney, Alyssa, and David Z. Albert, eds. *The Wave Function: Essays on the Metaphysics of Quantum Mechanics*. Oxford University Press, 2013.

Ngai, Sianne. *Theory of the Gimmick: Aesthetic Judgment and Capitalist Form*. Belknap Press, 2020.

Nochimson, Martha P. *David Lynch Swerves: Uncertainty from "Lost Highway" to "Inland Empire."* University of Texas Press, 2013.

Nochimson, Martha P. "Desire Under the Douglas Firs: Entering the Body of Reality in *Twin Peaks*." *Film Quarterly* 46, no. 2 (Winter 1992–1993): 22–34. https://doi.org/10.2307/1213005.

Nochimson, Martha P. *The Passion of David Lynch: Wild at Heart in Hollywood*. University of Texas Press, 1997.

Nochimson, Martha P. *Television Rewired: The Rise of the Auteur Series*. University of Texas Press, 2019.

O'Keefe, Madeleine. "Massless Particles Can't Be Stopped." *Symmetry*, July 23, 2019. https://www.symmetrymagazine.org/article/massless-particles-cant-be-stopped.

Olenina, Ana Hedberg. *Psychomotor Aesthetics: Movement and Affect in Modern Literature and Film*. Oxford University Press, 2020.

Perez, Gilberto. *The Material Ghost: Films and Their Medium*. Johns Hopkins University Press, 1998.

Perkins, Will. "*Westworld* (2016)." Art of the Title. October 12, 2016. https://www.artofthetitle.com/title/westworld/.

Pirnia, Garin. "The Epic Influence of David Lynch's *Eraserhead*, from Kubrick to *Star Wars*." *Esquire*, September 18, 2018. https://www.esquire.com/entertainment/movies/a30108/eraserhead-influence/.

Popkin, Gabriel. "Einstein's 'Spooky Action at a Distance' Spotted in Objects Almost Big Enough to See." *Science*, April 25, 2018. https://www.science

.org/content/article/einstein-s-spooky-action-distance-spotted-objects-almost-big-enough-see.

Potocki, Jan. *Tales from the Saragossa Manuscript (Ten Days in the Life of Alphonse Van Worden)*. Translated by Christine Donoughe. Dedalus, 1990.

Powell, Helen. *Stop the Clocks! Time and Narrative in Cinema*. I. B. Tauris, 2012.

Prigogine, Ilya. *From Being to Becoming: Time and Complexity in the Physical Sciences*. W. H. Freeman, 1980.

Prusak, Bernard. "What Is He Up To? Seeing as God Sees: Malick's 'Tree of Life.'" *Commonweal*, December 18, 2013. https://www.commonwealmagazine.org/what-he.

Renfro, Kim. "How the *Westworld* Main Titles Have Evolved with Each Season to Tell a New Story." Entertainment. *Business Insider*. August 18, 2020. https://www.businessinsider.com/westworld-title-sequence-designer-interview-patrick-clair-season-3-2020-8.

Ricoeur, Paul. *Time and Narrative*. 3 vols. Translated by Kathleen McLaughlin and David Pellauer. University of Chicago Press, 1984–1988.

Rieser, Martin, and Andrea Zapp, eds. *New Screen Media: Cinema/Art/Narrative*. Palgrave Macmillan on behalf of the BFI, 2002.

Rosen, Philip. *Change Mummified: Cinema, Historicity, Theory*. University of Minnesota Press, 2001.

Rovelli, Carlo. *The Order of Time*. Translated by Erica Segre and Simon Carnell. Riverhead Books, 2019.

Schrödinger, Erwin. *"What is Life?" with "Mind and Matter" and Autobiographical Sketches*. Cambridge University Press, 2012.

Sider, Theodore. *Four-Dimensionalism: An Ontology of Persistence and Time*. Clarendon Press, 2001.

Sinnerbrink, Robert. *Terrence Malick: Filmmaker and Philosopher*. Bloomsbury Academic, 2019.

Sitsky, Larry, ed. *Music of the Twentieth-Century Avant-Garde: A Biocritical Sourcebook*. Greenwood, 2002.

Skow, Bradford. *Objective Becoming*. Oxford University Press, 2016.

Smolin, Lee. *The Life of the Cosmos*. Oxford University Press, 1997.

South, James B., and Kimberly S. Engels, eds. *"Westworld" and Philosophy: If You Go Looking for the Truth, Get the Whole Thing*. Wiley Blackwell, 2018.

Stallworth, Ron. *Black Klansman: Race, Hate, and the Undercover Investigation of a Lifetime*. Flatiron Books, 2018.

Thain, Alanna. *Bodies in Suspense: Time and Affect in Cinema*. University of Minnesota Press, 2017.

Thorne, John. *Ominous Whoosh: a Wandering Mind Returns to "Twin Peaks."* Published by the author, 2022.

Tresch, John. *The Reason for the Darkness of the Night: Edgar Allan Poe and the Forging of American Science.* Farrar, Straus and Giroux, 2021.

Tucker, Thomas Deane, and Stuart Kendall, eds. *Terrence Malick: Film and Philosophy.* Continuum, 2011.

Van Ness, Sara J. *"Watchmen" as Literature: A Critical Study of the Graphic Novel.* McFarland, 2010.

Veder, Robin. *The Living Line: Modern Art and the Economy of Energy.* Dartmouth College Press, 2015.

Villarejo, Amy. *Ethereal Queer: Television, Historicity, Desire.* Duke University Press, 2014.

Voegelin, Salomé. *Listening to Noise and Silence. Towards a Philosophy of Sound Art.* Continuum, 2010.

White, Mark D., ed. *"Watchmen" and Philosophy: A Rorschach Test.* Wiley Blackwell, 2009.

Wierzbicki, James. *Terrence Malick: Sonic Style.* Routledge, 2019.

Williams, James. *Gilles Deleuze's Philosophy of Time: A Critical Introduction and Guide.* Edinburgh University Press, 2011.

Wright, David C., Jr., and Allan W. Austin, eds. *Space and Time: Essays on Visions of History in Science Fiction and Fantasy Television.* McFarland, 2010.

MEDIOGRAPHY

12 Monkeys, Terry Gilliam (1995)
2010: The Year We Made Contact, Peter Hyams (1984)
2046, Wong Kar-wai (2004)
32 Sounds, Sam Green (2022)
5 × 2, Francois Ozon (2004)
About Time, Richard Curtis (2013)
Adaptation, Spike Jonze (2002)
A.I. Artificial Intelligence, Steven Spielberg (2001)
Another Earth, Mike Cahill (2011)
Arrival, Denis Villeneuve (2016)
The Artist's Dilemma, Edwin S. Porter (1901)
Avengers: Endgame, Anthony Russo and Joe Russo (2019)
Back to the Future, Robert Zemeckis (1985)
Badlands, Terrence Malick (1973)
The Ballad of Buster Scruggs, Ethan Coen and Joel Coen (2018)
Battlestar Galactica, Glen A. Larson and Ronald D. Moore (2004)
Being John Malkovitch, Spike Jonze (1999)
BlacKkKlansman, Spike Lee (2018)
Blade Runner, Ridley Scott (1982)
Casablanca, Michael Curtiz (1942)
Un Chien Andalou, Luis Bunuel (1929)
Cloud Atlas, Tom Tykwer, Lana Wachowski, and Lilly Wachowski (2012)
Code Unknown, Michael Haneke (2000)
Conquest of Space, Byron Haskin (1955)
Copenhagen, Howard Davies (2002)
Cunk on Earth, Charlie Brooker (2022)
Days of Heaven, Terrence Malick (1978)
The Demolition of a Wall, Louis Lumière (1896)
The Discreet Charm of the Bourgeoisie, Louis Bunuel (1972)
Doctor Who, Donald Wilson and Sydney Newman (1963–1989)
Doctor Who, Sydney Newman (2005–)
Don't Look Up, Adam McKay (2021)
Dune, David Lynch (1984)

Dune, Denis Villeneuve (2021, 2024)
The East, Zal Batmanglij (2013)
Eternal Sunshine of the Spotless Mind, Michel Gondry (2004)
Everything, Everywhere, All at Once, Daniel Kwan and Daniel Scheinert (2022)
Forbidden Planet, Fred M. Wilcox (1956)
Game of Thrones, David Benioff and D. B. Weiss (2011–2019)
Gandhi, Richard Attenborough (1982)
Get Out, Jordan Peele (2017)
The Grapes of Wrath, John Ford (1940)
Groundhog Day, Harold Ramis (1993)
The Handmaid's Tale, Bruce Miller (2017–2025)
Harry Potter franchise, Chris Columbus, Mike Newell, Alfonso Cuaron, and David Yates, (2001–2011)
The Haunting of Bly House, Mike Flanagan (2020)
A Hidden Life, Terrence Malick (2019)
Hiroshima Mon Amour, Alain Resnais (1959)
Homecoming, Micah Bloomberg, Eli Horowitz, and Sam Esmail (2018–2020)
The Hour, Abi Morgan (2011–2012)
I'm Thinking About Ending Things, Charlie Kaufman (2020)
Inception, Christopher Nolan (2010)
Inland Empire, David Lynch (2006)
Into Great Silence, Philip Groning (2005)
Irreversible, Gaspar Noe (2002)
It Happened Tomorrow, René Clair (1944)
La Jetée, Chris Marker (1962)
La La Land, Damien Chazelle (2016)
The Last Czars, Nutopia (2019)
Last Year at Marienbad, Alain Resnais (1961)
A Letter to Three Wives, Joseph L. Mankiewicz (1949)
Lodge 49, Jim Gavin (2018–2019)
Lost, J. J. Abrams, Jeffrey Lieber, and Damon Lindelof (2004–2010)
Lost Highway, David Lynch (1997)
The Man in the High Castle, Frank Spotnitz (2015–2019)
The Matrix, Lana Wachowski and Lilly Wachowski (1999)
Matrix Isolation, Cheryl Lisa Bullock (2020)
The Matrix Reloaded, Lana Wachowski and Lilly Wachowski (2003)
Memento, Christopher Nolan (2000)
Miami Vice, Anthony Yerkovich (1984–1989)
Midnight in Paris, Woody Allen (2011)
Mulholland Drive, David Lynch (2001)
The New World, Terrence Malick (2005)
Night on Earth, Jim Jarmusch (1991)

Night Sky, Holden Miller (2022)
The OA, Zal Batmanglij and Brit Marling (2016–2019)
Once Upon a Time in America, Sergio Leone (1990)
Oppenheimer, Christopher Nolan (2023)
Orlando, Sally Potter (1992)
The Ox-Bow Incident, William A. Wellman (1942)
Palm Springs, Max Barbakow (2020)
Peggy Sue Got Married, Francis Ford Coppola (1986)
Portrait of Jennie, William Dieterle (1948)
Possession, Neil LaBute (2002)
The Prestige, Christopher Nolan (2006)
Pulp Fiction, Quentin Tarantino (1994)
The Romanoffs, Matthew Weiner (2018)
Roots, Alex Haley (1997)
Russian Doll, Leslye Headland, Natasha Lyonne, and Amy Poehler (2019–2022)
The Saragossa Manuscript, Wojciech Has (1965)
Solaris, Andrei Tarkovsky (1972)
Sorry to Bother You, Boots Riley (2018)
Sound of My Voice, Zal Batmanglij (2011)
Stargate SG-1, Jonathan Glassner and Brad Wright (1997–2007)
Star Trek franchise, Robert Wise, Nicholas Meyer, Leonard Nimoy, William Shatner, and Nicholas Meyer (1979–1991)
Stranger Than Fiction, Marc Forster (2006)
Stranger Things, Matt Duffer and Ross Duffer (2016–2025)
Synecdoche, New York, Charlie Kaufman (2008)
Tales of the Black Freighter, (2009)
Time Code, Mike Figgis (2000)
The Time Traveler's Wife, Robert Schwentke (2009)
Total Recall, Paul Verhoeven (1990)
Travelers, Brad Wright (2016–2018)
The Tree of Life, Terrence Malick (2011)
A Trip to Infinity, Jonathan Halperin and Drew Takahashi (2022)
The Truman Show, Peter Weir (1998)
Twin Peaks, David Lynch and Mark Frost (1990–1991, 2017)
Twin Peaks: Fire Walk with Me, David Lynch (1992)
Under the Hood, Eric Matthies (2009)
Voyage of Time, Terrence Malick (2016)
WandaVision, Jac Schaeffer (2021)
Watchmen, Damon Lindelof (2019)
Westworld, Michael Crichton (1973)
Westworld, Lisa Joy and Jonathan Nolan (2016–2022)
What Time Is It There?, Tsai Ming-liang (2001)

INDEX

Note: Page numbers in *italics* indicate figures.